Delphi™ Programming For Dummies®, 2nd Edition

D1128796

A Field Guide to Delphi Component Properties

Property Type	Symbol before Name	Symbol after Value	Example Property	Example Value
Exploding Object	+	▦	TForm.Font	(TFont)
List	▼		TForm.Cursor	crDefault
Numeric			TForm.Left	123
Object		▦	TForm.Icon	(TIcon)
Set	+		TForm.BorderIcons	[biSystemMenu].
String-list		▦	TMemo.Lines	(TStrings)
True/False		▼	TForm.Enabled	True
"Anything goes"			TForm.Caption	Whatever!

Amazing Secret Editor Keys

Key Combination	Effect
Ctrl+O,C	Enter column-marking mode
Ctrl+O,K	Leave column-marking mode
Alt+Shift+Arrow	Mark a rectangular column of text
Ctrl+K,I	Indent marked block
Ctrl+K,U	Un-indent marked block
Ctrl+K,N	Convert marked block to uppercase
Ctrl+K,O	Convert marked block to lowercase
Ctrl+O,U	Toggle marked block's case, e.g. *Up* becomes *uP*
Ctrl+K,F	Convert word at cursor to uppercase
Ctrl+K,E	Convert word at cursor to lowercase
Ctrl+E	Start incremental text search
Alt+[	Search for the closing parenthesis, bracket, or brace matching the opening parenthesis, bracket, or brace at the cursor (forward search)
Alt+]	Search for the opening parenthesis, bracket, or brace matching the closing parenthesis, bracket, or brace at the cursor (backward search)

. . .For Dummies: #1 Computer Book Series for Beginners

Delphi™ Programming For Dummies®, 2nd Edition

Cheat Sheet

Essential System Events for Forms

Event	Occasion	Usual Response
OnActivate	The form has just become the program's active window	Update any information displayed in the form
OnClose	OnCloseQuery already happened, and the form is being shut down	Last chance to refuse to shut down
OnCloseQuery	Windows asks the form whether it's willing to shut down	Prompt the user to save changed data, or *refuse* to shut down
OnCreate	The form is created	Perform any necessary initialization
OnDeactivate	The form has just stopped being the program's active window	Undo any actions taken in the OnActivate event handler
OnDestroy	The form is about to disappear for good	Clean up any resources the program allocated
OnPaint	The form needs to be redisplayed	Draw lines or other simple graphics directly on the form
OnResize	The form has been resized	Adjust the size or position of components

Essential Data Types

Type	Data Represented
LongInt	A whole number (no fractional part)
Extended	A number that may have a fractional part
Boolean	A True or False value
Char	One character, such as *A*
String	A string of characters, such as *'Delphi'*
PChar	A character string for use with a Windows API function

. . .For Dummies: #1 Computer Book Series for Beginners

DELPHI™
PROGRAMMING
FOR
DUMMIES®

2ND EDITION

DELPHI™
PROGRAMMING
FOR
DUMMIES®
2ND EDITION

by Neil J. Rubenking

IDG Books Worldwide, Inc.
An International Data Group Company

Foster City, CA ♦ Chicago, IL ♦ Indianapolis, IN ♦ Braintree, MA ♦ Southlake, TX

Delphi™ Programming For Dummies®

Published by
IDG Books Worldwide, Inc.
An International Data Group Company
919 E. Hillsdale Blvd.
Suite 400
Foster City, CA 94404

Text and art copyright © 1996 by IDG Books Worldwide, Inc. All rights reserved. No part of this book, including interior design, cover design, and icons, may be reproduced or transmitted in any form, by any means (electronic, photocopying, recording, or otherwise) without the prior written permission of the publisher.

Library of Congress Catalog Card No.: 96-75001

ISBN: 1-56884-621-5

Printed in the United States of America

10 9 8 7 6 5 4 3 2 1

2E/SW/QU/ZW/IN

Distributed in the United States by IDG Books Worldwide, Inc.

Distributed by Macmillan Canada for Canada; by Computer and Technical Books for the Caribbean Basin; by Contemporanea de Ediciones for Venezuela; by Distribuidora Cuspide for Argentina; by CITEC for Brazil; by Ediciones ZETA S.C.R. Ltda. for Peru; by Editorial Limusa SA for Mexico; by Transworld Publishers Limited in the United Kingdom and Europe; by Al-Maiman Publishers & Distributors for Saudi Arabia; by Simron Pty. Ltd. for South Africa; by IDG Communications (HK) Ltd. for Hong Kong; by Toppan Company Ltd. for Japan; by Addison Wesley Publishing Company for Korea; by Longman Singapore Publishers Ltd. for Singapore, Malaysia, Thailand, and Indonesia; by Unalis Corporation for Taiwan; by WS Computer Publishing Company, Inc. for the Philippines; by WoodsLane Pty. Ltd. for Australia; by WoodsLane Enterprises Ltd. for New Zealand.

For general information on IDG Books Worldwide's books in the U.S., please call our Consumer Customer Service department at 800-762-2974. For reseller information, including discounts and premium sales, please call our Reseller Customer Service department at 800-434-3422.

For information on where to purchase IDG Books Worldwide's books outside the U.S., contact IDG Books Worldwide at 415-655-3021 or fax 415-655-3295.

For information on translations, contact Marc Jeffrey Mikulich, Director, Foreign & Subsidiary Rights, at IDG Books Worldwide, 415-655-3018 or fax 415-655-3295.

For sales inquiries and special prices for bulk quantities, write to the address above or call IDG Books Worldwide at 415-655-3200.

For information on using IDG Books Worldwide's books in the classroom, or ordering examination copies, contact the Education Office at 800-434-2086 or fax 817-251-8174.

For authorization to photocopy items for corporate, personal, or educational use, please contact Copyright Clearance Center, 222 Rosewood Drive, Danvers, MA 01923, or fax 508-750-4470.

Limit of Liability/Disclaimer of Warranty: Author and Publisher have used their best efforts in preparing this book. IDG Books Worldwide, Inc., and Author make no representation or warranties with respect to the accuracy or completeness of the contents of this book and specifically disclaim any implied warranties of merchantability or fitness for any particular purpose and shall in no event be liable for any loss of profit or any other commercial damage, including but not limited to special, incidental, consequential, or other damages.

Trademarks: All brand names and product names used in this book are trademarks, registered trademarks, or trade names of their respective holders. IDG Books Worldwide is not associated with any product or vendor mentioned in this book.

 is a trademark under exclusive license to IDG Books Worldwide, Inc., from International Data Group, Inc.

About the Author

Neil Rubenking came to California seeking enlightenment, but got distracted along the way. Someone had to placate the tutelary deities of the Zen Master's brand-new IBM PC. Because he was too slow running from office, he served as vice president and president of the San Francisco PC User Group for three years.

In 1986, *PC Magazine* brought Neil on board to handle the torrent of Turbo Pascal tips submitted by readers. By 1990, he had become *PC Magazine's* technical editor and a coast-to-coast telecommuter. His "User-to-User" column showcases tips from readers on using DOS and Windows. Between editing articles and writing *PC Magazine* utilities in Pascal, Visual Basic, and Delphi, Neil has found time to write *Delphi Programming Problem Solver* (a book of solutions for problems in Delphi 1.0 and 2.0) and five other books covering Turbo Pascal, Windows, and DOS. (Batch files rule!)

In his occasional free moments, Neil likes to play with his children and read cheap fiction.

ABOUT IDG BOOKS WORLDWIDE

WINNER
Eighth Annual
Computer Press
Awards ≥ 1992

WINNER
Ninth Annual
Computer Press
Awards ≥ 1993

IDG BOOKS WORLDWIDE

Welcome to the world of IDG Books Worldwide.

IDG Books Worldwide, Inc., is a subsidiary of International Data Group, the world's largest publisher of computer-related information and the leading global provider of information services on information technology. IDG was founded more than 25 years ago and now employs more than 7,700 people worldwide. IDG publishes more than 250 computer publications in 67 countries (see listing below). More than 70 million people read one or more IDG publications each month.

Launched in 1990, IDG Books Worldwide is today the #1 publisher of best-selling computer books in the United States. We are proud to have received 8 awards from the Computer Press Association in recognition of editorial excellence and three from Computer Currents' First Annual Readers' Choice Awards, and our best-selling ...*For Dummies*® series has more than 19 million copies in print with translations in 28 languages. IDG Books Worldwide, through a joint venture with IDG's Hi-Tech Beijing, became the first U.S. publisher to publish a computer book in the People's Republic of China. In record time, IDG Books Worldwide has become the first choice for millions of readers around the world who want to learn how to better manage their businesses.

Our mission is simple: Every one of our books is designed to bring extra value and skill-building instructions to the reader. Our books are written by experts who understand and care about our readers. The knowledge base of our editorial staff comes from years of experience in publishing, education, and journalism — experience which we use to produce books for the '90s. In short, we care about books, so we attract the best people. We devote special attention to details such as audience, interior design, use of icons, and illustrations. And because we use an efficient process of authoring, editing, and desktop publishing our books electronically, we can spend more time ensuring superior content and spend less time on the technicalities of making books.

You can count on our commitment to deliver high-quality books at competitive prices on topics you want to read about. At IDG Books Worldwide, we continue in the IDG tradition of delivering quality for more than 25 years. You'll find no better book on a subject than one from IDG Books Worldwide.

John G. Kilcullen

John Kilcullen
President and CEO
IDG Books Worldwide, Inc.

IDG Books Worldwide, Inc., is a subsidiary of International Data Group, the world's largest publisher of computer-related information and the leading global provider of information services on information technology. International Data Group publishes over 250 computer publications in 67 countries. Seventy million people read one or more International Data Group publications each month. International Data Group's publications include: **ARGENTINA:** Computerworld Argentina, GamePro, Infoworld, PC World Argentina; **AUSTRALIA:** Australian Macworld, Client/Server Journal, Computer Living, Computerworld, Digital News, Network World, PC World, Publishing Essentials, Reseller; **AUSTRIA:** Computerwelt, PC TEST; **BELARUS:** PC World Belarus; **BELGIUM:** Data News; **BRAZIL:** Annuário de Informática, Computerworld Brazil, Connections, Super Game Power, Macworld, PC World Brazil, Publish Brazil, SUPERGAME; **BULGARIA:** Computerworld Bulgaria, Networkworld/Bulgaria, PC & MacWorld Bulgaria; **CANADA:** CIO Canada, ComputerWorld Canada, InfoCanada, Network World Canada, Reseller World; **CHILE:** Computerworld Chile, GamePro, PC World Chile; **COLUMBIA:** Computerworld Colombia, GamePro, PC World Colombia; **COSTA RICA:** PC World Costa Rica/Nicaragua; **THE CZECH AND SLOVAK REPUBLICS:** Computerworld Czechoslovakia, Elektronika Czechoslovakia, PC World Czechoslovakia; **DENMARK:** Communications World, Computerworld Danmark, Macworld Danmark, PC World Danmark, PC World Danmark Supplements, TECH World; **DOMINICAN REPUBLIC:** PC World Republica Dominicana; **ECUADOR:** PC World Ecuador, GamePro; **EGYPT:** Computerworld Middle East, PC World Middle East; **EL SALVADOR:** PC World Centro America; **FINLAND:** MikroPC, Tietoverkko, Tietoviikko; **FRANCE:** Distributique, Golden, Info PC, Le Guide du Monde Informatique, Le Monde Informatique, Reseaux & Telecoms; **GERMANY:** Computer Business, Computerwoche, Computerwoche Extra, Computerwoche Focus, Electronic Entertainment, GamePro, I/M Information Management, Macwelt, PC Welt; **GREECE:** GamePro, Macworld & Publish; **GUATEMALA:** PC World Centro America; **HONDURAS:** PC World Centro America; **HONG KONG:** Computerworld Hong Kong, PCWorld Hong Kong, Publish in Asia; **HUNGARY:** ABCD CD-ROM, Computerworld Szamitastechnika, PC & Mac World Hungary, PC-X Magazine; **INDIA:** Computerworld India, PC World India, Publish in Asia; **INDONESIA:** InfoKomputer PC World, Komputek Computerworld, Publish in Asia; **IRELAND:** ComputerScope, PC Live!; **ISRAEL:** PC World 32 BIT, People & Computers; **ITALY:** Computerworld Italia, Computerworld Italia Special Editions, Lotus Italia, Macworld Italia, Networking Italia, PC Shopping, PC World Italia, PC World/Walt Disney; **JAPAN:** Macworld Japan, Nikkei Personal Computing, SunWorld Japan, Windows World Japan; **KENYA:** East African Computer News; **KOREA:** Hi-Tech Information/Computerworld, Macworld Korea, PC World Korea; **MACEDONIA:** PC World Macedonia; **MALAYSIA:** Computerworld Malaysia, PC World Malaysia, Publish in Asia; **MEXICO:** Computerworld Mexico, GamePro, Macworld, PC World Mexico; **MYANMAR:** PC World Myanmar; **NETHERLANDS:** Computable, Computer! Totaal, LAN Magazine, Macworld, Net Magazine; **NEW ZEALAND:** Computer Buyer, Computerworld New Zealand, MTB, Network World, PC World New Zealand; **NICARAGUA:** PC World Costa Rica/Nicaragua; **NIGERIA:** PC World Africa; **NORWAY:** Computerworld Norge, Computerworld Privat, CW Rapport Klient/Tjener, CW Rapport Nettverk & Telecom, CW Rapport Offentlig Sektor, IDG's KURSGUIDE, Macworld Norge, Multimedia World, PC World Ekspress, PC World Nettverk, PC World Norge, PC World's Produktguide, Windows Spesial; **PAKISTAN:** Computerworld Pakistan, PC World Pakistan; **PANAMA:** GamePro, PC World Panama; **PARAGUAY:** PC World Paraguay; **P. R. OF CHINA:** China Computerworld, China Infoworld, Computer & Communication, Electronic Product World, Electronics Today, Game Camp, PC World China, Popular Computer Week, Software World, Telecom Product World; **PERU:** Computerworld Peru, GamePro, PC World Profesional Peru, PC World Peru; **POLAND:** Computerworld Poland, Computerworld Special Report, Macworld, Networld, PC World Komputer; **PHILIPPINES:** Computerworld Philippines, PC Digest, Publish in Asia; **PORTUGAL:** Cerebro/PC World, Correio Informático/Computerworld, Mac•In/PC•In Portugal; **PUERTO RICO:** PC World Puerto Rico; **ROMANIA:** Computerworld Romania, PC World Romania, Telecom Romania; **RUSSIA:** Computerworld Rossiya, Network World Russia, PC World Russia; **SINGAPORE:** Computerworld Singapore, PC World Singapore, Publish in Asia; **SLOVENIA:** MONITOR; **SOUTH AFRICA:** Computing S.A., Network World S.A., Software World; **SPAIN:** Computerworld España, COMUNICACIONES WORLD, Dealer World, Macworld España, PC World España; **SWEDEN:** CAP&Design, Computer Sweden, Corporate Computing, MacWorld, Maxi Data, MikroDatorn, Nätverk & Kommunikation, PC/Aktiv, PC World, Windows World; **SWITZERLAND:** ComputerWorld Schweiz, Macworld Schweiz, PCtip; **TAIWAN:** Computerworld Taiwan, Macworld Taiwan, PC World Taiwan, Publish Taiwan, Windows World; **THAILAND:** Thai Computerworld, Publish in Asia; **TURKEY:** Computerworld Monitör, MACWORLD Turkiye, PC WORLD Turkiye; **UKRAINE:** Computerworld Kiev, Computers & Software Magazine, PC World Ukraine; **UNITED KINGDOM:** Acorn User, Amiga Action, Amiga Computing, Amiga, Appletalk, CD Powerplay, CD-ROM Now, Computing, Connexion, GamePro, Lotus Magazine, Macaction, Macworld, Open Computing, Parents and Computers, PC Home, PC Works, The WEB; **UNITED STATES:** Cable in the Classroom, CD Review, CIO Magazine, Computerworld, Computerworld Client/Server Journal, Digital Video Magazine, DOS World, Electronic, InfoWorld, I-Way, Macworld, Maximize, MULTIMEDIA WORLD, Network World, PC World, PUBLISH, SWATPro Magazine, Video Event, WebMaster; **URUGUAY:** PC World Uruguay; **VENEZUELA:** Computerworld Venezuela, GamePro, PC World Venezuela; and **VIETNAM:** PC World Vietnam   10/17/95a

Dedication

To my family — you all helped!

Acknowledgments to First Edition

Borland's Delphi development team put up with a lot of bother from me. Each time a new field test version appeared, I revised the growing book and plagued the team with old and new questions. I'd like to thank the entire team — and especially Danny Thorpe — who gave this book a most thorough technical review.

My wife, Janet, deserves a medal for never once complaining about the fact that this book and our son are due to be "born" at almost precisely the same time. A medal? Make it a halo! My daughter Sophie and stepdaughter Katherine showed admirable restraint, leaving me free to work even when I wished for an interruption — thanks, kids!

Special thanks go to Trudy Neuhaus, my old friend and editor, for convincing me to write this book. Writing a book, even an enjoyable book such as this one, is a painful process; thanks to all the folks at IDG for easing the pain.

Author's Acknowledgments

The Delphi Development team did it again; they managed to crank out a version 2.0 that outshines their original effort. And again they've been patient with my questions and suggestions. Thanks to all!

Baby John, whose birthday is roughly the same as Delphi's, is a year old. He is walking, talking, running, climbing bookcases, eating books, and programming in Delphi. Well, perhaps he's not programming *yet*. My thanks go again to my family, who put up with me while I was attempting to simultaneously revise this book and write another.

And of course, thanks to all of you who bought the first edition. I'm especially grateful to those of you who sent me e-mail with your questions and problems. Cogitating on those conundrums is what inspired me to write *Delphi Programming Problem Solver* (also published by IDG Books). Thanks!

Publisher's Acknowledgments

We're proud of this book; send us your comments about it by using the Reader Response Card at the back of the book or by e-mailing us at feedback/dummies@idgbooks.com. Some of the people who helped bring this book to market include:

Acquisitions, Development, & Editorial

Project Editors: Susan Pink

Acquisitions Editor: Tammy Goldfeld

Assistant Acquisitions Editor: Gareth Hancock

Product Development Manager: Mary Bednarek

Editors: S. Diane Smith, William A. Barton

Technical Reviewer: Danny Thorpe

Editorial Managers: Kristin A. Cocks, Mary Corder, Seta K. Frantz

Editorial Assistants: Constance Carlisle, Chris Collins, Jerelind Davis

Production

Project Coordinator: Sherry Gomoll

Layout and Graphics: Linda M. Boyer, Cheryl Denski, Angela F. Hunckler, Todd Klemme, Drew R. Moore, Gina Scott, Kate Snell

Proofreaders: Melissa D. Buddendeck, Betty Kish, Christine Meloy Beck, Carl Saff, Robert Springer

Indexer: Richard T. Evans

General & Administrative

IDG Books Worldwide, Inc.: John Kilcullen, President & CEO; Steven Berkowitz, COO & Publisher

Dummies, Inc.: Milissa Koloski, Executive Vice President & Publisher

Dummies Technology Press & Dummies Editorial: Diane Graves Steele, Associate Publisher; Judith A. Taylor, Brand Manager; Myra Immell, Editorial Director

Dummies Trade Press: Kathleen A. Welton, Vice President & Publisher; Stacy S. Collins, Brand Manager

IDG Books Production for Dummies Press: Beth Jenkins, Production Director; Cindy L. Phipps, Supervisor of Project Coordination; Kathie S. Schnorr, Supervisor of Page Layout; Shelley Lea, Supervisor of Graphics and Design

Dummies Packaging & Book Design: Erin McDermitt, Packaging Coordinator; Kavish+Kavish, Cover Design

◆

The publisher would like to give special thanks to Patrick J. McGovern, without whom this book would not have been possible.

◆

Contents at a Glance

Cartoons at a Glance

By Rich Tennant • Fax: 508-546-7747 • E-mail: the5wave@tiac.net

"I THOUGHT HE WAS A VACUUM CLEANER SALESMAN. HE CAME IN, SPRINKLED DIRT ON THE CARPET, AND THEN TRIED TO SELL ME A SOFTWARE PROGRAM THAT WOULD SHOW ME HOW TO CLEAN IT UP."

page 7

"THE PRINTER AND DISK DRIVE ARE CONTAINED IN THE HAT. IT'S GREAT FOR KEEPING AN UNCLUTTERED DESK, BUT IT'S HARD GETTING MORE THAN THREE OF US ON AN ELEVATOR AT THE SAME TIME."

page 349

Real Programmers curse alot, but only at inanimate objects.

page 49

"I ALWAYS BACK UP EVERYTHING."

page 259

AFTER THE INITIAL MERGER OF TWO COMPANIES COMES THE DELICATE PROCESS OF SELECTING A DOMINANT SOFTWARE SYSTEM.

SOMEONE SAY "GO".

page 129

Table of Contents

Introduction

● ●

Congratulations! You've found *Delphi Programming For Dummies,* 2nd Edition, the book that puts *you* in control of your computer. Add your copy of Delphi itself, and you have everything you need to start creating your own Windows applications. You'll design programs right on the screen and let Delphi do most of the programming. Sound easy? It is!

About This Book

There are no prerequisites for reading and using this book. It isn't a textbook, and you don't need to be able to pass an entrance exam on arcane programming language syntax or Windows internal functions to understand the concepts discussed here. With this book and Delphi, you can get results right away and learn the technical stuff later on — if you need to. No long hours of preparation and study here; you'll build and run a program in Chapter 1.

You're not going to find syntax diagrams, exhaustive function lists, or dissertations on the painful technicalities of data types in this book. That stuff is all available in the Delphi manual and on-line help, and you can look it up if you *really* want to. Working with this book, you'll get personal with Delphi, learn all its features, and gain practical experience in constructing programs.

Who Are You?

You've wisely chosen to read this book, and that lets me guess a few things about you. First and foremost, you have a fair amount of experience using Windows and Windows programs. You're comfortable working in Windows, and you're ready to take a little more control of what's happening in your computer.

You may be skilled in using your primary application's macro language, but frustrated by its limitations. Or perhaps you've mastered Object Linking and Embedding (OLE), only to find that many fairly simple tasks can't be handled with OLE. Chances are good that your coworkers turn to you when they need help customizing their working environment. You could make your work and theirs more efficient, but the boss won't allow it unless you can show results right away.

You're too busy to study programming in night school or to spend time decoding cryptic expressions such as y—=x++. Possibly you're an accomplished DOS programmer just beginning to program in Windows. Or you may simply be interested in getting the most out of your computer. You have ideas for projects the computer could accomplish, but you don't know how to implement them.

Possibly you're already familiar with Delphi 1.0, but feel you need a refresher before you switch over to using Delphi 2.0 under Windows 95 or Windows NT. In truth, most of your knowledge will carry over from Delphi 1.0 to Delphi 2.0. However, all the examples and text in this second edition have been reviewed and retested using Delphi 2.0 and Windows 95, so you'll probably learn a thing or three.

Whatever your reasons for learning Delphi, welcome! If you want to *do* things in Windows, you've come to the right place.

Why Delphi?

Programming has long been a practice shrouded in mystery, with practitioners protecting their secrets by using languages unintelligible to normal human beings. Some overenthusiastic programmers delete sacrificial data files by the light of the full moon while chanting "GetPrivateProfileString! WritePrivateProfileString! AbortDoc! AbortProc! Pie! Chord! Yield!" But a new breed of visual programming tool is lifting the curtain and blowing away the smoke to let ordinary humans write programs. Delphi is the latest arrival in the visual programming field; Visual Basic (VB) is its main rival.

Deep down, both Delphi and VB rely on programming languages originally designed to *teach* programming. Delphi is a descendant of Pascal; VB, of BASIC. (Pascal promoters and BASIC boosters have been feuding longer than the Hatfields and the McCoys, but at heart they're not all that different.) Both products have a handy visual interface that eliminates a lot of unnecessary effort, but Delphi has certain key advantages.

To the neophyte, the two seem very similar. However, VB users eventually run into some major limitations. VB can use the function libraries called DLLs, but it can't create new DLLs. It can react to events that occur in Windows *only* if a response to those events was preprogrammed by Microsoft. Your VB programs can use Visual Basic custom controls (VBXs) to add functionality, but if you want to make your own VBXs, VB won't do the job.

Delphi has none of these limitations. It can use or create DLLs, and its programs can respond to and initiate absolutely any Windows event. Delphi components (the equivalent of VBXs) are written *in* Delphi, and you don't have to leave Delphi to create new or enhanced components. You don't even have to leave

Delphi to use Visual Basic VBX controls because Delphi programs can use VBXs! In fact, Delphi users can customize VBX controls in ways VB programmers only dream of.

In addition, Delphi does a complete job of compiling your programs into the machine code that your computer understands. VB does a halfway job, translating BASIC instructions into an intermediate language called p-code. When the VB program runs, it interprets the p-code into actual machine instructions. Delphi goes straight to the machine code level. What are the advantages of going straight to machine code? Speed, speed, and speed!

Now that Visual Basic 4.0 is here, I'll have to eat my words about the limitations of VB. . . NOT! In fact, the main limitation that's lifted in VB4 is that you can now write DLLs, but there's a catch. You must be willing to interface with those DLLs through OLE; the usual methods for connecting to DLL functions don't work. The resulting EXEs are still compiled to p-code, the programs still can't easily respond to an arbitrary Windows message, and you still can't write custom controls (OCXs rather than VBXs) using only VB4. And even though VB4 is a 32-bit program, it's got quite a few 16-bit limits remaining. A module can't contain more than 64KB of p-code, for example, and the maximum number of components in a list is 16,384.

Delphi 2.0, on the other hand, is in every way a 32-bit product, and it has kept pace with the new features of VB4. Programs written with Delphi 2.0 can use and enhance OCX controls just the way Delphi 1.0 programs did with VBX controls. Delphi 2.0 creates fully compiled 32-bit executables with full access to 32-bit Windows functions. And it supports OLE every bit as well as VB4, even including a special Remote OLE Automation technique that was invented by the VB4 development team.

Want to see an example of what Delphi can do? Just look at Delphi itself. In an amazing feat of self-referential programming, Delphi was written *using* Delphi. Any design element you see in Delphi, such as a pop-up menu or a paged dialog, is available to *you* for use in your own programs. You won't find another visual development tool that's written with itself! Some lack the necessary power or flexibility; others would just be impossibly *slow*.

How to Use This Book

Clear a space near your computer and grab something heavy to hold the book open — a brick, perhaps, or a Windows manual. That way you can try out the many exercises as you come to them. Or, if you prefer, relax with the book in your easy chair, hammock, or Jacuzzi (watch those bubbles!), and then come back to the computer and try out what you've learned. Either way, you *will* be spending time at the computer.

You'll find that later chapters build on concepts from earlier chapters, but don't be afraid to plow ahead even if you haven't quite mastered a particular chapter. There's nothing like some real-world practice to hammer home new concepts. After you've worked with Delphi a bit, you can reread any chapters that seemed tough at first.

You won't be typing interminable program listings into Delphi — Delphi isn't *about* typing. Most of the program design and layout in Delphi is accomplished by choosing and arranging components with the mouse, and setting properties that describe them. A minitable like this:

Property   **Value**

Caption   Fantastic Program

means you should set the property called Caption to the value Fantastic Program — you'll learn how to do that in Chapter 1.

When you do need to type in a few lines of program code, they'll be displayed like this:

```
Edit2.Enabled  := Edit1.Text = 'Delphi';
Edit3.Enabled  := Edit2.Enabled;
```

All you do is type the lines precisely as shown.

What Not to Read

Hi, my name is Neil, and I'm a technoholic. . . I know lots of boring things like what the TabTheTextOutForWimps function does, why the mysterious word "BurgerMaster" is buried deep inside Windows, and how to invoke the musical credits display hidden in Windows 95. This information isn't important or even necessary for you to know, but sometimes I can't resist talking about it anyway. Don't worry — you'll have plenty of warning so you can skip those parts. (And no, I wasn't kidding about that function name. There are a *lot* of weird names buried in Windows, including Death, Resurrection, Brute, Bunny_351, BozosLiveHere, and WinOldAppHackOMatic!)

How This Book Is Organized

This book is divided into five parts that more or less follow each other logically. You don't have to read the chapters in order, but if you skip ahead and find yourself confused, come back and work through the background material. The key concept here is understanding by *doing*. After you've been introduced to Delphi in general, you'll start writing programs that use each of Delphi's many components. When the book starts giving you instructions such as "place this component, set that property," that's your cue to plunk yourself down in front of Delphi and create a brand-new program. Only *after* you have several dozen programs under your belt will you learn about the programming concepts behind them. That way, you'll have some experience to hang those concepts on.

Part I: Getting Started

Part I tells you how to install Delphi's files on your system and how to configure it most effectively. It also introduces you to the *form,* the basic unit of visual programming, and gets you started running programs.

Part II: Programming with Components

Delphi's components have so much built-in power that the biggest task for a Delphi programmer is learning what all the components do. That's what Part II is all about. You'll *use* all the basic components in small but powerful programs.

Part III: More Components

Delphi's capabilities go far beyond simply managing the standard controls built into Windows. Part III introduces you to all the rest of Delphi's components and extends the range of projects you can build. It also includes a chapter on the snazzy Windows 95 interface components introduced with Delphi 2.0!

Part IV: Real Programming

Part IV gets into programming in the old-fashioned sense — writing statements in a programming language. It introduces basic programming concepts and shows how they're implemented in Pascal (the programming language that underlies Delphi). And it brings up the unsavory topic of debugging, or what to do when your program does what you *told* it to do instead of what you *meant* for it to do.

Part V: The Part of Tens

There's more to know about programming in Windows than just placing components and writing a few lines of code. However, you don't need to learn it all at once. Part V introduces some of the most useful functions found in Windows and in Delphi, along with common pitfalls to avoid.

Icons Used in This Book

This icon points out a dandy shortcut, a timesaving technique, or a hot tip.

This icon is a warning flag for text that talks about technical stuff. You can read it if you want, but you don't have to. If you start to feel lightheaded, or develop an urge to break your glasses and patch them with adhesive tape, stop reading!

Watch out — here's something you should *not* do!

When you see this icon, you can say "I knew that!" You learned this information earlier, and you need to remember it now.

Where to Go from Here

Get to your computer, get Delphi running, and start programming!

Part I
Getting Started

The 5th Wave   By Rich Tennant

"I THOUGHT HE WAS A VACUUM CLEANER SALESMAN. HE CAME IN, SPRINKLED DIRT ON THE CARPET, AND THEN TRIED TO SELL ME A SOFTWARE PROGRAM THAT WOULD SHOW ME HOW TO CLEAN IT UP."

In this part . . .

Getting used to a new program is like familiarizing yourself with a new car. At first, you don't know which lever is the cruise control and which is the turn signal. You may squirt the windshield when you meant to turn on the heat, or open the hood when you meant to lock the doors. You'll make a few mistakes at first, but even if you figuratively run into a lamppost, nobody will be hurt. And of course, you'll learn the rules of the road and tips for safe programming. Before long you'll be driving Delphi like a pro.

Part I helps you install Delphi and set its options for safe, effective programming. It introduces the many different elements that make up Delphi, shows how you can configure them to suit yourself, and points out areas you can personalize but shouldn't. You'll also meet the form — the canvas on which you lay out your Delphi programs. A form, like every Delphi component, is defined by properties and responds to events. You'll learn how to set properties and define events; these are skills you'll use every time you write a program in Delphi. And of course, you'll start building working programs right away!

If you already know and love Delphi 1.0, moving to Delphi 2.0 is a breeze. A few of the knobs and levers are in different places — such as choosing Options from the Project menu instead of Project from the Options menu — but the differences are surprisingly few.

Chapter 1

Meet Delphi

- -

In This Chapter

▶ Installing Delphi on your system

▶ Setting Delphi's options to ensure safe programming

▶ Discovering how to be an instant programmer

▶ Configuring Delphi's SpeedBar to suit your taste

▶ Looking through Delphi's windows

- -

Did you already install Delphi on your system? Good! With that kind of enthusiasm you'll go far! You can skip ahead to the "Don't Program without a Safety Net!" section. If you haven't installed Delphi yet, now's the time.

Installing Delphi

If you have a CD-ROM drive, installing Delphi is a snap. Just slide the CD-ROM into the drive and run the SETUP program from Program Manager. Or, if you've got the disk version, slip the first disk into your favorite disk drive, select Run from Program Manager's File menu, and run A:SETUP (or B:SETUP, if your favorite drive is B). Feed disks to the computer when the SETUP program demands them, and answer any personal questions it asks.

When the process is complete, you'll have a few dozen new Delphi icons placed inside a new Delphi Program Manager group. If you're running Windows 95, these will be transmuted into Delphi-related menu items in a new Delphi submenu of the Start Menu. To start Delphi, double-click the icon labeled Delphi.

If your Windows 3.1 configuration uses 24-bit color (also called "true color"), you may run into trouble when Delphi 1.0 tries to install its two dozen icons in Program Manager. Program Manager allows 50 icons per group, which is fine in 256-color mode, but another limit kicks in for advanced modes such as true color. In true color mode, Program Manager may allow as few as 13 icons per group; attempts to add more icons will either fail or produce black icons. To avoid this problem, use Windows Setup to downshift into 256-color mode while you're installing Delphi. When the installation is complete, create another group and move half the icons into it. Then switch back to true color.

Which Delphi?

Delphi 1.0 comes in two flavors, Delphi Desktop and Delphi Client/Server. The Client/Server version contains everything that's in the Desktop version, along with additional tools for advanced and networked database development. Either way, you get the whole Delphi cake; with the Client/Server version, however, you get extra icing.

Delphi 2.0, the new 32-bit version of Delphi, completely includes Delphi 1.0, so you don't have to give up 16-bit Windows programming. It adds a third flavor in between Delphi 2.0 Desktop and Delphi 2.0 Client/Server. This new option is called Delphi 2.0 Developer, and it's intended for network-based professional developers. As in Delphi 1.0, the Desktop version is a complete and fully functioning development environment, with one tiny exception — Delphi Desktop doesn't include the Multi Object Grid component (discussed in Chapter 11) or the Math unit (mentioned in Chapter 18). With those exceptions, this book concentrates on the vast portion of Delphi that's common to all the versions, and points out any differences between Delphi 1.0 and 2.0.

Don't Program without a Safety Net!

Life is full of trade-offs. The sporty car you yearn for is a gas-hog, and the fuel-efficient alternative looks like a butter dish on wheels. You can afford a health club membership to buff your bod *or* a beach vacation to show off your new physique — but not both. Delphi is no different. With Delphi's options, the main trade-off is between safety and speed. Your programs can be armored against error, but they'll be slower and larger. Or they can be svelte and speedy but more vulnerable to your programming oversights.

Setting compiler options for safety

While you're creating, editing, and testing a project, there's no question — safety is the Prime Directive. After the project is tested, debugged, and ready for production, you can remove the safety net to speed up and slim down the program.

To create your safety net, select Options from the Delphi 2.0 Project menu (or Project from the Delphi 1.0 Options menu) and click the tab that says Compiler. You'll be transported to Nerd Nirvana, a.k.a. the Compiler page in the Project Options dialog. Figure 1-1 shows Delphi 2.0's screenful of compiler-option choices. Fear not; the choices may look intimidating now, but your task is actually quite simple. Whether you're running Delphi 1.0 or Delphi 2.0, use the mouse to check off all the options *except* the Complete boolean eval option. Also check off the lonely box that says Default (near the OK button), to tell Delphi you want these options to be the default for all projects. Click OK and you're finished.

Figure 1-1:
Turn on all
but one of
Delphi's
compiler
options.

When a program is working perfectly and is totally bug-free . . . then pigs will fly! Let me rephrase that. When a program *seems* to be working perfectly and all *known* bugs have been corrected, you can turn off certain options to make the final version smaller and faster. To do this, choose Project from the Options menu again. In the Runtime errors panel, check off only I/O checking and blank out all the others. The improvement in size and speed will vary from program to program, but it can be dramatic.

Why does your program bloat and drag its feet when the Runtime errors options are turned on? Delphi adds machine code to your program to warn you when certain errors occur. For example, if you try to put ten gallons of data into a one-gallon variable, overflow checking will catch the mistake. And if you try to examine the seventh bullet in a six-shooter, range checking will stop you. But to make those things happen, every spot in your program that assigns a value to a variable needs to have overflow- and range-checking code added. If you call a function from within a function from within a function too many times, you'll run out of something called stack space; stack checking will catch that error. That's why every function call has stack-checking code added. In each of these cases, the error-checking code is just a few bytes, but those bytes add up!

The Project Options dialog actually has five pages, identified by tabs at the top or bottom of the window. You'll see a lot of these multipage tabbed windows in Delphi — in fact, Delphi includes these same multipage and tab components for you to use in your own programs. The options you've set thus far are all on the Compiler page, and they're by far the most important, but you'll need to know about the other options, too. Let's look at the linker options now; click the Linker tab in the Project Options dialog to display the Linker page shown in Figure 1-2.

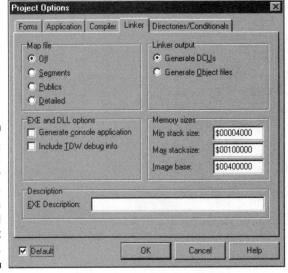

Figure 1-2: Keep the linker options the way Delphi's install program set them.

Here again the Delphi 2.0 dialog is shown, but in this case the options are a bit different between 1.0 and 2.0. In Delphi 1.0, the panel at the top right lets you set the link buffer to Memory or Disk. Old-time Turbo Pascal fans might be tempted to "save memory" by setting this option to Disk. However, if your available memory is so pitifully small that this truly helps, you desperately need to buy more RAM!

In Delphi 2.0, the choice is between generating DCU files (Delphi's own format for compiled units) and OBJ files (a format used by other compilers). Unless you're already a programming wizard *and* have a need for multilanguage programming, leave this one set to Generate DCUs.

TECHNICAL STUFF

Short-circuiting your logic

What's so bad about the Complete boolean eval option? Try this True-False test: "All cows are blue and all douroucoulis are yellow." If you answered False instantly because you know all cows aren't blue, you just performed a short-circuit Boolean evaluation, which is the opposite of complete Boolean evaluation! Because some cows are not blue, the color of douroucoulis is irrelevant — the combined statement is False. Complete Boolean evaluation would pointlessly force you to discover what are douroucoulis (they're nocturnal monkeys), and whether they're yellow (I'll leave that for you to discover).

Sometimes complete Boolean evaluation can even be dangerous. For example, take the expression "x is not zero and 1/x is less than 4." If x is zero, short-circuit evaluation returns False right away. However, complete Boolean evaluation would try to calculate 1/0 to see whether the result is less than 4. Computers just hate it when you divide by zero! Complete Boolean evaluation is both wasteful and dangerous — that's why it's the one option you should leave turned off.

Later, when you've mastered Delphi and its built-in debugger, you may graduate to an external debugging program. At that time (not now) you'll want to set the Map file option to Detailed, and check off the box that says Include TDW debug info.

When you're ready to compile a final version of your Delphi 1.0 program for distribution, check off the Optimize for size and load time option. Your program will take a tiny bit longer to compile, but it will be smaller and faster. In Delphi 2.0, Optimization is a compiler option, and you always leave it turned on.

The Directories/Conditionals page of the Project Options dialog, which is shown in Figure 1-3, tells Delphi where to find certain important files. The Delphi install program leaves these lines blank, because the files you need are in the same directory as Delphi. If you buy third-party component libraries to extend Delphi, you need to add the directory for those libraries to the Search path list on this page. To do that, just add a semicolon to the end of the existing line, followed by the new directory. For example, if the line were C:\DELPHI\UNITS, you might change it to C:\DELPHI\UNITS;C:\NEWUTIL. But hey: Don't go buying add-on libraries before you've mastered the substantial collection of components built into Delphi!

The panel labeled Aliases appears only under Delphi 2.0. Unit Aliases allow Delphi to treat one unit name as if it were another. Their main reason for existence is to let Delphi 2.0 compile Delphi 1.0 programs as painlessly as possible. You won't need to change the alias list any time soon.

Figure 1-3:
The
Directories/
Conditionals
page of the
Project
Options
dialog
normally
won't need
any changes
until you add
third-party
components.

The Output directory line on the Directories/Conditionals page starts out blank, and that's the way it should stay. If you put a directory name on this line, the compiled program files for all your projects will be dumped higgledy-piggledy into that directory. Leave it blank and the compiled files will be stored along with the source files, which is where they belong.

As Figure 1-4 shows, the Application page of the Project Options dialog lets you specify some important attributes for the final compiled program. Except for the layout of the components, it's the same in Delphi 1.0 and Delphi 2.0. The value that you fill in for Title is what will appear under the icon when you minimize the program, and the icon itself is displayed in the Icon field. You press the Load Icon... button to choose an icon that suits your program's style. A modern Windows program should always have a help file — you can automatically associate one with your program by filling in the Help file line.

What about the remaining page, the one labeled Forms? Well, a project can have one form or dozens, but one of them is always the boss form. That's the one named in the Main form combo box, and it's always the first one in the Auto-create forms list box. That box lists forms that will be automatically created when your program starts. The other list box holds forms that are available but don't exist until your program creates them. Figure 1-5 shows how this page looks for one of Delphi's sample projects. I know, I know, we've hardly talked about forms, but don't worry. Even when you *do* build multiform projects, you'll rarely need to meddle with this page.

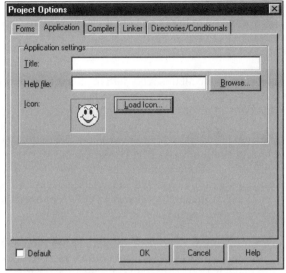

Figure 1-4:
The Application page in the Project Options dialog controls your program's icon, title, and help file.

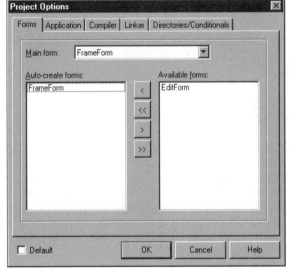

Figure 1-5:
The Forms page of the Project Options dialog lets you promote a new Main form, but you'll rarely need to do that.

Setting preferences for safety

The computer always does what your program tells it to do, but frequently that's not what you *meant* it to do. To put it bluntly, programs under development have bugs (whether the programs are written in Delphi, Visual Basic, or Swahili). If you have a buggy program that crashes, it's possible for the fallout from the crash to blow up Delphi itself, or even to bring all of Windows to a screeching halt. Windows 95 is somewhat less crash-prone than Windows 3.1, and Windows NT is quite skilled at avoiding fallout from exploding programs. Even in these Windows environments, however, you need to program defensively and assume the worst.

When Windows crashes, you lose all unsaved data in all applications, including the latest changes in the form layout and source code for your Delphi *program*. That is, you'll lose this data *unless* you've set your preferences correctly. Did that get your attention? Good. Here's how to set your preferences: Select Options from the Delphi 2.0 Tools menu (or Environment from the Delphi 1.0 Options menu) and look at the first page, titled Preferences. Make sure both check boxes in the Autosave Options rectangle are checked, and then click OK. Now each time you run a program, Delphi will automatically save all open files, the layout of your Delphi desktop, and any options you've changed. Whew! That's a relief!

There's one more precaution you should take, though. In the same Environment Options dialog, click on the Display tab (it's called Editor display in Delphi 1.0). A check box in the top panel is titled Create backup file; make sure this box is checked. Now each time Delphi saves a file, it will store the previous version with the extension ~xx, where xx are the first two letters of the file's extension. For example, the backup file for UNIT.PAS would be called UNIT.~PA, and UNIT1.DFM's backup would be UNIT1.~DF. You should round up and delete these backup files from time to time by deleting *.~*, but having a backup can sure save your bacon.

Delphi All over the Screen

Program Manager keeps its group windows nicely corralled, and Word for Windows wouldn't think of letting a document creep outside its frame. But as Figure 1-6 shows, Delphi is much more permissive. Like Visual Basic, it splatters windows all over the screen. Get used to it — this "Single Document Interface" is the latest style, recommended by Microsoft for Windows 95 and Windows NT programs.

The four primary Delphi windows are

- ✔ Form window
- ✔ Object Inspector window
- ✔ Code Editor window
- ✔ Main window

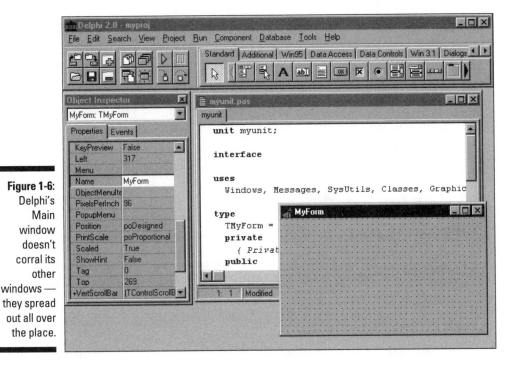

Figure 1-6:
Delphi's
Main
window
doesn't
corral its
other
windows —
they spread
out all over
the place.

Fire up Delphi and examine these windows. Move them around, stretch them, poke them a little and see what they do. These are your new friends — you're going to get to know them *very* well!

The multitude of Delphi windows can take up a lot of space on your desktop. If your video card supports 800-by-600 resolution, go into Windows Setup and try it — you'll find it gives you more space. If you have a huge monitor or *very* sharp eyes, you may even want to try 1,024-by-768 resolution, which lets you fit even more on the screen.

It's all happening at the Form window

Find a window with the caption Form1 and a bad case of measles — that's the Form window. It's already loaded with default properties that define an ordinary window for your program's use. Every normal Delphi program displays a main form when it loads, and many use secondary forms to display or exchange information with the user. You design a program by dropping buttons, labels, and other components on the form, adjusting the properties of the form and components, and adding code to respond to events that occur as the user interacts with the program. The black dots in the window aren't really measles, by the way. They define a grid that helps you line up components on the form.

To change, hide, or eliminate the grid, select Options from the Tools menu (or Environment from the Options menu in Delphi 1.0) and click the Preferences tab. A rectangular panel titled Form Designer contains check boxes that determine whether or not Delphi displays the grid and whether or not controls snap to the grid points when you size or move them. You can also set the distance between grid dots in the X (left/ right) and Y (up/down) directions; however, the default distance of 8 pixels usually works well. Hiding the grid can make it easier to visualize what your form will look like, but I don't recommend turning it off entirely. It's tough to make components line up nicely on the form without the grid's help.

Detailing with the Object Inspector window

After roughing out your Delphi program in the Form window, you can fine-tune your design by using the Properties page of the Object Inspector, shown in Figure 1-7. Initially the Object Inspector exposes the intimate details of the program's main and only form, named Form1 by default. Every property starts with a default value; you personalize your program by changing these properties. To change the form's caption, for example, you'd select the Caption property in the Object Inspector and type in a new value. Some properties define visible aspects of a form or component, such as its color and caption. Others define run-time behavior, such as whether or not a form will be resizeable.

The Object Inspector has a second page labeled Events. Flip to this page and you'll see that the event names have a dreary sameness — OnActivate, OnClick, OnCreate, and so *On*. Delphi forms can respond to a variety of events generated by the mouse, the keyboard, or the Windows system itself. *You* control the form's response by defining an *event handler* for a particular event — you'll be writing event handlers in the very next chapter.

Instant program — the Code Editor

You'll do a lot of "programming" without ever looking at the Code Editor because Delphi itself writes the code. Even in a brand-spanking new project, the Code Editor already contains a page of program source code generated by Delphi, with the inspiring name Unit1. Choose the Code Editor to take a peek at the code on this page, but don't make any changes — not yet, anyway.

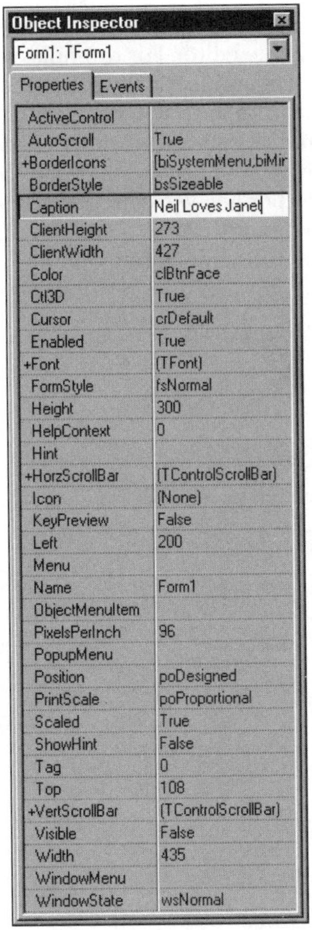

Object Inspector

Form1: TForm1

Properties | Events

ActiveControl	
AutoScroll	True
+BorderIcons	[biSystemMenu,biMin
BorderStyle	bsSizeable
Caption	Neil Loves Janet
ClientHeight	273
ClientWidth	427
Color	clBtnFace
Ctl3D	True
Cursor	crDefault
Enabled	True
+Font	(TFont)
FormStyle	fsNormal
Height	300
HelpContext	0
Hint	
+HorzScrollBar	(TControlScrollBar)
Icon	(None)
KeyPreview	False
Left	200
Menu	
Name	Form1
ObjectMenuItem	
PixelsPerInch	96
PopupMenu	
Position	poDesigned
PrintScale	poProportional
Scaled	True
ShowHint	False
Tag	0
Top	108
+VertScrollBar	(TControlScrollBar)
Visible	False
Width	435
WindowMenu	
WindowState	wsNormal

Figure 1-7:
The Object
Inspector
displays
properties
of a form or
component
and lets you
change
them.

Customizing the Code Editor

Select Options from the Delphi 2.0 Tools menu (or Environment from the Delphi
1.0 Options menu) and look at the tabs that name the dialog's pages. Three of
the seven tabs relate to the Code Editor — Editor, Display, and Colors (in Delphi
1.0, they're named Editor options, Editor display, and Editor colors, respectively). There's nothing you *need* to change on these pages, except possibly the
editor font (on the Display page). Delphi's editor uses only fixed-pitch fonts, and
changes to color and style are reserved for syntax highlighting. Thus the editor
font option just displays the available fixed-pitch fonts and possible sizes for
each. Set it to phone book-size font to cram tons of code onto one screen or
choose the Large Type edition for easy reading. Experiment and choose the size
you prefer.

The syntax highlighting options on the Colors page give different program elements different colors and text styles in the editor. For example, reserved words such as begin, end, and procedure are automatically displayed in boldface. Syntax highlighting is a handy feature once you get used to it — for example, if you accidentally type *procedrue* when you meant *procedure,* you'll notice the typo right away because the word won't snap into boldface as it's supposed to do. Unless you're addicted to fiddling with options, there's just no need to change the details of syntax highlighting. Figure 1-8 shows what can happen if you lose control while setting syntax highlighting options.

Figure 1-8: With syntax highlighting you can put comments in reverse video, give reserved words a gray background, and underline all identifiers — but you probably shouldn't.

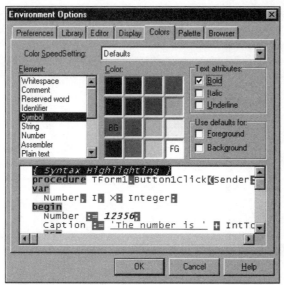

You'll notice a large number of other options for customizing the editor. You can change the keystrokes it responds to, change the colors, and so on. Here's a tip — *don't.* Customizing an editor is just an exercise in frustration. If you try working on someone else's system, your special layout won't be available, and when Delphi gets an upgrade, you may have to customize all over again. Your effort is better spent getting accustomed to the standard keystrokes.

Take action with the Main window

Stretched across the top of your screen is the big boss window, the Main window. You can tell this window's the boss because if you close it Delphi goes away. This is the window that keeps the other windows under control. It's divided into three parts:

    ✔ Main menu

    ✔ SpeedBar buttons

    ✔ Component palette

Figure 1-9 shows Delphi's Main window.

Figure 1-9:
Delphi's
Main
window
controls all
the other
windows,
but it
doesn't
contain
them.

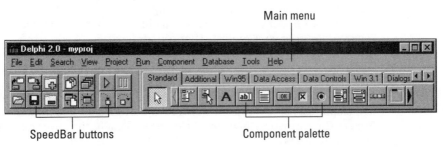

SpeedBar buttons   Component palette

Selecting from the menu

There's just no point in droning through a lengthy list of all the Delphi menu commands. Many of them will be familiar to any Windows user, and many others are self-explanatory. This book takes the practical approach of introducing individual menu commands as they're needed.

There's one aspect of the Delphi menus that might throw you off at first. In Delphi, the standard Windows File menu shortcut keys are instead assigned to options that deal with the current file in the Code Editor, *not* to the whole project. For example, Alt+F,S saves just the current file, and the shortcut key for Save All (Save Project in Delphi 1.0) is Alt+F,V. Until you get used to the difference, use the mouse to select directly from the menu.

SpeedBar buttons

We live in an instant society, and fast is never fast enough. Menus were invented to save you the trouble of remembering and typing complicated commands. And SpeedBar buttons (also known as speed buttons) save you the trouble of reading and clicking menu items! Delphi's SpeedBar buttons provide fast access to several especially useful menu items.

Most large and modern Windows applications have SpeedBar buttons under one name or another (SmartIcons, ToolBar buttons, HotCrossButtons, whatever). And all suffer from the same problem — the meaning of the button icon isn't always obvious. For instance, one of Delphi's buttons looks like a flea jumping into a box, and another button looks like a flea jumping over a box. Something to do with debugging, perhaps? Luckily you don't have to guess. Just place the mouse cursor on a button and leave it there for a second or two. A tiny help window (*flyover help*) will appear to remind you what the button does.

The six buttons in the left-hand block of the SpeedBar (see Figure 1-9) smooth your access to common file-related actions. You'll recognize the standard glyphs (graphics) for open file and save to disk, which load and save individual files. Two other buttons depict a folder emerging from and reentering a hard disk; these symbolize opening and saving a whole project. Finally, the buttons that display a folder emblazoned with a plus or minus sign let you add and remove files from your project. That sounds logical!

The next block of four buttons helps you navigate among the forms and unit files in a large project. One button shows several pieces of paper; pressing it displays a list of units to choose from. Another button depicts several forms and displays a list of forms. The lower left button takes you from the active form to the corresponding unit or vice versa. Finally, the lower right button creates and adds a shiny new, blank form to your project.

When there's just one unit and one form in your project, these buttons don't seem terribly important. Later, though, when you have a dozen forms and as many units in one project, you'll find them extremely helpful.

The last four standard SpeedBar buttons handle running and debugging your programs. The two that look like the play and pause buttons on a VCR do what you'd expect — run the program and pause its execution. Below them are the flea-jumping buttons mentioned previously. Yup, they're used for debugging!

The whole point of SpeedBar buttons is to let you work more efficiently. But you're not me, and neither of us works the same way as Delphi's authors. That's why the SpeedBar is completely configurable. Just right-click the bar itself, outside the buttons, and choose Configure... from the pop-up menu. You can add a button for any menu choice, or rearrange the buttons that are already there. If you never use a particular button, just drag it right *off* the SpeedBar. And when, in your excitement, you've utterly scrambled the SpeedBar, press the Reset Defaults button and start again, calmly this time.

The Component palette

Delphi's Component palette is like a cabinet stuffed with parts you can use to build programs. Every item on every page of the Component palette is a functioning gadget that you can drop into your program with the click of a mouse. Push buttons and scroll bars, data grids and text editors, they're all here. A major part of this book is dedicated to explaining and demonstrating each of the Delphi components.

Here again the meaning of the icons that Delphi uses to represent the components may not be crystal clear to you. Just leave the mouse cursor sitting on any one of them and in a second or two the flyover help will show you the name Delphi uses for that type of component.

If you experiment with the Options menu choices, you'll eventually find a page of the Options | Environment dialog called Palette. Don't mess with it! Yes, you can change the order of the pages in the Component palette and change the order of the components. Yes, you can rename the existing pages, add or delete pages, and add or delete components. However, there's just no *need* to fiddle around with these things. Leave them with the names they started with, and you'll be able to talk about them with other Delphi users. Keep their original positions and you won't be confused when an update to Delphi *restores* those positions. The same is true of the page called Library. The options on this page affect what happens when you rebuild the entire component library — which isn't a task for the neophyte!

Your First Program RIGHT NOW!

Windows mega-guru Charles Petzold, in his classic book *Programming Windows,* demonstrates that creating a minimal "Hello, World" Windows program in the C programming language requires writing 80 lines of code. Here's a little test: How many lines of code would you expect to write to convert a blank new Delphi form into a working program?

Add nothing, chill, and serve

Okay, the test is over. Put down your pencil and turn over your paper. Did you say absolutely none? You're right!

To create your first Delphi program, just click the Run button on the SpeedBar (the button with a picture of a right-pointing wedge; it looks like the Play button on a VCR). If you prefer to use menus, select Run from the Run menu, ignoring the redundancy. Or press the Run program shortcut key, F9. Delphi will first compile the program — that is, convert it into a self-contained EXE file — and then run it.

The resulting program, stored as PROJECT1.EXE on disk, displays a blank window with Form1 as its caption. You can maximize this window to fill the screen or shrink it down to an icon. Use the mouse to move it around and change its size, and when you get bored, double-click the system menu box at the top left corner to shut it down.

Delphi programs versus VB programs

There are two important differences between the EXE files created by Delphi and the EXE files created by Visual Basic (VB) version 3.0 or 4.0. Delphi creates pure machine code that's directly executed by your computer, but VB translates source code to an intermediate form called p-code. A VB-generated EXE file is actually a p-code interpreter program, with your program's p-code tacked onto the end of it.

The "run-time library" of standard functions for all VB programs is stored in the file VBRUN300.DLL or VB40032.DLL. Any VB program you distribute will have to include this file, or rely on the user to get ahold of this file. You'll also need to distribute VBX or OCX files for any VB controls that aren't included in the main support DLL.

Delphi programs contain the necessary portions of the Delphi run-time library within themselves, along with the components you've used. As a result, a Delphi EXE file will usually be larger than an equivalent VB EXE file, but it won't rely on any external files for its operation.

This instant program doesn't do anything *useful,* but consider the implications: You'll never have to write code to do any of the things it does! All the basic behaviors that make up a Windows program are already in place. Delphi's aim is to do everything for you that it possibly can.

Templates for instant programming

The do-nothing program you just built represents a kind of lowest common denominator for Windows programs. It's utterly generic, and you have to do a bit of work to turn it into a really useful program. Delphi 1.0's templates and Delphi 2.0's object repository provide another way for you to get started on a program, and they do more of the work for you.

If you're running Delphi 1.0, select Environment from the Options menu, flip to the Preferences page, and check off both check boxes in the rectangle labeled Gallery. Click OK — and nothing happens!

Now, though, when you start a new project, Delphi 1.0 asks whether you want to use one of the project templates from the gallery. When you create a new form, Delphi uses the dialog shown in Figure 1-10 to ask whether you want to use one of the form templates.

The Delphi 2.0 object repository expands the template concept. When you create a new form based on an object from the repository, your new form retains its relationship with the original. This can be extremely handy for building company-wide standardized forms. For example, suppose the standard form style for TechnoGrub, Inc. includes a picture of the company logo. When

TechnoGrub is acquired by DataSlug, a simple change to the original form in the object repository will put the *new* company logo on all forms derived from that original. By comparison, Delphi 1.0's templates are static; after you create a form based on a template, the connection is broken. Even if the template swells and turns purple, your form won't change.

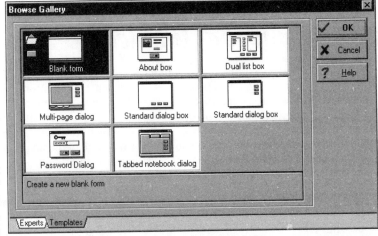

Figure 1-10:
Delphi 1.0
offers an
assortment
of
prepackaged
forms.

To pull a form or project from the Delphi 2.0 object repository, you select New... from the File menu, rather than one of the more specific choices such as New Form or New Application. Delphi displays the dialog shown in Figure 1-11, inviting you to choose an object. Notice that the project's name appears on one of the tabs — yes, you can use a form that's already in your project as a model for another form in the same project.

Figure 1-11:
The Delphi
2.0 object
repository
makes
reusing
forms and
other Delphi
objects
incredibly
simple.

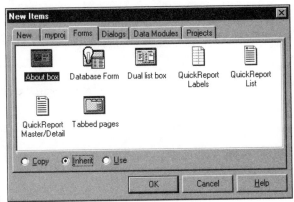

You won't be relying heavily on templates or objects from the repository as you do the exercises in this book; you'll learn more by building projects from scratch. Unless you're instructed otherwise, just choose New Application or New Form each time this book tells you to open a new project or a new form. In Delphi 1.0, choose the Blank Project or Blank Form each time, or simply turn off the Gallery options.

An Embarrassment of Windows

The Main window *is* Delphi — close it and Delphi is gone. Whenever Delphi is running, the Main window will be present. The Form, Code Editor, and Object Inspector windows are so important that you'll always keep them open as well. If you think that makes for a crowded screen, wait until you see the *rest* of Delphi's windows! Delphi provides a number of other windows that you can open for a specific purpose and close when you've finished using them. Figure 1-12 shows all the Delphi windows open at the same time.

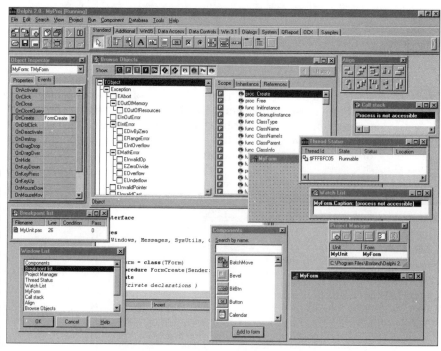

Figure 1-12: If you open all of Delphi's windows, there's no room on the screen for anything else.

The first section of the View menu is a list of Delphi windows. If you select a window from this menu, you'll open it (or you'll bring it into view if it's already open). The windows are

✔ Project Manager

✔ Project Source

✔ Object Inspector

✔ Align

✔ Browse Objects

✔ Breakpoint list

✔ Watch List

✔ Call stack

✔ Thread Status (Delphi 2.0 only)

✔ Components

✔ Window List

The Project Manager shows all the forms and units contained in your project. With it you can add or remove files from the project, or jump directly into the Form Designer or editor for a particular file. Most of the time, though, you can leave this window packed away.

Choosing Project Source adds the source code for the project file itself to the Code Editor. However, you rarely need to even see the project file, much less edit it!

You've already been introduced to the Object Inspector, so let's skip ahead to the next window. The Alignment palette is a specialized window used for lining up components that you've already placed on a form. You open it up when you're fine-tuning component placement, and close it when you're finished. You'll get the lowdown on using the Alignment palette in Chapter 3.

Delphi's forms and components are all related, and their family tree is called the *object hierarchy*. The Browse Objects window (*browser* for short) displays the entire hierarchy or details about any particular component. It's truly over-whelming! For the most part, the genealogical, anatomical, and referential information supplied by the browser won't be useful to you until you know more about Delphi's overall component architecture and programming model. Go ahead and look at it, but don't worry if it doesn't make sense yet. Note that the Browser window can't be opened until you've successfully compiled your project.

Three of the windows deal with debugging topics. The Breakpoint list window lists breakpoints, which are lines that you've specially marked so Delphi will drop into debugging mode before executing them. The Watch List window displays the value of specified variables as they change during a run of your program. Finally, the Call stack window lists the name of the function that's currently executing, the function that called it, the function that called it, and so on. Uh-oh. We haven't discussed variables or functions yet. You learn how to use these three windows in Chapter 15, the debugging chapter. Delphi 2.0 adds a fourth debugging window called Thread Status. In 32-bit Windows, threads let your program develop a split personality and run multiple processes at the same time. Sounds alarming? Fear not. You won't be writing any multithreaded programs in this book.

The Components list is simply an alternate way to add components to the form. It lists all available components alphabetically, so it's handy when you don't remember where to find a particular component. The Components list lets you get at all the components using just the keyboard, for those times when you get tired of wrestling with the minimouse on your laptop. (Did you remember to bring the mouse this time?)

When the impossible mass of windows on the screen has you tearing your hair, open the Window List window. This window just lists all the other open Delphi windows and lets you jump directly to the one you want.

All these multifarious windows have their uses, but they merely play supporting roles to the real star — the Form Designer window. The next chapter dishes the dirt on form design.

Chapter 2

Programming in Good Form

. . . .

In This Chapter

▶ Finding out how properties define a form

▶ Putting a Windows 95-style help icon on Delphi 2.0 forms

▶ Discovering the various types of properties

▶ Making one form the "child" of another form

▶ Assigning new values to different types of properties

▶ Identifying the events that forms can respond to

▶ Creating a project template for programs with a fixed-size main form

▶ Making a form respond to mouse-clicks or keyboard input

▶ Making a program ask "Are you sure?" before it terminates

. . . .

*E*very normal Windows program communicates with the user through a rectangular area on the screen — a window. Yes, that's where Windows gets its name. In Delphi's world, windows are represented by *form* components. Everything else depends on the form, so it's the first of Delphi's many components that you'll meet.

Blueprint for a Program

Before you build a new house, you draw up a plan that shows the size, shape, and other properties of the edifice you want to build. Markings on the plan show where various standard components will go — doors, windows, the Jacuzzi, and so on. When the design is complete, you hand it to a contractor and cross your fingers, hoping it will come out the way you want it.

A Delphi program's blueprint is the form. You design a program by setting the properties of the form and placing standard components on it. However, you don't have to wait for a contractor to build the final program to see what it will look like. Once you've worked up a design for the program, you can see immediately what it will look like. Don't like it? Change it! It's a snap to redesign when no lumber is involved, and it's smart to get the design right before you start adding code.

What if you like the house so much that you want another just the same? You have to call the contractor again (and find out that the cost of materials has gone up!). Delphi 2.0 users can get a duplicate *form* simply by using visual inheritance. The new form is identical to the old, yet you can still add to it. Still more amazing, enhancements made to the original form appear in the copy. It's as if you could add a swimming pool to your house and have an identical pool appear in other houses built to the same plan.

Most programs you create start with a main form, and many have secondary forms as well. The form is what holds your program together — everything else relies on forms. Without a form, you don't have a program.

Making a FORMal Inspection

Suppose you're going to meet an e-mail acquaintance at the airport — someone who's never seen you before. How do you describe yourself? You probably offer a list of *properties* — your height, hair color, tattoos, and so on. A Delphi form has properties, too; as Figure 2-1 shows, the Object Inspector window lists several dozen. For example, the form's caption, size, and on-screen position are properties. If you change a value in the Object Inspector window, the form changes accordingly. Making a form skinnier is a lot easier than reducing your own weight!

If you don't see the Object Inspector window on the screen, select Object Inspector from the View menu. The window has two pages, with tabs labeled Properties and Events. Click the Properties tab and move the scroll bar to see all the properties for the form. Depending on your video resolution, you may be able to stretch the window's height so that all the properties are displayed at once.

The left column of the Properties page lists property names, and the right column holds their current values. You make changes by entering new values in the right column. The way you enter a new value depends on the property — the list is designed to help you enter suitable values for each property.

When you click various properties, you notice differences in the way their values are displayed. For some, a down arrow appears next to the value; clicking it pulls down a list of possible values. Others display a button with an ellipsis (…). Pressing the button displays a dialog box for setting the property's value. Still others have a plus sign at the start of the property name. Double-clicking the name "explodes" the property into a number of subproperties. Figure 2-2 is a composite showing several different types of properties; the section later in this chapter called "A Field Guide to Properties" sums up the possibilities. You can experiment and become familiar with the important properties.

Component name

Component type

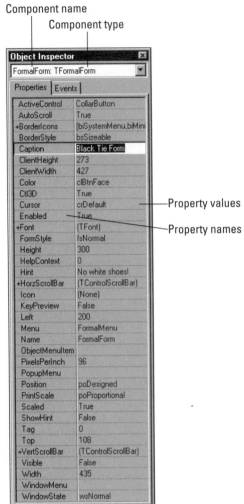

Property values

Property names

Figure 2-1:
The Object
Inspector
window
displays
properties
and lets you
change
them.

Tweaking visible properties

The most impressive form properties are those that affect the on-screen design
image of the form. When you change one of these, the effect is immediate. For
example, click the Caption property and enter your name — the change will
show up right away in the form's title bar. You always wanted your name in
lights, didn't you?

Changing the form's Color property also makes a big difference. There are three
ways to set the Color property: choose a color by name, match the color of a
Windows screen element, or choose any color of the rainbow. Press the down
arrow next to the current Color value and you get a list of possible values, all

Figure 2-2:
This composite figure shows properties with value lists pulled down and not pulled down, exploding properties exploded and not exploded, and an ellipsis button that brings up a property-setting dialog.

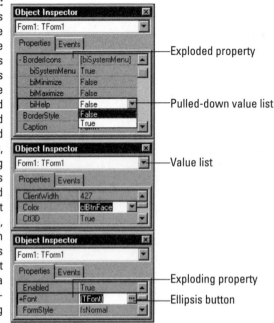

starting with the letters *cl*. The first 16 items on the list — clAqua, clNavy, clLime, clWhite, and so on — define actual colors. Choose one and the form's color changes to match. (The exact shade may vary slightly with different video drivers.)

The remaining items on the list have names such as clScrollBar and clBtnHighlight rather than particular colors. They correspond to the colors you can set using the Color module in the Windows 3.1 Control Panel, or the Appearance page of the Display Properties dialog in Windows 95. If you choose one of these, your form's color will vary depending on the user's color scheme. Delphi trusts you to make sensible color choices. For example, it doesn't really make sense to set a form's color to match the color of inactive window borders or highlighted menu items.

If you're using Windows 3.1, flip over to Program Manager, load the Windows Control Panel, and double-click the Color icon. In the Color module, press the Color Palette button. Note that each of the items listed under the label Screen Element corresponds to a possible value of the Color property. For example, Desktop matches clBackground, Button Face matches clBtnFace, and so on.

If Windows 95 is your current operating system, right-click on the desktop and select Properties from the popup menu. Click the Appearance tab at the top of the resulting dialog, and pull down the combo box labeled Items. Here again you get a list of screen elements whose colors are user-defined. In addition, Windows 95 lets you tweak the font for screen elements that include text and the size of elements such as scroll bars and window borders.

If you don't want to match your form to the color of a standard Windows screen element and the 16 basic colors don't excite you, you can choose any color that Windows is capable of showing. Just double-click the current color value and the special color-setting dialog shown in Figure 2-3 will pop up.

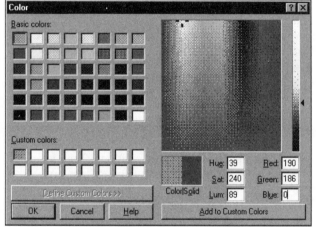

Figure 2-3:
The Color dialog lets you select from all the possible Windows colors.

Choose one of the colors shown, or press the Define Custom Colors button and mix the exact color you want. To save the color for future use, press the Add to Custom Colors button. When you've got it just right, click OK. The resulting custom color value will show up in the properties list as a hexadecimal number like $00BA0BAB.

Yes, Delphi does use those alarming hexadecimal (hex) numbers, with A's and F's mixed in with the 3's and 4's. Humans use decimal (base ten) because we have ten fingers. Computers have no fingers, but counting from zero to zero is deadly dull, so computers use binary numbers (base two). Programmers like hexadecimal numbers because one hex digit represents exactly four binary digits. Fortunately, Delphi handles converting decimal to hexadecimal and vice versa.

To convert a hexadecimal number to decimal, select Evaluate/Modify from Delphi's Run menu, type the hex number (including the dollar sign at the start) in the top line, and press Enter. To convert a decimal number to hex, type the decimal number in the top line, follow that with a comma and an *h* for hex, and then press Enter. Try it now. Bring up the Evaluate/Modify dialog and type 12648430,h in the Expression line, and then press Enter. You learn what nutrient is most important to programmers!

Double-click the value of the Ctl3D property to toggle it from False to True and back. Setting it to True doesn't have any visible effect except to change the form's color to clBtnFace. When you add components to the form, however, they take on the popular three-dimensional look. That is, the components appear to be chiseled into the surface of the form.

The colors used on the beveled edges of Ctl3D controls match the colors Windows 3.1 uses for push buttons. In the Windows 3.1 Control Panel's Color module, these are Button Face, Button Text, Button Shadow, and Button Highlight. These push buttons are normally shades of gray, black, and white, but they *can* be changed. The 3D Objects element in the Windows 95 Display Properties dialog controls the button face and button text colors; the shadow and highlight colors aren't exposed for meddling by the uninitiated.

That's about the size of it

Half a dozen properties define the size and position of your form on the screen. Most of the time you won't bother typing values for these properties — you just drag the form around with the mouse until it looks right. Move the form and you change the Left and Top properties. Resize it and you change the Width and Height. Resizing also changes the ClientWidth and ClientHeight properties, which are the dimensions of the inside of the form, not including the frame, caption, or menu. You can set these to particular numbers to create a form with specific interior dimensions.

Another pair of properties that relate to the form's size are HorzScrollBar and VertScrollBar. These are "exploding" properties — when you double-click the property name in the Object Inspector, they expand to display seven subproperties. The most important subproperty is Range. Any time the form's ClientWidth is smaller than HorzScrollBar.Range, the form displays a horizontal scroll bar. Any time the ClientHeight is smaller than VertScrollBar.Range, the form displays a vertical scroll bar. If you set the ranges to 1024 and 768, for example, you can create a form that uses the whole screen in 1024-by-768 mode, but is fully accessible to the user when it's smaller.

Scroll the Object Inspector window so that both Height and ClientHeight are visible and then use the mouse to tweak the form's height. Note that both properties change, but the difference between them remains the same. Set ClientHeight to a particular value and watch the form's size change.

Now try setting both the Left and Top properties to –32000. This hides the form by pushing it way off the screen. Bring it back into view by setting Left and Top to 0.

Delayed gratification

Some of the properties that change the way your form looks don't seem to have any effect at design time. That's because displaying those changes could interfere with the design process. To see the result of making changes to these properties, you have to run the program.

The BorderIcons property has a plus sign in front of it, which means that double-clicking explodes it into several subproperties. The subproperties that appear control whether or not your form will have a system menu box, a minimize button, and a maximize button. Your main form should always have a system menu box, and almost always a minimize button. If it's a resizeable window, it should have a maximize button as well. Delphi is smart — if you remove the minimize or maximize button, the corresponding item in the system menu is disabled.

The system menu box in Windows 3.1 occupies the top left corner of a window and contains a picture of the Spacebar. Why the Spacebar? Because Alt+Spacebar is one way to pull up the system menu. In Windows 95, the Alt+Spacebar keystroke still works, even though the system menu box displays a reduced version of the window's icon. The minimize and maximize buttons live at the top right corner of a window and contain wedge shapes that point downward and upward.

After you finish editing the border icons, double-click the BorderIcons property name again to hide the subproperties. If you look closely at the value of BorderIcons, you see that it consists of a pair of square brackets surrounding a list of the subproperties whose value is True. If you set them all to False, the value shrinks to [] (just the empty square brackets).

In Delphi 2.0, BorderIcons has a new subproperty called biHelp. When this property is True, the form displays context-sensitive help in popup panels rather than calling up the full WinHelp window. If the form has a system menu but no minimize or maximize button, a special question-mark icon appears on the form. Clicking this icon adds a question-mark to the cursor; clicking a component with this help cursor is an alternate way to bring up a context-sensitive help panel. Figure 2-4 shows an example of the help cursor in action.

Figure 2-4:
A user can get context-sensitive help automatically.

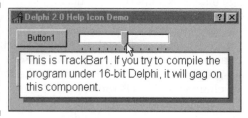

The question mark icon appears *only* when the form has a system menu but no minimize or maximize button. That means the form must have a BorderStyle of bsSizeable or bsSingle because in Delphi all other BorderStyle values suppress the system menu. (What's BorderStyle? Read on!)

The BorderStyle property is closely related to BorderIcons. It defaults to a border that the user can grab with the mouse and resize, just as you can resize it at design time. Sometimes, however, resizing the form just doesn't make sense. Suppose you spend all day agonizing over the placement of dozens of components on your form. You don't want the user to shrink the form so that half the components aren't visible or expand the form to put a useless expanse of blank space around the components. To make your program's main form nonresizeable, set its BorderStyle to bsSingle. To make a secondary form nonresizeable, use bsDialog.

Don't try to use the bsDialog style on a form that has a menu! Because of a quirk in Windows itself, this combination leaves a visible (and ugly) gap around the menu. Note, too, that you don't get the minimize or maximize border icons with this style.

Here again, Delphi 2.0 expands your options. The two new BorderStyle values, bsToolWindow and bsSizeToolWin, differ in that one is resizeable and the other is not. A form that uses one of these styles will have no system menu, maximize button, and minimize button, and its title bar will be smaller than usual. Figure 2-5 shows the difference. Use one of the two tool window styles for secondary windows such as floating toolbars and palettes.

Figure 2-5:
The right-hand window is a tool window.

The Position property tells Delphi whether or not you consider the size and position of the form at design time to be important. By default, its value is poDesigned, which means the form will initially be displayed at precisely the size and position it had at design time. A value of poDefault lets Windows choose the size and position; poDefaultSizeOnly and poDefaultPosOnly let Windows choose the size *or* the position, respectively. Finally, poScreenCenter retains the designed size but positions the form in the center of the screen, regardless of what screen resolution Windows is running in. Of course, if you set a form's BorderStyle to anything but bsSizeable or bsSizeToolWin, Windows can't give it a default size regardless of the value of Position.

Your program's initial appearance on the screen is determined by the WindowState property. Most of the time the default of wsNormal is correct. If you change it to wsMinimized, the program will load as an icon. If you set it to wsMaximized, it fills the whole screen.

Don't use the wsMaximized window state with a window that doesn't include a maximize button among its border icons. You end up with a window that covers the entire screen and has no restore button. (It can be restored to a smaller size only by double-clicking its caption.)

The default mouse cursor is the familiar arrow, pointing upward and just a bit to the left. If you change the form's Cursor property, the cursor will change to match, but only when it's over your form's client area. Try it. Select the different values and run the program to see the result.

Changing a form's Font property doesn't have any visible effect unless you add some components to the form. By default, components automatically display text using the font of the underlying form. There are two ways to change this property. You can click the ellipsis (...) button to display a standard Windows Font dialog, or you can double-click the property name to explode it into a set of subproperties. As you can see in Figure 2-6, Font is a double-bang property — its Style subproperty can also be exploded to let you set the bold, italic, underline, and strikeout styles.

Figure 2-6:
All the subproperties of a form's Font property are hidden until you "explode" them by double-clicking.

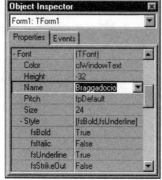

The default font for Delphi 1.0 forms and components is System. This is an awful choice because it comes in just one size and doesn't stretch or shrink. To change the default, open DELPHI.INI and add a DefaultFont= key to the [FormDesign] section, for example "DefaultFont=Arial, 8". Select any font you like, but make sure to use a TrueType font or a font such as MS Sans Serif that has many point sizes. Otherwise, you may find that your labels and components don't line up properly under certain video drivers. Delphi 2.0 uses MS Sans Serif as its default font. This isn't a TrueType font, but it comes in many different sizes, so it's a reasonable choice.

If you minimize a Delphi form, it appears as a default Delphi icon unless you set its Icon property to an icon specific to your application. Before you release any Delphi application for others to use, you definitely want to give each of its forms a distinctive icon. You can use one of the icons supplied with Delphi or draw your own using Delphi's Image Editor — just select Image Editor from the Tools menu. You also want Program Manager to use your icon when displaying your application in a group window. For that to happen, you must set the application's icon property to be the same as the main form's icon property.

To set the icon for your application, select Project from the Options menu and click the Application tab.

Frequently, you want to store some information about a form that's just not covered by the existing properties. If the information can be stored as a number, put it in the Tag property. Every component has a Tag property, and I use this property frequently in the examples.

Form families — the Multiple Document Interface

Sometimes one big window isn't enough. The Windows Multiple Document Interface (MDI) lets the program enlist the help of other windows that live inside the main window. The main window is called the parent, and the helpers are called child windows. An MDI program acts like a miniature version of the Windows desktop; it can tile or cascade the child windows within its boundaries, or minimize them to icons at the bottom of the main window. The child windows can be either the same type (for example, they could all be text editing windows but with a different file open in each) or different types (perhaps some text editing windows and some bitmap display windows). Program Manager is the most famous MDI program — its group windows are its children.

The FormStyle property controls whether a Delphi form is a normal window, an MDI parent window, or an MDI child window. You never define a program's main form as an MDI child.

Before starting the following set of instructions, select New Project from the File menu, so that you start with a new blank form. Do this *every* time you come to a set of instructions like this from now on, unless you're specifically told to use a program created previously.

Select New Form from the File menu — this adds a second form named Form2 to your project. Set the FormStyle property of Form2 to fsMDIChild and the FormStyle property of Form1 to fsMDIForm.

Run the program and try moving and resizing the secondary form. You find that it stays entirely within the parent MDI form. As Figure 2-7 shows, if any portion of the child form extends beyond the boundaries of the main form, the child form is cut off from view, and the main form sprouts scroll bars along the bottom, the right edge, or both, to let you bring the entire child form into view. If you minimize the child form, its icon appears at the bottom of the main form. Under Windows 95, a minimized child form turns into a tiny caption bar rather than an icon.

Figure 2-7:
This MDI form has three child forms; one is minimized, and another is cut off at the edge of the main form.

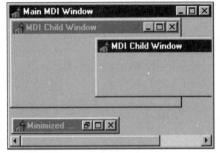

An MDI form created by Delphi has the built-in capability to tile or cascade its child windows and to arrange their icons neatly across its bottom edge. Because these features are normally invoked from the program's main menu, I wait until Chapter 6 (the menu chapter) to talk about them in detail.

But wait, there's more! FormStyle has one more possible value, StayOnTop. When you choose this value, your form will "float" on top of other programs even when it's not active, like the Windows Clock utility. This can be aggravating if there's something important under the floating form, so if you use the StayOnTop style, make the form as small as you can.

The WindowMenu property enables a handy feature. After creating a menu for the main form, you set this property to point to one of the top-level menu choices. Then, as each child window is created, its name is added to the tail end of the specified menu, and the currently active child window has a checkmark beside it. Again, you can take a good look at this property in Chapter 6.

A Field Guide to Properties

When you go stalking the wild property, you'll be more successful if you can recognize the common types. You see quite a few of them in this chapter — I review and categorize them now:

- ✔ *Exploding object properties* — The value is an object name such as (TFont), the name has a plus sign in front of it, and the value has an ellipsis button. Press the button to display a dialog or double-click the name to explode a list of subproperties. Example: Font.

- ✔ *List properties* — A down arrow appears next to the property value; clicking this arrow displays a list of possible values. Double-clicking the value selects the next item on the list; if the current value is the last, it jumps back to the first item. (The Color property looks like a list property, but it's a special case.) Examples: WindowState, Cursor, FormStyle.

- ✔ *Numeric properties* — You can type anything at all for the value, but non-numeric input will be rejected. In most cases, impossible numeric values will be converted to reasonable values. For example, a ClientHeight of –1 will be converted to 0. Examples: Left, Height, Top.

- ✔ *Object properties* — The value displayed is (None) or an object name such as (TIcon), and an ellipsis button (...) appears next to it. Pressing the button brings up a standard file-selection dialog. Example: Icon.

- ✔ *Set properties* — The property name has a plus sign in front of it, and the value is a list of words in brackets. If you double-click the name, the property explodes into a list of True or False subproperties. Examples: BorderIcons, HorzScrollBar, VertScrollBar.

- ✔ *String-list properties* — The value displayed is (TStrings), and an ellipsis button (...) appears next to it. Press the button to display a special editor that lets you enter a list of strings. The Form component doesn't include any properties of this type, but you see it in chapters to come.

- ✔ *True/False properties* — A down arrow appears next to the value; clicking this arrow displays a list containing just True and False. Double-clicking the value toggles it from True to False or False to True. Examples: Ctl3D, Enabled, Visible.

- ✔ *"Anything goes" properties* — A few properties accept *almost* anything you enter. If you type something that isn't valid, Delphi rejects it — try typing Visual Basic for the Name property, for example. Examples: Caption, Hint.

Every component has its own properties, and almost all of them fit one of these types, so you may want to review this list from time to time.

The Main Events

Raise your hand if you already learned programming under DOS. Did you raise your hand? If you *didn't,* you have an advantage. DOS programmers are accustomed to picturing a program as a sequential list of instructions: Go to the grocery, buy a dozen kumquats, IF they're on sale THEN buy two dozen — that sort of thing. They expect the computer to execute instructions in sequence, occasionally swirling in a loop or leaping into a subroutine. If you did raise your hand, pay special attention, because Windows programming is not what you're used to.

After a Windows program loads in memory and executes any initialization code, it doesn't do anything. Nothing at all. There is no "next step." Nothing happens until an event occurs, and then the program responds to the event. Instead of a list of instructions, it has a set of contingency plans that tell it what to do for each important event.

In Delphi, these contingency plans are called event handlers, and they respond to a variety of different events. Figure 2-8 shows the Events page of the Object Inspector window, which appears when you click the Events tab.

Figure 2-8:
The Events page of the Object Inspector lists all the events a Delphi component can respond to.

The events fall into three main categories: mouse events, keyboard events, and system events. Get your fingers warmed up, because you're going to be writing some very simple programs that respond to events in each of these categories.

Mouse events

For starters, you build a program that changes its cursor every time you click it with the mouse. If you click the Cursor property and then click the down arrow to look at its list of values, you notice that they run from crArrow (crAppStart in Delphi 2.0) through crVSplit. A little experimentation shows that for a form, crDefault is effectively the same as crArrow. Each value has a numeric equivalent ranging from –15 (crVSplit) to 0 (crDefault). In Delphi 2.0, the low end of the range is crHelp, with a value of –20.

 To learn the numeric value of a named constant such as crVSplit, press Ctrl+F7 to display the Evaluate/Modify dialog. Type the name of the constant into the Expression line and press Enter. Note that this works only after you compile or run the project successfully.

The first step in writing an event handler is to mentally plan out exactly what you want to happen. The computer always does precisely what you tell it to, nothing more, nothing less. If what you say isn't exactly what you mean, the computer can't second-guess you. So, for example, it's not enough to say that each time the user clicks with the mouse, the cursor changes to the next value in the list. You have to specify that when the cursor is on the *last* value (crDefault), it should wrap back to the first value (crVSplit). Expressing this concept in broken English, you get

> IF Cursor equals crDefault THEN
>> Set Cursor equal to crVSplit (crHelp in Delphi 2.0)
>
> OTHERWISE
>> Set Cursor equal to the next value.

As you'll see, this translates very nicely into Delphi code.

Click the Events tab in the Object Inspector and then double-click the event handler column next to the OnClick event. The Code Editor comes to the top, with the framework for an OnClick event handler already in place. Figure 2-9 shows the result — you just enter code between the event handler's begin and end lines.

Enter the following code at the cursor. (If you're using Delphi 2.0, replace crVSplit with crHelp.)

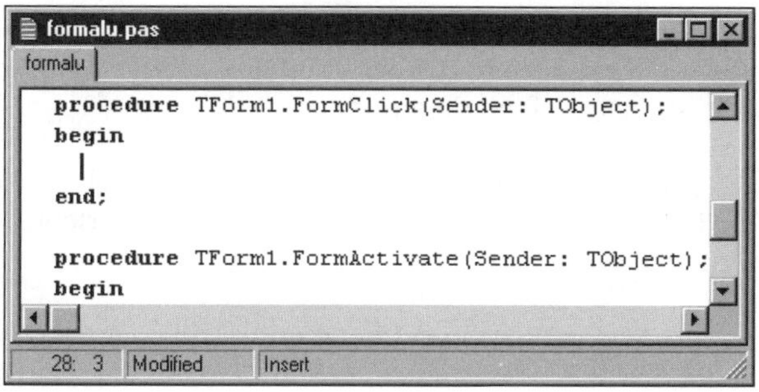

Figure 2-9:
Delphi
automatically
provides you
with the
framework
for an empty
event
handler —
all you do
is fill the
inside.

```
📄 formalu.pas                              _ □ ✕
 formalu

    procedure TForm1.FormClick(Sender: TObject);    ▲
    begin
      |
    end;

    procedure TForm1.FormActivate(Sender: TObject);
    begin                                           ▼
 ◄ |                                            ►
 28: 3    Modified       Insert
```

```
IF Cursor = crDefault THEN
   Cursor := crVSplit
ELSE
   Cursor := Succ(Cursor);
```

This is almost a direct translation of the pseudo-English code given previously. The equal sign (=) stands for testing equality in a comparison, and the := symbol stands for the act of moving data to make one thing equal to another. Weird, but you get used to it.

The built-in function Succ returns the successor of Cursor — the next available value. And the period at the end of the sentence is replaced by a semicolon. That's not too difficult now, is it?

You can break a line of Delphi code almost anywhere except in the middle of a word or in the middle of a literal string of text. The sample code you just typed is on four lines, but it can just as well be on one or two:

```
IF Cursor = crDefault THEN Cursor := crVSplit
ELSE Cursor := Succ(Cursor);
```

For that matter, you can put each of the 16 words and symbols on a separate line. The important thing is that the code should be easy to read and understand. When you type the code samples in this book just as they're shown, you're getting practice in a consistent and legible style.

Run the program and click the mouse on the form several times. Each time, the cursor changes to a new shape. After the cursor has taken on every shape (including the plain arrow shape *twice*), it starts over again. See? You've written a program that responds to mouse events! The other mouse events are OnDblClick, OnMouseDown, OnMouseMove, and OnMouseUp, along with OnDragOver and OnDragDrop. You use these events in later chapters.

Keyboard events

Now you can build a program that moves around on the screen when you press the arrow keys. It should respond to the left, right, up, and down arrows by moving eight pixels in the specified direction.

Shrink the form as narrow as it will go and make it about as high as it is wide. Set its BorderStyle to bsSingle and then double-click the BorderIcons property and set biMaximize to False.

Enter this code for the OnKeyDown event handler:

```
CASE Key OF
   VK_LEFT  : Left := Left - 8;
   VK_UP    : Top := Top - 8;
   VK_RIGHT : Left := Left + 8;
   VK_DOWN  : Top := Top + 8;
END;
```

To enter code for a particular event, double-click the event handler column to the right of the event's name. Delphi creates a framework for the event handler, and you enter code between the begin and end lines of the framework.

This CASE thing looks more complicated than the IF..THEN logic in the last example, but it's not. Delphi passes the event handler a variable called Key. The Key variable contains a code to identify which key was pressed, and the CASE statement compares that variable to four specific numbers.

What? You say VK_LEFT isn't a number? That's true. The four names beginning with *VK* are constants — descriptive names applied to numbers. We can replace them with 37, 38, 39, and 40. However, the bare numbers don't tell us anything about what's going on. The named constants make it clear that 37 here identifies the Virtual Key (VK) left arrow.

You can get the numeric value of a named constant using the Evaluate/Modify dialog, as long as you successfully compile or run the program. Just press Ctrl+F7, enter the name of the constant, and press Enter.

You can add one more keyboard event handler to make the program quit if you type the letter *Q*. You add this event handler to the OnKeyPress event. How is this different from OnKeyDown or OnKeyUp? The OnKeyPress event occurs after a key has been pressed (down), and the system has identified it as a simple typing key such as *A* or *!*, and not as an arrow key, a function key, an Alt+key combination, and so on.

Without starting a new project, create an OnKeyPress event handler for the form containing this single line:

```
IF UpCase(Key) = 'Q' THEN Close;
```

The UpCase function is built into Delphi. When you pass it a letter of the alphabet, it returns the uppercase version of that letter. When you pass it any other character, it just returns the character unchanged.

Run the program and take it for a walk. When you press the up, down, left, or right arrow key, the form obediently moves in the specified direction. Press *Q* and it quits. This is actually a weird and deviant use of the keyboard events — there are other ways to move and close a form. But it serves to give you an example of how keyboard events work.

The keyboard-driven form project you just built is a program whose main window retains the size you gave it at design time, resisting attempts to maximize it or tweak it with the mouse. In effect, the main form is a dialog. This style is very handy for the small programs you create in this book — handy enough to merit its own template in Delphi 1.0, and its own project stored in the Delphi 2.0 object repository.

Start a new blank project and set the form's BorderStyle to bsSingle and its BorderIcons.biMaximize property to False. Change the form's caption to Fixed-Size Form. Now select Project Manager from the View menu and right-click the Project Manager window. If you're running Delphi 1.0, select Save As Template… from the resulting pop-up menu. Under Delphi 2.0, select Add Project to Repository… from the pop-up menu. Whichever version you're using, fill in FIXFORM for the name, Fixed-Size Form for the template title, and enter your own description. If you're a Delphi 2.0 user, you also select Projects from the Page combo box and fill in your own name in the Author box. Use the default bitmap to represent this project and click OK.

OOPs — what about fields and methods?

If you cut through the hype in the media's treatment of object-oriented programming (OOP) and grasp what it's really about, you may notice a certain similarity between objects and forms. An object has fields that hold data values and methods that act on the data. A form has properties that hold data and event handlers that act on the data. In fact, Delphi is an OOP system. A property is a kind of data field, an event handler is a kind of method, and a form is a type of object called TForm.

Forms and other Delphi program components can also have data fields that are not properties and methods that are not event handlers. For example, in the keyboard event example you saw earlier to shut down the program, Close is a method of the form object.

Properties and event handlers are the important elements of Delphi programming, and this book concentrates on them. However, in writing the code to respond to events, from time to time you use data fields that aren't properties and methods that aren't event handlers. You dig into objects, fields, and methods in Chapter 14. By the time you get there, you have plenty of experience using them in the sample programs.

From now on, you'll use this stored project to create fixed-size forms for the exercises in this book. Of course, Delphi supplies a variety of stored projects, but using your own gives such a feeling of power! The fixed-size form project you just built creates a program in which the main form's size is fixed.

System events

The mouse and keyboard events are triggered by things the user does with the program. System events come straight from Windows, so their use is a little less obvious. Table 2-1 describes the most important system events.

Table 2-1	Important System Events	
Event	*Occasion*	*Usual Response*
OnActivate	The form has just become the program's active window	Update any information
OnClose	OnCloseQuery already happened, and the form is being shut down	Last chance to refuse to shut down
OnCloseQuery	Windows asks the form whether it's willing to shut down	Prompt the user to save any changed data or refuse to shut down
OnCreate	The form is created	Perform any necessary initialization
OnDeactivate	The form has just stopped being the program's active window	Undo any actions taken in the OnActivate event handler
OnDestroy	The form is about to disappear for good	Clean up any resources the program allocated
OnPaint	The form needs to be redisplayed because, for example, it has just been uncovered or restored from an icon	Draw lines or other simple graphics directly on the form
OnResize	The form has been resized	Adjust the size or position of components when the form is resized

Many Windows programs interrupt your attempt to shut them down by asking whether you're sure that's what you want to do. Your Delphi programs can ask for this kind of confirmation in the OnCloseQuery event handler.

Insert these lines in a new form's OnCloseQuery event handler:

```
CanClose := MessageDlg('Are you sure?',
    mtConfirmation,
    [mbYes, mbNo], 0) = IDYES;
```

Run the program and then double-click the system menu box to shut it down. A message dialog like the one in Figure 2-10 appears, asking for confirmation. If you choose No, the program won't terminate.

Figure 2-10:
A single call to the Delphi function MessageDlg produces this dialog.

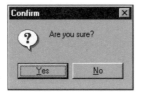

MessageDlg is a function supplied by Delphi to let programs communicate with the user. This is a more complicated function than the UpCase function you used earlier, and you have to pass it four pieces of information, called parameters or arguments.

The first parameter is the message you want to display, enclosed in single quotation marks. The second parameter is a constant that determines what kind of message box this is: possible values are constants named mtWarning, mtError, mtInformation, and mtConfirmation. Each constant has a specific icon associated with it, and a specific title for the message box. In this case, the icon is a large question mark and the title is Confirm.

The third parameter is a set of constants specifying what buttons should appear in the dialog. Brackets surround the list, and your choices are mbYes, mbNo, mbOk, mbCancel, and mbHelp. Delphi 2.0 adds mbAbort, mbRetry, mbIgnore, and mbAll. If mbHelp is among the choices and your program has a Windows help file associated with it, pressing the Help button displays the help topic associated with the number in the fourth parameter. Finally, the MessageDlg function *returns* a constant identifying which button the user pressed. If the returned value isn't IDYES, the program is not permitted to close. You use the MessageDlg function quite a bit.

A program with just a main form is like a house with no furniture. It keeps the rain off, but it's not very comfortable! The next part of this book explains how to furnish your forms with Delphi's components. You become an instant interior decorator and learn to move furniture without straining your back.

Part II
Programming with Components

Re'al Pro'gram·mers

Real Programmers curse alot, but only at inanimate objects.

In this part . . .

Delphi supplies you with a huge number of prefabricated program components. Some are simple, such as push buttons, check boxes, and labels. Others incorporate amazing power, such as displaying a complex dialog box to let users choose which file to open. The biggest step in programming with Delphi is understanding how incredibly much Delphi can do for you.

Part II introduces Delphi's most basic components and shows off their capabilities. You'll gain experience in laying out Delphi forms, and you'll become familiar with the process of writing event handlers to tell the components what to do. Along the way, you'll use all the basic components in programs ranging from tiny demo projects to a text editor comparable to the Windows Notepad.

Chapter 3

Hooking Up Components

· ·

In This Chapter

▶ Designing a program by arranging components on the form

▶ Lining up groups of components

▶ Learning which properties and events are common to most components

▶ Giving your programs a three-dimensional look

▶ Adding drag-and-drop functionality to programs

▶ Making the Tab key move between components in the order *you* choose

· ·

*I*t's always satisfying to find that your workbench has exactly the right screw or bolt or wing nut on hand to deal with your current project. Imagine the thrill of building programs with Delphi: You never have to run to the hardware store for parts! The Component palette is your multidrawer parts chest, and the only tool you need is a mouse.

The Component Palette

Delphi's basic Component palette has seven pages labeled Standard, Additional, Data Access, Data Controls, Dialogs, System, and Samples. Another page is provided to hold Visual Basic components — yes, Delphi 1.0 can use VBXs and Delphi 2.0 can use OCXs!

✔ *Standard* — Most components on this page correspond directly to on-screen elements of Windows itself. Menus, push buttons, scroll bars — they're all here. The Delphi versions, however, have some handy extra features built in.

✔ *Additional* — This page contains more advanced components. For example, the outline component is handy for displaying data that's organized in some kind of hierarchy, and the amazing media player component lets your programs play sounds, music, and video. This page also holds components whose main purpose is to display graphical information. The image component loads and displays bitmaps, and the shape component decorates your form with circles, squares, and so on.

✔ *Data Access and Data Controls* — Delphi uses the Borland Database Engine (BDE) to access database files in a variety of file formats. The components on these two pages make it easy for Delphi programs to tie into the database services provided by the BDE, such as multiuser reading, writing, indexing, and querying of dBASE and Paradox tables. It takes almost no programming at all to write a program for browsing and editing the information in a database.

✔ *Dialogs* — Windows 3.1 introduced standardized common dialogs for file operations, font selection, color selection, and so on. However, using them in an ordinary Windows program can require a substantial amount of setup code. The Dialogs page gives Delphi programs easy access to these common dialogs.

✔ *System* — Not every file-handling need can be shoehorned into the standard common dialogs, so Delphi's System page lets you mix and match individual elements such as drive, directory, and file lists. The System page also holds the components that handle high-level communications between programs using DDE (Dynamic Data Exchange) and OLE (Object Linking and Embedding). And the System page's timer component can trigger events at preset time intervals.

✔ *Samples* — This is a catch-all page for components that aren't intrinsic to the Delphi package, but do demonstrate the power of the component system. On-line help for these components isn't built in. Still, you'll find they're just as useful as their companion components on the other pages.

Delphi 2.0 adds some pages and changes a few others:

✔ *Win 95* — This page holds the shiny new components that let Delphi programs take advantage of Windows 95 user-interface enhancements such as the tree view, list view, and status bar used in the Windows 95 Explorer, and the rich text editor found in WordPad.

✔ *Win 3.1* — Components that existed in Delphi 1.0 but have been superseded by fancy Windows 95 components get sent to Siberia, otherwise known as the Win 3.1 page.

✔ *Additional* — Most of the components that were put out of a job by the advent of Windows 95 *used* to reside on this page. It's substantially less populous in Delphi 2.0 than it was in Delphi 1.0.

The chapters that follow this one introduce you to components from all of these pages. This chapter provides general information about components.

Placing Components

It's very simple to place components. You just click the tab of the Component palette page you want, push the speed button for the component you want to place, and click the form. That's it! Or if you prefer, you can click the component and then drag a rectangle on the form; the component will appear inside the rectangle. If the component's size is adjustable, it will appear sized to match the rectangle.

If you can't remember which page a particular component is on, select Components list from the View menu for an alphabetical listing.

Placing, moving, and resizing a single component

When you click a component in the Component palette, its button appears pushed in. When you click on a different component, the first button pops out — only one component at a time can be selected. To pop all the buttons out and regain normal use of the mouse, click the selection arrow that appears at the left end of every page in the palette (see Figure 3-1).

Figure 3-1:
To return to normal use of the mouse, click the selection arrow.

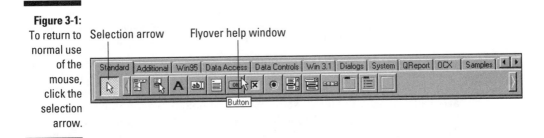

Select the Standard page on the Component palette and put the mouse cursor on the square that shows a button with the word OK on it. After the mouse has been still for a second or two, a tiny flyover help window will appear to identify this component as a Button — you can see it in Figure 3-1. Click it, and then click your form. An average-sized button captioned "Button1" will appear.

Click the button component again, but this time use the mouse to draw a big rectangle on the form. Button2 will fill the rectangle. Note that the button has little square sizing handles at each corner and in the middle of each edge. Use these to resize the button using the mouse. Now click Button1 and drag it to a new position.

You'll notice that when you move and resize components, they snap to the grid points on the form. Most of the time this is a good thing — it helps avoid that snaggle-toothed look. If you want to turn off this feature, or change the spacing of the grid points, select Environment from the Options menu. The first page of options relates to your preferences, and it includes a rectangular panel called Form Designer. The Display grid and Snap to grid check boxes control whether the grid is visible and whether it's active. You can also change the values of Grid Size X and Grid Size Y to change the size of the grid.

To get finer control over the placement and size of your components, try this. Set the grid size values to 4 instead of 8, turn off the visible grid, but leave the Snap to grid check box active.

Nonvisible components

Not every component shows up on the form at run time. For example, the menu component causes the form to have a menu, but the corresponding square icon doesn't show up on the form when the program runs. The common dialog components don't appear on the form at all at run time. A nonvisible component can't be resized — it always shows up as a simple icon.

Stash your nonvisible components in a nonbusy corner of the form, where they'll be easy to find.

Twins, triplets, quadruplets, and beyond

It's simple enough to add two or three components to a form. You click the item in the palette, click the form, click the item, click the form, and so on, back and forth. But if you're placing a dozen components of the same type, you want to avoid all that back-and-forth. No problem. Just hold down the Shift key when you choose the component from the palette and its button will *stay* pressed in. Then you can place any number of that type of control on the form. Click the selection arrow on the Component palette when you're finished. Don't forget that last step, or the next time you drag with the mouse, you'll unexpectedly create another component!

Scientists announce cloning breakthrough!

After you have correctly sized and placed a component, with all its properties set precisely to your taste, you can clone it easily. Just click the component, press Ctrl+C to copy it to the Clipboard, and press Ctrl+V to paste a copy into the form. The clone will be identical to the original in all properties except a few that are required to be unique, such as the component's name. So as not to hide the original, the clone is positioned a little to the right and down, as you can see in Figure 3-2.

Figure 3-2:
This form
contains ten
buttons
cloned from
the original
button in the
top left
corner.

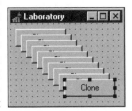

The keystrokes Ctrl+C, Ctrl+X, and Ctrl+V are standard Windows keys for Copy, Cut, and Paste. If you've rashly selected a key mapping other than the default in Delphi's Environment Options, you'll be using different keystrokes. It's really best to use the default key mapping!

To see a still more amazing trick, select a component, press Ctrl+C, and then switch to the Editor window. Move to the very end of the unit, beyond the line that reads *end*. Now press Ctrl+V. You've just inserted a text description of the component. You can edit this description, cut or copy it to the Clipboard, and paste the edited component back into the form. You can even mutate the component from one type to another, if the two types are similar to start with.

Find the list box button in the Standard page of the Component palette and place a list box on a new form. Press Ctrl+X to cut it to the Clipboard, switch to the tail end of a file in the editor, and press Ctrl+V. The first line of the text description should be `object ListBox1: TListBox`. Change this to object `ComboBox1: TComboBox`. Select and cut the modified text block to the Clipboard, switch back to the Form Designer, and press Ctrl+V. The combo box will appear right where the original list box was, because its Left and Top properties are the same as those of the list box. Hey presto! You've transformed a list box into a combo box.

Selecting multiple components

It's a snap to select one component on the form — you just click it. Selecting several components at once isn't any more difficult. If you drag a rectangle that intersects all the components you're interested in, they'll all be selected. Or if you want to pick and choose, hold down the Shift key while you click each component in turn. You can even combine the two methods. If your dragnet catches more components than you want, as seems to have happened in Figure 3-3, just Shift+click the undesirables to throw them back.

Figure 3-3:
You can select a group of components all at once, and then deselect any that don't belong.

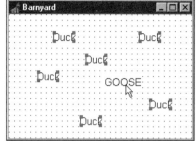

When you've got a group of components selected, you can move them as a group. They'll all stay in the same position in relation to each other. So, for example, if you get the urge to place a new component at the top of the form, it's easy to select *all* the other components and drag them down to make room.

One size fits all

After a flurry of placing components, you're likely to find that they're not all the same size, or not all the size you *want* them to be. To correct this, start by setting one of the components to the desired final size. Then select all the components whose size you want to adjust, either by dragging a rectangle that encloses them or by Shift+clicking on them. Select Size from the Edit menu and make your choices from the Size dialog, shown in Figure 3-4.

Unless the instructions say otherwise, start each set of instructions — like those that follow — on a new blank form in a new project.

Figure 3-4:
With the Size dialog, you can adjust the width and height of several components at once.

Shift+click the button item on the Component palette and place six or eight standard-sized buttons on a new form. Click the selection arrow to stop placing buttons. Select Button1 and shrink it so the caption just barely fits inside. Drag a rectangle that selects all the buttons, and then select Size from the Edit menu. Select the Shrink to smallest option in both the Width and Height columns of the Size dialog, and click OK. Now all the buttons are the size of the smallest one.

You can also enter the width and height for all selected components directly in the Size dialog. By doing this, however, you forfeit the advantage of using the sizing grid. As you'll see later, you can also use the Object Inspector window to set the width and height for a group of components. In fact, it's often better to use the Object Inspector window for this task because the width and height of the first component you select show up as default values.

Most of the time, the components you're nudging into shape will be the same type, but that's not a requirement. You can adjust, for example, the width of a whole column of different type components.

Putting your ducks in a row

If you enjoy stacking alphabet blocks and solving jigsaw puzzles, you may find the process of lining up your components on the form by hand both soothing and entertaining. But if you don't have time for that, Delphi's Alignment palette, grandly displayed in Figure 3-5, will help. If the icons on the speed buttons don't make sense to you, just rest the mouse cursor on each in turn and read the flyover help.

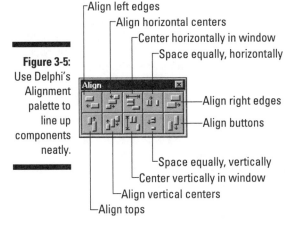

Figure 3-5:
Use Delphi's Alignment palette to line up components neatly.

Align left edges
Align horizontal centers
Center horizontally in window
Space equally, horizontally
Align right edges
Align buttons
Space equally, vertically
Center vertically in window
Align vertical centers
Align tops

The pictures for the buttons that align components on one of the four edges suggest that selected items will move to line up with the item that extends farthest in the direction of the arrow, but it's not so! Rather, all selected components line up with the first selected component, along the specified edge. The two buttons that align the centers of a group of selected components align them with the center of the first selected component. (You probably won't use this pair very much.)

You can center one component or a group of components in the window, horizontally or vertically. If it's a group, the components in the group stay in the same relationship to each other. Finally, the buttons that equalize the horizontal or vertical spacing of the selected components do so by adjusting the amount of space between the top or left edges of the components, *not* the actual space between them. These two buttons, therefore, work best when the selected components are all the same size.

If you have ten edit boxes in a row and accidentally align them at the top instead of the left, they'll all be stacked on top of the first edit box. Any time you slip and choose the wrong alignment option, you can end up with a group of controls all stacked up in the same place. It's always a good idea to *save* your form before performing major alignment tasks, because there's no undo for slips like this.

Enforcing component conformity

You might notice a flash from the Object Inspector window when you select more than one component. The flash occurs because the list of properties was redrawn, usually with fewer items on the list. What's going on? Let's find out.

Place two buttons on the form. Select one of them, and position the cursor above the other one. While watching the properties page of the Object Inspector window like a hawk, Shift+click the second button several times and watch what changes. A little experimentation will show that the Name and TabOrder properties disappear from the list when both buttons are selected.

Now, with both buttons selected, set the Width property to double its present value. Both buttons expand to the new width.

When more than one component is selected, the list of properties shrinks to include only the properties the two items have in common. Suppose you selected a dragon component and a horse component; the resulting properties list would include legs and tail, but not scales or mane. Also, properties that must be unique disappear from the list. In the previous exercise, the Name property disappeared because Delphi won't let two components have the same name (how would it tell them apart?). The TabOrder property disappeared because it, too, must be different for every component on the form.

If a property remains on the list when more than one component is selected, it's fair game. You can set that property for all the selected components at once. That's what happened when you changed the width — both buttons got the new value.

The more different kinds of components you select, the fewer properties will be common to all of them, and the shorter the property list will be. For example, select a check box along with the two push buttons you selected at the beginning of this section, and the Cancel, Default, and ModalResult properties will disappear. That's because these properties have no meaning for a check box. It's even possible to select a set of controls that have *no* properties in common except the ubiquitous Tag property.

Common Component Properties

If you flip through the Properties list for a number of different components, you notice certain items coming up again and again. Just about every component has Height and Width properties, for example. Many of the common properties should be familiar from the preceding chapter because the Form component has them too. In the next chapter, we start digging into the properties specific to individual components. For now, though, let's look at what they have in common.

A rose by any other caption

The most visible property of many components is the Caption property. You can enter just about anything as a value for the Caption property — a word, a phrase, a sentence, even a short poem, such as "Fleas: Adam had 'em." The kind of caption that's appropriate depends on the particular component. For example, push buttons tend to have short action words for captions, but check boxes and radio buttons sometimes have complete sentences describing the options they control.

The ampersand (&) has amazing powers when used in a component caption. It turns the next character into a mnemonic access key for the component. If a button's caption is &Press Me, the *P* will show up underlined, and pressing Alt+P will have the same effect as pressing that button. Naturally, no two components on a form should have the same mnemonic key.

What if you want an ampersand in a caption, as in Save & Exit, or Ham & Eggs? No problem — just use *two* ampersands in the Caption property, for example, Ham && Eggs.

Any component that displays text will have a Font property, just like a form has. However, if the ParentFont property is True, the component will automatically display its text in the font that was selected for the main form, and changing the main form's font will change the font used by the component. Most of the time, you'll leave ParentFont set to True.

As Figure 3-6 shows, you can use a nontext font such as Wingdings for a component's caption, but there are a few pitfalls. The character in the font that's in the position normally occupied by the ampersand will be treated as the ampersand. It will cause the following character to be underlined, and the access key for the component will be the text-font key corresponding to that character. If you want to use the character that corresponds to the ampersand, you have to use *two* of them, the same as with an ampersand. "&L" in the Wingdings font is an underlined unhappy face, and Alt+L triggers it. Don't use mnemonic access keys with nontext fonts!

Figure 3-6:
You can use a symbol font for Delphi's button captions, but don't try to give them mnemonic access keys.

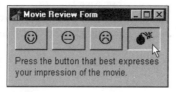

Color me beautiful

Most components have a Color property that works just like the Color property for the form itself. You can select one of 16 named colors, or match the component's color to a Windows on-screen element, or choose any custom color that Windows can display. However, unless you're writing a program for designing patchwork quilts, chances are good you won't want to set a different color for every component on the form. The True/False ParentColor property saves you the trouble of having to do so. When this property is True (which it is by default), the component takes on the color of the form. Change the form's color and the component changes to match. If you change the Color property of a component to something different than the form's color, Delphi automatically flips ParentColor to False.

Most components also have a Ctl3D property and the corresponding Parent-Ctl3D property. As you might expect, when ParentCtl3D is True, the Ctl3D property is tied to the corresponding property of the main form. You'll almost always want to leave ParentCtl3D set to True.

Start with a new form, and set its Ctl3D property to False. Find the group box button on the Standard page of the Component palette. Place a group box on the form. It will appear as a black rectangle with the name GroupBox1 displayed on the top line, near the left corner. Now click the form and change its Ctl3D property to True. The group box changes too — now its border appears to be incised into the imaginary surface of the form. Figure 3-7 shows the same form with and without Ctl3D.

Figure 3-7:
A form's
Ctl3D
property
gives a 3-D
look.

Don't ever set a component's Ctl3D property to True and leave ParentCtl3D set to False. The three-dimensional look is a cooperative effort between the form and its components.

That's about the size of it

Every component that shows up on the form when the program runs has dimension and location properties — Height, Width, Left, and Top. All four properties are expressed in pixels, and the Left and Top properties are measured relative to the top left corner of the form. If you snuggle a component right up into that top left corner, its Left and Top properties are both 0.

You can control the alignment and size of a group of components by setting these properties. If you know that a particular component is already the size you want, select it first and then Shift+click the others. Now when you go to set one of the dimension or location properties for the group, the value used by that first component appears as the default.

Some components, such as list boxes and memo boxes, have a property called Align, which controls the way they grab real estate from the form. Setting Align to alTop, alBottom, alRight, or alLeft causes the component to stick to the specified edge. For example, if Align is alBottom, the component will stay snuggled up against the bottom of the form. When the form's size changes, the component will keep its height as designed, but change its width to fill the form's width. If another component is already aligned on the same edge, the two will not overlap — they'll stack against that edge. Setting Align to alClient causes the component to fill the form's client area (or at least, the part of the client area that's not already occupied by components aligned on the edges). Figure 3-8 shows a form completely filled by components aligned in various ways.

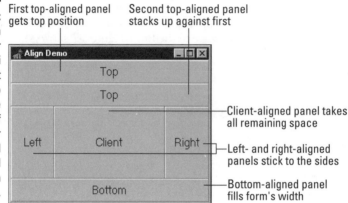

Figure 3-8: The Align property for a Delphi component causes it to hug one edge of the form or to fill all unoccupied space on the form.

First top-aligned panel gets top position

Second top-aligned panel stacks up against first

Client-aligned panel takes all remaining space

Left- and right-aligned panels stick to the sides

Bottom-aligned panel fills form's width

Behind the scenes

Quite a few of the common properties have no visible effect at design time, but quite an effect at run time. If you set the Enabled property to False, for example, the component rolls over and plays dead. It acquires a gray, deathly pallor, and it doesn't respond to any events.

If you set the Visible property to False, the component becomes invisible at run time. It's still present, and the program can make it visible later on. The most common reason to make components invisible is to put more than one at the same location on the form, and make just one of them visible at a time.

You may be tempted to make controls invisible when they're not available. For example, a File Save button may be invisible when no file is loaded. Don't do it! Components that appear and disappear confuse the user. Instead, if a component is not available, disable it (set Enabled to False).

When you've mastered programming with Delphi, you can turn your energies toward a *truly* difficult task — creating Windows help systems for your programs. With the right tools this is a moderately onerous task, but alas, the tools don't come with Delphi. Assuming you've managed to build a help file for your program, you can link a component to a topic in the help system by assigning the topic number to the component's HelpContext property. When you do that for all the program's components, the user can just press F1 for context-sensitive help. Under Delphi 2.0, if you enable the Windows 95 help button by setting the form's BorderIcons.biHelp property to True, the user can also get help by pressing the Help button and then clicking a component.

If you don't feel ready to attack the Windows help system, consider giving hints. Just enter a pithy phrase describing each component into that component's Hint property. To have these hints displayed as flyover help, set the main form's ShowHint property to True, and leave each component's ParentShowHint property set to True. Don't meddle with the component's own ShowHint property; if you don't want a hint for a particular component, simply leave the Hint property blank. Your program can also display a hint for the active component or menu item on its status bar. You find out how to do this in Chapter 7.

To store information that doesn't correspond to any existing property, you can use the Tag property. This capacious property holds any number from –2,147,483,647 to 2,147,483,648! You can represent a lot of different things with 4 billion numbers to choose from.

Pop-up menus are all the rage these days. If you click an object on the screen with the right mouse button, a menu related to that object pops up. Not surprisingly, this menu is called the pop-up menu. The PopupMenu property defines a Delphi component's pop-up menu, but you can't just type in a value. You have to create a pop-up menu component (you learn how to do that in Chapter 6) before you can select it as a component's PopupMenu property. If you're not familiar with this type of menu, turn to Delphi itself. Display the Code Editor and right-click it. The items in the pop-up menu will be enabled or disabled depending on where you clicked and whether any text is selected.

The mouse is essential to using Windows, but sometimes you don't want to take your hands off the keyboard. The TabStop and TabOrder properties help make programs work efficiently without a mouse. Pressing the Tab key moves the focus to the next component that has TabStop set to True. The word *next* in this case means the component with the next higher value for TabOrder. If you enter a value for TabOrder that's already in use by another component, Delphi adjusts the TabOrder of other components to make room for your new value.

As much as possible, all of your programs should be usable with or without a mouse.

The DragMode and DragCursor properties automate drag-and-drop for components. If DragMode is set to dmAutomatic, you can click the component and drag a cursor representing the object. If the component the cursor is over can accept dropped objects, the cursor displays as whatever you chose for DragCursor; otherwise it displays as a slashed-circle universal No symbol: ⊘.

Start with a new form and place a label component on it. (The glyph for a label is just a big letter *A*.) Set the label's caption to Drag me! and double-click its DragMode property to change it to dmAutomatic.

Click the form and flip to the Events page in the Object Inspector. Double-click the OnDragOver event and insert this code:

```
Accept := Source IS TLabel;
```

This means that the form will accept dragged components as long as the type of the component is TLabel. Now double-click the OnDragDrop event line in the Object Inspector and insert these lines:

```
WITH Source AS TLabel DO
  BEGIN
    Left := X;
    Top := Y;
  END;
```

These lines move the dragged component to the coordinates the cursor is pointing at.

Run this program and drag the label around. Note that when you first press the mouse button, the cursor changes to the no-drag symbol. That's because it's over the label itself, and you didn't tell the label to accept dragged components. As soon as the cursor moves off the label, it turns into the default drag cursor, an arrow with a rectangle attached. When you release the mouse button to drop the label on the form, the form's OnDragDrop event handler moves the label to its new location. (Try dragging the label so it protrudes off the right edge of the form; a horizontal scroll bar will appear like magic.)

Every component has a unique Name property. Initially, Delphi assigns a default name such as Form1 or Button2, choosing the first number that's not in use. You can replace this with a name of your own choice, subject to certain restrictions: The name can't already be in use by another component; it must be composed solely of letters, digits, or the underscore character; and it can't begin with a digit. You can also delete the name entirely, if your program has no need to refer to the component by name — this is often true of label components. In general, you'll find it's just as easy to stick with the default names Delphi provides.

You can't delete the name of *every* component of a given type. If your program uses labels, for example, you need to leave a name on at least one label. Delphi needs this information to decide which of its many code modules your program depends on.

Common Events

Like forms, most components respond to mouse, keyboard, and system events. There are exceptions — for example, static text labels don't respond to the keyboard, and Timer components respond only to the OnTimer event.

Most components have a default event; double-clicking the component in the Form Designer transports you instantly to the code for the default event. The three standard default events are OnChange, OnClick, and OnCreate, in that order. The first of these that's available will be the component's default. If a component doesn't respond to any of the three, it doesn't have a default event.

Mouse events

As your sore index finger well knows, the most common mouse event is clicking, specifically clicking the left button. The OnClick event is definitely the most popular mouse event. A component receives the OnClick event when the left mouse button is released while the mouse pointer is over the component. As a bonus, Delphi also sends an OnClick event to many components when they're activated from the keyboard.

Occasionally you'll want the more detailed information that comes with the OnMouseDown and OnMouseUp events. These two tell you which mouse button was pressed, where the mouse cursor was positioned, and even which Shift keys were held down, if any. You can also use OnMouseUp instead of OnClick if you need to distinguish an actual mouse-click from a press of the access key.

Oddly enough, when mouse-clicking is *not* the primary occupation of a component, it's more likely to respond to the OnDblClick event as well as OnClick. It's important to remember that OnDblClick is always preceded by OnClick. Windows can't read your mind, so it sends an OnClick event with the first click and then sets an internal timer. If another click comes before the timer runs out, it sends an OnDblClick event.

Drag and drop events

Drag and drop events are a variety of mouse event, but they're specialized enough to deserve separate mention. As you've seen in the discussion of the DragMode property (in the "Behind the scenes" section), a component's OnDragOver event is triggered when the user drags another component over it. Commonly, this event responds by setting the Accept parameter to True or False, indicating whether or not it can accept the particular component. A component's OnDragDrop event occurs when the user actually drops another component on it.

OnEndDrag, on the other hand, is received by the component that's being dragged, and it's triggered when the user stops dragging, whether or not the component was successfully dropped. Delphi 2.0 adds an OnStartDrag event to signal the start of dragging. There isn't a corresponding event in Delphi 1.0, but a component can detect the beginning of dragging by noting an OnDragOver event initiated by the component itself.

Place a label on a new form, change its caption to Drag Me!, and set its DragMode to dmAutomatic. Place several more labels on the form, select them all, and change the caption for all of them to Target. Then flip to the Events page in the Object Inspector and create an OnDragOver handler for the target labels; it should contain just one line:

```
Accept := True;
```

Select the Drag Me! label and give it an OnDragOver event handler containing these lines:

```
WITH Sender AS TLabel DO
  Caption := 'Dragging';
Accept := False;
```

Create an OnEndDrag method for it like this:

```
IF Target <> NIL THEN
  WITH Target AS TLabel DO
    Caption := 'A HIT!';
WITH Sender AS TLabel DO
  Caption := 'Drag Me!';
```

The WITH Sender AS TLabel DO expression takes the Sender variable (which could theoretically be any draggable component) and treats it as a TLabel. Using it is like a promise to Delphi that the sender *is* a TLabel. If it's not, Delphi will complain that you've made an invalid typecast.

Run the program and try dragging the Drag Me! label around. Its caption changes to Dragging. The form itself doesn't accept drag-drop events, so the cursor displays a slashed-circle No symbol. When the dragged label is over a Target label, the cursor changes to an arrow, indicating that the Target label will accept a drop. Drop on the target and its caption changes to A HIT! Whether you drop on a target or not, when you release the mouse button the original label changes back to Drag Me!

To review, OnEndDrag and Delphi 2.0's OnStartDrag are events aimed at the component being dragged. OnStartDrag occurs at the beginning of the dragging process, and OnEndDrag occurs when the dragging process ends, whether or not the component was dropped on another component. OnDragOver and OnDragDrop are events aimed at the component upon which another component is dropped. Drag and drop is where it's at; all the coolest programs use it.

Keyboard events

For most components, the built-in processing of access keys is all the keyboard input you need. For components that accept text input from the keyboard, advanced Delphi users can filter or modify text input through the keyboard events, as you see in the next chapter. Here's a little project that should help you see how the mouse and keyboard events interact.

Place a single button on an empty form. Set its caption to &Up, and set its Default property to True. Fill in its event handlers as follows:

Event Handler	*Code*
OnClick:	MessageBeep(0);
OnMouseDown:	Button1.Caption := '&Down';
OnMouseUp:	Button1.Caption := '&Up';
OnKeyDown:	IF Key = 32 THEN Button1.Caption := '&Down';
OnKeyUp:	IF Key = 32 THEN Button1.Caption := '&Up';

Run the program and play with the button. When you press the mouse down while pointing at the button, the caption changes to Down; when you release the mouse, the caption changes back to Up. Press the Spacebar and the caption changes to Down; release the Spacebar and the caption changes back to Up. When you release the mouse button or Spacebar, an OnClick event occurs and you hear a beep. Press Alt+U or Enter and the OnClick event occurs audibly, with no other key or mouse event.

Nine times out of ten, the OnClick method is sufficient to handle mouse and keyboard interaction with a component. As you can see, however, the other events give you finer control.

System events

The form is a program's big boss, and it does most of the negotiating with the Windows bureaucracy. Individual components don't have the wealth of system events that a form has. For the most part, when a component gets the focus, it receives an OnEnter event; when it loses the focus, it gets an OnExit event. That's it for system events. Let's see just how this works.

Shift+click the edit box icon in the Component palette. Its glyph looks like a tiny edit box with the letters *ab* inside. Place five or six edit boxes on the form. Select them all, set their AutoSelect property to False, and insert these lines as their OnEnter event handler:

```
WITH Sender AS TEdit DO
  Font.Color := clRed;
```

Use these lines as their OnExit event handler:

```
WITH Sender AS TEdit DO
  Font.Color := clWindowText;
```

Run the program, and try selecting the different edit boxes with the mouse, or press Tab repeatedly. The text of the active edit box always shows up in red. Remember this trick when you're writing big data entry forms with dozens of edit boxes!

Special events

For the occasional component that responds to the OnChange event, OnChange takes precedence over OnClick as the default event for that component. If you double-click an edit box in the Form Designer, for example, you get the skeleton of an OnChange event handler. For an edit box, OnChange is triggered any time the text changes, whether it's due to the user's input or a command from the program itself.

Place a label above an edit box on a new form and stretch them both to fill the width of the form. Double-click the edit box and insert this line in its OnChange event handler:

```
Label1.Caption := UpperCase(Edit1.Text);
```

Run the program and type some text in the edit box. The label's caption will faithfully echo what you type, converted to uppercase.

Entering the Fourth Dimension

The position of components on a form is determined by their Left and Top properties. These are like the X and Y dimensions you may remember from graphs in high-school algebra (assuming you stayed awake). There are actually two more dimensions involved in component positioning, Tab order and Z-order.

We've already talked briefly about Tab order — it's the order defined by the TabOrder property of the components on your form. One component at a time has the focus; that component receives the user's keyboard input. TabOrder controls the order in which the focus moves when the user presses Tab. The Tab order usually flows logically from left to right and top to bottom. Naturally, no two components can have the same TabOrder.

Unfortunately, the normal style of building a form is to add components as you think of them, not in a logical order. Each component gets the next unused TabOrder value, so the result is a Tab order that's based solely on *when* you placed the components, not on their order within the form. Before you can call a form finished, you need to adjust the Tab order of its components. To do this, select Tab Order from the Edit menu (or from any component's local menu), and simply shove components up and down in the resulting Edit Tab Order dialog, shown in Figure 3-9, until you get them in the right order. The easiest way to do that is to select the component that ought to be first in Tab order and drag it to the top slot in the list box. Then select the component that should be second and drag *it* into place, and so on.

Figure 3-9:
Use Delphi's
Edit Tab
Order dialog
to put your
components
in correct
Tab order.

If you have trouble relating the list of component names in the Edit Tab Order dialog to the components on your form, you can try another method. Here's what you do. First, decide how you want the focus to move around your form — remember that left to right and top to bottom is the standard. Now click the last component in your chosen order and set its TabOrder to 0. Delphi finds the component that had a TabOrder of 0 before and changes its TabOrder to 1, and this change ripples through all the other components as necessary to avoid duplication. Click the next-to-last component and set its TabOrder to 0. Again Delphi adjusts all the other components. Continue until you reach the first component; now every item has the correct TabOrder for your chosen order.

A combination of mouse and keyboard agility will make this process easy. Click the very first component and then click TabOrder in the Object Inspector, type 0, and press Enter. For all the rest of the components, the sequence is click, type 0, press Enter. You don't have to go back to the Object Inspector, because Delphi assumes you want to type a new value for the property you used most recently.

Z-order can probably best be described as a dimension. The X dimension runs left to right, the Y dimension runs top to bottom, and the Z dimension runs straight out of the screen and hits you between the eyes. Place a few components on a form and move them so their boundaries overlap. One component is on top of all the rest — it has the highest Z-order. The component that's overlapped by only the one that has the highest Z-order has the next-highest Z-order, and so on.

Z-order is rarely as important as Tab order — it's not even a property. But when you need to set Z-order, it's just as easy as setting Tab order. Suppose you have three components that overlap each other. Click the one that should be on top of all the rest and choose Send to Back from the Edit menu. Click the one that should be in the middle and send it to the back. Finally click the one that should be below the other two and send it to the back. That's all there is to it!

Chapter 4
Standard Components

* *

In This Chapter

▶ Deciding which standard components to use

▶ Grouping radio buttons and check boxes so they work together

▶ Learning how one Delphi component can enable and disable another

▶ Creating a password-entry dialog

▶ Creating a program that lets you edit AUTOEXEC.BAT and keep a backup

▶ Using a list box to sort the lines of a text file in order

▶ Adding color and graphics to a list box

▶ Controlling the form's color using scroll bars

* *

Delphi's standard components are a perfect match for on-screen elements shared by Windows 3.*x* and Windows 95 — and they come with some added features that make them especially easy to use. Because just about every Windows program uses these components, it's important that you learn how to select the right component for the job. As Figure 4-1 shows, Delphi puts the components you'll use the most on the first page of the Component palette.

Figure 4-1:
The Standard page on Delphi's Component palette.

Choosing Standard Components

At first it might seem like the Delphi Component palette gives you *too* many choices. In fact, every component has a particular purpose, and there's rarely any doubt about which is best for any given circumstance. To see these components in use, you can look at any Windows program, including Delphi itself. Refer to Table 4-1 any time you're not sure which standard component to choose.

Table 4-1	Problems Solved by Standard Components
Task	*Component*
Activate a feature in your program.	Push button. See "You're Pushing My Buttons!"
Choose between two or more mutually exclusive options.	Radio button. See "Punching Radio Buttons."
Choose one or more nonexclusive options.	Check box. See "Checking Off Your Options."
Associate groups of related radio buttons, check boxes, or other components.	Group box. See "Join the In Group."
Add an identifying label to a component.	Label. See "Pinning Labels on Components."
Take one-line input from the user.	Edit box. See "Fill in the Blank in an Edit Box."
Take multiline, justified, or scrolling input from the user.	Memo box. See "Take a Memo."
Display a list of items for single or multiple choice.	List box. See "I've Got a Little List."
Display a list of items for single choice using minimal space on the form; optionally allow the user to enter a value not on the list.	Combo box. See "A Two-Player Combo (Box)."
Display or adjust the value of a continuous numeric quantity.	Scroll bar. See "Belly Up to the (Scroll) Bar."

Okay, if you looked really closely, you noticed that the panel component on the Standard page in the Component palette isn't covered in this chapter. Panel is *not* a standard Windows component, and its purpose is mostly related to the look and feel of a form, so I discuss it in Chapter 7, the chapter on graphical components. And the menu and pop-up menu components, also on the Standard page, are so important that all of Chapter 6 is devoted to them.

You're Pushing My Buttons!

In the real world, push buttons make things happen. Press a doorbell and a chime sounds. Punch an elevator button and off you go to the floor of your choice. Hit the History Eraser button and . . . wait, don't press that one! Use Delphi's push button component to make things happen in your program.

Properties

The most visible property for a push button is its Caption property. A caption for a push button should be a short action word that describes what the button does. If you're undecided about a particular caption, try picturing it as a line of dialog for the Terminator: OK, Yes, No, Load, Run, Shoot — these are all good possibilities.

An ampersand in a button caption makes the character that follows a mnemonic access key for the button. Pressing Alt with the access key is the same as clicking the button.

Some captions have evolved special meanings based on the way most Windows programmers use them. OK means shut down the form and accept its data, Cancel means shut down the form and throw away its data, Help means HELP! Don't use different words for these functions, or your program will be ostracized for talking funny.

Of course, the captions you select yourself must be consistent. If you use Load for the name of a button that opens a file in one form, and Replicate for the same purpose in another form, you confuse the poor user.

Setting a button's Cancel property to True associates that button with the Esc key — Esc becomes the access key for the button. Commonly, the caption for a button with Cancel set to True will be . . . Cancel. (Big surprise, yes?)

A button with the Default property set to True will be activated when the user presses Enter, unless the user has tabbed to another button. The standard caption for a Default button is OK. Only one button with the Cancel property and one button with the Default property should be active at any given time — one per form or one per page on a multipage form. (This default button behavior sounds a little complicated, but you've been *using* it for as long as you've been using Windows.)

When a form has lots of components, it can be difficult to find enough distinct access keys to go around. Don't bother giving an ampersand-style access key to a button with the Default or Cancel property.

A push button doesn't have a Color property because its color is rigidly dominated by the color settings in the Windows Control Panel. Separate Control Panel settings exist for the button face, the text on the button, the shadow along the bottom and right edges, and the highlight along the top and left edges. You can control the font used for the button's caption as far as size and type-face go, but don't bother setting a font color. No matter what vivid color you choose, Windows will sneer and discard your choice, replacing it with the button text color set by Control Panel.

The ModalResult property is useful only in secondary forms that function as modal dialogs. A modal dialog is a form that gets in the user's face and won't go away until it gets a response, like a door-to-door salesperson. The rest of the program can't continue until the user closes the modal dialog. When you set a button's ModalResult property to a nonzero value, pressing that button closes the modal dialog and returns the ModalResult value to the calling program.

Events

It's no surprise that the big event for a push button comes when you push it. Most push buttons need to respond only to the OnClick event, nothing more. When you double-click a push button in the Form Designer, Delphi creates a skeleton for an OnClick event handler in the Editor window.

On a new form, first place an edit box and then place a button; change the button's caption to OK. Double-click the button. You'll be flipped into the Code Editor with the cursor on a line between the words begin and end. Type

```
Close;
```

Run the program. Press Enter vigorously, and note that nothing happens. Click the button to end the program. Now change the button's Default property to True and run the program again. This time when you press Enter, it wipes out the program, just like clicking the button. What a difference Default makes!

Start a new project and then select New Form from the File menu. Drop a button on the secondary form. Set the button's Caption property to OK, set its Default property to True, and set its ModalResult property to mrOK. Size the secondary form so it's just a little bigger than the button and set its properties as follows:

Property	*Value*
BorderIcons.biSystemMenu	False
BorderIcons.biMinimize	False
BorderIcons.biMaximize	False
BorderStyle	bsDialog
Position	poScreenCenter

Now switch to the main form and place a push button with the caption &Show
Form2. Put this line in its OnClick event handler:

```
Form2.ShowModal;
```

In the Code Editor page for Unit1, the first form's unit, scroll all the way to the
top and find a line that contains the lone word uses. Add the word Unit2 and a
comma to the end of this line (don't forget the comma). Or, if you're using
Delphi 2.0, select Use Unit... from the File menu and choose the secondary
form's unit.

The short way to describe what you did by inserting the name Unit2 is: "Add
Unit2 to the uses clause." You'll be doing this from time to time. When you run
this program, clicking the Show Form2 button displays the secondary form, and
clicking the OK button on that form closes it. You didn't have to write any code
to close Form2; setting the OK button's ModalResult property to mrOk was
enough.

When you see a table of property names and values like the one in the preceding instructions, simply set each property to the specified value. If a property
name contains a period, such as BorderIcons.biMaximized, it means you should
find the first portion of the property name and double-click to explode it, and
then find the second portion in the exploded list.

Join the In Group

Group boxes keep other components neatly corralled on the form. They
associate related components visually and logically. In fact, a group box takes
on some of the capabilities of a form — it's a kind of straw boss to the components it contains. When you place a component in a group box, its ParentColor,

ParentShowHint, ParentFont, and ParentCtl3D properties refer to the group box, not to the form. The Left and Top properties of a component in a group box are relative to the top left corner of the group box. If you move the group box, all the components it contains will move too.

On a brand new form, place a group box. Now place one radio button on the group box and another on the form outside the group box. Drag the second radio button onto the group box. Move the group box and watch what happens — the first radio button moves with it, but the second is left behind.

This little experiment reveals that you can't fool a group box. If you want a group box to contain a particular component, you have to create the component in the group box. Dragging it in after the fact just won't work. If you've invested time and effort in setting a component's properties only to realize later that it should be inside a group box, there *is* hope. Click the component and press Ctrl+X to cut it to the Clipboard. Then click the group box and press Ctrl+V to paste the component into the group box.

Often when you paste a component into a group box, it will seem to disappear. That's because its Left and Top properties are now measured from the top left corner of the group box, and the group box isn't as big as the form. The easiest way to avoid this problem is to *move* the component to the top left corner of the form before you cut it to the Clipboard. If you've already pasted the component and forgotten to move it first, use the Object Inspector to set the Left and Top properties of the component to 0. Ah, but how do you use the Object Inspector when you can't see the component in the first place? It's easy. Just pull down the component list at the top of the Object Inspector — you'll find your little lost component there.

Group boxes have no important properties beyond the common ones described in the preceding chapter. They *can* respond to the common keyboard, mouse, and system events, but they almost never do.

Punching Radio Buttons

These days, car radios are digitally controlled miniatures of home stereo systems, with dozens of hidden speakers, CD audio, and digitally controlled tuning. *Some* of us remember when you had to twist a knob to tune the radio, or punch a button to choose a favorite station. It took some oomph to push those buttons because they had to drag the tuner to the specified location. And when you pushed in one button, any other pushed-in button would pop out — ka-chunk!

The point of this trip down nostalgia lane is that car radio buttons are the origin of the name for Windows radio buttons. They always come in groups (visibly marked by a group box), and only one button per group can be pushed in at a time. Each radio button has a circle next to its caption, and the one that's pushed in has a filled circle.

You use a group of radio buttons to let the user choose between two or more options that are mutually exclusive. For example, Delphi's own Find dialog uses radio buttons to let you choose a forward or backward search. At any given time, you can search in one direction or the other, but never in both.

Properties

The Alignment property for a radio button determines whether the caption appears to the right or left of the circle. Normally it's on the right, but if Ctl3D is False, you can set Alignment to taLeftJustify to put the caption on the left. In Delphi 2.0, this works even when Ctl3D is True.

A radio button's most important property is the Checked property. This property is True only for the one radio button in the group that's selected. It's possible for all the radio buttons in a group to start off with Checked set to False, but if you try to set a second button's Checked property to True, even at design time, Delphi will change the first one to False.

Place a group box and a push button on a form and then add three radio buttons inside the group box. Give the three radio buttons different captions, each with a different access key, for example, &Curly, &Larry, &Moe. For each button in turn, set the Checked property to True — note that it remains True only for the button you set last.

Run the program. Press Tab repeatedly and note how the focus moves back and forth between the push button and the selected radio button. Press the access keys for the radio buttons — they all work. Now fool around with the arrow keys. The down and right arrow keys move the selection through the group of radio buttons, staying within the group box. The up and left arrow keys do the same thing in reverse.

Events

The average radio button doesn't need to do anything except show whether or not it's the lucky selected button. That's all handled without any effort on your part. When the program needs to know which button is selected, it peeks and sees which one of them has Checked set to True. However, you may want to tweak other components on your form, depending on which radio button is checked. Adding a handler for the OnClick event enables you to tweak the components on your form.

On a new form, first place a group box and then place a push button. Set the push button's caption to OK and its Default property to True. Double-click the push button and fill in its OnClick event handler with the single line

```
Close;
```

Now put two radio buttons in the group box, with captions &Enabled and &Disabled. Set the Checked property of the first to True. Double-click the Enabled radio button and fill its OnClick event handler with this line:

```
Button1.Enabled := True;
```

Double-click the Disabled button and do the same for its OnClick event handler, but replace True with False.

Now run the program. If you click Disabled, the OK button is disabled; click Enabled and it works again.

Radio buttons and group boxes have a special relationship that Delphi cele-brates by marrying the two in its RadioGroup component. A RadioGroup is a group box whose purpose in life is to display radio buttons. Its Items property is a list of captions for the radio buttons, and its ItemIndex property indicates which button is checked. If ItemIndex is –1, none of the radio buttons is checked. The radio buttons will be neatly arranged in as many columns as the Columns property specifies. Any time you want a group box with only radio buttons inside, it's much simpler to just use a RadioGroup.

By the way, if you find yourself longing to use a lone radio button for a single yes-or-no option, what you really need is a check box. Coming right up!

Checking Off Your Options

Like radio buttons, check boxes normally come in groups. However, you can check off as many of them as you like. For example, a form for ordering pizza may use radio buttons to choose a thick or thin crust, but check boxes to select any or all of the dozens of available toppings.

Usually the check box caption is to the right of the box itself, but if Ctl3D is False or if you're using Delphi 2.0, you can reverse their positions with the Alignment property. Besides a True/False Check property, check boxes also have a State property with three values: cbChecked, cbUnchecked, and cbGrayed.

You use the cbGrayed state to show that the choice represented by the check box is not clearly one way or the other. For example, suppose the check box indicates that the text in your word processor is Politically Correct. If the selected text is "The old horse is dead," the box won't be checked. If the text is partially Politically Correct, say, "The temporally gifted horse is dead," the box should be grayed. Clicking on a grayed check box causes it to be checked; in this example it would also translate the sentence to "The temporally gifted equine companion is metabolically challenged."

Clicking a checked check box causes it to be unchecked. (Say that ten times fast!) If the AllowGrayed property is True, clicking an unchecked check box turns it to grayed; otherwise, it turns it to checked. Most of the time you can avoid this confusion by leaving AllowGrayed set to False.

Like radio buttons, check boxes are occasionally used to control the status of other items on the form through an OnClick event handler. Most of the time, though, your programs will simply peek at the Checked or State property.

Pinning Labels on Components

The label component has two main purposes. First, it can serve as a caption for another component that doesn't *have* its own caption, such as the list box or edit box components later in this chapter. Second, it can display read-only information for the program's user; an example of this is the score in a Solitaire game. A label can have a mnemonic access key too, but pressing that key gives the focus to the caption-impaired component associated with the label. If you'd rather forego the mnemonic access key and gain the ability to use the ampersand freely in the label's Caption, set the ShowAccelChar property to False.

The Alignment property determines whether a label's caption is left, right, or center justified within the space allowed. When the AutoSize property is True (as it is by default), the label automatically sizes itself to fit its Caption. Setting an autosized label to right alignment essentially pins the right edge of the label to the form. If a right-aligned autosized label needs to grow larger, it grows to the left.

The FocusControl property determines which of the other components on the form will get the focus when the label's access key is pressed. Click the down arrow next to its value and choose from a list of components on the form. If you later change the name of that component, Delphi won't complain. It just cleverly changes the FocusControl property to match the new name.

Occasionally, you'll want to use a multiline label rather than several single-line labels. In that case, set the WordWrap property to True and be sure to make the label tall enough to accommodate multiple lines.

A label's background color is normally controlled by the Color property. If you set the Transparent property to True, though, the background disappears.

Place a large rectangular label on the form so it nearly fills the left half of the form and place another that nearly fills the remaining space. Set the Color property of one to clFuchsia and of the other to clLime. (All right, all right, you don't *have* to use clFuchsia and clLime. Choose any two colors that strike your fancy.) Now create a third label that overlaps both of the first two. Repeatedly double-click the third label's Transparent property, toggling it from False to True and back. You can use this property to place labels on top of Image components and other graphical components, as Figure 4-2 shows.

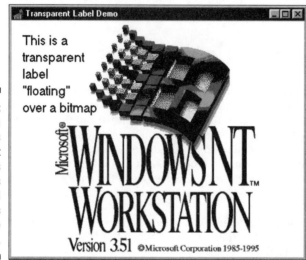

Figure 4-2:
When a label's Transparent property is True, its background vanishes and only the text shows.

Fill in the Blank in an Edit Box

Computer programs are always asking questions. What is your name? What is your quest? What is your favorite color? You may select a quest or color from a list of what's available, but no computer can offer a list of all possible names. The user must be permitted to enter absolutely anything — and that's what an edit box is for.

Properties

An edit box has no caption — its most important property is called Text. When you first place an edit box on the form, the Text property is set to the edit box's name. You can delete this initial value, change it to a different default value, or have your program set the value just before displaying the edit box. In Delphi 1.0, the user can enter a string of as many as 255 characters, unless you set the *MaxLength* property to a lower value.

It's actually possible to enter many more than 255 characters in an edit box. By using the GetTextBuf and SetTextBuf methods, you can edit a text buffer that's almost 64K. However, this task is rarely necessary and requires some programming techniques that haven't been discussed yet.

Delphi 2.0 doesn't impose a 255-character limit on the Text property's length — it can be as long as the operating system allows. In Windows 95, 32,767 characters is the limit; in Windows NT, text length is limited only by available memory. In either version of Delphi, you can enter more text in an edit box than will fit in the boundaries of the box, but it's awkward to do so. As you add text at the end of the string, the beginning gets shoved out of sight. It's best to use MaxLength to restrict the number of characters that can be entered and to set the physical size of the edit box large enough to hold that many characters. Make the edit box a little extra large, because different combinations of screen resolution and font size will change the meaning of "large enough." If you need one super-long line of text or multiple lines, use a memo box, described in the next section.

By default, an edit box has a single-line border around it. This border helps users estimate just how much text they can enter. You can get rid of the border by setting the BorderStyle property to bsNone, but don't — it will only confuse users.

If the PasswordChar property is anything but ASCII character zero (#0), every character that's typed will show up as that character. This way, someone looking over the user's shoulder can't learn what was entered. The asterisk (*) is the usual password character, but you can use X or / or even a smiley face — any character will do.

ReadOnly means what it says — look but don't touch. The user can peruse the edit box's text, select and copy parts of it, and scroll it around, but that's all. Your program can turn this property on and off at run time, if necessary.

If AutoSelect is True (as it is by default), the text in the edit box is automatically selected any time the user tabs to the edit box. Be careful: This makes it easy to wipe out the contents of the edit box. That's because Tab followed by any character wipes out the selected text and replaces it with that character. It's your choice: Do you want to make it easy for your users to replace text in edit boxes, or do you want to protect them from trashing text accidentally?

Normally when an edit box isn't the active control, you can't see whether any text is selected. That helps the user keep track of which box is active. If you set the HideSelection property to False, however, the selection shows up even when the edit box isn't active. This can be handy when your program displays another dialog that acts on the selected text, such as a Find and Replace dialog.

AutoSize is also True by default, but you probably want to set it to False. When this property is True, the edit box's height automatically increases if necessary to accommodate a larger font. The problem is that the other components on the form don't automatically move to make room for the taller edit box, so this action may result in some territorial squabbling. It can get ugly!

Events

Most of the time, an edit box just gathers its input without any intervention from the programmer. The OnChange event occurs every time the value of the Text property changes, which can be useful. And you can use the OnKeyPress event to modify or prohibit certain keystrokes.

Be extremely careful if you put code in an OnChange event handler that makes a change to the Text property. Why? Because that change will trigger another OnChange event, which may trigger another, and another, indefinitely. Your program could go off to chase its own tail forever and lock up Windows 3.1 or crash Windows 95. Windows NT is more durable — a tail-chasing program can't knock it out!

Place an edit box on a new form and set its MaxLength property to 4. Put these lines in its OnKeyPress event handler:

```
IF ((Key < '0') OR (Key > '9')) AND (Key <> #8) THEN
   BEGIN
     MessageBeep(0);
     Key := #0;
   END;
```

Use these lines for its OnChange event handler:

```
WITH Sender AS TEdit DO
   IF (Length(Text) > 0) AND
      (StrToInt(Text) > 4999) THEN
   BEGIN
     MessageBeep(0);
     Text := Copy(Text, 1, Length(Text)-1);
     SelStart := Length(Text);
   END;
```

Click the edit box and press Ctrl+C. Then press Ctrl+V twice to paste two copies of the edit box into the form. Arrange the three edit boxes so they don't overlap and delete the Text property of all three.

The edit boxes in this program accept only numeric keys, and you can't enter a number greater than 4999. Try it! If the OnKeyPress event handler detects a key that's neither a digit nor a backspace (#8), it beeps and sets the Key parameter to ASCII #0. This tells Delphi to censor the key — it never reaches the edit box. And if the user types a digit that brings the number above 4999, the OnChange event handler beeps and cuts off that last digit. Delphi doesn't have a cut-off-last-character function, so you use the built-in Copy function to copy everything except the last digit.

Yes, I warned you earlier not to change the Text property in an OnChange event handler, and now I'm doing it. You probably think I've got a lot of nerve to do that. Not really. In this case, cutting off the last digit of the text does indeed trigger a second OnChange event. However, no infinite tail-chasing chain of changes occurs because the second OnChange event doesn't make any further changes to the text.

Now, let's really exercise the edit box control by building a password-entry dialog.

Start a new project and select the Fixed-Size Form template, the one you created back in Chapter 2. Or, if you're using Delphi 2.0, select New from the File menu, flip to the Projects page, and select the Fixed-Size Form project. Change the form's Ctl3D property to False, and change its caption to Change Password. Add three labels, three edit boxes, and two buttons to a new form, arranging them as shown in Figure 4-3 and assigning their captions as shown. Create the labels and edit boxes from top to bottom, and the buttons from left to right. (This arrangement is important because in the following code, we assume that the first button is Button1, the third label is Label3, and so on.)

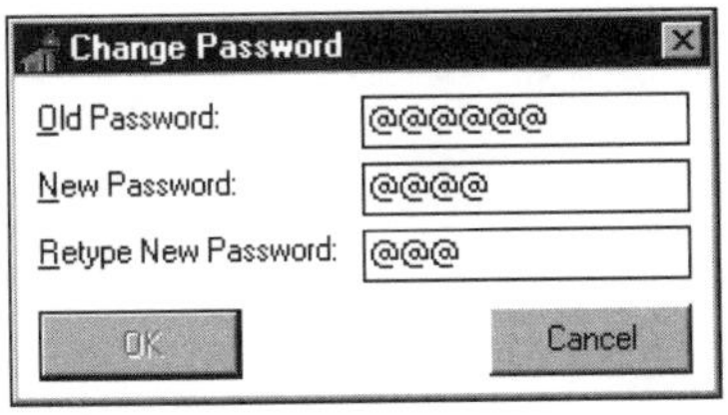

Figure 4-3:
Retype the final character of the password; the OK button will be enabled instantly.

Set the OK button's Default property to True, and set the Cancel button's Cancel property to True. Select the OK button and the lower two labels and edit boxes, and set their Enabled property to False. Now select all three edit boxes, delete their text, set AutoSize to False, and set their PasswordChar property to the @ symbol. Set each label's FocusControl property to the corresponding edit box.

Double-click the OK button and set its OnClick event handler to the single command

```
Close;
```

Do the same for the Cancel button. Double-click the top edit box and insert these lines in its OnChange event handler:

```
Edit2.Enabled   := Edit1.Text = 'Delphi';
Edit3.Enabled   := Edit2.Enabled;
Label2.Enabled  := Edit2.Enabled;
Label3.Enabled  := Edit2.Enabled;
```

Select both of the lower edit boxes, flip to the Events page in the Object Inspector window, and double-click the OnChange event. Insert the following lines in the resulting event handler, which will be called when the value of *either* of the two edit boxes changes:

```
Button1.Enabled := (Edit2.Text <> '') AND
    (Edit2.Text = Edit3.Text);
```

Now run the program. The lower two edit boxes are disabled until you enter the super-secret password *Delphi* in the first edit box. The OK button is disabled until you enter the same new password in the lower two edit boxes.

The password dialog you just created is similar to the dialog Windows 3.1 uses for changing the screen saver password. You can't change the password until you've entered the existing password, and it won't accept the new password until you've typed it twice exactly the same.

Take a Memo

An edit box is good for getting one fairly short line of text from the user. For anything fancier, you need a memo box. A memo box holds multiple lines of text and has quite a few properties that an edit box doesn't, making it much more flexible. In fact, the Windows Notepad accessory is hardly more than a memo box with a menu slapped on.

Several memo box properties behave exactly the same as the corresponding edit box properties: BorderStyle, ReadOnly, HideSelection, and MaxLength.

The text you enter in an edit box is always aligned with the left edge of the box's border. If you want right or center justification, even if it's just for a single line of text, use a memo box and set the Alignment property to the style you want.

Don't confuse the Alignment property with the Align property. With the Align property, you can set a memo box so that it automatically sizes itself to fill either a portion of the form along any of the four edges, or the entire available area of the form.

The ScrollBars property lets you give the memo box a horizontal scroll bar, a vertical scroll bar, both, or neither. The WordWrap True/False property determines whether the text you enter will automatically wrap at the end of the visible line. If you set WordWrap to True, you must not give the memo box a horizontal scroll bar — the two concepts are contradictory. You wouldn't want a neurotic memo box, would you?

Normally the Tab key moves the focus around among the various components on a form, and the Enter key activates the default button. If your memo box needs to accept Tab as just another character, set the WantTabs property to True. If you want Enter to simply start a new line in the memo box, set the WantReturns property to True.

Even if you don't set WantTabs or WantReturns to True, you can enter Tab characters by pressing Ctrl+Tab, and you can start a new line by pressing Ctrl+Enter. This is true in Delphi's own memo boxes as well.

The most important property for a memo box is the Lines property. This is a new type of property, one you haven't run into before. Click the ellipsis button (...) and a dialog opens that lets you type numerous lines of text, each up to 255 characters long. (Delphi 2.0 doesn't limit the number of characters per line.) These lines will show up in the memo box at design time, and they'll be its initial contents at run time. When your program needs to refer to the contents of the memo box, it will look at the Lines property.

The memo box's Lines property is actually an object itself, with its own special capabilities. Most impressively, it can load itself with text from a file and write its contents back to a file!

Place a memo box on a new form and change the form's caption to AUTOEXEC Editor. Set the ScrollBars property of the memo box to ssBoth and its Align property to alClient. Now insert these lines in the form's OnCreate event handler:

```
Memo1.Lines.LoadFromFile('C:\AUTOEXEC.BAT');
Memo1.Lines.SaveToFile('C:\AUTOEXEC.BAK');
```

And insert this line in the OnCloseQuery event handler:

```
Memo1.Lines.SaveToFile('C:\AUTOEXEC.BAT');
```

Do you realize what you just did? You've created a simple editor devoted to editing AUTOEXEC.BAT! If perchance your system marches to a different drummer and boots from a different drive, change each occurrence of C: to the boot drive for your system. Now, did you think you'd be writing a text editor this quickly?

I've Got a Little List

A list box stores a list of items and lets the user select one or several of them. You can preload the list at design time, or your program can add and remove items. A single-selection list box serves much the same purpose as a set of radio buttons — it lets the user select one of a number of mutually exclusive choices. But a list box can easily hold dozens or even hundreds of items, whereas the same number of radio buttons would overflow even the largest form. Also, you can easily build the list of choices at run time.

A multiple-choice list box lets the user select any number of choices, like a group of check boxes. Again, you'd use a list box instead of the check boxes when there are more than eight or ten choices, or when the choices aren't known at design time.

Properties

Delphi's list box component has an Align property, just like the memo box. You can set it to hug any of the four sides of the form, or to occupy all available space on the form.

The Items property in a list box is like the Lines property in a memo box. It's a collection of lines that you can preload at design time, and your programs can call on the Items property to load itself from a file or save its contents to a file. Your programs can treat Items as an array of strings, and the run-time-only ItemIndex property is the index of the selected item. For example, this line in an OnClick event handler would display the selected item in the label Label1:

```
Label1.Caption :=
  ListBox1.Items[ListBox1.ItemIndex];
```

Most of the time you'll leave the Style property set to its default of lbStandard. If it's lbOwnerDrawFixed, your program must take over the task of drawing the list box items (normally handled by Windows). If it's lbOwnerDrawVariable, your program has to draw the items and let Windows know how high each item is.

If you set the Sorted property to True, items inserted into the list box at run time will automatically be put in sorted order. At design time, any lines you've entered in the Items property are put into order when you set Sorted to True. If you then add more lines that aren't in order, Delphi cleverly sorts them as soon as you click OK to close the list editor.

You can use nonvisible sorted list boxes for minor sorting tasks in your programs. Windows 3.1 does impose a limit of 5,440 or so items in a list box — fewer if the lines average longer than 10 or 11 characters. Technical wizardry can stretch this limit to a bit over 8,000 items, but there's no point in forcing that many items into a list box when a grid component (which you meet in Chapter 9) can handle them so much better. Things are a bit different for Delphi 2.0 programmers — Windows 95 permits over 32,000 items per list box and puts no limit on the total string length. Windows NT doesn't even limit the number of items!

Place a label in the top left corner of a new form, with an edit box to its right. Put another label and edit box just below the first pair. Set each label's FocusControl property to the adjacent edit box. Caption the labels &Input file and &Output file and delete each edit box's text. Now place a list box on the form and set its Visible property to False and its Sorted property to True.

Place a push button on the form with the caption &Sort, and fill in its OnClick event handler with these lines:

```
ListBox1.Items.LoadFromFile(Edit1.Text);
ListBox1.Items.SaveToFile(Edit2.Text);
MessageDlg(Edit2.Text + ' sorted!',
  mtInformation, [mbOk], 0);
```

Run the program and type into the first edit box the name of an existing small-to-medium text file. Type a file name that's not already in use into the second edit box. Press the Sort button and Presto! The file is sorted.

With just three lines of code, you've written a simple file-sorting program. But that's not all you've accomplished. Some potent protection against errors is built into any Delphi program, including the one you just wrote. If you omit the input or output file name, or use an invalid name, your program automatically pops up a warning to the user. The user also gets a warning if the input file is too big to fit in the list box.

The fancy name for this protection is exception handling. Try it and see what it's like. But first, open the Environment dialog under the Options menu and clear the box next to the Break on exception option. If you don't do that, Delphi's debugger will trap the exception and display a scary message box.

When the MultiSelect property is False, only one item in the list can be selected. If you click another item, the first one is deselected. If you set this property to True, though, you can select any or all of the items. Just how you select depends on another property, ExtendedSelect. When ExtendedSelect is True, you just click one item and Shift+click another to select the two items and all items between them. And you Ctrl+click any item to select or deselect it without affecting other items. When ExtendedSelect is False, each click on an item in the list box turns the selected state of that item on or off. You get a more versatile multiple selection list box when ExtendedSelect is True.

The Selected property isn't available at design time, but when your program is running it tells which items of a multiple choice list box are selected. For example, to find out if item number 10 is selected, you could do something like this:

```
if ListBox1.Selected[10] then...
```

Setting the Columns property to a nonzero value substantially changes the look of a list box. The box's items are lined up in as many columns as you specified, and the scroll bar is horizontal. Not many Windows programs use this type of list box, but it *can* come in handy. The four small list boxes in Figure 4-4 contain the same list of items but have different values for the Columns property.

If IntegralHeight is set to True, the list box automatically adjusts its height so as not to show a partial item at the bottom; see the rightmost list box in Figure 4-4 for an example of this. The height of items can change depending on the user's

Figure 4-4:
The four small list boxes at the left have different values for the Columns property; the two taller list boxes differ in their IntegralHeight settings.

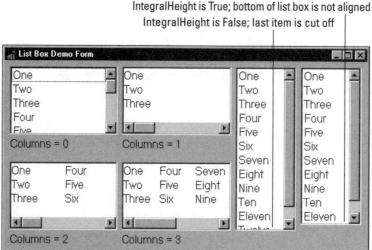

IntegralHeight is True; bottom of list box is not aligned
IntegralHeight is False; last item is cut off

Windows setup, so adjusting it on your system at design time isn't enough. Note that it isn't possible to make a list box line up top and bottom with another component if IntegralHeight is True. The next-to-right list box in Figure 4-4 lines up correctly with its neighbors to the left, but the bottom portion of its last item is cut off.

List boxes are made for displaying text, but that's not all they can do. If you set the Style property to lbOwnerDrawFixed, your program can draw anything at all for the list box's items. Well, anything that fits in a rectangle. The ItemHeight property controls how high the items in an owner draw list box are. Set Style to lbOwnerDrawVariable and the items don't even have to be the same height.

Events

A list box's OnClick event is triggered, logically enough, when you click it with the mouse. However, it's also conveniently triggered when you change the selection using the arrow keys.

In addition to the usual mouse, keyboard, and system events, list boxes respond to OnDrawItem and OnMeasureItem. These events occur when the list box has one of the two owner draw styles. A program responds to OnMeasureItem by indicating the height of the specified item. It responds to OnDrawItem by drawing the item. In the stone age of Windows programming (before Delphi), owner draw list boxes were terribly complicated; now they're simple!

Place a list box on the form, set its Align property to alClient, and set its Style to lbOwnerDrawVariable. Enter 16 items in the Items property. It doesn't matter what they are, as long as there are precisely 16 of them — you can enter the names of your 16 closest friends, for example. Now flip to the Events page and enter this line of code for the list box's OnMeasureItem event handler:

```
IF Odd(Index) THEN Height := 2*Height;
```

Create an OnDrawItem event handler containing these lines:

```
WITH ListBox1.Canvas DO
  BEGIN
    IF odFocused IN State THEN Brush.Color := 0
    ELSE Brush.Color := $FFFFFF;
    FillRect(Rect);
    Rect.Left := Rect.Left + 12;
    Brush.Color := $111111 * Index;
    FillRect(Rect);
  END;
```

Run the program and scroll through the items in the list box. Because of the OnMeasureItem event handler, every odd-numbered line is double-height. Because of the OnDrawItem event handler, instead of text each item contains a different shade of gray, with a black marker at the left of the selected item.

A Two-Player Combo (Box)

A combo box is a combination of an edit box and a list box. Combo boxes come in three types: simple, drop down, and drop-down list. The simple type looks like a list box with an edit box grafted onto its head. The drop-down type keeps the list rolled up out of sight like an old-fashioned window shade until you press the down arrow button to the right of the edit box. And the drop-down list type doesn't let you type anything in the edit box part — all you can do is choose an item from the list.

The simple type of combo box isn't very common because it doesn't provide the main advantage of a combo box — reduced space on the form. A combo box of any other type keeps its list portion rolled up, so it takes very little space, yet manages to display its current selection.

Naturally, the combo box shares many properties and events with the list box and edit box. Its Text property holds the text for the edit box portion. Items, ItemHeight, and Sorted behave just like the corresponding list box properties.

The Style property in a combo box determines whether or not this combo box will keep its list rolled up, and whether the user will be able to enter a value in the edit portion. If Style is csSimple, the list is always visible, like a list box, and the user can either choose from the list or type into the edit box. A style of csDropDown tells the combo box to keep the list rolled up when not in use. And csDropDownList keeps the list rolled up and restricts the user to choosing from the list instead of typing in any old thing. The DropDownCount property determines how many items will appear at once in the list.

The csOwnerDrawVariable and csOwnerDrawFixed styles give you a drop-down list type combo box in which you control what's displayed, just like in an owner draw list box. If either of the owner draw styles is selected, you use the OnDrawItem event handler to draw the individual items. And if lbOwnerDrawVariable is the style, the event handler for OnMeasureItem lets you set the height of each item separately.

Place a combo box on the form and set its Sorted property to True. Set its Style to csSimple; you have to resize it to see the list part. Flip to the Events page and double-click OnKeyPress. Type this code:

```
IF Key = #13 THEN
  BEGIN
    ComboBox1.Items.Add(ComboBox1.Text);
    ComboBox1.Text := '';
    Key := #0;
  END;
```

Run the program and enter some lines into the combo box. When you press Enter (which is the key whose code is #13), the line you typed will be inserted into the list portion of the combo box, in sorted order.

Belly Up to the (Scroll) Bar

Memo, list box, and combo box components can have scroll bars built in, but you can also place independent scroll bars on a form. You use these for setting a value that can vary continuously between two fixed extremes, like the volume sliders on your stereo's graphic equalizer. You can grab the movable "thumb" with the mouse and drag it to a new position, or you can click the scroll bar to move in predefined increments. Clicking the arrows at either end moves the thumb a small increment, whereas clicking the bar itself either above or below the thumb moves it a large increment.

Properties

Scroll bars can be horizontal or vertical, depending on the value of the Kind property. A newborn scroll bar is always horizontal — when you switch the Kind to sbVertical, it pivots on the top left corner. The Max and Min properties control the range of the scroll bar, and Position reports the current position in that range. SmallChange determines how far the thumb will move in response to a click on the arrows at the end of the scroll bar, and LargeChange affects how far it moves when you click the scroll bar itself. There is no SpareChange property.

Events

The big event for a scroll bar is OnChange. Any change to the position of the thumb causes an OnChange event. OnScroll is a more low-level scroll bar event triggered by *any* activity on the scroll bar, even if it doesn't move the thumb. For example, if the scroll bar's thumb is already at the top, clicking the up arrow generates an OnScroll event but not an OnChange event.

Start a new project using the Fixed-Size Form template and set the form's properties like this:

Property	*Value*
Caption	Color Changer
Ctl3D	False
Color	clWhite

Place three horizontal scroll bars on the form, spacing them evenly and sizing them to almost the full width of the form. Select all three and set their properties as follows:

Property	*Value*
LargeChange	16
Max	255
Position	255

Keeping them all selected, flip to the Events page and double-click OnChange. Put this statement in the OnChange event handler:

```
Color := RGB(ScrollBar1.Position,
    ScrollBar2.Position,
    ScrollBar3.Position);
```

When you run the program, it will look like Figure 4-5. Use the mouse to tweak the scroll bars: The top one controls the amount of red in the form's color, the middle one the amount of green, and the bottom one the amount of blue. Now try the arrow keys. The left and up arrow keys scroll the focused scroll bar left one unit (SmallChange); the right and down arrow keys scroll right one unit. PgUp scrolls left 16 units (LargeChange) and PgDn scrolls right 16 units. Finally, Home and End go to the left and right ends of the scroll bar, respectively.

These standard components are the lowest-level building blocks of the Windows interface. Master them and you've graduated from Windows novice to journeyman.

Figure 4-5:
Scroll bars control values such as the amount of red, green, and blue in a form.

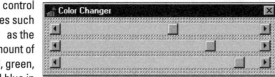

Chapter 5

A Dialog with Windows

*S*tandardized Windows on-screen elements such as buttons, list boxes, and menus have always given Windows applications a helpful consistency. It's a bit humdrum, compared to the exciting world of DOS-based programs, where you never know whether help is F1, F3, ?, or Ctrl+Alt+Shift+H. But when you know how to use one Windows application, you have a head start on using every other Windows application.

Windows 3.1 raised this consistency to new heights with *common dialogs*. Now every Windows program can use the same dialogs for selecting files, choosing fonts or colors, finding text, and printing. Windows 95 adds more power to the common dialogs, and Delphi 2.0 makes these super-charged dialogs available. Use the common dialogs whenever you can; you'll save time and effort.

Common Habits of Common Dialogs

Delphi's common dialog components all live together on the Dialogs page in the Component palette and have a lot of traits in common. At design time they all appear on your form as little icons that can't be resized, and at run time none of them appear. To make a common dialog component show up in response to an event, you execute it. No, put down that guillotine! You call its Execute method. For example:

```
OpenDialog1.Execute;
```

The File, Color, and Printer dialogs basically take over. Your program can't continue until you click OK or Cancel, at which point the Execute function returns True (if OK was clicked) or False (otherwise).

The Find and Replace dialogs are more egalitarian. Their Execute function returns right away, and the dialog shares space with your program until you get tired of it. That way, you can leave the dialog open and press Find Next repeatedly to continue finding occurrences of the item you're looking for.

All the common dialog components have a Ctl3D property. In Delphi 1.0, it controls whether the whole dialog is displayed in a 3-D style. The updated Windows 95 common dialogs used in Delphi 2.0 are always 3-D, but the property still exists so existing code won't have to be rewritten. All common dialog components also have a HelpContext property, and each component's Options property has a subproperty that enables a Help button. When that subproperty is True, pressing the button brings up the help system page whose number matches HelpContext. (That is, this happens if you have a help system attached to your program.) Each common dialog except the Print Setup dialog has its own specialized Options property that explodes into a set of True or False properties specific to the component.

The File, Color, and Printer dialogs don't have any events associated with them. Your program simply executes them and acts on the user's choices. The Font, Find, and Replace dialogs all have associated events, triggered by pressing buttons on the dialog. For example, pressing the Font dialog's Apply button generates an OnApply event, giving you the opportunity to apply the user's changes to some text without closing the Font dialog. Now let's get down to details.

Opening Data Files

It's a rare program that doesn't use some kind of file storage for data. Thanks to the Open File common dialog shown in Figure 5-1, all Windows 3.1 and Windows 95 programs can open files in similar ways. And the overwhelming set of options lets you fine-tune the dialog to address your program's particular needs.

Properties

By default, the caption of an Open File common dialog is just Open. You'll probably want to change that to something appropriate to your program. That's easy — just set the Title property to, for example, Open Completely Different File (which is the caption used in Figure 5-1).

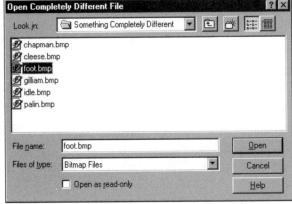

Figure 5-1:
The
Windows 95
Open File
common
dialog, set
up for
loading
various
types of
graphics
files.

The Filename property is the payoff for using the dialog. After the user clicks OK, the dialog disappears from view, and your program can retrieve the selected file from the Filename property. If you want the dialog to start with a particular filename displayed, your program should fill in the Filename property just before executing the dialog. Otherwise, your program retains the value it had the last time the dialog was used.

InitialDir specifies what directory the dialog should display at first. If you leave it empty, the dialog starts in the directory that your program last accessed. If you put a value in it, the dialog always starts in the specified directory.

Setting a default extension with the DefaultExt property isn't all that useful, but you may as well do it. If the user painstakingly types in a file name, rather than simply pointing and clicking, and runs out of steam before typing an extension, the Open File common dialog appends the default extension. Also, the dialog warns you if the user chose a file with an extension different from the default extension.

You probably noticed that file common dialogs display a set of choices at the bottom left — a drop-down list box labeled Files of type (see Figure 5-1). The Filter property lets you create a list like this for yourself. Until Delphi came along, creating this list was a laborious process. You had to build one long string containing the description and file specification for every type. One misplaced character could throw the whole thing off. In Delphi, though, you just double-click the Filter property and fill in the names and file specifications as in Figure 5-2. Notice that one filter can include multiple file specifications, separated by semicolons.

FilterIndex indicates which of the filter items should be selected initially. Just leave it at its default value of 1 and put the most popular filter at the beginning of the list.

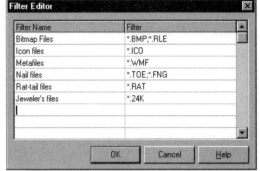

Figure 5-2:
Delphi's
Filter Editor
simplifies a
tedious
Windows
programming
task.

The FileEditStyle property lets you enhance the basic Windows file common dialog by changing the file name edit box into a combo box. The HistoryList property gives access to the combo box's list of items. The name gives it away; you normally use the list to store recently loaded files.

That leaves only the Options property, but what a property it is! When you double-click it, it explodes to over a dozen individual True or False properties.

Options that affect the display

Some elements of the Open File dialog are optional. The Help button, for example, is absent unless you set the ofShowHelp option to True. The Read Only check box disappears if the ofHideReadOnly property is True. This check box is useless by itself, in any case. If it's present, your program is responsible for opening the file in a way that doesn't permit changes. Unless you really *need* to allow read-only file viewing, you want to hide the check box. The Open File dialog in Figure 5-1 has ofShowHelp set to True and ofHideReadOnly set to False.

Delphi 2.0 adds a few more options. The standard Windows 95 Open File dialog has a Network button and displays long file names. You can suppress the Network button by setting ofNoNetworkButton to True, and force old DOS-style file names by setting ofNoLongNames to True. You can even go for the totally retro-chic Windows 3.1 style by setting ofOldStyleDialog to True!

Options that affect what you can do

If your user politely chooses a file from the list using the mouse, you're pretty much guaranteed a safe and correct result. However, users are permitted to improvise by typing a file name directly into the common dialog, and users are amazingly talented at creating improper file names. By default, the Open File dialog rejects an entry that contains invalid characters. You can turn off this behavior by setting ofNoValidate to True, but why would you want to?

If you don't want to deal with read-only files, just set ofNoReadOnlyReturn to True and the dialog won't allow the user to choose read-only files. Note that this is unrelated to the read-only check box on the dialog. ofNoReadOnlyReturn controls what files can be selected; the check box simply carries a message saying whether the user wants to open the selected file in a read-only mode.

What will your program do if the user tries to open a file that doesn't exist yet? You need to decide whether this is permitted or not. If not, set ofFileMustExist to True and the common dialog rejects nonexistent files. If new files are allowed, you may want to set ofCreatePrompt to True. This action causes the dialog to ask for confirmation before creating a new file — a handy wake-up call in case users thought they were typing an existing file name.

Even if you feel expansive enough to allow users to create new files, you'll probably draw the line at creating new directories to hold those files. Set ofPathMustExist to True and the common dialog won't accept a file name unless it's in an existing directory.

Set ofShareAware to True if you'll be using the dialog to choose database files that may be in use by some other person or application. Delphi's database file components have file-sharing capability built in. If this option is False, the Open File dialog won't allow the user to choose a file that's already in use. That's the more prudent course if your program is opening a file without using the database components.

Other options

The Open File dialog has a few other useful options, and a few that aren't good for much. If you set ofNoChangeDir to True, the dialog returns to its starting directory when it's finished. And ofAllowMultiSelect lets the user select multiple files; the list of files turns up in a run-time-only property named, appropriately, Files.

The ofOverwritePrompt option doesn't mean anything in an Open File dialog — it's there only because the Save File dialog uses the same set of options. The same is true of ofNoTestFileCreate. You can check ofExtensionDifferent after executing the Open File dialog to see whether the user selected a file with a different extension from the default, but there's rarely any reason to do so.

The ofReadOnly option holds the state of the read-only check box in the dialog. The expression for checking it is

```
IF ofReadOnly IN OpenDialog1.Options
```

The common dialog is just a messenger here — it's up to your program to *do* something about this check box. Unless the program actually provides some method for opening a file for nothing but viewing, you should hide the read-only check box.

Brother, Is Your Data Saved?

Every time a program opens an existing file, it should use the Open File dialog. And every time a program saves a file for the first time or saves it under a new name, it should use the Save File dialog. The two dialogs have a lot in common — in fact, their property lists are identical.

Properties

The only difference between the properties of the Save File dialog and the Open File dialog is in the meaning of some of the options. OfCreatePrompt isn't relevant here, but ofOverwritePrompt causes the dialog to warn users if they choose to save to an existing file name. OfReadOnly is simply irrelevant in this dialog.

Build a simple text editor

You can use these components to make a simple text editor. In the process, you're going to use a bevel component. You haven't been properly introduced to the bevel yet, but don't be shy. Pretend you're friends now; you get a full introduction in Chapter 7. You find the bevel on the Additional page of the Component palette.

Place a bevel component on a new form and set its Align property to alTop. Place four buttons on the bevel. Caption them &Ope..., &Save, Save &As..., and E&xit. (The three-dot ellipsis at the end of two of the names is a secret Windows code that means pressing the button displays a dialog, rather than performs some action immediately.)

Drop a memo box on the form with its properties set like this:

Property	Value
Align	alClient
ScrollBars	ssBoth
Lines	(blank)

Change the form's Caption to My Editor. Now drop an Open File dialog on the form and give it these properties:

Property	Value
DefaultExt	TXT
FileEditStyle	fsComboBox
Options.ofHideReadOnly	True
Options.ofFileMustExist	True
Options.ofNoReadOnlyReturn	True
Title	Open Text File

Double-click the Filter property to open the Filter Editor. Fill in the first two lines in the Filter Name column with Text files and All files and type the corresponding filters *.TXT and *.* in the Filter column.

Place a Save File dialog on the form and give it almost the same set of properties:

Property	Value
DefaultExt	TXT
Options.ofHideReadOnly	True
Options.ofOverwritePrompt	True
Options.ofNoReadOnlyReturn	True
Title	Save Text File

Fill in the same set of filters as you did for the Open File dialog.

Create an OnClick event handler for the Exit button with just the command Close; in it. For the Open button, use these lines:

```
WITH OpenDialog1 DO
  IF Execute THEN
    BEGIN
      Memo1.Lines.LoadFromFile(Filename);
      HistoryList.Add(Filename);
```

(continued)

```
      Caption := 'My Editor - ' +
         ExtractFilename(Filename);
      SaveDialog1.Filename := Filename;
      Filename := '';
   END;
```

Double-click the Save button and enter this line for its OnClick event handler:

```
Memo1.Lines.SaveToFile(SaveDialog1.Filename);
```

Finally, use these lines for the Save As. . . button:

```
WITH SaveDialog1 DO
   IF Execute THEN
      BEGIN
         Memo1.Lines.SaveToFile(Filename);
         Caption := 'My Editor - ' +
            ExtractFilename(Filename);
      END;
```

Leaping Lizards! As Figure 5-3 shows, you've written a simple text editor. It can load, edit, and save small to medium files; its capacity is roughly the same as the Windows Notepad accessory. You can cut, copy, and paste text using the standard Windows keystrokes. And each file you open is added to a history list in the Open File dialog, in case you want to open it again soon. You'll be returning to this project, so save it now. Name the unit MYEDITU.PAS and the main project MYEDIT.PRJ.

Figure 5-3:
Building this
simple text
editor is a
snap.

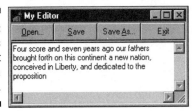

Taking Advantage of Windows Fonts

If you use any Windows word processor, you've probably seen the Font common dialog many times. Even the puny little Windows 3.1 Write accessory uses it. Select Fonts... from Write's Character menu and you see the Font common dialog. (You can access the Font dialog also by double-clicking the Font property of any Delphi component.) Figure 5-4 shows a Font common dialog with all its elements in use.

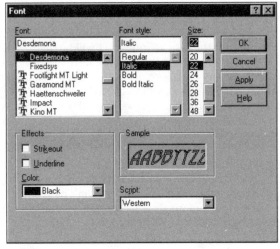

Properties

Some fonts are designed to display beautifully on the screen, some are optimized for printing, and some are good for both. The Font dialog's Device property determines which types of fonts will be displayed: screen, printer, or both.

The Font dialog component has a Font property, just like most other Delphi components, but this particular Font property doesn't control the font for the dialog itself. Rather, you use it to pass font information into and out of the dialog. Typically, you copy the current font into the Font property before calling the dialog, and you retrieve the selected font from this property after the dialog closes.

Like the two file common dialogs, the Font dialog has an Options property that explodes into a number of True or False options.

Options that affect screen elements

If you set fdShowHelp to True, a Help button appears on the dialog. Pressing this button displays the program's Help file at the page specified in the Font dialog's HelpContext. The fdEffects option is the only option that's True by default. If you set it to False, the portion of the Font dialog that enables you to set the Underline and Strikeout effects disappears.

Options fdNoFaceSel, fdNoSizeSel, and fdNoStyleSel eliminate the initial display of a default value in the Font (typeface), Font size, and Style sections of the dialog. You use these options only if you are using the dialog to set the font for a chunk of text that currently includes more than one typeface, size, or style.

Options that affect which fonts are available

The remaining options restrict the type of fonts that will be displayed. The fdAnsiOnly option limits the list to fonts that use the normal Windows character set, in case you don't see any need for your users to type their memos in Symbols or Wingdings or other nontext fonts. And fdTrueTypeOnly rejects fonts that aren't the flexible Windows TrueType style. The fdFixedPitchOnly option cuts out variable-pitch fonts, leaving only the fonts in which every character is the same width.

TrueType fonts make it especially easy for the user to choose a ridiculously huge or tiny font size. The fdLimitSize option lets you ban fonts so big that one letter fills the screen or so small that the characters can't be read. Set it to True and put your desired minimum and maximum sizes in the MinFontSize and MaxFontSize properties.

You need a master's degree in fontology to understand the restrictions corresponding to fdNoOEMFonts, fdNoSimulations, fdNoVectorFonts, and fdWysiwyg. Best bet: leave these set to False.

Finally, fdForceFontExist means the Font dialog should display an error message if the user types in a typeface name that doesn't exist. Always set this option to True, unless you happen to develop an amazing technique for automatically inventing fonts based on nothing but the name. Let's see, how would you represent Slartibartfast Bold Italic?

Events

The Font common dialog responds to one special event, OnApply. This event is triggered when you press the Apply button on the dialog. Don't get frantic looking for the Apply button; in Delphi 1.0 it doesn't appear until after you define an OnApply event handler. The Options.fdApplyButton property, new in Delphi 2.0, lets you pointlessly force an Apply button to appear even without an OnApply method. The purpose of this button and its event is to apply the changes you've made in the Font dialog without closing the dialog.

Load the MyEdit project again and place a Font dialog on the form. Move the Exit button to the right and insert a button captioned &Font between Save As and Exit. Put this code in the new button's OnClick event handler:

```
WITH FontDialog1 DO
  IF Execute THEN
    Memo1.Font := Font;
```

Put this single line in the Font dialog's OnApply event handler:

```
Memo1.Font := FontDialog1.Font;
```

Run the program again and load a file into it. Select a font using the Font button. Choose something wild — use all the options. The file is displayed in the typeface, size, style, and color you selected. Bring up the Font dialog again and move it so that it doesn't obscure the editor itself. Make some changes and press the Apply button. The change takes effect right away, but the Font dialog doesn't close. This makes it easier to fiddle around with different possibilities. Note that in this sample program, after you've used the Apply button, you can no longer truly cancel your changes. That's not a problem; if you don't like the font you applied, just reselect the one you were using before.

Save the updated MyEdit project; now it includes the capability to change fonts!

You may be wondering if you're going to be giving the simple editor the capability to apply fonts to just *some* of the text. Maybe you'd like to put the heading in bold 16-point type and underline every occurrence of your name. The answer is — you're not going to be doing that yet. The memo component at the heart of our editor depends completely on the Windows multiline edit box element, which simply doesn't have the capability to display more than one font at a time. In Chapter 12, you look at the Windows 95 rich edit component, which has text formatting capabilities to rival most word processors, along with nearly unlimited capacity.

A Rainbow of Color Dialog

You probably already used the Color common dialog in Delphi itself. If you double-click the Color property of any component, you see the Color dialog. If your programs need to let users choose a color, this dialog — shown in Figure 5-5 — does the job for you.

The Color dialog's Color property doesn't affect the color of the dialog itself. Instead, it determines what color will be selected initially. After the user has made a selection, this property contains the chosen color.

The CustomColors property is a list of up to 16 strings that have the same format as the lines in the Custom Colors section of CONTROL.INI. Each line consists of a color name (from ColorA to ColorP), an equal sign, and the hexadecimal value of the particular custom color. For example:

```
ColorA=5AEBD6
```

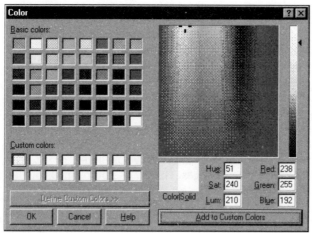

Figure 5-5:
The Color
common
dialog can
also display
only its left
half; here it
is fully
opened.

As you'll see shortly, Delphi makes it easy to load the color dialog with CONTROL.INI's official custom colors and to save any changes back to CONTROL.INI.

After the first three dialogs, which were jam-packed with options, you may dread the thought of another Options property. But this time it's no big deal. If cdFullOpen is True, the dialog starts life fully open, with the gaudy "curtain" of all possible colors showing. If cdPreventFullOpen is True, the Define Custom Colors button is disabled, and the user is forced to choose from existing basic and custom colors. And if cdShowHelp is True, a Help button appears on the dialog. Pressing it opens the program's help system to the page whose number is stored in the dialog's HelpContext property.

The Windows 95 Color dialog, available in Delphi 2.0, adds the cdSolidColor and cdAnyColor options, but they're fairly lame. Use cdAnyColor and the user can choose colors that won't display properly in the current video mode. And rather than forcing all the colors in the dialog to the nearest solid color with cdSolidColor, you'd be better off using Delphi's own Color Grid component, introduced in Chapter 7.

Drop a Color dialog on a new form and set its Color property to clWhite. Set the form's Ctl3D property to False and make its color clWhite as well. Put these lines in its OnDblClick event handler:

```
IF ColorDialog1.Execute THEN
  Form1.Color := ColorDialog1.Color;
```

Run the program and double-click the form to change its color. That's all you have to do to add a Color dialog to your program.

If you want to load and save the custom colors from CONTROL.INI, you need a little more code. Delete the lines you just entered and replace the begin..end pair for the OnDblClick event handler with the following lines:

```
VAR N, P : Word;
begin
  WITH TIniFile.Create('CONTROL.INI') DO
    try
      WITH ColorDialog1 DO
        BEGIN
          ReadSectionValues('Custom Colors',
            CustomColors);
          IF Execute THEN
            BEGIN
              Form1.Color := Color;
              FOR N := 0 TO CustomColors.Count-1 DO
                BEGIN
                  P := Pos('=', CustomColors[N]);
                  WriteString('Custom Colors',
                    Copy(CustomColors[N], 1, P-1),
                    Copy(CustomColors[N], P+1, 255));
                END;
            END;
        END;
    finally
      Free;
    END;
end;
```

Now page up to the top of the file and add IniFiles to the uses clause. (Remember, that means you find the word *uses* at the start of a line and add *IniFiles* and a comma after it.) Now each time you double-click the form, the color dialog's custom colors are loaded from CONTROL.INI. If you add or change custom colors and click OK, the changes are written to CONTROL.INI. Do note that although Windows 95 still has a CONTROL.INI file, it stores its *internal* custom colors as a chunk of binary data in the registry. I am not going to discuss modifying the registry; the potential for disabling your system is simply too great!

Calling on Windows to Configure Printers

In the old DOS days, many a programmer sank into terminal despair on confronting the Printing Problem. To send anything but the most basic plain text to a printer, you needed to know the control codes for that printer. But there were hundreds of sets of codes, with more appearing every month. Not only that, there was no way to query the printer to find out what set of codes it knew.

The great thing about Windows is that it is in charge of printing. Your programs don't have to know the detailed control codes for a zillion and one printers, because Windows knows. The Print Setup dialog component (its icon has a picture of a printer and a wrench) gives you an easy way to select and configure Windows printers.

The Print Setup dialog gives you a break — it doesn't respond to any events, and you don't need to set values for any of its handful of properties.

Load the MyEdit project again and drop a Print Setup dialog on it. Stretch the bevel component downward so there's room for a second row of buttons. Place two new buttons labeled &Print... and P&rint Setup... in the second row. Create the Print Setup button's OnClick method with this single line of code:

```
PrinterSetupDialog1.Execute;
```

Run the program and push the Print Setup button (the Print button doesn't do anything yet). You see a dialog like the one shown in Figure 5-6. Now press Properties or Options (one or the other will be present) and you get a further dialog; its look varies depending on your printer driver. Note carefully what the existing options are before you make any changes.

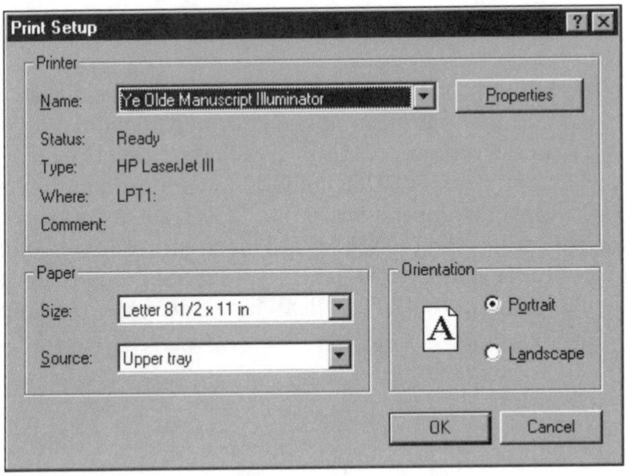

Figure 5-6: In the Print Setup common dialog, you can select which of the installed printers to use.

Preparing to Print

You use the Print Setup dialog to select and configure the printer. When it comes to what gets printed, the Print dialog, shown in Figure 5-7, is in charge. Just in case you get a last-minute urge to change printers, the Setup... button in the Windows 3.1 style Print dialog displays the Print Setup dialog.

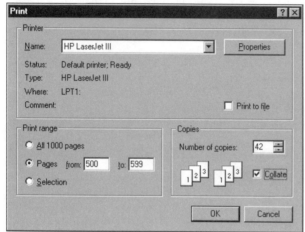

Figure 5-7: In the Print common dialog, you can select what will be printed.

Several of the remaining properties control the initial values of items in the dialog and report those values after the user's changes. If Collate is True, the Collate check box is checked, and multiple copies of multi-page documents are printed a whole document at a time. If Collate is False, all copies of page 1 are printed, and then all copies of page 2, and so on. The check box is disabled if the selected printer doesn't support uncollated copies.

The Copies property corresponds to the Number of copies box on the dialog, and should generally be set to 1. If the user increases this number, your program is responsible for printing multiple copies. FromPage and ToPage control the range of pages that will get printed, and MaxPage and MinPage define the valid range for FromPage and ToPage.

The value of PrintRange corresponds to one of the three radio buttons in the Print Range group box; FromPage and ToPage are ignored unless the PrintRange property's value is prPageNums. Finally, PrintToFile goes with the Print to file check box on the dialog. If this box is checked, your program is responsible for getting a file name from the user and performing the print to file operation.

You don't always need all the information that the Print dialog can gather, so the Options property's subproperties let you selectively disable portions of the dialog. The Print to file check box disappears if poPrintToFile is False. If poPageNums is False, the Pages radio button isn't available. If poSelection is False, the option to print only the selected text is turned off. When poWarning is True, the dialog automatically warns if there's no default printer selected. And poHelp determines whether or not a Help button appears on the dialog.

Add a Print dialog to the MyEdit project, leaving all of its properties set to their default values. Double-click the Print button and replace the begin..end pair supplied by Delphi with this code:

```
VAR
  POutput : TextFile;
  N       : LongInt;
BEGIN
  IF PrintDialog1.Execute THEN
    BEGIN
      AssignPrn(POutput);
      Rewrite(POutput);
      Printer.Canvas.Font := Memo1.Font;
      FOR N := 0 to Memo1.Lines.Count - 1 DO
        Writeln(POutput, Memo1.Lines [N]);
      CloseFile(POutput);
    END;
END;
```

Scroll to the top of the unit and add Printers to the uses clause. (Find the line near the top of the file that starts with the word *uses*. Add the unit name after this word, and follow it with a comma.) Select the Font common dialog and set its Device property to fdBoth to restrict its choices to fonts that are available for both the printer and the screen.

You just added printing to the simple editor. It doesn't attempt to print or collate multiple copies, but you can print the editor's contents in the font of your choice. And with the Print Setup dialog, you can select the printer, paper orientation, and configuration options that are specific to your printer.

Searching for Text in All the Right Places

What if you loaded a good-sized text file into your simple editor and you needed to search for a particular word or phrase in the file? You wouldn't want to page through the whole file; after all, you may blink and miss what you're looking for.

Finding stuff is the kind of job computers are good at, so Windows and Delphi provide a Find common dialog. Unfortunately, all the dialog does is find out what the user wants to look for; your program has to do the legwork to actually find it.

Properties

The FindText property holds the text the user entered in the dialog. Most of the time, you won't set this in advance. The only properties you normally set for a Find dialog are the numerous options.

The basic Find dialog has two check boxes that let users choose whether to match the exact case (so they don't find *CAT* when they're searching for *Cat,* for example) and whether to match whole words only (so they don't find *catastrophe* when they're looking for *cat*). It also includes a pair of radio buttons that let users specify whether they want to search forward or backward from the current cursor position.

If you want to hide these three options from users, you can use the frHideMatchCase, frHideWholeWord, and frHideUpDown properties to do so. If you'd rather tantalize users by displaying the three user-option controls without allowing input, just disable the controls. The options for this purpose are frDisableMatchCase, frDisableWholeWord, and frDisableUpDown. There's also the frShowHelp option — if it's True, a Help button appears.

The remaining options are used in the Find dialog's OnFind event to let you know which button the user pressed and which options are current. frMatchCase, frWholeWord, and frDown indicate the current state of the user options. If frFindNext is True, the user pressed the Find Next button. The remaining options, frReplace and frReplaceAll, are used only by the Replace dialog. (I get to that dialog in a minute.)

Events

A Find dialog responds to just one event, OnFind. When the user presses the Find Next button, it triggers the OnFind event. That's all the help you get from this component — your program is responsible for doing the required searching.

Making Replacements

A Replace dialog is almost the same as a Find dialog. It has all the same properties plus ReplaceText, which holds the text entered by the user on the Replace line. And it has one added event, OnReplace, which is triggered by pressing the Replace or Replace All buttons.

Load the MyEdit project and set the memo box's HideSelection property to False. Drop a Find dialog and a Replace dialog on the form and select them both. Double-click the Options property and set frHideMatchCase, frHideWholeWord, and frHideUpDown to True. Add buttons labeled Fi&nd... and Rep&lace... to the second row of buttons. Use this line for the Find... button's OnClick event:

```
FindDialog1.Execute;
```

and this line for the Replace. . . button:

```
ReplaceDialog1.Execute;
```

Run the program and try the Find. . . and Replace. . . buttons. Each displays the corresponding dialog, but using them is frustrating; they don't do anything yet.

Select the Find dialog, flip to the Events page and double-click the OnFind event. Replace the begin..end pair inserted by Delphi with the following rather formidable-looking block of code:

```
VAR
  Buff, P, FT : PChar;
  BuffLen : Word;
begin
  WITH Sender AS TFindDialog DO
    BEGIN
      GetMem(FT, Length(FindText) + 1);
      StrPCopy(FT, FindText);
      BuffLen := Memo1.GetTextLen + 1;
      GetMem(Buff, BuffLen);
      Memo1.GetTextBuf(Buff, BuffLen);
      P := Buff + Memo1.SelStart + Memo1.SelLength;
      P := StrPos(P,  FT);
      IF P = NIL THEN MessageBeep(0)
      ELSE
        BEGIN
          Memo1.SelStart := P - Buff;
          Memo1.SelLength := Length(FindText);
        END;
      FreeMem(FT, Length(FindText) + 1);
      FreeMem(Buff, BuffLen);
    END;
end;
```

When you're finished, click the Replace dialog, flip to the Events page in the Object Inspector, and press the down arrow next to the slot for the OnFind event handler. From the resulting list, select the same event handler you just created for the Find dialog. Create an OnReplace event handler for the Replace dialog that contains these lines:

```
WITH Sender AS TReplaceDialog DO
  WHILE True DO
    BEGIN
      IF Memo1.SelText <> FindText THEN
        FindDialog1Find(Sender);
      IF Memo1.SelLength = 0 THEN Break;
      Memo1.SelText := ReplaceText;
      IF NOT (frReplaceAll IN Options) THEN Break;
    END;
```

Wow, that was quite a handful of code. It would have been simpler if it didn't have to compile under both Delphi 1.0 and Delphi 2.0. But it would have been even more complicated if we hadn't skipped the various options, such as match case and search up or down! Save the program, run it, and load a file. Now you can use the Find button to locate a given string in the loaded file. It has to be an exact match, and only the text after the current cursor position will be searched.

Press Replace and you can use the dialog to replace a particular string with another. In the Replace dialog, Replace All replaces every instance that occurs after the current cursor position. We could make the find and replace code more complicated, but this should be enough for now. Hey, Notepad doesn't even offer replace!

Figure 5-8 shows the final form of the MyEdit project with a Replace dialog in action. Be sure to save the project, because you'll continue to enhance it.

What's missing in that last picture? What does almost *every* Windows program have that our simple editor doesn't? A menu, of course. On to the next chapter!

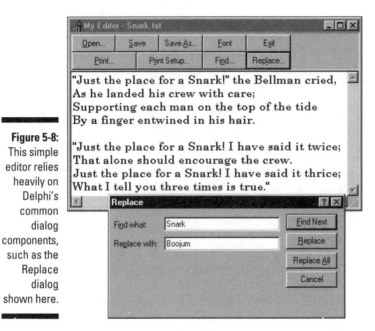

Figure 5-8:
This simple
editor relies
heavily on
Delphi's
common
dialog
components,
such as the
Replace
dialog
shown here.

Chapter 6

What's on the Menu?

*W*hen it comes to push buttons, two's company, six or eight's a crowd. In a big and complicated program, a push button for every feature may leave no room on the form for anything else. And finding a particular button among the huddled masses is tough. You can solve both problems by using a menu to launch your program's features. The main menu lists general categories of activity in a menu bar that's always visible across the top of the form. When you click each main menu item, a submenu appears; it disappears when you make a selection.

Preparing a Tasty Menu

The main menu component is the first item on the standard Component palette — its icon looks like a menu with a submenu pulled down. Dropping a main menu component on your form has no immediate visible effect, but as soon as you add a menu choice to the component, the main menu appears across the top of the form. Even during the design phase, you can pull down submenus, and if you click a submenu item, Delphi takes you to the OnClick event handler for that item.

The main menu component

A main menu component has just four properties — AutoMerge, Items, Name, and Tag — and responds to no events. Name and Tag are introduced in earlier chapters; you look at the AutoMerge property later in this chapter. The Items property is the list of menu items. When you push the ellipsis button next to the Items property or double-click the menu component's icon, Delphi fires up the Menu Designer, which is shown in Figure 6-1.

Add a main menu item here

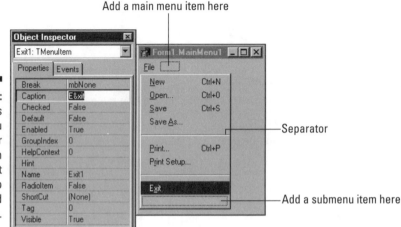

Figure 6-1:
Delphi's
Menu
Designer
works with
the Object
Inspector to
let you build
menus.

Separator

Add a submenu item here

Like everything else in Delphi, the Menu Designer is visually oriented. To start creating a new menu, just type the caption for the first item on the menu bar. After you type that first caption, you add new main menu items in the empty rectangle at the right end of the menu bar. You add submenu items in the empty rectangle at the bottom of the active submenu. You can see both of these rectangles in Figure 6-1. To insert a series of submenu items, click the Caption line in the Object Inspector, click the empty rectangle at the bottom of the submenu, and just start typing captions. Each time you press Enter, you move to the next item.

When the items in a submenu fall naturally into groups, you can insert a separator line (visible in Figure 6-1) by adding a menu item with a lone hyphen for its caption.

Chances are good that your first attempt at a menu structure won't be perfect. That's not a problem, though, because redecorating is simple — you just move individual items or whole submenu structures by dragging them around with the mouse. You can also right-click anywhere on the Menu Designer to display a pop-up menu that (among other things) lets you insert and delete menu items. Note that the Insert command inserts a new item before the highlighted item, and the Delete command deletes the highlighted item.

Remember that right-clicking *doesn't* select the item you right-clicked. Get in the habit of left-clicking to select and then right-clicking to bring up the pop-up menu.

Menu item components

Every item on the main menu bar and every item in a submenu is represented in your program by a menu item component. These components don't appear on the Component palette; only the Menu Designer can create them. However, after they're created, you use the Object Inspector to set their properties and events just like ordinary components.

The absolutely essential property of a menu item is its Caption property, which tells the user what this item does. Top-level menu items must have one-word captions; that's because two-word captions can easily be mistaken for two items. You can be a bit more verbose with submenu items, but captions should still be as short as possible. Delphi automatically derives a name for the item from the caption.

As with other components, an ampersand (&) in the caption underlines the following character and makes it into a mnemonic access key. For main menu items, the access key is Alt plus the underlined character. To select a submenu item, pressing Alt is optional. For example, to select the &Open item from the &File menu you can either press Alt+F and then Alt+O or press just Alt+F,O.

The ShortCut property defines an always-available shortcut key for a submenu item. Pressing this key has the same effect as selecting the menu item, but without having to open the menu. As Figure 6-2 shows, when you choose a shortcut key for a submenu item, Delphi puts the name of the shortcut key to the right of the caption in the menu, lined up against the right edge of the submenu.

You can pull down a list of values for the shortcut key, but that list contains only the simplest keystroke combinations. Instead, try typing key combo names that aren't on the list, such as Ctrl+Up or Ctrl+Shift+Alt+A. If Delphi doesn't gripe, the combination is valid.

If a menu item's Checked property is True, a check mark appears to the left of the caption. The last two items on Delphi's own View menu are good examples of checkable menu items. It's common practice to separate related groups of checkable items with separator lines, such as the line above SpeedBar in Delphi's View menu.

Menu item components have a property called GroupIndex that, in Delphi 1.0, is strictly related to the AutoMerge property of a main menu component. The use of GroupIndex with AutoMerge is discussed later in this chapter. In Delphi 2.0, GroupIndex is used with the new RadioItem property to create groups of menu items that act like radio buttons — only one at a time can be checked. (As you can see later in Figure 6-3, the check mark morphs into a circle for menu items that use the RadioItem property. We call them "checked" menu items regardless, because the Checked property controls the mark.)

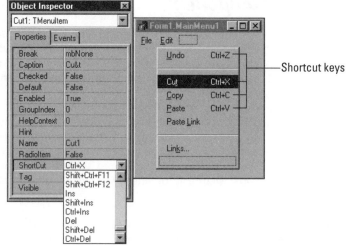

Figure 6-2:
The shortcut
key for a
submenu
item
appears
right-aligned
after the
caption and
is available
even when
the
submenu is
not pulled
down.

—Shortcut keys

Sometimes a group of checkable menu items represent independent options, such as the SpeedBar and Component palette items in the View menu. Other times they're mutually exclusive choices, such as the different Sort by items in File Manager's View menu. In either case, it's up to your program to check and uncheck the items.

If your submenu is overloaded with items, you can set the Break property of an item to mbBreak. This forces the submenu to begin a new column of menu items. Setting the Break property to mbBarBreak does the same thing and also places a vertical bar before the new column (peek ahead to Figure 6-3 for an example). Always leave this property set to mbNone for top-level menu items — they never get a break!

Drop a main menu component on a new form and double-click it to enter the Menu Designer. Give the first main menu item the caption &Test. Click on the blank submenu item just below it and type captions &A, &B, &C, &I, &J, and &K, pressing Enter after each. This should create a submenu with six items. Note that Delphi has named the items A1 through K1. Now, if you like, replace each caption with a word that starts with that letter, such as &Apple, &Bridge, and so on.

Don't skip a step and give your menu items personalized captions right off the bat. Delphi assigns a default *name* to menu components based on their initial caption, and the code that follows assumes that those names are &A, &B, &C, and so on.

Click the item that starts with *I*, right-click to display the pop-up menu, and select Insert. Set the caption of the inserted item to a single hyphen (-) to create a separator. Then click on the A item and set its Checked property to True.

Click on A, and then Shift+click on C to select the first three items. If you're using Delphi 2.0, set the RadioItem property to True and GroupIndex to 1 for all three items. Flip to the Events page in the Object Inspector and double-click the OnClick event. Put these lines in the event handler (Delphi 2.0 users should omit the first three lines):

```
A1.Checked := False;
B1.Checked := False;
C1.Checked := False;
WITH Sender AS TMenuItem DO
  Checked := True;
```

Now select items I, J, and K and create an OnClick method for all of them with just this line:

```
WITH Sender AS TMenuItem DO Checked := Not Checked;
```

If you're using Delphi 2.0, set the GroupIndex for these three items to 2. When you first run the program, only the A menu item will have a check beside it; in Delphi 2.0 it will be a solid circle. Choosing the B or C item will *move* the mark to that item. Items A, B, and C act like radio buttons; only one of them can be checked. Any time you want mutually exclusive checked menu items like this in Delphi 1.0, use an OnClick handler like the one for A, B, and C. In the event handler, you turn off the Checked property for all items in the group, and then turn it on for the item that you clicked. For Delphi 2.0 programs, simply set RadioItem to True for all related menu items and give them a GroupIndex different from all the other items. In their OnClick event handler, set Checked to True for the item that you clicked; Delphi handles unchecking the other items.

Choosing I, J, or K from the menu toggles the check mark — if the check mark is there, it disappears; if it's not there, it appears. Items I, J, and K act like check boxes. Any time you want a menu item to toggle its checked state on each click, use an OnClick event handler like the one for I, J, and K.

Using the same project, bring up the Menu Designer again. Assign the shortcut key Ctrl+A to the A item, Ctrl+B to B, and so on. Click the separator item and either press the Del key or right-click and select Delete. Click the menu item that starts with I and set its Break property to mbBarBreak. (You won't see the result of changing the Break property until the program runs.)

Run the program again and press Ctrl+I, Ctrl+J, and Ctrl+K. Click Test or press Alt+T and you see that all three of those items are now checked, just as if you selected them from the menu. Also, as you can see in Figure 6-3, the two sets of three items are in two parallel columns, with a vertical bar separating them.

Figure 6-3:
Two types of
checkable
menu items,
each with a
shortcut
key.

Only one of the items in this
column can be checked

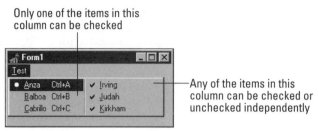

Any of the items in this
column can be checked or
unchecked independently

As the figure shows, if you're using Windows 95, the shortcuts for the second column of menu items won't be visible. You think that looks bad? Break the menu into three columns and it gets worse, much worse. The shortcuts for items in the second column appear in the third column! The problem lies in the combination of Windows 95, multicolumn menus, and menu shortcuts. Eliminate any one of the three and there's no problem. Because Windows 95 is here to stay, the simplest rule is to avoid using multicolumn menus and menu shortcuts together.

Go back to the Menu Designer for the same project and add another main menu item called &SuperTest. To do this, click the empty rectangle to the right of the Test item and type the caption. Use the mouse to drag the Test item to the submenu location below SuperTest. Don't get frustrated if the submenu hanging from Test obscures the place you want to drag to. If you drag directly to the right and then down, you are able to see the target.

You just created a cascading submenu. Run the program and select SuperTest. Note that the Test submenu item has a sort of cuneiform wedge after its name, like the one in Figure 6-4. That's the signal that it has a cascading submenu. Click Test and the original six submenu items appear. Note that the shortcut keys Ctrl+A and so on still work even though the corresponding menu items are one level deeper in the menu. Another way to create a cascading submenu is to highlight any submenu item, right-click, and select Create Submenu from the pop-up menu.

Figure 6-4:
One
cascading
submenu is
open and
another is
indicated by
the symbol
to the right
of its name.

Cascading submenu indicator

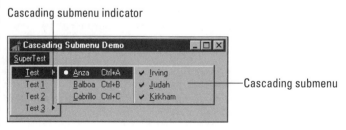

Cascading submenu

Standard Menu Templates

Part of the charm of Windows is that programs *try* to always do things the same way. In all but the most antisocial programs, the submenu option to load a file from disk is called &Open..., and it's in a main menu named &File. Delphi makes it extremely easy for you to conform to standard usage by letting you store menu layouts as templates. You can use templates provided by Delphi or build your own.

Unless your program is totally bizarre, you find that some elements of the standard templates fit your needs. Start your menu by installing all appropriate templates. Then simply delete any of the standard items that don't apply and add items specific to your program.

To add a template using the Menu Designer, first click the empty rectangle on the menu bar where the template should go. Then right-click and select Insert From Template... from the pop-up menu. Choose the template you want, click OK, and you're done.

File menu

Just about every program uses files in some way. For the rare program that doesn't, it's common to have a File menu anyway, with just the Exit item. You can now create a template for the File menu. (Yes, Delphi already includes templates for File, Edit, and Help menus, among others, but you'll learn more by building them yourself.)

Drop a menu component on a new form and double-click it to enter the Menu Designer. Type &File and press Enter. Now look back at Figure 6-1 and type each of the menu item captions below File (New, Open, Save, and so on). Insert an ampersand (&) before the underlined character in each name and press Enter after each. Remember to enter a hyphen for each separator line's caption and don't try to include the shortcut keys in the item name. When you finish entering the captions, go back and add the shortcut keys, if you want. Then right-click and select Save as Template... from the menu that pops up. Name this template My File Menu.

That's it! You created a reusable menu template. If you made a mistake, or if you want to fine-tune the template later on, load it into an otherwise empty main menu, make your changes, and save the modified menu as a template again.

As I mentioned in Chapter 5, some menu items have an ellipsis (...) after the item name to let you know that choosing this item displays a dialog. Follow this convention when you create menu items of your own. For any item that activates a dialog, tack those three dots onto the end of the item name.

Edit menu

After you load a file, you probably want to edit it, so the Edit menu comes next. You can build this template as well.

If the Menu Designer is still open from the previous exercise, select the File menu and delete it. Click the Caption line in the Object Inspector and then click the empty rectangle at the top left of the Menu Designer. You're ready to type in another list of menu captions. This time use the items shown in Figure 6-2, starting with &Edit for the top-level item name.

Assign the standard shortcut keys to Undo, Cut, Copy, and Paste (these keys are, respectively, Ctrl+Z, Ctrl+X, Ctrl+C, and Ctrl+V). Now save this template as My Edit Menu.

Most of these items should be familiar to you from Delphi's own Edit menu. A few of them, Paste Link and Links…, are strictly related to OLE. You may want to create a separate template without these two items and use the template for projects that don't require OLE.

Help menu

In a perfect world, every Windows application would have a standard Windows help file. Alas, we don't live in a perfect world, but our world *does* contain utilities that ease the process of creating help files. When you've managed to build a help file for a project, the first three choices on the standard help menu invoke the Windows help program in three specific ways. You can use either Delphi's Help menu template or build your own to match Figure 6-5.

Figure 6-5: The Help menu standardizes access to the application's help file.

The Contents item displays the help file's contents page, just like the corresponding item on Delphi's own Help menu, and the Search for Help On… item is equivalent to Topic Search on Delphi's menu. Selecting How to Use Help brings up a help file associated with the Windows help program itself.

You always rename the About <program>... item to refer to your program's name. The item should display an About box, which is a secondary form that tells the name and version number of the program and supplies copyright information. In Chapter 17, you build a fancy About box that displays all kinds of useful information.

Add a menu component to a new form and double-click it to enter the Menu Designer. Right-click and add the Help menu template. Use these three lines of code as the OnClick event handlers for the three standard menu choices:

Menu choice	*OnClick event handler*
Contents	Application.HelpCommand (HELP_CONTENTS, 0);
Search for Help On. . .	Application.HelpCommand (HELP_PARTIALKEY, 0);
How to Use Help	Application.HelpCommand (HELP_HELPONHELP, 0);

Choose Options from the Project menu (or Project from the Options menu in Delphi 1.0) and turn to the Application page. Press the Browse button next to the Help File combo box and choose Delphi's own help file, DELPHI.HLP.

If you're using Delphi 1.0, select New Form from the File menu, and choose the About Box template. Delphi 2.0 users should select New... from the File menu, click the Forms page, click the Copy radio button, and choose the About Box template. Put this line in the About menu item's OnClick event:

```
AboutBox.ShowModal;
```

Now add Unit2 to the main form's uses clause.

When you run this program, you find that the standard Help menu items work fine. You can bring up the contents page of the Delphi help system, search for help on a given topic, or get help on using help in general. And clicking the About menu item brings up the as-yet-unfinished About box.

Beautify the simple text editor

Remember the MyEdit project from the last chapter? Remember how busy it looked, with so many buttons across the top? Load it up again; you're going to build a menu for it using the templates.

Drop a menu component on the MyEdit form and double-click it to enter the Menu Designer. Place a standard File menu template in the menu, click the separator after Save As..., and select Insert from the pop-up menu — use &Font... as the caption for the new menu item. Now add a top-level menu item named Fi&nd, with submenu items Fi&nd... and &Replace... below it.

For each item on the menu except File|New, attach the existing OnClick method for the corresponding button. For example, the Open button was named Button1, so in the Object Inspector's Events page for the Open menu item, you click the right arrow next to OnClick and select Button1Click. If you're not sure which name was used for a particular button, just click on the button and look in the Object Inspector.

Double-check to be sure that you connected each of the menu items to the correct event handler. Now delete all nine buttons and the bevel they rode in on. Instead of wasting space on the form with buttons, you've put all the actions into a tidy menu. You'll find that you can open, edit, save, and print files just fine.

Take a moment to add some polish to the tiny editor. Right now, it lets you exit or switch to a new file without reminding you to save your existing file, and the File|New menu item doesn't do anything. You can fix that!

In the event handler for the Open menu item, find the line that begins

```
Memo1.Lines.Load...
```

and insert this line after it:

```
Memo1.Modified := False;
```

The event handler for the Save menu item contains just one line at present. Replace that line with:

```
IF SaveDialog1.Filename = '' THEN
  SaveAs1.OnClick(Sender)
ELSE
  BEGIN
    Memo1.Lines.SaveToFile(SaveDialog1.Filename);
    Memo1.Modified := False;
  END;
```

In the event handler for the Save As menu item, find the line that begins

```
Memo1.Lines.Save...
```

and insert this line after it:

```
Memo1.Modified := False;
```

Now create an OnCloseQuery event handler for the form, with these lines:

```
IF Memo1.Modified THEN
  CASE MessageDlg('File ' +
      ExtractFileName(SaveDialog1.Filename) +
      ' has changed. Save now?',
      mtConfirmation, mbYesNoCancel, 0) OF
    idYES    : Save1.OnClick(Sender);
    idNO     ::
    idCANCEL : CanClose := False;
  END;
```

Highlight the lines you just typed and press Ctrl+C to copy them to the Clipboard. Go back to the event handler for the Open menu choice, place the cursor immediately after the begin line, and press Ctrl+V to insert a copy. Then change the line that begins with the word idCancel to:

```
idCancel : Exit;
```

Again highlight all the lines you typed for the form's OnCloseQuery event handler and press Ctrl+C for another copy. Click on the New item in the File menu to start an OnClick event handler for it, and paste in a copy of the confirmation code. Again, change the line that begins with the word idCancel to:

```
idCancel : Exit;
```

Now add these three lines after the pasted-in code:

```
Memo1.Clear;
SaveDialog1.Filename := '';
Caption := 'My Editor';
```

With those additions, this simple editor is now a *safe* editor. You won't accidentally throw away your work without saving. Speaking of saving, save the MyEdit project now. You may even want to add an icon for MYEDIT.EXE to one of your Program Manager groups.

Pop-Up Menus

All visible Delphi components have a property called PopupMenu. When you right-click the component, the attached pop-up menu pops into view. Of course, before you can hook up a pop-up menu, you have to build it. That's what you do next.

The most important property of a pop-up menu is AutoPopup. If this property is True, as it is by default, right-clicking a component that's hooked to this menu causes it to pop up. The Alignment property determines where this menu pops up. The top edge of the menu will be at the height of the cursor, and — depending on whether Alignment is paLeft, paCenter, or paRight — either the left, center, or right of the top edge will be at the cursor.

Designing a pop-up menu is similar to designing a main menu but easier, because no menu bar is across the top. Although you can add cascading submenus to the pop-up using the Create Submenu choice from the Menu Designer's *own* pop-up menu, don't do it. Pop-up menus are supposed to be speedy and convenient.

Most of the time, pop-up menu items don't have mnemonic access keys because there's no built-in way to pop up the menu itself using just the keyboard. However, you *can* get a lot of mileage out of assigning shortcut keys to pop-up menu items. Naturally enough, you do this with the ShortCut property. Even if the menu itself isn't hooked to any component and never shows its face on the screen, the shortcut keys will be available throughout your program.

A pop-up menu component receives the OnPopup event just *before* it appears on the screen. This is the chance for the pop-up menu to make any last-minute preparations, such as disabling unavailable items or adjusting check marks.

Drop a memo component and a pop-up menu on a new form. Double-click on the pop-up menu to enter the Menu Designer, and put three items in the menu; name them Cut, Copy, and Paste. In their OnClick methods, use the lines:

```
Memo1.CutToClipboard;          (in the Cut item)

Memo1.CopyToClipboard;         (in the Copy item)

Memo1.PasteFromClipboard;      (in the Paste item)
```

Delete the contents of the memo's Lines property, set its ScrollBars property to ssBoth, and set its PopupMenu property to the name of the pop-up menu component. Set its Align property to alClient.

Run the program and type some text. Highlight a word or two by dragging with the mouse and then press the right mouse button. Select Cut from the pop-up menu and the text disappears. Move the text insertion point and right-click again, this time selecting Paste. The text reappears. You created a pop-up menu that lets you cut and paste with the mouse in one hand while holding an ice cream cone in the other. Cool, huh?

Using the same program, select the pop-up menu from the list in the Object Inspector. Flip to the Events page, double-click the OnPopup event, and insert this code:

```
Cut1.Enabled := Memo1.SelLength > 0;
Copy1.Enabled := Cut1.Enabled;
Paste1.Enabled := Clipboard.HasFormat(CF_TEXT);
```

Add ClipBrd to the uses clause of the unit.

Run the program again and you see that the pop-up menu's Cut and Copy items are disabled when there's no selected text to cut or copy, and the Paste item is disabled when there's no text to paste. That's the point of the OnPopup event — it lets you tweak the pop-up menu to match current conditions.

Many different components on the form can be associated with the same pop-up menu through their PopupMenu property. The pop-up menu's PopupComponent property makes that connection in reverse. It tells the pop-up menu component which component it's popping up over.

Place a pop-up menu and six or eight edit boxes on a new form. Make sure the form's font is one that supports both bold and italic (not the nasty old System font). Now select all the edit boxes and set their PopupMenu property to point to the pop-up menu.

Double-click the pop-up menu itself and add four menu items with captions Bold, Italic, Underline, and Strikeout (their names will be Bold1, Italic1, and so on). Set the Tag property of the four items to 0, 1, 2, and 3, respectively. These numbers directly correspond to the font style constants fsBold, fsItalic, fsUnderline, and fsStrikeout.

Put this code in the pop-up menu's OnPopup event handler:

```
WITH (PopupMenu1.PopupComponent AS TEdit).Font DO
  BEGIN
    Bold1.Checked := fsBold IN Style;
    Italic1.Checked := fsItalic IN Style;
    Underline1.Checked := fsUnderline IN Style;
    Strikeout1.Checked := fsStrikeout IN Style;
  END;
```

Highlight all four of the submenu items in the Menu Designer, flip to the Events page in the Object Inspector, and create an OnClick handler for all of them containing this code:

```
WITH (PopupMenu1.PopupComponent AS TEdit).Font DO
  BEGIN
    Style := Style - [TFontStyle((Sender AS TMenuItem).Tag)];
    IF NOT (Sender AS TMenuItem).Checked THEN
      Style := Style + [TFontStyle((Sender AS
              TMenuItem).Tag)];
  END;
```

Run the program and right-click one of the edit boxes. The choices in the pop-up menu are checked or unchecked depending on the edit box you clicked. Click any of the menu items to *change* the box's font.

Caution: Merging Menus

Now that you have some menu experience under your belt, you can tackle two advanced items: the main menu's AutoMerge property and the GroupIndex property of individual menu items. In a plain, simple program with just one form, AutoMerge is useless. It's only when you have a main form and one or more secondary forms that menu merging makes sense. If a secondary form menu's AutoMerge property is True, its menu items merge with the main form's menu when that secondary window is active. Suppose you write a program that includes secondary windows for limerick editing and graffiti design. When the limerick window is active, the Limerick menu item appears among the items of the main window's menu bar. When the graffiti window is active, that item is replaced by the Graffiti item.

Never set AutoMerge to True in the main form's menu. If you do this, at run time the menu attempts to merge with the cosmic even-more-main form . . . and it disappears.

In Delphi 1.0, GroupIndex is relevant *only* for top-level menu items — the ones that show on the menu bar even when nothing is pulled down. In either Delphi version, the GroupIndex of top-level menu items controls how the secondary form's menu merges into the main menu. Going from left to right across the menu bar, the GroupIndex for each item must never be less than the GroupIndex for the previous item. For example, if you raise one item's GroupIndex to 3, Delphi checks all items to its right and makes sure that their GroupIndex is at least 3. If you attempt to set an item's GroupIndex lower than the previous item, Delphi slaps your wrist.

Items with the same GroupIndex form a group. When a group from a secondary menu merges into a main menu, one of two things happens. If the main menu has a group with the same index, the group from the secondary menu completely replaces the group from the main menu. If no same-numbered group is in the main menu, the secondary group is inserted into the main menu in GroupIndex order. It sounds complicated, but the process is easier to understand when you see it happening.

On-again off-again merging

Start a new project and select the MDI Application template. You are presented with a working skeleton of a Multiple Document Interface program. Try it — run the program and select File | New a few times. Now quit the program.

Back in the Form Designer, double-click the main window's main menu. Select the Help menu item and set its GroupIndex to 2. Now bring up the MDI child form. (If you don't see the child form, select Forms... from the View menu.) Drop a menu component on the child window and open the Menu Designer. Name the top-level menu &Test and set its GroupIndex to 1. Invent some creative item names to put in the Test item's submenu.

Run the program again. When you open a child window, the Test menu appears in the main window's menu, as you can see in Figure 6-6. When you close the last child window, the Test menu disappears again. Exit the program and change the Test menu item's GroupIndex to 2. Now when you run the program, the Test menu *replaces* the Help menu anytime a child window is open.

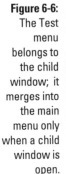

Figure 6-6:
The Test menu belongs to the child window; it merges into the main menu only when a child window is open.

With no child window, the Test menu is absent

Child window

The Test menu appears when the child window is open

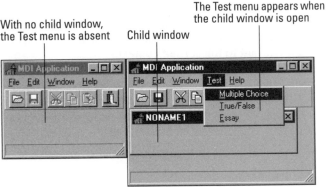

Multiple-choice merging

The aphorism "Different strokes for different folks" becomes "Different menus for different venues" in Windows. All the child windows in the MDI example were the same type, but nothing says they *have* to be the same. Delphi itself has *lots* of different window types: the Form Designer, the Code Editor, the Object Inspector, and so on. If you want, you can give each type of child form its own set of menu items. Whichever child form is active will have its menu merged into the main form's menu.

Put this code in a new form's OnCreate event handler:

```
Left := 0; Top := 0;
Width := Screen.Width;
ClientHeight := 0;
```

Place a menu component on the form with just two top-level menu items, &File and &Help. Set the GroupIndex property of the second one to 2. (Don't worry about submenus; this is just a demonstration.) Now choose the New Form item from Delphi's File menu twice, to add two more forms to the project. For each of them, set Visible to True and BorderIcons.biSystemMenu to False. Drop a menu component on each form and set the menu's AutoMerge property to True.

In the menu for Form2, create a top-level menu item and then set its caption to Form&2 and give it a GroupIndex of 1. Do the same for Form3 but set the menu item's caption to Form&3.

The commands in the main form's OnCreate method cause it to take over the top of the screen, just like Delphi does. The two secondary windows appear wherever Windows chooses to place them. When you click one of the secondary windows to activate it, its menu merges into the main menu. This can be a handy way to keep the menu activity for a multiform application centralized, while keeping it relevant to the current context.

In the next part, you meet components that you can use to build *extraordinary* programs, starting with the graphical components in the next chapter.

Part III
More Components

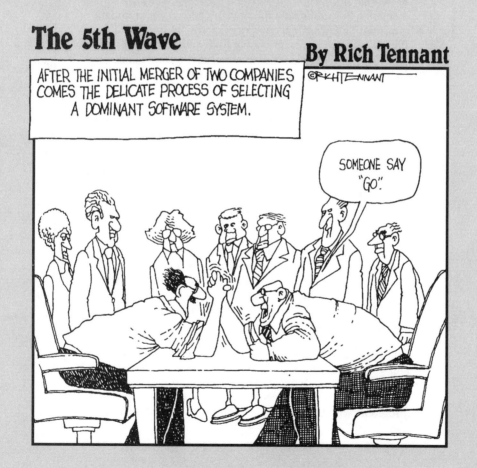

In this part . . .

At the Delphi Diner, you can order bland components that duplicate and enhance the basic Windows screen elements. But that's only the beginning for the component gourmet. The graphical components you'll learn about in Part III spice up forms and serve to display information visually. The tedious task of loading, saving, and displaying bitmap images is a snap with Delphi's help.

There are components to implement simple controls that Windows forgot, and components to let you create customized file-selection forms. At the top of the food chain, you'll find potent components such as the media player, which plays any multimedia file or device. Along the way, you'll experience interprogram communion through Dynamic Data Exchange, and you'll activate OLE objects in your own programs.

To top off this feeding frenzy, you'll work with Delphi's powerful and versatile database components. Delphi's database support is modern and high-tech. It supports specialized field types, such as images and variable-length memos, and can easily scale up from local database applications to client/server. Just hook up a handful of components and write a line or two of code!

For dessert, those lucky enough to be running Delphi 2.0 can dip into the delicious collection of Windows 95 user interface components. Whether you're running under Windows 95 itself or Windows NT, these components enhance your programs with truly up-to-the-minute power and flexibility.

Chapter 7

Look-and-Feel Components

In This Chapter

▶ Using shape components to stack up a Towers of Hanoi puzzle

▶ Building unlimited shapes with the paint box component

▶ Creating a simple graphic file viewer

▶ Creating a toolbar with flyover help, just like the Delphi toolbar

▶ Building a status line that automatically displays hints for the current component or menu choice

▶ Using the bevel component to set off form elements with 3-D "dips" and "bumps"

▶ Controlling your form's scrolling with a scroll box

*T*he standard components, dialogs, and menus handle all the mundane aspects of building a Windows user interface for your programs. Useful? Indubitably! Exciting? Alas, no. Computer users these days are jaded. Even the most supremely effective program gets short shrift unless it *looks* like the user's idea of a supremely effective program.

In this chapter, you examine some components that add color and style to your forms and that provide new ways to organize mundane components. These components deal with the "look and feel" of your program, not with accomplishing its grunt work. You can use them to add crown moldings, decorative finials, tailfins, a good paint job, or whatever it takes for your programs to grab the attention of even the most finicky user.

Choosing Look-and-Feel Components

Use Table 7-1 to locate the component that best suits your needs. You find most of these components on the Additional page of the Component palette, although a few appear on the Samples page.

Table 7-1	Problems Solved by Look-and-Feel Components
Task	*Component*
Place a simple geometric shape on your form	Shape. See "Get into Shape with Shapes."
Display a nonstandard or complex shape	Paint box. See "Paint Any Shape You Like."
Let the user choose one of the 16 simple solid colors for the foreground and the background	Color grid. See "Color Control with Color Grid."
Put a pretty picture on your form	Image. See "Image Is Everything."
Display the progress of an ongoing process	Gauge. See "Gauging Your Progress."
Create a toolbar or status bar, with optional flyover help	Panel. See "Introducing Our Panel."
Create dividing lines or rectangles on your form	Bevel. See "Bumpy and Dippy Forms."
Limit the portion of your form that can scroll	Scroll box. See "Controlling Scrolling."

Get into Shape with Shapes

The shape component can take on six shapes, all of them variations on the ellipse and rectangle. Sorry, no triangles, hexagons, or enneagrams. Shape components are often used to create backgrounds and borders for other components. For example, you could put a gray rectangle behind a data entry field to give it a shadow effect. You can also create wholly visual programs in which the user interacts with the program by manipulating shapes.

Properties

The most important properties of a shape component are Shape, Pen, and Brush. The Shape property determines the shape that is displayed — ellipse, circle, rectangle, square, round-cornered rectangle, or round-cornered square. Pen is an exploding property that determines how the shape's border is drawn, with subproperties Color, Mode, Style, and Width. Color is the border's color, and Width is the width of the border. Style selects a solid, dotted, or dashed line for the border, but the nonsolid styles have no effect unless the pen's width is 1.

Drop two Shape components on a new form. Select them both, set their shape to stEllipse, and set the pen width to 16. Then select just one of them and set its pen style to psInsideFrame.

In Windows, when you draw a shape using a wide pen, the border is drawn so its *center* comes right to the edge of the shape's boundary rectangle, and any bits that hang outside the boundary are unceremoniously chopped off. The psInsideFrame style exists to avoid this problem. However, Delphi automatically fits the whole shape inside its boundary, so the psInsideFrame style makes the shape too small, as Figure 7-1 demonstrates.

Figure 7-1:
If you set a shape component's pen style to psInside-Frame when the width is 2 or more, it won't fill the entire boundary rectangle.

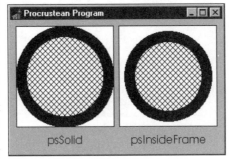

The Brush property controls what's drawn inside the shape. This, too, is an exploding property, with subproperties Color and Style. If Style is bsClear, the interior of the shape is transparent; if Style is bsSolid, the interior is filled in with the brush's Color. The other styles yield various line and crosshatch patterns. (You can see one of the crosshatch patterns in Figure 7-1.)

Events

A shape component responds only to the OnMouseDown, OnMouseUp, and OnMouseMove events, along with the drag and drop events. The following exercise is a classic graphics-only puzzle program called the Towers of Hanoi, implemented using shapes that can be dragged and dropped.

If you made any changes to the Form Designer's sizing grid, select Environment from the Options menu. On the Preferences page, in the Form Designer rectangle, put an X next to Display Grid and Snap to Grid, and set both grid sizes to 8 pixels. Now your grid settings match the assumptions in the instructions that follow.

Start a new project, but instead of choosing the blank project template, choose the fixed-size form template you built back in Chapter 2. Place eight shapes on the new form, as shown in Figure 7-2. (You probably need to look at the figure as you follow the next few instructions.) First draw a rectangle three grid units high and eight grid units wide. Draw five more rectangles below it, each one extending one grid unit farther to the left and one grid unit farther to the right than the rectangle above it. Finally, select the largest rectangle, copy it to the Clipboard, and paste two copies of it onto the form, lining them up in a horizontal row with the original.

Figure 7-2:
This is the
Towers of
Hanoi
puzzle,
implemented
using
Delphi's
shape
components.

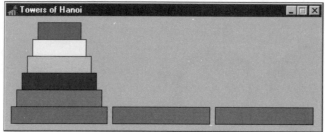

Select the three largest rectangles and set their Brush.Color property to clGray. Set the Brush.Color property of each of the other five rectangles to a different bright color. (I used clRed, clYellow, clLime, clBlue, and clFuchsia, but you can choose any colors you like.)

Does this look like anything to you? Perhaps a Mayan pyramid, with two parking lots for tourists? Well, it's supposed to be an edge-on view of three flat bases with five disks of decreasing size stacked on the left-hand base. This is a replica of a very old puzzle called the Towers of Hanoi. All you have to do is move the disks from the left base to the right base. That would be simple, except that there are two restrictions. First, you can move only one disk at a time. Second, you can never, even for an instant, stack a larger disk on top of a smaller disk.

Change the form's caption to Towers of Hanoi and size the form so that it fits nicely around the shapes you drew. Change the Name property of the left, middle, and right large rectangles at the bottom of the form to *L*, *M*, and *R*, respectively. Change the Name property of the five disk rectangles stacked on top of the large rectangle on the left to *A*, *B*, *C*, *D*, and *E*, going from top to bottom.

Set the DragMode of the smallest disk, *A*, to dmAutomatic, meaning this disk can be moved. This is the only disk that can be moved at the beginning of the game.

To force obedience to the rules, your program is going to have to know how each disk is related to the disk above it and to the disk below it. You can use the Hint property for this purpose, because it's not otherwise occupied. Set each shape's Hint to a two-letter string in which the first letter is the name of the shape below it and the second letter is the name of the shape above it; use *X* when there is no shape either above or below it:

Rectangle	*Setting*
A (top)	BX (B is below it and nothing is above it.)
B	CA (C is below it and A is above it.)
C	DB (D is below it and B is above it.)
D	EC (E is below it and C is above it.)
E	LD (L is below it and D is above it.)
L (left base)	XE (Nothing is below it and E is above it.)
M (middle base)	XX (Nothing is above it or below it.)
R (right base)	XX (Nothing is above it or below it.)

Select all the shapes except the smallest (*A*) and create an OnDragOver event handler for them containing these lines:

```
Accept := ((Sender AS TShape).Hint[2] = 'X') AND
  ((Source AS TShape).Width < (Sender AS TShape).Width);
```

Remember the rule that forbids placing a larger disk on a smaller one? This event handler already enforces that rule. It says that a disk (Sender) will accept having another disk (Source) dropped on it only if the width of the dragged disk is smaller. And, of course, the disk must be at the top of its stack, with nothing above it.

Source and Sender are important parameters passed by Delphi to every OnDragOver event handler. Source is the component that's dragged; Sender is the component that's dragged over. These could be any old type of component, but we know they are both shapes, so we use the AS keyword to share that knowledge with Delphi. So (Source AS TShape) refers to the dragged disk and (Sender AS TShape) is the dropped-on disk. Got that?

Run the program and try dragging the top disk around the form. The cursor turns to the slashed-circle No symbol at first. Drag the disk over either of the two empty bases, though, and they welcome it by changing the cursor to an arrow with a rectangle. Sorry, nothing happens if you try to drop the disk; you write the code to do that next.

Again select all the shapes except the smallest. Switch to the Events page of the Object Inspector and double-click the OnDragDrop event. Replace the begin..end lines of the OnDragDrop event handler supplied by Delphi with this code:

```
VAR Moved, Still : TShape;
begin
  Moved := Source AS TShape;
  Still := Sender AS TShape;
  Moved.Top := Still.Top - Moved.Height + 1;
  Moved.Left := Still.Left + (Still.Width DIV 2)
    - (Moved.Width DIV 2);
  WITH FindComponent(Moved.Hint[1]) AS TShape DO
    BEGIN
      IF Name <= 'E' THEN DragMode := dmAutomatic;
      Hint := Hint[1] + 'X';
    END;
  Moved.Hint := Still.Name + 'X';
  Still.Hint := Still.Hint[1] + Moved.Name;
  Still.DragMode := dmManual;
  IF (L.Hint = 'XX') AND (M.Hint = 'XX') THEN
    Caption := 'Towers of Hanoi - DONE!';
end;
```

The OnDragOver event handler was a little clunky because of all the repetitions of (Source AS TShape) and so on. This new event handler would have been even clunkier, so we solved that problem by declaring a pair of local variables. The Moved variable represents the shape that moved and the Still variable represents the shape that stood still; the first two lines of the event handler set these variables to the Source and Sender parameters passed by Delphi. The rest of the handler uses these simple names to refer to the two disks.

The first step is to set the Top and Left properties of the moved disk to center it above the shape it was dropped on. Next, you use the handy FindComponent method of the main form to locate the disk that was previously beneath the moved disk. The FindComponent method locates a component on the form by name, and the desired name here is the first character of the moved shape's Hint.

If the newly uncovered shape isn't one of the three base rectangles, you set its DragMode to dmAutomatic, making it movable. You also set the second character of its Hint to *X*, because now nothing is above it. You adjust the Hint properties of the moved and still shapes to reflect that one is now above the other, and you set the still shape's DragMode to dmManual so it can't be moved. Finally, you check to see if all the disks are now stacked on the right-hand base, in which case the puzzle is solved.

That's it! The program is complete. The OnDragOver event handler enforces the rules of the puzzle by allowing only valid moves, and the OnDragDrop handler takes care of shuffling the disks around when you make a move. The minimum number of moves to solve this puzzle is 31 — can you get all the disks to the right-hand base in just 31 moves?

To increase the difficulty, you can add more disks between disk *E* and the left-hand base, naming them *F, G,* and so on. Adjust all the Hint properties to include the new disks. For each additional disk, you double the previous minimum number of moves and add one. For example, with 6 disks the puzzle takes 63 moves (which is $31 \times 2 + 1$). With 16 disks (the most you can use without suffering a "name collision" with the base named *L*), the puzzle would require 65,535 moves.

The legendary Towers of Hanoi reside in an undisturbed temple deep in the jungle. (Which jungle? It doesn't matter!) There are 64 polished brass disks, and shifts of silent black-robed monks continually move one disk at a time from one stack to another. When they finish, the universe will end. Well, that's what the story says! If they manage one move per second, the solution will take about half a trillion years, so you needn't change your plans for the weekend.

Paint Any Shape You Like

Shape components can be useful, but they're limited to representing variations on the ellipse and rectangle. Also, they have only two colors, one for the border and one for the interior. The paint box component lets you draw any shape or combination of shapes in any color you want. Of course, along with control comes responsibility — you're completely in charge of painting every aspect of the paint box component.

A paint box has all the common properties, but the only ones that show a visible effect at design time are the ones controlling on-screen size and position: Left, Top, Width, Height, and Align. The Color property becomes the default brush color; you can use Font.color to pass a pen color into the paint box's OnPaint method. This essential method gets called whenever the paint box needs to repaint itself. The code in the OnPaint method completely determines what a particular paint box looks like.

Place a paint box component on a new form, making it roughly square. Set its Color property to clWhite and create an OnPaint event handler for it using this code:

```
WITH Sender AS TPaintBox, Canvas DO
  BEGIN
    Brush.Color := Color;
    Pen.Color := Font.Color;
    Polygon([Point(Width DIV 2, 0),
      Point(Width DIV 5, Height),
      Point(Width, 2U(Height DIV 5)),
      Point(0, 2U(Height DIV 5)),
      Point(4U(Width DIV 5),Height)]);
  END;
```

When you run the program, it displays a five-pointed star. The interior of the star matches the paint box's Color, and the border matches its Font.Color. There is one little problem; the points of the star are filled in, but not the center.

Go back to the OnPaint event handler and insert this line just before the line that begins with the word Polygon:

```
SetPolyFillMode(Handle, WINDING);
```

Now the star is completely filled in. SetPolyFillMode is a function of Windows itself — it's not part of Delphi. But Delphi automatically gives you access to every one of the thousands of functions built into Windows. This particular function determines what method Windows uses to fill a polygon whose border lines cross each other.

In the OnPaint event handler you just built, you're directly calling methods and setting field values for the paint box's run-time-only Canvas property. This property is an object itself, but it's not a visible component that can stand alone on the form. Look up TCanvas sometime in Delphi's on-line help to see a list of properties and methods for this object. There's a lot it can do! Now, though, you can teach the paint box a few more tricks.

Place another paint box on the same form and make this one twice as wide as it is high. Start an OnPaint event handler for it and replace Delphi's begin..end pair with this code:

```
VAR
  R : TRect;
  N : Word;
CONST
  Rainbow : ARRAY[0..4] OF TColor =
    (clRed, clYellow, clLime, clBlue, clFuchsia);
begin
  WITH Sender AS TPaintBox, Canvas DO
```

```
   BEGIN
     R := ClientRect;
     R.Bottom := 2UR.Bottom;
     Pen.Width := 8;
     Pen.Style := psInsideFrame;
     FOR N := 0 TO 4 DO
       BEGIN
         Pen.Color := Rainbow[N];
         WITH R DO
           Ellipse(Left, Top, Right, Bottom);
         InflateRect(R, -8, -8);
       END;
     END;
 end;
```

Most of the time when you type in the code for an event handler, you just enter lines between the begin..end pair supplied by Delphi. Be alert for examples like the one here, in which you *replace* the begin..end pair with lines you type.

This event handler is a little more complicated than most you've written, but that's the price of using a paint box. You can draw whatever you want, as long as you can figure out how to write the code to do it. This code draws a rainbow. Actually, it draws five ellipses of different colors, one inside the other, but since the bottom half of each ellipse is outside the paint box, it looks like a rainbow.

Add yet another paint box to the project you are working on. Set its properties like this:

Property	*Value*
Align	alTop
Color	clYellow
Font.Name	Arial
Font.Style.fsBold	True
Height	41

Create an OnPaint event handler for this paint box, replacing the begin..end pair supplied by Delphi with these lines:

```
VAR
  a16th, N, X : Word;
begin
```

```
(continued)
  WITH Sender AS TPaintBox, Canvas DO
    BEGIN
      Brush.Color := Color;
      FillRect(ClientRect);
      WITH ClientRect DO
        Rectangle(Left, Top, Right, Bottom);
      a16th := PixelsPerInch DIV 16;
      N := 0; X := 0;
      WHILE X < Width DO
        BEGIN
          MoveTo(X,1);
          LineTo(X, 6U(1+(Byte(N MOD 2=0) +
            Byte(N MOD 4=0) +
            Byte(N MOD 8=0) +
            Byte(N MOD 16=0))));
          Canvas.Font := Font;
          IF (N > 0) AND (N MOD 16=0) THEN
            TextOut(PenPos.X+3, PenPos.Y-16,
              IntToStr(N DIV 16));
          N := N + 1;
          X := X + a16th;
        END;
    END;
end;
```

Try to guess what that event handler does before you run the program. Did you guess? It draws a ruler across the top of the form. The FillRect function fills the entire paint box with color, and the Rectangle function draws a border. (So far, this isn't doing anything a shape component couldn't do.) Next you calculate approximately how many pixels correspond to 1/16 inch. You set variables N and X to 0 and start a loop that draws a vertical line every 1/16 inch across the width of the paint box.

Within the loop, the MoveTo function moves the pen to the top edge of the paint box, at the pixel position defined by X. The LineTo function draws a line from that position down; the longest lines come at the 1-inch marks, the next shorter lines come at 1/2-inch marks, and so on down to the shortest lines at 1/16-inch marks. For a 1-inch mark, the TextOut function writes the correct number just to the right of the mark. Each time through the loop, variable N increases by 1 and variable X increases by the number of pixels in 1/16 inch.

The very first line is numbered 0, so look at line number 1, the first 1/16-inch mark. It's not divisible by 2, 4, 8, or 16, so its length is 6. How about the 1-inch mark (line 16)? It is divisible by 2, 4, 8, and 16, so its length is 5×6, or 30 pixels. This handy calculation yields the correct length for lines representing whole inches and for each fraction down to 1/16 inch.

Color Control with Color Grid

The Color common dialog lets you or your users choose any of the 16,777,216 colors that Windows is theoretically able to display. That's about 16 million more choices than you'll ever need. When your system is set up to display 256 or fewer different colors, Windows usually gives you a dithered color instead of the exact color you chose. That is, it displays a pattern of dots in two or more solid colors that, when viewed through frosted glass or smudgy spectacles, approaches the color you asked for. If you just want to select a solid color, the color grid component is a better bet.

You find the color grid on the Samples page of the Component palette. Components that live on this page aren't as tightly integrated into Delphi as the rest of the components. For example, the help system doesn't have help for them. Borland supplies them for your use and edification without claiming that they're as essential as the rest of the component library. Personally, I find these "second-class citizens" to be just as useful and worthy of note as their mainstream companions.

Properties

If you drop a new color grid onto a form, you get a 4-by-4 array of colored boxes. The GridOrdering property lets you rearrange the boxes in 8 or 16 rows or columns instead. By default, the color grid tracks foreground and background colors, but you can set ForegroundEnabled or BackgroundEnabled to False to disable one of these. Don't disable both unless your users have shown a tendency to choose really vile combinations. The ForegroundIndex and BackgroundIndex properties indicate which of the 16 boxes is selected for each, and the run-time-only ForegroundColor and BackgroundColor properties hold the actual color. This component sadly lacks the PopupMenu property found in almost all visible components; Delphi 2.0 cures its inferiority complex by adding the PopupMenu property.

Events

A left-click on a color box sets a new foreground color, and a right-click sets a new background color. When the user changes the foreground or background selection, the color grid receives an OnChange event. You can also respond to the OnClick event, which occurs anytime the user clicks the grid, but OnChange is usually all you need.

Place a good-sized shape on the form and set its properties like this:

Property   ***Value***

Shape   stEllipse

Pen.Width   8

Place a color grid on the form below the shape, and set its GridOrdering property to go8x2. Match its width to that of the shape, and set its height so the boxes are roughly square. Set its BackgroundIndex property to 15. Put these lines in the color grid's OnChange event handler:

```
WITH Sender AS TColorGrid, Shape1 DO
  BEGIN
    Pen.Color := ForegroundColor;
    Brush.Color := BackgroundColor;
  END;
```

Run the program (shown in Figure 7-3) and try left- and right-clicking the color grid. When you left-click, the outline of the shape changes to match the color, and *FG* appears in the box you clicked. When you right-click, the shape's interior changes color and *BG* appears in the box. If you make the foreground and background the same, the box holds *FB*. Note, too, that you can use the arrow keys to move the highlight around the color grid and press the *F* or *B* key to set the foreground or background color.

Figure 7-3:
The color
grid
component
lets users
choose
foreground
and
background
colors from
a set of 16
solid colors.

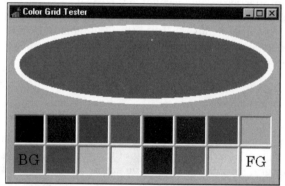

Image Is Everything

An image component displays a bitmap, an icon, or a Windows metafile. Delphi wizards can even arrange to register other graphic file formats for the image component's use. If you ever meet any old-time Windows programmers, *don't* show them the image component! You'll be letting yourself in for an hour-long harangue about how difficult it was to display bitmaps in the "good old days," and how kids these days just don't know the value of honest work.

Properties

An image component's *Picture* property is an object that holds the bitmap, icon, or metafile to be displayed. You can load an image into the Picture property at design time or at run time. If the Stretch property is True, the picture stretches or shrinks to fit the bounds of the image component. Otherwise, the picture retains the size you gave it at design time. If the picture is too big, it is clipped at the bounds of the image; if it's too small, there is blank space around it.

Events

Images respond to the standard mouse events — clicks, double-clicks, dragging, and so on. Most of the time, though, they don't have to do anything except display a pretty picture.

Drop an image component on a new form, set Stretch to True, and set its Align property to alClient, so it fills the form. Set the form's caption to Image Viewer and add an Open File dialog with these properties:

Property	Value
DefaultExt	BMP
Options.HideReadOnly	True
Options.FileMustExist	True
Title	Open Image File

Double-click the dialog's Filter property to bring up the filter list and create filters named Bitmaps, Icons, and Metafiles, with values *.BMP, *.ICO, and *.WMF, respectively.

Place a menu on the form and give it a simplified File menu, with just the &Open... and E&xit items. Put the single command Close; in the Exit menu item's OnClick event handler and these lines for the Open item:

```
WITH OpenDialog1 DO
  IF Execute THEN
    BEGIN
      Screen.Cursor := crHourglass;
      try
        WITH Image1.Picture DO
          BEGIN
            LoadFromFile(Filename);
            WindowState := wsNormal;
            ClientWidth := Width;
            ClientHeight := Height;
          END;
        Caption := ExtractFilename(Filename);
      finally
        Screen.Cursor := crDefault;
      end;
    END;
```

Loading a bitmap from disk can take a little time, so you set the cursor to an hourglass while the loading is going on. Rather than change the cursor for the form or one of its components, you change it globally for the Screen object. Run the program and load any bitmaps you have handy. To start with, the form sizes itself to match the image. But if you resize or maximize the form, the image stretches to fit. Oh, one thing — icons don't stretch.

If you use this viewer on some of the tiny bitmaps designed to be Windows wallpaper, the result is some squashed-looking, very tiny pictures. That's because the size of the bitmap is tied to the size of the form, and the form can't shrink small enough to display these particular bitmaps at their actual size.

Gauging Your Progress

Computers are supposed to be fast — they do things in the blink of an eye that you or I would take hours to do by hand. Still, some tasks would take a person years, and those tasks take more than moments even for a computer. It behooves a program that's cranking away at a job to keep the user apprised of its progress. That's what the gauge component is for. It represents a process's progress visually in several different ways. Like the color grid, the gauge resides on the wrong side of the tracks, in the Sample page of the Component palette.

The Kind property determines which type of gauge is displayed:

- A pie-type gauge gradually fills a circle as the process progresses.
- A bar-type gauge fills either horizontally (from left to right) or vertically (from bottom to top).

✔ A needle-type gauge is like the gas gauge on your car; it's shaped like a semicircle and has a needle that moves to track the process.

✔ A text-only gauge displays the percentage-complete information as text only. (All the gauges — not just this one — display this information as text, unless you set the ShowText property to False.)

You want to set BorderStyle to bsNone for the nonrectangular gauges (the pie and the needle gauges). Otherwise, a rectangular border surrounds the circular or semicircular gauge.

The BackColor property sets the color of the entire gauge, and the ForeColor property sets the color of the filled portion of the gauge. Properties MaxValue and MinValue determine the range of values reported by the gauge, and your program reports progress by setting the aptly named Progress property. The percentage displayed is relative to the position of Progress between MinValue and MaxValue. As with the Color Grid, the gauge has a PopupMenu property in Delphi 2.0, but not in Delphi 1.0.

Shift+click the gauge component's icon and place five gauge components on a new fixed-size form, arranged as in Figure 7-4. Here's the value of the Kind property for each component:

Gauge component	*Value of the Kind property*
Big circle	gkPie
Half circle	gkNeedle
Small square	gkText
Horizontal bar	gkHorizontalBar
Vertical bar	gkVerticalBar

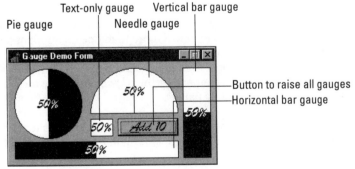

Figure 7-4: The gauge component offers five ways to report the progress of a process.

Pie gauge

Text-only gauge

Needle gauge

Vertical bar gauge

Button to raise all gauges

Horizontal bar gauge

Set the BorderStyle property for the two nonrectangular gauges to bsNone. Place a button on the form next to the small square gauge and give it the caption &Add 10. Double-click the button and put the following code in its OnClick event handler:

```
Gauge1.Progress := (Gauge1.Progress + 10) MOD 100;
Gauge2.Progress := Gauge1.Progress;
Gauge3.Progress := Gauge1.Progress;
Gauge4.Progress := Gauge1.Progress;
Gauge5.Progress := Gauge1.Progress;
```

Run the program and press the button repeatedly. The gauges go up by 10% with each press of the button. When they pass 100%, they reset to 0%. Notice how the percentage-complete text changes color as the color bar passes it. You use the gauge control in other projects.

Introducing Our Panel

The panel component is the building block from which status bars and SpeedBars are built. If you place a panel component at the top of your form and drop a few speed buttons (introduced in the next chapter) on it, you have a SpeedBar. If you place a panel component at the bottom of the form and arrange to have useful information displayed on it, you have a status bar.

Properties

The most important property of a panel component is Align. If you set it to alTop, the panel moves to the top of the form and expands to the form's full width. If you set it to alBottom, the panel fits itself to the bottom of the form. AlLeft and alRight snug the panel against the left and right edges, respectively, and alClient causes it to fill the entire client area of the form.

But wait, there's more! When you run the program and resize the form, the panel automatically resizes to match. If more than one component has the same Align value, they stack up along the specified edge. A panel with the alClient Align value fills the entire client area of the screen that's not occupied by other panels. And MDI child forms (remember them?) correctly use only the part of the form that's not occupied by panels.

Don't confuse the Alignment property with Align. Alignment simply determines where the panel's Caption is displayed: left, right, or center. Frequently you delete the caption entirely.

A panel automatically has a 3-D look and a handful of properties dedicated to adjusting that look. BevelInner and BevelOuter set the panel's inner and outer edges to look raised, lowered, or flat. BevelWidth and BorderWidth set the width of the bevel and the panel's border.

Place a panel on a new form and set its height to 57 and its width to 97. Now make eight copies of the panel and arrange the nine panels in three rows of three. Select them all, delete their captions, and set their BevelWidth and BorderWidth properties both to 2. Select the top row of three and set BevelInner to bvLowered and Caption to *H* (make sure it's a capital *H*). Select the middle row of three and set BevelInner to bvNone and Caption to *m* (small *m*). For the bottom row of three, set BevelInner to bvRaised and Caption to *G* (capital *G*). Why these captions? You'll find out shortly!

Now select the left column of three and set bevelOuter to bvLowered. Set BevelOuter for the middle and right columns to bvNone and bvRaised. Select each panel in turn and append a letter to its caption — capital *H* if it's in the first column, small *m* for the second column, and capital *G* for the third column.

Now select the form itself and double-click its Font property. Choose Wingdings for the font and set the size to 20.

Surprise! With that last step, it all makes sense. As you can see in Figure 7-5, each bevel contains two pictographs from the Wingdings font. The first represents the value of bevelInner and the second the value of bevelOuter. A down-pointing hand means bvLowered, an up-pointing hand means bvRaised, and a big zero means bvNone. Save this project and load it up any time you need to check what a particular combination of bevel styles looks like.

Figure 7-5:
By adjusting the inner and outer bevels of Delphi's panel component, you can get a variety of different effects.

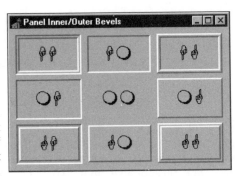

The ShowHint property is especially useful when you've got a panel full of speed buttons or other components. You can set the panel's ShowHint property to True without enabling hints for every component on the entire form.

The background color of all hint boxes in your program is controlled by the HintColor property of the invisible Application object. The Application object's HintDelay property is the number of milliseconds the mouse must rest on a component before the flyover help appears. You can use all these properties shortly.

Events

Frequently, a panel doesn't have to respond to any events. It does its job by maintaining its alignment, holding other components, and displaying flyover help. What more could you want? Occasionally, you add an OnResize event handler, to take care of the arrangement of components contained in the panel.

Panels that display information directly are more likely to respond to OnClick or OnDblClick events. For example, in Word for Windows, a subpanel of the bottom status bar indicates whether overwrite mode is on, and double-clicking that panel toggles overwrite mode on or off.

Place a panel on a new form and delete its caption. Set its Align property to alTop and its ShowHint property to True. Insert this line in an OnCreate event handler for the form:

```
Application.HintColor := clAqua;
```

Put a smaller panel inside the first panel and set its properties as follows:

Property	*Value*
BevelOuter	bvLowered
Caption	CAP
Font.Color	clGray
Hint	"Toggles CapsLock"
Tag	20

Size it to fit snugly around the caption and center it vertically in the larger panel. Now make two copies of the subpanel but be sure that they're owned by the same big panel. To do that, click the subpanel, press Ctrl+C, click the main panel, and press Ctrl+V. Drag the copies into a horizontal line. Change the captions of the other two panels to NUM and SCR and their Hints to Toggles NumLock and Toggles ScrollLock. The Tag for the NUM panel should be 144; for the SCR panel, 145. (In case you're wondering, the values 20, 144, and 145 are the numbers Windows uses internally to represent the CapsLock, NumLock, and ScrollLock keys, respectively.)

Run the program and move the mouse cursor over any of the three subpanels. When it's been still for 8/10 second, the flyover help appears. However, clicking the panels doesn't *do* anything yet.

Select all three subpanels and create an OnClick method for them, replacing the default begin..end pair with this code:

```
VAR KS : TKeyboardState;
begin
  GetKeyboardState(KS);
  WITH Sender AS TPanel DO
    KS[Tag] := KS[Tag] XOR 1;
  SetKeyboardState(KS);
end;
```

Now when you click one of the subpanels, it toggles the corresponding light on your keyboard — try it and see! Each time you click the CAP panel, for example, the CapsLock light turns on or off. And it's functional too, as you notice if you type anything.

Unfortunately, you can't yet make this project *display* the current state of the three shift locks. You haven't been introduced to a component that's essential for fixing up that kind of display. Save the project as LOCKS, and you can add the state-display capability in the next chapter.

Status symbols

One popular style of window dressing is a status line at the bottom of the form that displays a brief hint for the control or menu item that has the focus. Setting up this kind of status bar in Delphi 2.0 is simple; you just use the status bar component! In Delphi 1.0, it's still relatively simple, but it involves a little programming of a type you haven't worked with yet.

Drop a panel on a new form and set its properties like this:

Property	Value
Align	alBottom
Alignment	taLeftJustify
BevelInner	bvLowered
Caption	(none)

Create an OnClick event handler for the panel; it should contain this single line:

```
Panel1.Caption := Application.Hint;
```

Now comes the tricky part. First, go to the Object Inspector's Events page and *delete* the panel's connection to this event handler. Use the editor's Find and Replace feature to change every occurrence of Panel1Click to DoShowHint. Put the following line in an OnCreate event handler for the form:

```
Application.OnHint := DoShowHint;
```

Before you continue, let's look at what just happened. You created a method for your form that is *not* an event handler for the form or any of its components. Rather, it's an event handler for the *Application* object — the power behind the throne, the invisible object that owns all forms. When the mouse passes into or out of a component that has a Hint property, the OnHint event is triggered.

Drop a bunch of components on the form — it doesn't matter what type as long as they're visible when the program runs. Set the Hint property of each to a short descriptive string or to any short string. Be creative! Drop a menu on the form and open the Menu Designer. Add a template or two and fill in a short hint for each menu item.

Run the program and move the mouse around. Whenever the cursor is over one of your components, the hint for that component appears in the status line. Skid the mouse up and down a pull-down menu and the hint for the highlighted menu item shows up on the status line.

You could run into trouble if you use flyover help and status bar help at the same time, because the text for a status bar hint is usually longer than the text for flyover help. Don't worry! Delphi lets you have the best of both worlds. For each component's Hint property, use the short flyover help text, a vertical bar character (|), and then the longer status bar hint text. Your program uses the short hints for flyover help and the longer ones for status bar help.

A template with status

That status line form is pretty darn valuable, and you're sure to want to use it again. Clean it up and save it as a template. First, delete the mess of components you dropped on the form for experimental purposes. Change the panel's name to StatusLine and make any final adjustments in the size, font, and so on for the panel.

If you're using Delphi 1.0, select Project Manager from the View menu and right-click on the Project Manager window. Choose Save As Template... from the pop-up menu. Call the project HINTED, enter Hinted Form as the title for this template, type in a description, and click OK.

Delphi 2.0's object repository stores projects and forms in a similar fashion. First, save the status line form and the project that contains it into a new subdirectory of the OBJREPOS directory, which is below the main Delphi 2.0 directory. Make sure that this directory contains *only* files related to the status line form project. Now open the Project Manager, right-clicking it, and choose Add To Repository… from the pop-up menu. Enter Hinted Form as the title and type a description. Select Projects from the Pages combo box and enter your name under Author. Then click OK.

From now on, when you open a new project, you can optionally start out with a working status line already in place.

Bumpy and Dippy Forms

Often you don't need all the features that the panel component brings along — sometimes you don't even need all four sides of a panel! In that case, the bevel component may be just what you need. A bevel doesn't own components the way a panel does; when you move the bevel, the components stay put.

Like a panel, a bevel has an Align property. Its Style can be simply bsLowered or bsRaised. But the most important property is Shape. The bsBox shape is like a simple panel that's just raised or lowered relative to the form. BsFrame yields a rectangle with a raised or lowered rim. The remaining four styles display just one of the four sides of the rectangle, again either raised (a bump) or lowered (a dip). That can be handy for creating a dividing line on your form. Figure 7-6 shows a form with raised and lowered frames and lines.

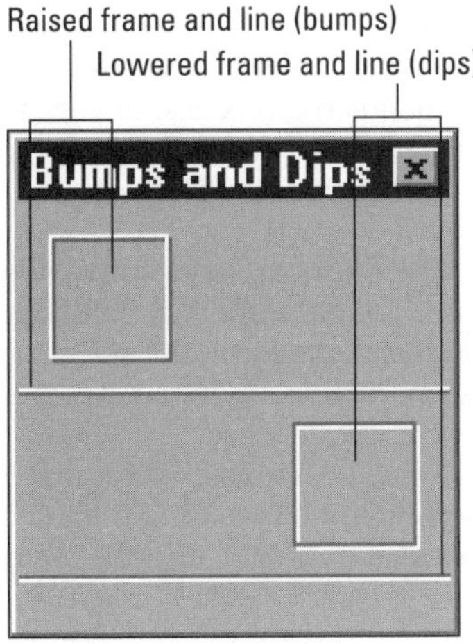

Raised frame and line (bumps)
Lowered frame and line (dips)

Figure 7-6:
Use the bevel component to define areas of your form with frames and lines.

Drop a bevel component onto a new form, set its Align property to alTop, and set its Shape property to bsBottomLine. You now have a horizontal dip on your form. Change the Style property to bsRaised and the dip becomes a bump.

In general, to create a dividing line that maintains a constant distance from one side of the form, set the Align property to that side and the Shape property to the opposite side. For example, to make a line that stays in place relative to the left side of the form, set Align to alLeft and Shape to bsRightLine.

Bevels don't do as much as panels, so they don't consume as much of the resources of Windows. Always use a bevel rather than a panel unless you *need* a feature that a bevel just doesn't have.

Controlling Scrolling

A Delphi form is smart — if any of its components protrude off the edge of the form, it automatically sprouts scroll bars, so the user can scroll around and see the entire form. Unfortunately, this isn't always the right behavior. Want to see something ugly? Try the following.

Place two panels on a new form, setting their Align properties to alTop and alBottom. These represent the SpeedBar and status bar of an elegant program. Now place a button near the bottom right corner of the form. Shrink the form so the button hangs off its right edge. A horizontal scroll bar appears and pushes the status line up. Widen the form again and resize it so the button is off the bottom of the available space. Now a vertical scroll bar appears on the right, cutting off the tips of the two panels.

Clearly the SpeedBar and status line should not be included in the part of the form that scrolls. That's why the scroll box component exists — to let you redefine the scrolling portion of the form. A scroll box is similar to a panel minus the 3-D effect. It has many of the same properties and events, but most of the time you can leave its properties set at their default values.

Using the same form, cut the button to the Clipboard and drop a scroll box in the middle of the form. Set the scroll box's Align property to alClient and paste the button back onto it. Now when you resize the form, the scroll bars that appear are restricted to the area between the SpeedBar and status bar panels.

The gorgeous graphical components discussed in this chapter make programs look better, but they don't necessarily contribute to getting the job completed. In the next chapter, you return to the workaday world, into the realm of specialized and powerful components.

Chapter 8

Additional Components

* *

In This Chapter

▶ Building your own digital clock

▶ Using a Delphi program to generate bitmap glyphs that can be used in other Delphi programs

▶ Using data entry components that force correct input

▶ Creating multi-page forms like the ones Delphi uses

▶ Adding headers that allow resizing of columnar information on your form

▶ Decorating your programs with speed buttons and bitmap buttons

▶ Enhancing the simple editor with a SpeedBar

* *

*T*he last chapter's graphical elements add pizzazz to user interfaces built using standard Windows components. The real fun begins with this chapter, though, because the sky's the limit as far as what a Delphi component can accomplish.

This chapter discusses the simpler additional components — the more advanced additional components are discussed in Chapter 9.

Choosing Additional Components

Naturally, you find *most* of the additional components on the Additional page in the Component palette. However, a few are on other pages, and several move to the Win 3.1 page in Delphi 2.0. You can consult Table 8-1 anytime you're not sure which of these components to use.

Table 8-1:	Problems Solved by Simple Additional Components
Task	*Component*
Trigger an event every so often or create a delay	Timer. See "Use a Timer Component for a Wake-Up Call."
Let the user enter a numeric value or tweak an existing value up or down	Spin edit. See "Putting the Best Spin on Things."
Send general up or down messages to a component	Spin button. See "Putting the Best Spin on Things."
Force the user's input to match a predefined mask (for example, for phone numbers)	Masked edit box. See "Who Was That Masked Edit Box?"
Create a form with multiple tabbed pages	Tabbed notebook. See "Compositions in a Tabbed Notebook."
Create a form with multiple pages, a set of tabs, or both	Tab set and notebook. See "Gluing Tabs on a Notebook."
Display a header with resizable columns	Header. See "Using Your Header."
Trigger a program feature with a button that has a picture or colored text	Bitmap button. See "Brighten Your Forms with Bitmap Buttons."
Launch processes from buttons on a SpeedBar	Speed button. See "Get Up to Speed with Speed Buttons."

Use a Timer Component for a Wake-Up Call

They say Windows is a cooperative multitasking system, but Windows 3.1 is anything but cooperative. What this term really means is that, if even one program *doesn't* cooperate, the whole system comes to a grinding halt. Experiencing this kind of crash is a rite of passage for Windows programmers. Typically it happens because of a program loop that continues until a particular Windows event occurs. The result is that the program spins madly in its loop, like a gerbil in a cage, giving Windows no chance to process messages. And because Windows can't process messages, the program never gets the message that would allow it to break out of the loop. Catch-22! Tight loops are still a problem in 32-bit programs, but they don't bring the whole system to a halt, just the offending program.

The solution to this problem lies in Delphi's timer component, which ties directly into the built-in Windows timer. If your program has to perform a long, repetitive task, you set a timer for a very short time and perform one portion of the task each time the timer ticks. Windows won't be tied up, because it processes all other pending messages before getting around to your timer.

You can use the timer also to update your program's display, perhaps reporting its progress with a gauge or updating an on-screen clock. Finally, you can set up a timer for a one-shot time delay, simply by turning the timer off when the OnTimer event occurs.

Properties and events

The timer component has just four properties. The Tag and Name properties are familiar from the other components you studied. The Interval property specifies a number of milliseconds (thousandths of a second) — it's initially set to 1000, or one second. Roughly each time that interval passes, the timer receives an OnTimer event. Why "roughly"? Windows queues up events as they happen, but it allows most other events to cut in line ahead of timer events. Setting the Enabled property to False turns off the timer and stops the flow of OnTimer messages.

Don't bother setting Interval to a value less than 55. Windows uses the hardware timer interrupt as the basis for its timers, and that interrupt occurs about every 55 milliseconds. What? You don't like approximations? Okay, the timer interrupt occurs once every 1,193,180/65,536 second. Better, yes?

Inside Windows, timers are a limited resource. Windows 3.0 had just 16 timers, which were shared by all applications in the system. Windows 3.1 doubled that to 32, and in 32-bit Windows there's virtually no limit, but you still shouldn't use more timers than necessary. It's possible to use one timer for multiple time intervals, if you choose the interval correctly. For example, to set timers at 8, 24, and 60 seconds, you could set the interval to 4000 milliseconds (4 seconds), and trigger the 8-second action every other event, the 24-second action every 6th event, and the 60-second action every 15th event.

Start a new project using the fixed-size form template. Place a label on the form, set its caption to 00:00:00 PM, and make sure its AutoSize property is True. Now choose an interesting font for the label, and make it big — I used 72 points.

Set the label's Align property to alClient and its Alignment property to taCenter. Size the form so it nicely surrounds the label and set its caption to Digital Clock. Locate the timer component on the System page of the Component palette and drop one on the form, leaving its Interval property set to the default of 1000. Create an OnTimer event handler containing this single line of code:

```
Label1.Caption := TimeToStr(Now);
```

Give the form an OnCreate event handler containing just this line:

```
Timer1Timer(Timer1);
```

With just two lines of code, you built an attractive digital clock. Figure 8-1 shows one possible clock — yours will look different depending on the font you choose.

Figure 8-1:
This clock
never needs
winding — a
timer
component
keeps it
ticking.

Locks again

In the last chapter, I promised you would teach the shift-lock program to stay synchronized with the keyboard. The timer component is the missing piece for this puzzle.

Load the LOCKS project you saved before. Drop a timer on the form, set its Interval to 100, and give it an OnTimer event, with these lines replacing the begin..end pair supplied by Delphi:

```
VAR KS : TKeyboardState;
begin
  GetKeyboardState(KS);
  IF Odd(KS[VK_CAPITAL]) THEN
    Panel2.Font.Color := clBlack
  ELSE Panel2.Font.Color := clGray;
  IF Odd(KS[VK_NUMLOCK]) THEN
    Panel3.Font.Color := clBlack
  ELSE Panel3.Font.Color := clGray;
  IF Odd(KS[VK_SCROLL]) THEN
    Panel4.Font.Color := clBlack
  ELSE Panel4.Font.Color := clGray;
end;
```

When you run the new Locks program, you see that the panels corresponding to the three shift locks are gray when the corresponding shift is off, and black when it's on. And when you toggle the shift state from the keyboard, the corresponding panel synchs up within 1/10 second. Timer components are great when your program needs to stay current with real-world events.

Putting the Best Spin on Things

Computers love numbers, but it's really easy for computer users to enter numbers *incorrectly*. In earlier chapters, you build an edit box component that accepts numbers only in a certain range. That's handy when users are entering brand-new numbers. When your aim is to tweak an existing numeric entry up or down, a spin edit box is a better choice. Users can still enter numbers directly in a spin edit box, but they can also finagle the number up or down by clicking an attached spin button. For other situations that involve tweaking values up and down, you can skip the edit box entirely and use a standalone spin button.

The SpinButton and SpinEdit components both reside on Delphi's Samples page. You won't find them built into the help system, but you *will* find them useful! Many Windows applications use them, even though they're not a built-in part of Windows 3.x. Windows 95 *does* have a spin button control built in; Delphi 2.0 implements it as the UpDown component. You meet this component in Chapter 12 — for projects that don't need backward compatibility with Delphi 1.0, the UpDown component replaces both SpinButton and SpinEdit.

Properties

The properties special to a spin button include DownGlyph and UpGlyph, which represent the glyphs on the down and up arrow portions of the spin button. By default these glyphs are boring little down- and up-pointing triangles, but you can draw your own glyphs to replace them. If you increase the size of the spin button you at least want to use a *larger* pair of triangles! The tiny default triangles look dopey when the spin button gets big. The FocusControl property determines which control gets the focus when the spin button is selected.

A spin edit box's properties mostly mirror those of a regular edit box, and you can't change the glyphs for the built-in spin button. A few properties are absent, most notably Text. If you want to check or set the text of a spin edit box, you work with its Value property. Properties special to a spin edit box include MaxValue, MinValue, and Increment. As you'd expect, the first two control the range available to the spin edit, and the last is the amount by which the value changes when you click the up or down button.

Events

A spin edit box responds to precisely the same set of events that a regular edit box does. The special events for a spin button are OnUpClick and OnDownClick, which are triggered by a click on the up or down portion of the button. Note that you can click and hold the button to spin through its values rapidly — hence the name.

Place four spin edit components on a new form. Set the MaxValue of the last three to 100, set the Increment of the third to 10, and set the MinValue of the fourth to 50.

Run the program and try entering values into the four spin edit boxes. Note that you can't enter nonnumeric characters in the edit boxes. You can enter values outside the range from MinValue to MaxValue, but when you move the focus to another component or tweak the value using the spin buttons, it snaps into range.

The first spin edit box in this sample program has MaxValue and MinValue at their default value, 0. You can spin this spin edit box through the full range of $-2,147,483,648$ to $2,147,483,647$ (that is, if you're prepared to spend the next ten years or so with your finger on the mouse button). The others are restricted to the range 0..100 or 50..100. The third spin edit box spins by tens rather than ones.

By the way, I did base that ten-year figure (in the preceding paragraph) on real facts. I observed that the numbers spin by at about ten per second. 429,496,729 seconds is actually more like thirteen years than ten, but I figure if you make it to ten, another few years won't matter.

There's not much more to say about spin edit boxes. Use them any time you want the user to either enter a number or adjust an existing number.

Delphi as artiste

Anytime you make a spin button bigger than the rather tiny default size, you need to supply it with up and down glyphs appropriate to its size. I don't know about you, but I'm no artist. Anytime I need to draw a bitmap, I try to find a way to make Delphi draw it for me.

Drop two image components on a new form. Set the height of both to 33. Set the width of the first to 17 and the second to 33. Put these lines in the OnCreate method for the form itself:

```
WITH Image1, Canvas DO
  BEGIN
    Font.Name := 'Wingdings';
    Font.Size := 20;
    TextOut(0,0,'G');
    Picture.SaveToFile('FINGUP.BMP');
    TextOut(0,0,'H');
    Picture.SaveToFile('FINGDOWN.BMP');
  END;
WITH Image2, Canvas DO
  BEGIN
    Brush.Color := clLime;
    Pen.Color := clLime;
    Polygon([Point(1, Height),
      Point(Width DIV 2, 0),
      Point(Width-1, Height)]);
    Picture.SaveToFile('TRNGUP.BMP');
    Brush.Color := clWhite;
    FillRect(ClientRect);
    Brush.Color := clRed;
    Pen.Color := clRed;
    Polygon([Point(0, 0),
      Point(Width DIV 2, Height),
      Point(Width, 0)]);
    Picture.SaveToFile('TRNGDOWN.BMP');
  END;
```

Run the program and watch Delphi mix its paints, daub them on the palette, measure the subject with squinted eye and thumb . . . whoops! It goes by too fast to see all that. In fact, as soon as the program comes up on the screen, it has finished generating the four bitmap files (though you only see two of them). The first two contain the up- and down-pointing finger characters from the Windows Wingdings font, and the second two contain large up- and down-pointing triangles. Hang onto this program in case you want to generate different bitmaps. Play around with it; change the size and color of the triangles or choose different characters for the character-based glyphs.

If you have sharp eyes, you may notice that the up-pointing triangle is two pixels narrower than the down-pointing one. That's because the spin button component checks the color of the bottom left pixel of the glyph and treats that color as transparent anywhere it appears in the glyph. If we hadn't made the triangle narrower, its *green* color would be treated as transparent — ugly!

Organizing the vertically challenged

A lone spin button can have its uses independent of any edit box. For example, it can be used to move the selected item up and down in a list box.

Start a new form and place two spin buttons on it. Stretch them both to several times their normal size. Set the UpGlyph and DownGlyph properties of one spin button to FINGUP.BMP and FINGDOWN.BMP and the other to TRNGUP.BMP and TRNGDOWN.BMP. Adjust the size of the spin buttons to match the glyphs. Now decide which one you prefer and delete the other.

Place a list box on the form and double-click its Items property. Enter the names of Snow White's seven vertically challenged companions (if you don't remember their names, check Figure 8-2). Set the FocusControl property for the spin button to the name of the list box and create an OnUpClick event handler, replacing Delphi's begin..end pair with these lines:

```
VAR I : Integer;
begin
  WITH ListBox1 DO
    IF ItemIndex > 0 THEN
      BEGIN
        I := ItemIndex - 1;
        Items.Move(ItemIndex, I);
        ItemIndex := I;
      END;
end;
```

Highlight the code you just typed and press Ctrl+C to copy it to the Clipboard. Now start an OnDownClick event handler for the spin button. Highlight the begin..end pair supplied by Delphi and press Ctrl+V to replace those lines with a copy of the OnUpClick event handler. In the copy, replace ItemIndex-1 with ItemIndex+1. Find the line "IF ItemIndex > 0 THEN" and replace it with this line:

```
IF (ItemIndex >= 0) AND (ItemIndex < Items.Count-1) THEN
```

Figure 8-2 shows the final program, with spin buttons displaying both pairs of specialized glyphs. Anytime you write a program that needs to let the user reorder items in a list, steal this code!

Who Was That Masked Edit Box?

Even without its spin button, the spin edit has a useful talent — it accepts only numbers. Well, the masked edit box can do that trick and quite a few more. You

Figure 8-2:
This
program
uses either
of the two
spin buttons
to move the
selected list
box item up
or down.

can set it up to automatically format input as phone numbers, zip codes, and so on, using a coded text string called a *mask* that controls what characters are permitted. If none of the prebuilt masks suit your purposes, you can create your own.

The event list for a masked edit box is identical to that of a plain edit box, and the property list is almost the same. A few properties are absent, and the essential property EditMask is added. The EditText property contains the text the user entered, with any literal characters from the mask incorporated. If the Save Literal Characters option for the mask is True, the Text property's value is the same as that of EditText; otherwise, Text contains precisely the text the user entered, without any additions.

Place several masked edit boxes on a new form, with a label next to each. For each one, double-click the EditMask property and choose a different predefined mask type from the resulting dialog. Double-click the first box to create an OnChange event handler with this single line of code:

```
Label1.Caption := MaskEdit1.Text;
```

Create a parallel OnChange event handler for each of the other masked edit boxes, setting the corresponding label's Caption property to the value of the masked edit box's Text property.

Run the program and try entering data in the various edit boxes. It's easy to see which is a zip code, which is a date, and so on. Enter a partial value, such as a single digit of a phone number, and try to move to another field. The program complains that the input isn't valid, because it's incomplete. However, enter a time such as 99:99:99PM, and you see that it's accepted. Masked edit boxes don't care about anything beyond making sure that the right type of character is in each position. Note, too, that the label associated with each edit box holds the exact contents of the box.

Go back into the same little program. For each masked edit box, double-click the EditMask property and uncheck the Save Literal Characters check box.

Now when you run the program, only the characters typed into the masked edit box appear in the label's caption. For example, the phone number (800)555-1212 appears as 8005551212. The phone number string with separators is 30% longer than without. If you plan to store thousands or millions of phone numbers, that 30% may represent megabytes of disk space.

Add a new masked edit box to the same form and set its EditMask property to

```
!>0LLL000;0;_
```

When you run the program, you find that the new masked edit box accepts only strings that start with a digit, followed by three uppercase letters and three digits. That's the current format for auto license plates in California. But how does that mask produce this effect?

The mask is broken into three fields, separated by semicolons. Working backward from the end, the underscore is the character that displays blanks. You can change it to anything you want, as long as you don't confuse users. The middle field is 0 if you want to strip the mask characters from the Text property, 1 if you don't. The first field is the mask itself, with each cryptic character having a special meaning. The following shows what the characters in this particular case mean:

!	Leading blanks are removed.
>	All alphabetic characters are changed to uppercase (until a < character is encountered).
0	The user must enter a digit.
L	The user must enter an aLphabetic character.

There are lots more hieroglyphics you can use in edit masks; check the on-line help for EditMask. Most of the time, though, you find that the built-in collection of masks serves you well.

Compositions in a Tabbed Notebook

Delphi uses many multi-page dialogs — in the Object Inspector, the Editor window, and most of the options dialogs, to name a few. Each page has a tab with its name, and clicking a tab flips to that page. You can add this absolutely fabulous feature to your own programs in two ways. The simpler way is to place a tabbed notebook component on your form, enter a list of names for the pages, and just start placing components on the different pages. The business of flipping pages and moving rows of tabs is handled for you. The other method, discussed in the next section, involves writing code to manage the connection between two separate components that represent the tabs and the pages.

In Delphi 2.0, these tab and notebook components are shoved off onto the Win 3.1 page of the Component palette. Their place in the limelight is usurped by the Windows 95 TabControl and PageControl components; Delphi 2.0 itself uses these new components. If your programs need to stay compatible with Delphi 1.0, however, you have to forego the thrill of using the Windows 95 components directly. In Delphi 2.0, however, the tabbed notebook is actually a PageControl in disguise. So if you use tabbed notebooks in your Delphi 1.0 programs, they automatically modernize themselves when compiled under Delphi 2.0!

The Pages property of the tabbed notebook component is an array of strings containing the names for the tabs on the notebook's pages. You enter the names in a special dialog that includes the capability to reorder the pages if necessary.

Once you start placing components on the pages, do *not* try to move a page by deleting its name and inserting it elsewhere in the list! Doing so will destroy all the components on that page.

ActivePage contains the name of the currently active page, and PageIndex contains its index, starting with 0 for the first page. The Font property for a notebook is passed along to any components on the pages that have ParentFont set to True. If you want to set the font for the tabs, use the TabFont property.

Place a tabbed notebook on a new form and set its Align property to alClient. Double-click the Pages property to enter a list of page names. Press the Edit button and change the first page's name from Default to One. Add pages named Two through Eight. Try reordering the pages using the Move Up and Move Down buttons (but make sure you organize them correctly before you close this dialog).

Set the TabsPerRow property to 4 and watch the tabs line up in two rows. Set it to 8 and they all scrunch into the same row. Try setting it to 2 — whoops! Delphi won't allow that, because the minimum is 3. (Alas, in Delphi 2.0 the tabbed notebook's TabsPerRow property has no effect.)

Right-click the tabbed notebook and notice that its pop-up menu has a few handy items titled Next Page and Previous Page. These enable you to flip through the pages at design time. Add a few components to each page.

Run the program and flip through the pages. You notice that if you choose a page whose tab isn't in the front row, the tabs shift to bring that row to the front. The top half of the form in Figure 8-3 is a tabbed notebook with eight pages, just like what you built. This component makes it incredibly easy to organize complicated forms by putting each set of related components on a different page.

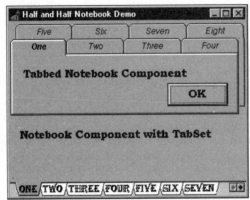

Figure 8-3: The top of this figure is a tabbed notebook component, and the bottom half is a notebook component connected to a tab set component.

Gluing Tabs on a Notebook

The bottom half of the form in Figure 8-3 is a notebook component with a tab set component glued onto it. A few lines of code are required to keep the tabs and notebook pages in synch, but the effort is minimal. Delphi's own multi-page dialogs are built this way. One more thing — tabs in a tab set point down, tabbed notebook tabs point up.

It's possible to use the tab set and notebook separately. For example, you might use a set of radio buttons or a list box full of page names to select which page to display in a notebook component. You could also use the tab set to provide a quick way to jump around in a phonebook database. However, tab sets and notebooks really shine when used together.

Properties

Both the notebook and the tab set components have the Align property. You almost always want the tab set aligned at the bottom and the notebook aligned to occupy the rest of the window's client area. The tab set's Tabs property is the list of names for the tabs. It corresponds directly to the notebook's Pages property, and generally the two lists should be the same. Tab set's TabIndex and Notebook's PageIndex both represent the selected tab or page. In addition, Notebook's ActivePage property holds the name of the active page.

That's about it for shared properties. Tab set has a number of other properties related to its on-screen image. EndMargin and StartMargin define the distance from the edge of the window to the first and last visible tab, and SelectedColor and UnselectedColor define the colors used for tabs. You almost always leave AutoScroll set to True — if the window gets too small to show all the tabs, this property causes left and right arrows to appear for scrolling through the tabs. (You can see the arrows at the bottom of Figure 8-3.) If you set AutoScroll to False, your program must take charge of the dreary task of displaying off-screen items by changing the value of FirstIndex, which controls which tab is drawn at the leftmost position.

If you change the Style property from tsStandard to tsOwnerDraw, you can take charge of how the tabs are drawn. No, you can't round them or make *any* change to the basic tab shape, but the tsOwnerDraw style does let you draw pictures on the tabs or color-code them. Tabs in a Delphi tab set always point downward; you can have any orientation you want, as long as it's down.

Events

The main event for a tab set is OnClick — when the user clicks a tab, you want something to happen. This method always includes a line like:

```
NoteBook1.PageIndex := TabSet1.TabIndex;
```

This causes the notebook to flip to the corresponding page when the user clicks a tab. If you forget this line, your tab set becomes an ineffectual milquetoast, good for nothing.

An OnChanging event occurs just before the TabIndex changes. This is an opportunity to validate the data on the page that's losing visibility, and refuse to let the pages flip if the data isn't valid.

The special event for a notebook is OnPageChanged. Whereas the tab set's OnChanging event occurs just *before* the active page changes, the notebook's OnPageChanged occurs just *after*. Your programs can respond to this event by making any necessary preparations for displaying the newly activated page.

 When you actually start building a multi-page form using these two components, you have to set the notebook's PageIndex property to the page that's under construction. Nine times out of ten you'll forget to reset it before running the program. The result? The highlighted tab won't match the active page. To avoid embarrassment, insert this line in the form's OnCreate event handler:

```
NoteBook1.PageIndex := TabSet1.TabIndex;
```

Drop a tab set on a new form and set its Align property to alBottom. Add a notebook and set its Align property to alClient. Double-click the notebook's Pages property and create pages named One, Two, and Three. Put these lines in the form's OnCreate method:

```
TabSet1.Tabs := Notebook1.Pages;
Notebook1.PageIndex := TabSet1.TabIndex;
```

You almost always want the tabs to have the same name as the corresponding pages, so the easiest thing to do is set them the same at run time, in the form's OnCreate event handler. That way, if you add or reorder pages, the tab set automatically matches up.

Put this line in the tab set's OnClick event handler:

```
NoteBook1.PageIndex := TabSet1.TabIndex;
```

Set the notebook's ActivePage property to One. Drop a label on it, set the label's caption to This Is Page One, and set its FontSize to 24. Right-click the notebook and choose Next Page from the pop-up menu. The label disappears, because the first page isn't showing. Place a similar label on the page that *is* displayed (the second page) and set the label's caption to This Is Page Two. Give the last page a label captioned This Is Page Three.

There are two other important events for a tab set, OnMeasureTab and OnDrawTab. Your tab set receives these events only if its Style is set to tsOwnerDraw. By default, tabs are just wide enough to hold their text — you can change that width by responding to OnMeasureTab. As for what gets displayed on the tab, you take charge of that by responding to OnDrawTab.

Use the same project as before. Change the tab set's Style property to tsOwnerDraw. Set the Font.Color property of the labels on the three pages to clRed, clBlue, and clLime, respectively.

In the tab set's OnMeasureTab event handler, put this single line:

```
TabWidth := 48;
```

This action gives you tabs 48 pixels wide. In the OnDrawTab handler, put these lines:

```
WITH TabCanvas, Brush DO
  BEGIN
    CASE Index OF
      0 : Color := clRed;
```

```
    1 : Color :=clBlue;
    2 : Color :=clLime;
  END;
  FillRect(R);
END;
```

Now when you run the program, the three tabs are marked with red, blue, and lime green rectangles instead of names. Clicking a tab brings up the page whose label is the same color.

It takes work to meld a tab set and a notebook into a multi-page form. Unless you're desperate for down-pointing tabs, owner-draw tabs, or some other special feature, use a tabbed notebook instead.

Using Your Header

To see an example of a header component, bring up Delphi's Project Manager view. Just below the SpeedBar, there's a gray bar with the headings Unit, Form, and Path. When you put the mouse cursor over one of the vertical lines on this bar, it turns to a left-right arrow, and you can drag the bar left or right to control the relative widths of the three headings, which in turn control the width of the columns below them. (In Delphi 2.0, the gray bar in Project Manager is actually a Windows 95 HeaderControl. Chapter 12 shows off the HeaderControl and its Windows 95 cohorts.)

Properties

The most important property of a header component is Sections, a list of heading strings naming the sections. AllowResize determines whether or not users are allowed to resize the headings at run time. If you set it to False, you pretty much defeat the purpose of having a header component. There's also a run-time-only SectionWidth property, which gives your program access to the widths of the individual sections.

Events

The two big events for a header are OnSized and OnSizing. OnSizing is triggered by every incremental mouse-move while the user is resizing the sections. OnSized occurs when the user stops resizing the headers.

Place a header component on a new form and set its Align property to alTop. Double-click the Sections property and enter two strings, Section One and Section Two. Place a list box on the form with Align set to alLeft, and then add another list box with Align set to alClient. With the *right* mouse button, drag the dividing line between the header's two sections until it's right above the line that separates the two list boxes. (You have to use the right button to resize the sections during form design because the left button is dedicated to the form design process.)

Enter this single line in an OnSized event handler for the header:

```
ListBox1.Width := Header1.SectionWidth[0];
```

Run the program and drag the header's dividing line back and forth (using the *left* mouse button). When you stop dragging, the list boxes resize so that their shared edge is just below the dividing line. While you're dragging, the header and the list box are out of synch, as Figure 8-4 shows.

Figure 8-4:
If a header component acts only on the OnSized event, it can get out of synch with the form.

Using the same project, click the header and flip to the Events page in the Object Inspector. Click the down arrow next to the OnSizing event and select the OnSized event handler you already created. This time when you run the program and drag the header's dividing line, the list boxes resize while you're dragging.

If the screen elements that are being resized in response to changes in the header are *slow* to redraw themselves, resize them only in the OnSized event. If, like the list boxes here, they can redraw themselves quickly, your program will seem more responsive if you resize them in the OnSizing event as well.

Brighten Your Forms with Bitmap Buttons

Standard push buttons are sartorially dismal. You can dress them up with a fancy font, and you can set their text to any color you want — as long as you want black. Bitmap buttons spice things up a bit. Not only can you set their text color, you can actually put a picture on the button. Standard pictures for buttons that mean Yes, No, OK, and so on are provided automatically.

Bitmap buttons respond to all the same events as regular push buttons. They also have all the same properties, plus a few more. Most important is the Kind property, which tells what kind of button this is. The values bkAbort, bkAll, bkCancel, bkClose, bkHelp, bkIgnore, bkNo, bkOk, bkRetry, and bkYes give you standard pictures appropriate to these ten standard buttons. Choosing any except bkHelp or bkClose sets the ModalResult property to the corresponding value. If you want to take control of the picture yourself, leave Kind set to bkCustom.

The Glyph property is the bitmap picture displayed on the button. You can draw simple button pictures for bkCustom buttons yourself using Delphi's Image Editor, or you can write short programs to create them (as you did earlier for the spin button component). To match the glyphs on the standard buttons, set your bitmap's size to 18 by 18.

The NumGlyphs property indicates how many different glyphs are in the bitmap you supplied. A bitmap button can have different bitmaps for its normal state, disabled state, and pressed-down state. If your bitmap is precisely two or three times as wide as it is high, Delphi automatically assumes it contains two or three bitmaps. (You see how this works shortly.)

By default, the glyph is to the left of the caption, but with the Layout property you can put it on the right, the top, or the bottom. The Spacing and Margin properties control the location of the glyph and the caption within the button. Margin is the distance of the glyph from the layout edge; if it's –1, the glyph and caption are centered on the button face. Spacing is the distance from the glyph to the caption; if it's –1, the two are centered between the margin and the opposite edge. If you have a vertical row of bitmap buttons, the glyphs and captions line up best if you set both margin and spacing to a small positive value, perhaps 4 or 6.

Because it's possible for the user to change the color of button faces, you've got a problem if you want the background of your glyph to match the button face background. If you select the default gray, it looks awful when a user with no color sense has selected maroon! Delphi gets you out of this dilemma by checking the color of the bottom left pixel in the glyph and treating all pixels of that color as transparent. Any part of the glyph that matches this color won't be drawn — the button face shows through.

The Style property determines whether the bitmap button uses the standard Windows 3.1 button style or emulate Windows 95. Leave it set to its default of bsAutoDetect and your buttons automatically match the operating system in use. That is, they look like Windows 3.1 buttons under Windows 3.1, and they look like Windows 95 buttons under Windows 95.

Place ten bitmap buttons in two columns of five on a new form and set their Kind properties to bkAbort, bkAll, and so on, skipping bkCustom. Start a new column of two buttons and set their captions to Left and Right. Place two more buttons side-by-side below these. Set their width to the height of the standard buttons and set their height so they line up as shown in Figure 8-5. Set the captions of these last two buttons to Top and Bot.

Figure 8-5:
Bitmap
buttons give
you
standard
pictures,
custom
pictures,
and colored
text.

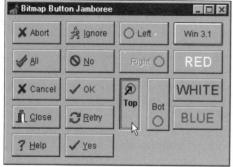

Now draw a 54-by-18 bitmap with three equal-sized sections representing, from left to right, the normal glyph, the disabled glyph, and the pressed-down glyph. This triptych doesn't have to be a work of art — I drew a red circle, a gray circle, and a red circle with an arrow in it. Set the Glyph property of the last four buttons — the buttons whose Kind property has the default value bkCustom — to this bitmap. Note that you have to set them one at a time — normally you wouldn't be using the same bitmap for multiple buttons. Set the layout of the Right button to blGlyphRight and set its Enabled property to False. Set the layout of the two vertical buttons to blGlyphTop and blGlyphBottom. Select all the buttons and set their Margin properties to 4.

Add four more bitmap buttons in a fourth column. Set the caption of the first button to Win 95 and set its Style to bsNew. Or if you're running under Windows 95, set the caption of the first button to Win 3.1 and set its style to bsWin31. Set the captions of the remaining three buttons to RED, WHITE, and BLUE. Select those three buttons, set Font.Size to 12, and then set Font.Color for each to the color corresponding to its caption.

Get Up to Speed with Speed Buttons

Speed buttons are another special type of button, specifically designed to provide fast access to menu choices. If you place a few of them on a panel component, you have an instant SpeedBar.

Properties

Speed buttons can function like radio buttons, so that pressing one button in a group causes the others to pop up. Several speed button properties are devoted to managing this behavior. Buttons with the same nonzero value in their GroupIndex property are treated as a group. The property determines whether it's permissible for none of the buttons in the group to be pressed down. AllowAllUp is False by default, and it's ignored if GroupIndex is zero. The Down property is True for the button in a group that's "stuck" down, and False for the rest.

If you set AllowAllUp to True and GroupIndex to a nonzero value that's different from every other speed button, you get a speed button that acts like a check box. One click and it sticks down, another click and it pops up again.

Like a bitmap button, a speed button has a picture defined by its Glyph property, and any pixels in the picture whose color matches the color of the pixel in the lower left corner of the glyph are see-through. NumGlyphs defines how many separate glyphs are included in the bitmap. However, a speed button has a fourth possible bitmap for a fourth possible state — stuck down.

The next little program builds an 18-by-72 bitmap containing four glyphs. If you're feeling creative, you can draw the bitmap yourself. Remember, from left to right, the bitmaps represent a button that's normal, disabled, pushed down, and stuck down. (What's the difference, you say? A button that's pushed down pops out when you release the mouse button; a button that's stuck down won't.)

Place an image component on a new form and set its width to 72 and height to 18. Put these lines in an OnCreate event handler for the form:

```
WITH Image1, Canvas DO
  BEGIN
    FillRect(ClientRect);
    Font.Name := 'Wingdings';
    Font.Size := 12;
    Font.Style := [fsBold];
```

```
(continued)
    TextOut(0,0,'K');
    TextOut(36,0,'m');
    TextOut(54,0,'J');
    Font.Color := clGray;
    TextOut(18,0,'L');
    Picture.SaveToFile('FOURGLYP.BMP');
  END;
```

Run the program to generate the bitmap file, and then start a new project.

Place a panel component on the form, delete its caption, and set its Align property to alTop. Place a speed button on the panel and sets its Glyph property to FOURGLYP.BMP. Press Ctrl+C to copy it to the Clipboard, click the panel, and press Ctrl+V repeatedly to paste four copies onto the panel. Place the first three buttons so they're touching, and place the fourth and fifth so they're separate. Select the three that are touching and set their GroupIndex property to 1. Set the first button's Down property to True, and the very last button's Enabled property to False.

Run the program and look at the buttons. As you can see in Figure 8-6, two of the first three buttons show neutral faces; one appears pushed in and shows a happy face. When you push one of the first three, the one that was pushed before pops out. The last button is disabled and shows a gray frowning face. When you click and hold the mouse on the fourth button (or any of the first three), it shows a blank circle.

Go back into the Form Designer and set the AllowAllUp property to True for the three grouped speed buttons. Now when you run the program, you can click the button that's down to pop it up again.

Events

OnClick is the default event for a speed button. If you're using the speed button to launch a process in your program, you do it in the OnClick event handler. Speed buttons also respond to OnDblClick, but only when they're stuck down. You won't use OnDblClick very often.

Load the MyEdit project yet again; that's the project you enhanced in the last few chapters. Drop a panel on the form, delete its caption, and set its alignment to alTop.

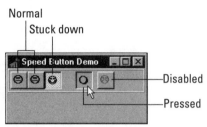

Figure 8-6:
The first three speed buttons are like radio buttons; the other two are independent.

Normal

Stuck down

Disabled

Pressed

Starting from the left, place two speed buttons on the panel so they don't touch each other. Place three more speed buttons on the panel so they do touch each other, set their AllowAllUp property to True, and set their GroupIndex properties to 1, 2, and 3. Place three more speed buttons so they touch each other and set the GroupIndex property of all of them to 4. Set the Down property of the first one in this last group to True.

Set the Font.Name for the first two buttons to Wingdings, and their captions to 1 and <, which will be displayed as an open folder and a diskette. Set the captions for the next three buttons to *B, I,* and *U,* and set their font styles to bold, italic, and underline, respectively. Set the captions of the last three to <, =, and >. Now go back and adjust the font size for each button individually so that the single-character caption fills the button.

Set the first button's OnClick event handler to the existing handler used by the Open menu choice, and the second to the handler for the Save menu choice.

Set the Tag properties of the next three buttons to 0, 1, and 2, respectively. Create an OnClick event handler for all three like this:

```
WITH Sender AS TSpeedButton, Memo1.Font DO
  IF Down THEN
    Style := Style + [TFontStyle(Tag)]
  ELSE
    Style := Style - [TFontStyle(Tag)];
```

For the next set of three buttons, assign Tag properties 0, 2, and 1 (in that order) and create an OnClick event handler for these three:

```
WITH Sender AS TSpeedButton DO
  Memo1.Alignment := TAlignment(Tag);
```

Replace the code for the Font menu choice's OnClick event with the following:

```
FontDialog1.Font := Memo1.Font;
WITH FontDialog1 DO
  IF Execute THEN
    BEGIN
      Memo1.Font := Font;
      SpeedButton3.Down := fsBold IN Font.Style;
      SpeedButton4.Down := fsItalic IN Font.Style;
      SpeedButton5.Down := fsUnderline IN Font.Style;
    END;
```

Finally, for each speed button, fill in the Hint property with a short phrase that describes what the button does. Set the panel's ShowHint property to True.

You just added a SpeedBar to the simple editor. The speed buttons let you open and save files, change font styles, and choose left, center, or right justification for the text. The file open and save speed buttons launch an action, because their GroupIndex is 0. The font style buttons can be up or stuck down independently of each other, because they have AllowAllUp set to True and they each have a unique GroupIndex. And precisely one of the justification buttons can be selected at a time, because they have the same group index and AllowAllUp is False.

I used simple characters on these speed buttons just to show that it's not always necessary to provide a glyph bitmap. You are welcome to draw and use tiny bitmaps for each. Remember, I'm not an artist!

It's worth noting that you can make speed buttons and bitmap buttons do almost the same things. Take a bitmap button, delete its caption, and shrink it to speed button size, and you hardly know the difference. Or take a speed button, give it a caption, and stretch it. The main difference is that speed buttons can act in groups, like radio buttons, and bitmap buttons have handy types OK, Cancel, and so on predefined. Speed buttons are also designed to use up fewer Windows resources, so if you need gobs of buttons, use speed buttons.

With all the enhancements we've added, the MyEdit project is hardly a simple editor any more. It has dozens of components and hundreds of lines of code. How many components do you suppose it would take to do something really complicated, such as play multimedia sound or video files? If you answered "One," you're ready for the next chapter.

Chapter 9
Advanced Additional Components

- -

In This Chapter

▶ Playing sound files, movies, and audio CDs on your multimedia computer

▶ Displaying Windows INI files in outline form

▶ Building a quick stand-in for the Windows character map accessory

▶ Building a program to extract the icons from other programs

▶ Displaying and choosing dates from a perpetual calendar

▶ Creating programs that converse with each other using Dynamic Data Exchange (DDE)

▶ Activating OLE objects inside your programs

- -

Certain areas of Windows programming have long been the domain of experts only, because they're just so darn hard to work with. The high-level super-powerful Delphi additional components blow the lid off these so-called difficult topics and make them as simple as anything else!

Choosing Additional Components

If you've got an idea for a project but don't know which component to use, be sure to check Table 9-1.

Table 9-1   Problems Solved by Advanced Additional Components

Task	*Component*
Play or record with multimedia devices	Media player. See "The Media Player Is the Message."
Display hierarchical data in outline form	Outline. See "Let Me Outline My Plan. . . ."
Display in grid form items that are either stored elsewhere or calculated	Draw grid. See "Cookin' with the Draw Grid(dle)."
Display in grid form strings or objects that are stored with the grid	String grid. See "Super Lists in a String Grid."
Display a calendar and choose a date	Calendar. See "I'll Check My Calendar."
Get information from other programs using Dynamic Data Exchange	DDE Client. See "Meeting with a DDE Client."
Supply information to other programs using Dynamic Data Exchange	DDE Server. See "I'll Be Your DDE Server Tonight. . . ."
Communicate with other programs using Object Linking and Embedding	OLE control. See "¡Ole! ¡Ole! ¡Ole!"

The Media Player Is the Message

If your computer doesn't jabber at you, you're not on the cutting edge. Multimedia is *the* hot topic in computers today. In fact, you can hardly find a new system that doesn't at least have a sound card, and most CD-ROM drives can play audio CDs as well. The massive removable storage capacity of CD-ROMs also makes it possible for applications to incorporate video clips without overflowing your hard disk.

Multimedia programming in Windows is a convoluted topic that rates a whole volume of its own in the Windows Software Development Kit documentation. Delphi's media player component handles the tough stuff *for* you, and gives instant access to this incredible sensory world. Play WAV and MIDI files, audio CDs, digitized video, or any multimedia file or device that can be controlled through the Windows MCI (Media Control Interface).

Properties

A media player component shows up on your form as a button bar containing up to nine buttons. The button bar resembles the control panel for a VCR or CD player. VisibleButtons, ColoredButtons, and EnabledButtons are exploding properties that define what buttons will be displayed, and how. All three have the same set of subproperties, btPlay, btPause, btStop, btNext, btPrev, btStep, btBack, btRecord, and btEject, and all are initially True. If the particular device you're writing for doesn't support a particular button, just set it to False in VisibleButtons. For example, you can't eject a WAV file, and you can't record on an audio CD. ColoredButtons gives default colors to the buttons — green for play, red for stop and record, yellow for pause, and blue for the rest. When this property is False, the corresponding button is black. Finally, EnabledButtons determines whether each button is initially enabled. Disabled buttons are grayed.

Leave the AutoEnable property set to True; this makes the media player automatically enable and disable the buttons sensibly. For example, the pause and stop buttons are disabled when nothing is playing. Leave AutoRewind True as well, so the media player will reset to the start when it finishes playing. DeviceType identifies which of the many multimedia device types the component is controlling. If the particular device type is file-related, such as a WAV or video file, the Filename property specifies what file, and the device type can be automatically determined from the filename.

If AutoOpen is True, the media player tries to open the selected device as soon as the program starts. Set it to False unless you're playing from a device or filename that's available when the program starts. For example, set AutoOpen to True for CD audio, and to False for playing WAV files.

The media player has a large collection of run-time-only properties as well. By default, video plays in a separate window, but you can force it into your own program's window using Display and DisplayRect. TimeFormat determines the format that will be used for reporting the Length, Position, and several other properties. TrackLength, Tracks, and TrackPosition relate to the tracks on an audio CD. There are more properties, but these are the essentials.

Events

The OnClick event comes with an indication of which button was pressed, and OnPostClick occurs when the action caused by a click has finished. If your program calls media player methods like Play, Rewind, and so on directly, and if it sets the property Notify to True beforehand, an OnNotify event occurs when the method finishes. In practice, though, you can do most of your multimedia programming without using any of these events.

Join the audio-visual club

Time to dive in and see just how easy multimedia programming can be with Delphi. You start with a general-purpose sound player.

Start a new project based on the fixed-size form template and drop a media player component on the form. Double-click the VisibleButtons property to explode it, and set all but the first three subproperties to False. Set AutoOpen to False. Position the media player near the top left corner of the form.

Place a speed button to the right of the media player. Set its caption to the digit 1 and its font to 9-point Wingdings. (Surprise! An open folder glyph appears on the speed button.) Put a horizontal bar gauge to the right of the speed button. Select all three components, choose Size from the Edit menu, and under Height choose Shrink to smallest. Set the gauge's ForeColor to clAqua and stretch it to almost the width of the form. Reduce the height of the form so there's about the same amount of space around the components on all sides. Set the form's caption to My Media Player.

Drop an Open File dialog and a timer on the form. Set the timer's Interval to 100 milliseconds, and set Enabled to False. Set the Open File dialog's properties like this:

Property	Value
DefaultExt	WAV
Options.ofHideReadOnly	True
Options.ofFileMustExist	True
Title	Open Sound File

Double-click the Filter property and create two filters named WAV files and MIDI files, with corresponding file masks *.WAV and *.MID.

Put this code in the speed button's OnClick event handler:

```
WITH OpenDialog1 DO
  IF Execute THEN
    BEGIN
      Caption := 'My Media Player - ' +
        ExtractFilename(Filename);
      MediaPlayer1.Filename := Filename;
      Filename := '';
      WITH MediaPlayer1 DO
        BEGIN
          Open;
          Gauge1.MaxValue := Length;
          Gauge1.Progress := 0;
          Timer1.Enabled := TRUE;
        END;
    END;
```

Put this single line in the timer's OnTimer event handler:

```
Gauge1.Progress := MediaPlayer1.Position;
```

That's all you have to do. Figure 9-1 shows the resulting program. As long as your system has a sound card and Windows drivers installed, you should be able to play the sample WAV and MIDI files that come with Windows, or any other sound files you might have acquired. As the music plays, the gauge component tracks its progress.

Figure 9-1:
This program plays any WAV or MIDI file.

What's the difference between WAV files and MIDI files? A WAV file is like a tape recording of a series of sounds converted to digital form. A MIDI file is more like sheet music — a set of *instructions* for producing that series of sounds. MIDI files can pack a vast amount of music into a small amount of space because the synthesizer on the sound card is responsible for producing the sound. On the other hand, WAV files can hold digitized voice, sound effects, and other non-musical sounds that MIDI files can't handle.

These days, many Windows systems include drivers for playing video clips in one format or another. How much work do you suppose it would take to make your sound player show movies as well?

If you guessed absolutely none, you win the prize! Simply select an AVI, QTW, or other video file for which your system has a driver loaded, and press the play button. The video clip will play in its own window. You can enhance the media player just a little, though, to put the video inside its boundaries.

Start with the sound player project you were just working on and update the Open File dialog's Filter property by adding three new names, Video for Windows files, Movies, and QuickTime files, with corresponding file masks *.AVI, *.MOV, and *.QTW. Change the dialog's title to Open Multimedia File. Explode the media player's VisibleButtons property and set btStep and btBack to True. You have to rearrange the speed button and gauge to make room for the expanded media player.

Stretch the form to make it higher and place a bevel component on the form below the media player. Set its shape to bsFrame and return the form to its original height so that the bevel is just out of sight.

Double-click the speed button to jump into its OnClick event handler. Find the line that contains only `Open;` and insert these lines of code immediately after it:

```
Display := Form1;
DisplayRect := Rect(Bevel1.Left+4,
   Bevel1.Top+4,0,0);
Bevel1.Width := DisplayRect.Right + 8;
Bevel1.Height := DisplayRect.Bottom + 8;
IF Bevel1.Height = 8 THEN
   Self.ClientHeight := Bevel1.Top
ELSE
   Self.ClientHeight := Bevel1.Height +
     Bevel1.Top + 8;
```

A few lines down you see `Timer1.Enabled := True;`. Just after that line, add these two lines:

```
Frames := 1;
Step;
```

As Figure 9-2 shows, the media player is now equipped to play movie-type files using itself as the screen. It resizes itself to match each video clip's preferred size, and returns to its original size if you play a simple sound file. The Step command you added causes the video clip to display its first frame so that you can see what's coming before you press Play.

Figure 9-2:
With just a few added lines of code, the media player program plays video.

Turn your PC into a boom box

Playing audio CDs using the media player is a little different from playing multimedia files. Mostly, it's easier. Hard to believe? Let's do it!

Start a new project based on the fixed-size form template and place a media player component on it. Double-click the VisibleButtons property and set btStep, btBack, and btRecord to False. Set DeviceType to cdAudio and set AutoOpen to True. Change the form's Caption to CD Player. Resize the media player and the form so that they fit together nicely.

Here's a list of the steps you have to follow before you can use this program to play audio CDs:

1. Put an audio CD in the CD-ROM drive.

Long list of steps, eh? That's really all you have to do. Try it now. You can start and stop the music, skip tracks forward and back (as long as the CD is playing) and even eject the CD from the drive. Without writing a single line of code, you've created an application that lets you luxuriate in sounds ranging from Mozart to Pink Floyd to Weird Al Yankovic.

What's that great song that's playing right now? Can't tell? Add a track indicator, and you don't have to guess.

Set the form's Ctl3D property to False. Put a bevel on the form below the media player, with Style set to bsFrame. Make it the same width as the media player and give it a height of 49.

Place a label inside the left end of the bevel. Set its properties like this:

Property	*Value*
Caption	00
Font.Color	clLime
Font.Name	Courier New
Font.Size	16
Font.Style.fsBold	True
Transparent	True

Copy this label to the Clipboard and paste a copy onto the form. Set its caption to 00:00, position it inside the right end of the bevel, and set Alignment to taRightJustify. Now set the form's color to clBlack.

Put a timer component on the form, with its Interval set to 100. Replace the begin..end pair of an OnTimer event handler with these lines:

```
VAR Trk, Min, Sec : Word;
begin
  WITH MediaPlayer1 DO
    BEGIN
      Trk := MCI_TMSF_TRACK(Position);
      Min := MCI_TMSF_MINUTE(Position);
      Sec := MCI_TMSF_SECOND(Position);
      Label1.Caption := Format('%.2d',[Trk]);
      Label2.Caption := Format('%.2d:%.2d',[Min, Sec]);
    END;
end;
```

Add MMSystem to the uses clause at the top of Unit1.

Figure 9-3 shows the completed audio CD player with its minimalist display. On the left you see the number of the track that's playing; on the right, the amount of time this track has been playing. You've turned your PC into a boom box!

Figure 9-3:
The media
player plays
audio CDs
on your
computer.

Let Me Outline My Plan . . .

Some kinds of information are best presented in outline form, so that you can choose the level of detail you want. For example, the Windows File Manager uses an outline to display the directory structure of your disk. You can collapse the outline right down to the root directory, expand it to show *every* directory, or display anything in between. Delphi's outline component is a flexible tool for displaying this kind of information. It still exists in Delphi 2.0, though it's been shoved aside into the Win 3.1 page of the Component palette. You'll read about its replacement, the ListView component, in Chapter 12.

Properties

The essential function of the outline component is to display lines of text that have a hierarchical relationship to each other. The Lines property contains these lines. The lower an item is in the hierarchy, the farther to the right it will be indented. The OutlineStyle property determines what other graphical elements are used to display the outline. Text is always present; other choices are a tree of lines, plus and minus icons indicating whether a particular icon can be expanded or collapsed, and folder and document icons that distinguish "leaf" items (those with no branches below them) and whether an item with branches below is open or closed. Figure 9-4 shows four of the possible combinations.

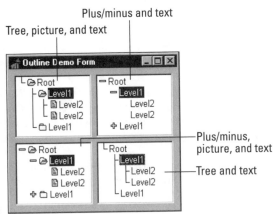

Figure 9-4: The outline component can represent the hierarchical relationship of its elements in several different ways.

Plus/minus and text

Tree, picture, and text

Plus/minus, picture, and text

Tree and text

Place an outline component on a new form and double-click its Lines property to enter the string list editor. Type President on the first line. At the start of the second line, press Ctrl+Tab to insert a tab character and type Vice President. On the next two lines, insert two tabs at the start and type Bureaucrat. Click OK to close the string list editor.

Now use the Object Inspector to select each possible value of the outline's OutlineStyle property in turn. Take note of the different styles.

For further control over the look of the outline, you can set the PicturePlus, PictureMinus, PictureLeaf, PictureClosed, and PictureOpen properties to different bitmaps.

Note that the Lines property has LoadFromFile and SaveToFile methods, just like the Items property of a list box. In the resulting file, the number of tab characters at the start of each line indicates the depth of that line in the outline.

The Options property explodes into three True and False subproperties. In Figure 9-4, a line connects the root of each outline to an unseen source beyond the top of the outline. If you set the ooDrawTreeRoot property to False, this line does not appear. The ooDrawFocusRect property controls whether a dotted focus rectangle appears around the selected outline item; it, too, is True by default. You generally want to set the ooStretchBitmaps property to True as well. This causes the bitmap pictures to adjust to the size of the text. If ooStretchBitmaps is False, the pictures may be cut off at the bottom.

The FullPath method of an item in the outline returns the full path from the outline's topmost level to that item. That is, it returns the item's text, preceded by the text of the item's parent, and before that the text of the parent's parent, all the way back to the primordial root of the outline. The individual item strings are separated by the string specified in the ItemSeparator property. By default, this is a backslash (\ ).

Sneak a peek at INI files

Just about every Windows 3.1 application summarily dumps an INI file in your Windows directory, and some of them are as long as Bill Gates's stretch limo. When you skim through a big one like WIN.INI in Notepad, it's easy to miss what you're looking for. Wouldn't it be nice if you could view just one section at a time?

Place an outline component, an Open File dialog, and a menu on a new form. Set the outline's OutlineStyle to osPlusMinusText and its Align property to alClient. Set the Open File dialog's properties thus:

Property	*Value*
DefaultExt	INI
InitialDir	C:\WINDOWS
Options.ofHideReadOnly	True
Options.FileMustExist	True
Title	Open INI File

This time the Open File dialog gets just a single filter with the name INI Files and the mask *.INI. Set the form's caption to INI Viewer.

Double-click the menu to enter the Menu Designer. Create a simplified &File menu with just two submenu items, &Open... and E&xit. In the OnClick event handler for the Exit menu choice, put this single line:

```
Close;
```

Replace the begin..end pair supplied by Delphi for the Open item's OnClick event handler with these lines:

```
VAR
  S : String;
  N, First, Last : Word;
  TS : TStringList;
begin
  WITH OpenDialog1  DO
    IF Execute THEN
      BEGIN
        Outline1.Clear;
        TS := TStringList.Create;
        try
          TS.LoadFromFile(Filename);
          TS.Insert(0, ExtractFileName(FileName));
          FOR N := TS.Count - 1 DOWNTO 1 DO
            BEGIN
              S := TS[N];
              First := 1;
              WHILE (First < Length(S)) AND
                ((S[First] = ' ') OR
                (S[First] = #9)) DO Inc(First);
              Last := Length(S);
              WHILE (Last >= First) AND
                ((S[Last] = ' ') OR
                (S[Last] = #9)) DO Dec(Last);
              IF Last >= First THEN
                BEGIN
                  S := Copy(S, First, Last-First+1);
                  IF (S[1]='[') AND
                    (S[length(S)]=']') THEN
                    S := #9 + S
                  ELSE S := #9#9 + S;
                  TS[N] := S;
                END
              ELSE TS.Delete(N);
            END;
          Outline1.Lines := TS;
        finally
          TS.Free;
        END;
      END;
end;
```

Run the program, select File I Open, and choose an INI file. The outline displays the INI file name along with the closed folder icon. Double-click that icon and the outline expands to show the names of the INI file sections. Double-click one of the sections and it opens to show the key values it contains. Double-click the INI file name again to close the whole outline.

You can also use the keyboard to manipulate an outline component. Use the arrow keys to highlight the INI file name at the top and press the minus key; the entire outline collapses into that one line. Now press the asterisk and every branch of the entire outline expands. To expand or collapse just the current line, press the plus or minus key.

If something went wrong during the file loading process, your program would normally just display an error message and merrily continue without executing the rest of the function. That would be bad, because the function is responsible for freeing up the memory it allocated in creating the string list. The try..finally block beginning right after the call to TStringList.Create solves that problem. Even if a problem occurs within the *try* part of the block, the *finally* part is always executed. In this case, the string list is always freed. This is an example of *exception handling,* a topic you can dig into in Chapter 15.

Events

Outline components don't *have* to respond to any events to be useful, as the foregoing program shows. If your program needs to respond to changes in the selected outline item, use the OnClick event. For example, you might display the value of the currently selected item in a label.

The OnExpand and OnCollapse methods occur when a branch of the outline is expanded or collapsed, either by the user or by the program itself. To expand the tenth item in the outline, the program would set Outline1.Expanded[10] to True.

Using the INI viewer project you just created, place a panel on the main form with the properties set as follows:

Property	*Value*
Align	alTop
Alignment	taLeftJustify
BevelInner	bvLowered
Caption	(none)

In the outline's OnClick event handler, insert these lines:

```
WITH Outline1 DO
  IF SelectedItem > 0 THEN
    Panel1.Caption := Items[SelectedItem].FullPath
```

Next, change the ItemSeparator property of the outline to space, asterisk, space (*).

Run the program and click various lines in the outline. Figure 9-5 shows the result — when you click on a key line, the panel's caption displays the INI file name, section name, and key separated by asterisks. Now the next time a tech-support person asks you the value of the MaxRTEncodeSetting key in the [msacm.imaadpcm] section of your SYSTEM.INI, you can find it fast with this INI file viewer!

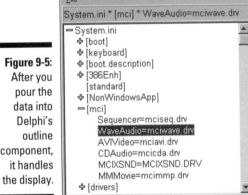

Figure 9-5: After you pour the data into Delphi's outline component, it handles the display.

Cookin' with the Draw Grid (dle)

The two grid components are grown-up relatives of the familiar list box. Like a list box, they can hold a list of items. But unlike a list box, the number of items is virtually unlimited, and the items can be in a grid of multiple columns. The draw grid component is used when the contents of a cell can be calculated from the cell's position, or when the contents of the cell are stored elsewhere. The string grid component stores strings and objects for display within itself.

Properties

The grids have a huge number of properties, but some are more important than others. You can hit the high spots in this section. The ColCount and RowCount properties define the number of columns and rows in the grid. FixedCols and FixedRows tell how many of each are fixed nonscrolling headers — normally you use one or none of these. There's a special FixedColor property that defines the background color for the fixed rows and columns.

By default, all columns and rows are the same size; this size is controlled by DefaultColWidth and DefaultRowHeight. DefaultDrawing (True by default) means the grid handles the basics of drawing cells, such as indicating whether a cell is focused or selected.

The Options property contains a huge collection of options that control the looks and action of the grid. The goRowSizing and goColSizing options determine whether rows and columns can be resized individually. If goRangeSelect is True, the user can select a range of cells with the mouse, and if goDrawFocusSelected is True, the focused cell will be the same color as the rest of the selection. When the goRowSelect option is True, the user must select whole rows of cells.

The goThumbTracking option controls whether the contents of the grid "track" as the scroll bars move or simply snap into place when the user releases the scroll bar. The former (tracking) makes it easier to find a particular position in a large grid; the latter (snapping into place) is more practical when drawing the cells is time-consuming.

A draw grid has some other useful properties available only at run time. Row and Col are the row and column of the currently selected cell. TopRow and LeftCol are the row and column of the cell at the top left of the scrollable part of the grid. They are both zero initially, but if some of the grid scrolls out of view, they change. ColWidths and RowHeights are arrays of integers holding the width and height of the individual columns and rows when sizing is permitted.

You must be reeling under this deluge of properties; I'll stop, I'll stop! You'll run across other properties for fine-tuning your grids after you start to use them in programs.

Events

The big event for a draw grid is OnDrawCell. The OnDrawCell event handler is completely responsible for putting whatever text or image you want in each cell.

Start a new project and select the fixed-size form template. Place a bevel on the form, and then set its Align property to alTop and its shape to bsFrame. Now place a draw grid on the form with these properties:

Property	Value
Align	alClient
ColCount	32
DefaultColWidth	18
FixedCols	0
FixedRows	0
Options.goRangeSelect	False
RowCount	7
ScrollBars	ssNone

Size the form big enough so that the grid doesn't need scroll bars, but make the form small enough so that there's no blank space outside the array of cells.

Create an OnDrawCell event handler for the grid. Put these lines in it:

```
WITH DrawGrid1.Canvas DO
  TextRect(Rect, Rect.Left, Rect.Top,
    Char((Row+1)*32 + Col));
```

Place a combo box on the bevel, set its Style to csDropDownList and Sorted to True, and stretch it so it fills most of the width of the bevel. Put these lines in the form's OnCreate event handler:

```
WITH ComboBox1 DO
  BEGIN
    Items := Screen.Fonts;
    ItemIndex := Items.IndexOf(Font.Name);
  END;
Caption := 'Font Display - ' + Font.Name;
```

Now create an OnClick event for the combo box like this:

```
DrawGrid1.Font.Name := ComboBox1.Text;
Caption := 'Font Display - ' +
  DrawGrid1.Font.Name;
```

You've just created a program that displays all the characters in a font, like the Windows CharMap accessory. Run the program and you see every character in the draw grid's current font. Choose various fonts using the combo box. Figure 9-6 shows all the characters in the fabulous Wingdings font.

Figure 9-6:
With just a few lines of code, this draw grid displays every character in the font of your choice.

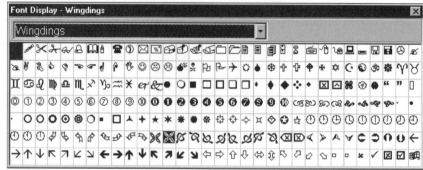

A bevel uses fewer Windows resources than a panel. In a program like this one, where the specialized events and properties of a panel aren't needed, always use a bevel.

Super Lists in a String Grid

A string grid is just like a draw grid, except you can store a string of text, an object, or both for every cell. You can set it up with one column and a zillion rows to create a list-box equivalent without the size limits of a list box. Or you can store an object such as an icon along with a descriptive string in each cell.

Properties and events

At design time, a string grid has the same set of properties and events as a draw grid, but it has a few additional run-time properties. The Cells property is a two-dimensional array of strings, and the Objects property is the corresponding array of objects. Another way to view the cells is through the Rows and Cols properties, which contain string lists corresponding to each row and column in the grid.

Four of the Options really make sense only in a string grid: goRowMoving, goColMoving, goEditing, and goAlwaysShowEditor. The first two options enable users to move rows and columns around at run time by dragging with the mouse. When goEditing is True, users are permitted to edit the contents of the cells. Pressing F2 displays the editor, unless you've set goAlwaysShowEditor to True, in which case F2 isn't needed.

The OnGetEditMask event gives you a chance to control the editing of cell data. This event occurs just before editing begins for a particular cell, and the event handler receives the row and column of the cell being edited. All your program needs to do is return an edit mask string (like those used by the masked edit box component) for cells whose data you want to control.

Place a string grid on a new form and set these properties:

Property	Value
Options.goRowSizing	True
Options.goColSizing	True
Options.goRowMoving	True
Options.goColMoving	True
Options.goEditing	True
Options.goAlwaysShowEditor	True
Options.goTabs	True

Now create an OnGetEditMask for the string grid containing these lines:

```
WITH StringGrid1 DO
  IF ACol = FixedCols THEN
    Value := '00000;1;_';
```

Run the program and start typing — your input goes into the selected cell. If the cell is in column 1, the first nonfixed column, you can enter only 5-digit numeric strings. Press Tab to step through the cells, left to right and top to bottom. Enter something in each cell. Click and drag the header cell of a column or row to move that column or row, or drag the line between header cells to resize.

Here we go gathering icons in May

Create a new project based on the fixed-size form template. Place a bevel on the form, set its Align property to alTop, and set its shape to bsFrame. Place a string grid on the form and set its properties like this:

Property	Value
Align	alClient
ColCount	4
DefaultColWidth	144
DefaultRowHeight	64
FixedRows	0
FixedCols	0
Font.Name	MS Sans Serif
Font.Size	8
Options.goRangeSelect	False
RowCount	4

Size the form high enough so that exactly three of the grid's four rows show, and just wide enough so that a horizontal scroll bar doesn't appear.

Change the form's caption to Icon Collector. Add an Open File dialog to the form, and set its properties as follows:

Property	Value
DefaultExt	ICO
InitialDir	C:\WINDOWS
Options.ofHideReadOnly	True
Options.ofFileMustExist	True
Title	Open Icon File

Double-click the Filter property and enter two filter names, All Icon files and All files, with corresponding masks *.ICO; *.EXE; *.DLL (for All Icon files) and *.* (for All files). Note that you separate multiple file specifications with a semicolon.

Place a push button on the bevel and set its Default property to True. Change its caption to &Gather Icons..., stretching it so the caption fits.

Double-click the push button and replace the begin..end pair supplied by Delphi with this longish block of program code:

```
CONST CurItem : LongInt = 0;
VAR
  pName : ARRAY[0..255] OF Char;
  fName : String[13];
  N     : Word;
  IcoH  : hIcon;
begin
  WITH OpenDialog1 DO
    BEGIN
      IF NOT Execute THEN Exit;
      fName := ExtractFilename(Filename);
      StrPCopy(pName, Filename);
    END;
  N := 0;
  WITH StringGrid1 DO
    REPEAT
      IcoH := ExtractIcon(hInstance, pName, N);
      IF IcoH <= 1 THEN Break;
      Col := CurItem MOD ColCount;
      IF (CurItem DIV ColCount) >= RowCount THEN
        RowCount := RowCount + 1;
      Row := CurItem DIV ColCount;
      Cells[Col,Row] := fName + ' #' + IntToStr(N);
      Objects[Col, Row] := TIcon.Create;
      WITH Objects[Col, Row] AS TIcon DO
        Handle := IcoH;
      CurItem := CurItem + 1;
      N := N + 1;
    UNTIL FALSE;
end;
```

Stop a second to let your fingers cool off. And don't worry; that's almost the entire program. The only other thing you need to do is give the string grid an OnDrawCell event handler like this:

```
IF StringGrid1.Objects[Col,Row] IS TIcon THEN
  StringGrid1.Canvas.Draw(
    Rect.Left+56, Rect.Top+24,
      TIcon(StringGrid1.Objects[Col,Row]));
```

Finally, scroll to the top of the Unit1 file and add ShellApi to the uses clause. (This gives your program access to the all-important ExtractIcon function.)

Run the program and choose any ICO, EXE, or DLL file. If the file contains icons, they show up in the string grid. For a real bonanza, choose PROGMAN.EXE or MORICONS.DLL from the Windows directory. Each icon is identified with the name of the file that contains it and the index of that icon in the file (as you can see in Figure 9-7).

Having succeeded beyond all your expectations in extracting icons from files on disk, you might wonder if viewing is *all* you can do with them. Well, of course not!

Add a Save File common dialog to the Icon Collector project with these properties:

Property	Value
DefaultExt	ICO
Options.ofOverwritePrompt	True
Options.ofHideReadOnly	True
Options.ofPathMustExist	True
Title	Save Icon File

Give the dialog just one filter named Icon files with *.ICO as the file mask.

Place a push button on the bevel with the caption &Save Icon..., and use these lines for its OnClick event handler:

```
IF SaveDialog1.Execute THEN
  WITH StringGrid1 DO
    WITH Objects[Col,Row] AS TIcon DO
      SaveToFile(SaveDialog1.Filename);
```

Figure 9-7 shows the resulting program with a number of icons loaded. Run it yourself and extract icons from EXE or DLL files, and then choose an icon and press the Save Icon... button to save it to an icon file. Of course it wouldn't be right to simply commandeer these icons for your own use, but you can use them for inspiration when you design your own icons.

The icon collector program can yank icons from either 16-bit or 32-files. Occasionally, though, a 32-bit file contains an icon whose format doesn't match what Delphi's TIcon component expects. The highlighted icon in Figure 9-7 is an example. Save this icon to an ICO file and you've got pure poison. The Image Editor gags on it, you can't use it as an icon for your Delphi forms, and Resource Workshop reports that its dimensions are 0 by 222 pixels! Fortunately, icons like this are rare.

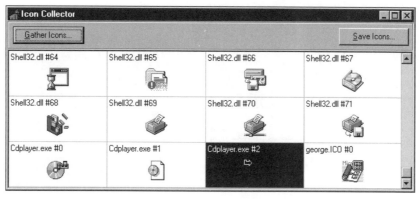

Figure 9-7:
This
program
uses a
string grid to
store icons
extracted
from EXE
and DLL
files.

I'll Check My Calendar

Delphi's generalized grids have the potential to become just about anything in your programs. You can almost hear them chanting "I can be a chessboard . . . I can be a spreadsheet . . . I can be a calendar . . . ." Wait, did someone say calendar? Delphi actually supplies a specialized grid that functions as a calendar. This grid, found on the Samples page of the Component palette, is a fully functional calendar that you can use in any program.

Properties and events

It would be alarming if the main properties of a calendar were anything but Year, Month, and Day. The run-time-only property CalendarDate holds the entire date in Delphi's own cryptic compressed form. And the OnChange event occurs when the user chooses a new date. When you've decided how your program lets the user change the month and date, the PrevMonth, NextMonth, PrevYear, and NextYear methods handle the dirty work.

Place a calendar component on a new fixed-size form. Place two panels on the form and set their BevelInner property to bvLowered. Delete their captions and place them as shown in Figure 9-8, above the calendar component. Place spin buttons to the right of the two panels as shown.

Create a one-line OnDownClick event handler for the left spin button containing this line:

```
Calendar1.PrevMonth;
```

Use this line for the left spin button's OnUpClick event handler:

```
Calendar1.NextMonth;
```

Figure 9-8:
Double-click
any of the
five masked
edit boxes in
the main
form, and
the date-
selection
calendar
form
appears.

The OnDownClick event handler for the right spin button should contain this line:

```
Calendar1.PrevYear;
```

Give it an OnUpClick event handler with this single line:

```
Calendar1.NextYear;
```

Drop two bitmap buttons on the form and set their Kind properties to bkOK and bkCancel. Put a panel in line with the bitmap buttons and sized the same. Delete its caption and set its BevelInner property to bvLowered.

Double-click the calendar and put these lines in its OnChange event handler:

```
WITH Calendar1 DO
  BEGIN
    DateStr := DateToStr(CalendarDate);
    Panel1.Caption := LongMonthNames[Month];
    Panel2.Caption := IntToStr(Year);
    Panel3.Caption := DateStr;
  END;
```

Locate the comment { Public declarations } near the top of the unit and add this line below it:

```
DateStr : String;
```

Create an OnActivate event handler for the form itself; the handler should contain these lines:

```
try
  Calendar1.CalendarDate := StrToDate(DateStr);
except
  On EConvertError DO;
end;
Calendar1.OnChange(Calendar1);
```

Set the form's caption to Choose Date and its Name property to PickDate.

If you're running Delphi 1.0, right-click the form and choose Save As Template… from the pop-up menu. Under Delphi 2.0, you right-click the form and choose Add To Repository… from the menu.

Now start a new project and place a masked edit box on the form. Double-click the EditMask property and select the Date mask. In Delphi 1.0, choose New Form from the File menu and add the date-selection form to the project. In Delphi 2.0, choose New… from the File menu, flip to the Forms page, and choose the date-selection form.

Create an OnDblClick event handler for the masked edit box:

```
WITH PickDate, Sender AS TMaskEdit DO
  BEGIN
    DateStr := Text;
    IF ShowModal = mrOK THEN
      Text := DateStr;
  END;
```

Now go to the top of the program file and add Unit2 to the uses clause.

Run the program and type a date, and then double-click the masked edit box. If the date you typed was invalid or incomplete, the calendar form just uses today's date. When you click OK, the date from the calendar is inserted in the masked edit box. You can use this form in any project that needs date input.

Meeting with a DDE Client

DDE stands for Dynamic Data Exchange. No, that's not a new consciousness cult — it's the way Windows applications share information. Delphi programs can call on applications that support DDE and get information from them. To hold a DDE conversation with an application, however, you need to know in advance just what topics it's prepared to talk about. This kind of information is usually buried deep in the application's manual, if it's available at all.

There are two sides to every DDE conversation, the client and the server. The client asks the server for data, and the server graciously or grudgingly provides it. (Actually, a saucy client can poke data back at the server.) Another handy property of DDE is its capability to execute macros in the server. What macros? You have to consult the server application's documentation to find out — be prepared to spend some time searching for this information.

Delphi supports the client side of DDE with two components called DdeClientConv and DdeClientItem. DdeClientConv is what you need to initiate a conversation and execute macros; DdeClientItem links up with an individual data item in the server.

Properties, events, and methods

The essential properties of a DdeClientConv are DdeService and DdeTopic. If you enter values for these at design time and ConnectMode is set to DdeAutomatic, the connection is made right then and there. Don't try to type in a value for just one of them. You need to click the ellipsis box next to either one and enter both at the same time.

DdeClientConv responds to just two events, OnClose and OnOpen, but you can generally ignore them. It has quite a few nonevent methods, the most important of which are OpenLink and CloseLink. These serve to open and close a DDE link when the ConnectMode is DdeManual. SetLink sets the service and topic at run time. This method is especially important because calling CloseLink clears those two fields. The ExecuteMacro method sends a DDE macro to the client application, and ExecuteMacroLines sends a whole collection of commands. RequestData makes a one-time request for data without establishing an active DDE link.

A DdeClientItem component relies on DdeClientConv named in its DdeConv property. When its DdeItem property contains the name of a valid item in the server, DdeClientItem receives an OnChange event every time that item's value changes. DdeClientItem appears in the next set of examples. Right now, you can try a simple request for data.

Wheedling Program Manager for data

Place two list boxes on the form and set the Align property of the first to alTop and the Align property of the second to alClient. Set the first list box's Sorted property to True.

Drop a DdeClientConv on the form and set its DdeService and DdeTopic both to ProgMan. Start an OnCreate method for the form and replace the begin..end pair supplied by Delphi with these lines:

```
VAR P : PChar;
begin
  P := DdeClientConv1.RequestData('Groups');
  ListBox1.Items.SetText(P);
  StrDispose(P);
end;
```

Use almost the same lines in the OnClick event handler for the first list box:

```
VAR P : PChar;
begin
  WITH ListBox1 DO
    P := DdeClientConv1.RequestData(
      Items[ItemIndex]);
  ListBox2.Items.SetText(P);
  StrDispose(P);
end;
```

Run this program and the top list box displays a list of all your Program Manager groups in alphabetic order. Click a group name and the bottom list box fills with detailed information about that group and its items, as Figure 9-9 shows. Amazing what you can do with DDE, isn't it?

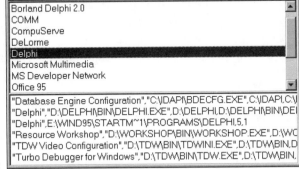

Figure 9-9: Your Delphi programs can acquire all kinds of information through DDE.

Most DDE sample programs assume that you have some particular application on your system, such as Excel or Quattro Pro for Windows. If you don't have that particular application, you're out of luck. I chose Program Manager for this example because *everybody* has it. Even if you're running Norton Desktop or some other alternate Windows shell, you can switch to Program Manager temporarily to try this demo. It even works in Windows 95! Explorer puts on a false nose and imitates Program Manager as far as DDE messages go. It responds to the request for a list of program groups by listing the submenus directly beneath Programs in the Start Menu. And it responds to a request for a list of items in one of those groups by listing the items in the corresponding menu, omitting any nested menus. This imitation fools most programs, including the one you just wrote!

Bullying Program Manager for data

While you've got Program Manager on the brain, get bossy and make it jump through a few hoops.

Drop a DdeClientConv on a new fixed-size form and set its ddeService and DdeTopic both to ProgMan. Place two ordinary buttons side by side on the form with captions &Create and &Destroy. Change the form's caption to Program Manager Macro Demo.

In the OnClick event handler for the Create button, replace Delphi's begin..end pair with these lines:

```
VAR
  N : Word;
  S : String;
begin
  WITH DdeClientConv1 DO
    BEGIN
      ExecuteMacro('[CreateGroup(Phony Group)]',True);
      WHILE WaitStat DO Application.ProcessMessages;
      ExecuteMacro('[ShowGroup(Phony Group,1)]',True);
      WHILE WaitStat DO Application.ProcessMessages;
      FOR N := 1 TO 45 DO
        BEGIN
          S := Format('[AddItem(NOTEPAD.EXE,#%.02d' +
            ',PROGMAN.EXE,%d)]'#0, [N, N]);
          ExecuteMacro(@S[1], True);
          WHILE WaitStat DO
            Application.ProcessMessages;
        END;
    END;
end;
```

Double-click the Destroy button and put these lines in its OnClick event handler:

```
WITH DdeClientConv1 DO
  BEGIN
    ExecuteMacro('[ShowGroup(Phony Group,1)]',True);
    WHILE WaitStat DO Application.ProcessMessages;
    ExecuteMacro('[DeleteGroup(Phony Group)]',True);
  END;
```

When you run this program and press the Create button, it sends a flurry of macro commands to Program Manager. These commands create a new group called Phony Group, shown in Figure 9-10, and fill it with 45 phony program items. The program items all have NOTEPAD.EXE as their command line, a label from #01 to #45 as their description, and one of Program Manager's 45 built-in icons as their icon. Be patient — it can take a little time to build this massive collection. When you tire of gazing upon this array of icons, simply press the Destroy button.

If you use a Windows shell other than the Windows 3.1, Windows for Workgroups Program Manager, or the Windows 95 Explorer (such as Norton Desktop for Windows or Central Point's PC Tools), this program might not behave correctly. Alternate Windows shells generally attempt to emulate Program Manager for DDE purposes, but their emulation might not be perfect. If your Windows shell is not Program Manager, you can try the Create button anyway to see what happens, but it's probably safer to avoid the Destroy button.

Figure 9-10:
The Windows 95 Explorer also responds to ProgMan macro commands from this Delphi application.

Clearly you can use the ExecuteMacro method in your programs to create happy Program Manager groups and populate them with contented icons. And doing the same thing under Windows 95 automatically creates serene submenus populated with merry menu items. The AddItem macro can take up to nine parameters, but only the first four are really important. First comes the all-essential command line. Next is the description that appears under the icon. After that is the name of the file that contains the icon for the program, followed by the index of the icon within that file.

I'll Be Your DDE Server Tonight . . .

Your Delphi applications can share their data with other applications (Delphi-spawned or otherwise) just as easily as they can go fishing for data. The heroes of this story are the DdeServerConv and DdeServerItem components.

The DdeServerConv component has only two properties, Name and Tag. It responds to the events OnOpen, OnClose, and OnExecuteMacro, which occur when a DDE conversation is opened or closed, or a client sends a macro comment. You need to include one of these components in your DDE server if you want to execute macros at the request of other programs, or if the caption of the form might change at run time.

Besides Name and Tag, DdeServerItem has a ServerConv property, which points to the DdeServerConv component if one is present. You set its Text property to the value you want shared using DDE; if the value is multiline, use the Lines property instead.

From a client's point of view, your DDE server's service name is the name of the program, minus the extension. Its topic name is the DdeServerConv's name or the form's caption. And the item name is the name of the DdeServerItem. Let's give this a whirl, so you can see how it works.

Put a DdeServerConv on a new fixed-size form and set its name to MyServer. Place a DdeServerItem on the form and set its ServerConv property to MyServer. Set its Name property to MyItem and its Text property to 0. Put a label in the form's top-left corner with its caption set to 0 (zero). Place a scroll bar just after the label and stretch it to fill the remaining width of the form. Now put these two lines in the scroll bar's OnChange event handler:

```
MyItem.Text := IntToStr(ScrollBar1.Position);
Label1.Caption := MyItem.Text;
```

Save the project as DDESERVE, and then compile it. (Two lines of code for a DDE server — that's pretty good!)

Now start a different project, also based on the fixed-size form. Drop a horizontal bar gauge and a DdeClientConv on it and set DdeService and DdeTopic to DDESERVE and MyServer. At this point the DDE server demo should appear on the screen, like magic.

Connect a DdeClientItem to the DdeClientConv and set its DdeItem property to Politics. Whoops! As soon as you press Enter, the text disappears. That's because Politics is not a valid item for DDE conversation with this server. Enter MyItem, and note that *this* value sticks (until the next time you restore the project from disk). Replace the begin..end pair of the DdeClientItem's OnChange method with these lines:

```
VAR S : String;
begin
  WITH DdeClientItem1 DO
    BEGIN
      S := '0' + Text;
      WHILE S[Length(S)] = ' ' DO
        S := Copy(S, 1, Length(S)-1);
      Gauge1.Progress := StrToInt(S);
    END;
end;
```

Run the DDE client program — if the DDE server isn't loaded, it gets launched automatically. When you move the scroll bar in the DDE server, the gauge in the client tracks perfectly! Now, just to see how easy it is, you can make the server respond to simple macro commands.

Open the DDE server demo project, select the DdeServerConv component, and double-click the OnExecuteMacro line in the Object Inspector's Events page. Put this single line in the event handler:

```
ScrollBar1.Max := StrToInt(Msg[0]);
```

When this server receives a macro, it sets the scroll bar's maximum to the numeric value of the received string. Press Ctrl+F9 to compile this project, save it, and then open the DDE client demo project.

Put a radio group on the client program's form and set its caption to Range. Double-click its Items property and enter the three strings 100, 500, and 1,000. Set its ItemIndex property to 0 (zero). Create an OnClick event handler for the radio group, replacing Delphi's begin..end pair with these lines:

```
VAR S : String;
begin
  WITH Sender AS TRadioGroup DO
    BEGIN
      S := Items[ItemIndex] + #0;
      DdeClientConv1.ExecuteMacro(@S[1], False);
      Gauge1.MaxValue := StrToInt(Items[ItemIndex]);
    END;
end;
```

Run the client program again. As before, the gauge automatically tracks changes to the position of the scroll bar in the server. Now, though, choosing a different radio button changes the range for the scroll bar in the server. Figure 9-11 shows both programs, though the links between them are invisible.

Figure 9-11:
Delphi can handle both ends of a DDE conversation.

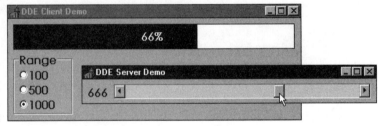

¡OLE! ¡OLE! ¡OLE!

OLE (Object Linking and Embedding), it's said, is the future of computing. When the Good Times arrive, you won't use monolithic one-style-fits-all monster applications. Rather, you'll snap together OLE-compliant miniprograms to create your own personal program.

This lovely dream may or may not come to pass, but right now your Delphi applications can link or embed OLE objects of any type available on your system, from Paintbrush pictures to media clips to spreadsheets. Implementing OLE in a program is extremely complex, and even with Delphi's help some of the complexity remains. Still, you can build a simple OLE container demo without straining your code muscles.

Embed the missing link

Right about now you'd expect to see a list of properties and events for the OLE container. Yes, this container has quite a few properties, and it responds to a number of different events, but in Delphi 1.0 the only property that's significant in the example that follows is PInitInfo. This is a complex internal OLE structure that you (thankfully) don't really have to understand. It's created by a few OLE helper functions and passed to the OLE container, like a sealed diplomatic pouch.

The example program in this section is specific to Delphi 1.0 — skip to the next section for the Delphi 2.0 version.

Drop a menu on the form, and double-click it to enter the Menu Designer. Add a &File menu with just the one item E&xit under it. Set the OnClick event handler for the Exit menu item to this single line:

```
Close;
```

Add another top-level menu item called &Edit, set its GroupIndex to 1, and put these five items below it:

- &Select OLE Object...
- &Paste Special...
- &Links...
- - (hyphen)
- Object

Close the Menu Designer and set the form's properties as follows:

Property	*Value*
Caption	My OLE Demo
ObjectMenuItem	Object1

Place two panels on the form and delete their captions. Set the Align property of one panel to alTop and the other panel to alBottom. (An in-place activated OLE object may take over these panels for its SpeedBar and status bar.)

Place an OLE container component on the form and set its Align property to alClient. Put these lines in an OnCreate event handler for the form:

```
ClipFmtEmbed := RegisterClipboardFormat(
  'Embedded Object');
ClipFmtLink  := RegisterClipboardFormat(
  'Link Source');
```

Page up until you see the comment { Private Declarations } and insert these lines just after it:

```
ClipFmtEmbed : Word;
ClipFmtLink  : Word;
```

Flip to the Events page in the Object Inspector and then pull down the list of
components and find Edit1. This is the top-level menu item captioned &Edit.
Put these lines in its OnClick event handler:

```
PasteSpecial1.Enabled :=
   PasteSpecialEnabled(Self,
   [OleFormat(ClipFmtEmbed,'%s','%s',TRUE),
    OleFormat(ClipFmtLink,'%s','%s',TRUE)]);
Links1.Enabled := LinksDlgEnabled(Self);
```

Replace the begin..end pair in an OnClick event handler for the Paste Special
menu item with these lines:

```
VAR
   Fmt    : Word;
   H      : Thandle;
   Pinfo  : Pointer;
begin
   IF PasteSpecialDlg(Self,
     [OleFormat(ClipFmtEmbed,'%s','%s',TRUE),
      OleFormat(ClipFmtLink,'%s','%s',TRUE)],
      0, Fmt, H, Pinfo) THEN
        OleContainer1.PInitInfo := Pinfo;
   ReleaseOleInitInfo(PInfo);
end;
```

Put this single line in the OnClick event handler for the Links menu choice:

```
LinksDlg(Self, 0);
```

Finally, create an OnClick event handler for the Select OLE Object menu item
and replace the begin..end pair with these lines:

```
VAR Pinfo : Pointer;
begin
   IF InsertOleObjectDlg(Self, 0, Pinfo) THEN
     OleContainer1.PInitInfo := Pinfo;
   ReleaseOleInitInfo(PInfo);
end;
```

Well, that was a bit of work, but not *too* bad. Yes, you're ready to run the program. First try the Select OLE Object menu choice. Figure 9-12 shows the result; you get a fancy dialog listing all the types of OLE objects registered on your system, and an invitation to create a new object or select a file. If you choose a file, you can either embed a copy of the file in your program or create a link to an existing file. And you can choose to display the object itself or just an icon in your program.

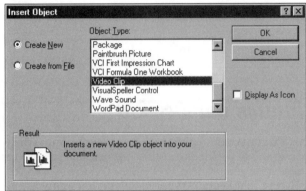

Figure 9-12:
This Insert
Object
dialog is
built into the
Delphi OLE
component.

After the object is linked or embedded in your program, double-clicking it launches the appropriate program. For example, if you link or embed a bitmap, double-clicking it launches Paint. Also, the Object menu choice under Edit is replaced by a menu specific to the type of object.

When you embed an object, your program *owns* the embedded data. Any changes you make exist only within your program. When you link an object, the link just points to an external file. All changes are stored in the external file.

The Paste Special menu choice is probably grayed, indicating that it's not available. Load a bitmap into the Windows 3.1 Paint accessory, select all or part of it, and copy to the Clipboard. Now come back to the OLE demo and you see that Paste Special is enabled. When you click it, you can either paste a link to the bitmap file or embed the copied bitmap as an object.

The Links menu choice is enabled only if you've either pasted a link to a file or linked a file using the Select OLE Object menu choice. Clicking Links displays the dialog shown in Figure 9-13, which lets you fool around with the links.

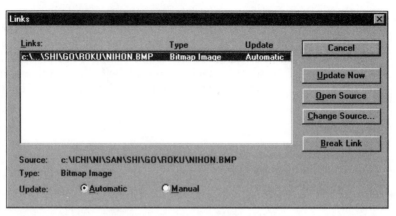

Rev-OLE-ution number 2.0

The Delphi 1.0 OLE container component is a bit rough around the edges. It's not quite as suave and debonair as most of the components you've met. Those rough edges have been smoothed off in Delphi 2.0 at the expense of backward compatibility. To use the Delphi 2.0 OLE container, you pretty much have to start fresh.

Drop a menu on a new form, and give it a &File menu with just E&xit below it. Double-click the Exit item and put this line in its OnClick handler:

```
Close;
```

Add another top-level menu item called &Edit, and set its GroupIndex to 1. Add these menu items below it:

- &Select OLE Object…
- &Paste Special…
- &Object Properties…
- &Change Icon…
- - (hyphen)
- Object

Set the form's caption to Delphi 2.0 OLE Demo, and set its ObjectMenuItem property to Object11. Put a panel on the form aligned alTop and delete its caption; add another captionless panel aligned alBottom. Place an OLE container component on the form and set its Align property to alClient.

Flip to the Events page in the Object Inspector, and select Edit1 from the pull-down list of components. Create an OnClick event handler for Edit1 using these lines:

```
PasteSpecial1.Enabled := OleContainer1.CanPaste;
ChangeIcon1.Enabled := OleContainer1.State <> osEmpty;
ObjectProperties1.Enabled := ChangeIcon1.Enabled;
```

The OnClick handlers for the four menu items below Edit are each a single line. In order, they are:

```
OleContainer1.InsertObjectDialog;

OleContainer1.PasteSpecialDialog;

OleContainer1.ObjectPropertiesDialog;

OleContainer1.ChangeIconDialog;
```

That's it! The dialog box displayed by the Select OLE Object menu choice was shown previously in Figure 9-12. When you choose Object Properties from the Edit menu, you get a dialog similar to the one shown in Figure 9-14.

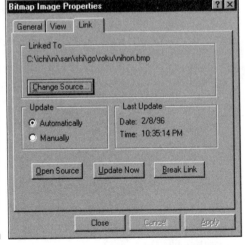

Figure 9-14: The Object Properties dialog lets you control the updating and display of an embedded OLE object.

This Object Properties dialog effectively replaces the Links dialog, but with a new twist or two. It adds the capability to convert the object to a different format (if conversion is available) or display it as an icon. Just which icon represents the object is determined by the Change Icon dialog, which is shown in Figure 9-15.

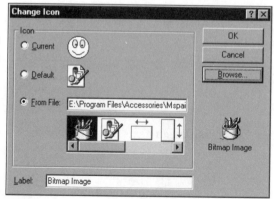

Figure 9-15:
Use the
Change Icon
dialog to
give the
embedded
object a
different
icon.

And now we return to our regularly scheduled program. The modifications in the next section apply equally to the Delphi 1.0 and Delphi 2.0 OLE examples.

Saving embedded objects to disk

The OLE container object has one more surprising capability: It can save and load its contents to disk.

Load the OLE demo program's main menu into the Menu Designer, highlight the Exit menu item, and press the Insert key four times. Fill in the new blank menu choices with &Open..., &Save, Save &As... and a lone hyphen separator. Place an Open File dialog and a Save File dialog on the form. Set the Filter property for both dialogs to a single line with the name OLE files and the mask *.OLE. Set the rest of the Open File dialog's properties like this:

Property	Value
DefaultExt	OLE
Options.ofHideReadOnly	True
Options.ofFileMustExist	True
Title	Open OLE file

Set the Save File dialog's properties like this:

Property	Value
DefaultExt	OLE
Options.ofOverwritePrompt	True

Property	*Value*
Options.ofHideReadOnly	True
Options.ofPathMustExist	True
Title	Save OLE file

Find the File1 top-level menu item in the list of components in the Object Inspector and put these lines in its OnClick event handler:

```
WITH OleContainer1 DO
  BEGIN
    Save1.Enabled := OleObjAllocated;
    SaveAs1.Enabled := Save1.Enabled;
  END;
```

If you're using Delphi 2.0, replace the third line with:

```
Save1.Enabled := State <> osEmpty;
```

Write an OnClick event handler for the Open menu item with these lines:

```
WITH OpenDialog1 DO
  IF Execute THEN
    BEGIN
      OleContainer1.LoadFromFile(Filename);
      OleContainer1.Refresh;
      SaveDialog1.Filename := Filename;
    END;
```

For the Save As menu item, use these lines as an OnClick event handler:

```
WITH SaveDialog1 DO
  IF Execute THEN
    OleContainer1.SaveToFile(Filename);
```

Put these lines in the OnClick handler for the Save menu choice:

```
IF SaveDialog1.Filename = '' THEN
  SaveAs1Click(Sender)
ELSE OleContainer1.SaveToFile(SaveDialog1.Filename);
```

And finally, go back to the OnClick handler for the Select OLE Object menu item and insert this line just before the end; line:

```
SaveDialog1.Filename := '';
```

Gee! I warned you this OLE stuff could get complicated. Run the program now and you can save your OLE objects to a file and load them again. If you transfer such a file to a different system, though, that system must have the required server present.

The OLE container objects in Delphi 1.0 and Delphi 2.0 use different file formats when they save stuff to disk. It's possible for a Delphi 2.0 program to convert files saved by a Delphi 1.0 object, but for simplicity's sake, this program won't do it.

Here's a free bonus. Server applications that are compatible with the OLE 2.0 specification have a capability called *in-place activation*. This means that when you activate the object, the server appears *within* your program. Its menu merges with your program's menu, and its SpeedBar and status bar do likewise.

Wow! OLE is certainly a lollapalooza. Too many programmers have accidentally burned out their brains trying to program OLE without Delphi. Even with Delphi's help, OLE is complicated, but manageable. Delphi 2.0 also simplifies the creation of OLE server programs and takes the pain out of OLE automation (using OLE to remote-control other programs).

In this chapter, you've seen components display almost magical capabilities — playing CDs, gathering icons, displaying the calendar, even communicating using DDE and OLE. You probably need a little time to absorb it all. Fear not; the next chapter will be gentle with you. It's all about the mundane but essential Delphi file components.

Chapter 10

File Components

*W*hen you turn off your computer, everything that's in memory goes pffft! All that's left is the information stored in files on the hard disk. When you crank up the computer again, it loads its operating system from *files* on the disk. The vast majority of programs deal with files in one way or another, whether it's to look up preferences in an INI file or to load and save scripts for the latest Hollywood extravaganza.

You've learned about Delphi's common dialog components; they're great for common file-related tasks. Unfortunately, if you need to do anything even slightly out of the ordinary, the common dialogs won't help you. They're like seamless black boxes; there's no easy way to put anything into them or take anything out of them. The Windows 95 common dialogs handle additional tasks, such as renaming files and creating directories, but adding features yourself requires wizardly programming skills. They're still black boxes — they're just *bigger* boxes.

To help you with *un*common tasks, Delphi skillfully separates the four major elements of the Windows 3.1-style file common dialogs (the file list, directory list, drive list, and filter list) and lets you use each separately, according to your own program's requirements. If the file common dialogs don't do *quite* what you want, you can just patch together the necessary file components.

Choosing File Components

The four main file components correspond to the four major elements of a file common dialog, and they reside on the System page of the Component palette. As a bonus, Delphi provides a sample directory outline for choosing any directory on your disk. Use Table 10-1 to quickly select the right component.

Table 10-1	Problems Solved by File Components
Task	*Component*
Display or process a list of files matching a file specification box. See "Flipping through the File List."	File list
Select any directory in the current drive list box. See "Directory Assistance."	Directory
Display the available disk drives and their drive types combo box. See "A Combo Box with Real Drive."	Drive
Select from predefined file specification masks combo box. See "Filter Your Files with a Combo Box."	Filter
View and navigate through the entire directory tree outline. See "More Directory Assistance."	Directory

Flipping through the File List

The instant you drop a file list box on a form, it displays a list of files in the current directory. Aieee! It's alive! The obvious way to use such a thing is to let your program's users make choices from the displayed files. Perhaps less obvious is the fact that you can also *hide* a file list box and use it as a clandestine source of information about the files on disk.

Properties

If you set the ShowGlyphs property to True, the file list immediately displays a picture (a glyph) to the left of each file name. Executable files get a picture of a miniwindow, directories show a folder, and data files display as a piece of paper.

The FileType property lets you choose which files show up in the box, based on their file attributes. ftNormal is the default — this selects files with no attributes or with the read-only or archive attributes. You can include hidden or system files, directories, or the volume label by setting the appropriate options to True. If you want to display only read-only or archive files, just say No to ftNormal files.

The Mask property and the run-time-only Directory property also determine which files you see. The Directory property naturally specifies the directory in which you're seeking files. Mask is the wildcard file specification for the files. It's *.* (all files) by default, but you can specify any one or more wildcard file specifications. Multiple file specifications are separated by semicolons, like *.FOO;*.BAR. And the Filename property at run time contains the currently selected file name. The FileEdit property associates an edit box on your form with the file list box. The edit box automatically displays the selected file name; before any file is selected, it displays the value of the Mask property.

If you set MultiSelect to True, users can choose multiple files from the file list. In most other ways, the file list box is similar to any list box. For example, to determine which files are selected when MultipleSelect is True, you peek at the Selected property. You get the list of files through the Items property.

Delphi 2.0 completes the picture with an ExtendedSelect property that controls how multiple files are selected. It's True by default, which means you can select multiple files by dragging, or by clicking while holding Shift and Ctrl. If ExtendedSelect is False, each click on a file name reverses its selection state.

Events

The most important event for a file list box is OnChange. When the selected file name changes, this event is triggered. Somewhat less useful is the OnClick event that occurs any time the user clicks on the file list, even if the chosen file name doesn't change. And you frequently hook the OnDblClick event to the same event handler used for a button that chooses the current file.

Start a new project using the fixed-size file template you created back in Chapter 2. Set the form's Font to MS Sans Serif, 8 point, bold. Place a label near the top left corner of the form, and an edit box just below it. Set the label's caption to File &Name:, and set its FocusControl property to point to the edit box.

Now place a file list box below the edit box, and set its ShowGlyphs property to True. Stretch it so it's wide enough to fit any file name, and make the edit box the same width. Under Delphi 1.0, the file list box is wide enough when a file name with the full eight-character name and three-character extension fits. The Delphi 2.0 version of this component supports long file names, so you'll have to settle for making the file list box wide enough for *most* file names. Set the file list's FileEdit property to the name of the edit box. Change the form's caption to File Dialog.

Run the program and click file names in the list. As you select a name, it appears in the file name edit box. If a Windows 95 file name is too wide for the file list box, click it and view it in the edit box. You can scoot it back and forth using the arrow keys to see the whole thing. Well, that's a start! Save this project as FILEDLG; you're going to add to it throughout this chapter.

Using the File Dialog form you just created, place a group box to the right of the file list box and set its caption to Attributes. Put seven check boxes in it with the captions Read Only, Hidden, System, Volume ID, Directory, Archive, and Normal, in that order. Set the Tag field for the seven check boxes to the numbers 0 through 6, and set the Normal one's Checked property to True. Select all seven and create a single OnClick event handler for them using these lines:

```
WITH Sender AS TCheckBox DO
  IF Checked THEN
    FileListBox1.FileType :=
        FileListBox1.FileType + [TFileAttr(Tag)]
  ELSE
    FileListBox1.FileType :=
        FileListBox1.FileType - [TFileAttr(Tag)];
```

Put this single line in an OnCreate event handler for the form:

```
FileListBox1.Directory := 'C:\';
```

When you run this program, it initially displays all the normal files in the root directory of your C: drive. Fiddle with the check boxes and the program displays directories, the volume ID, and files with special attributes. Figure 10-1 shows the read-only, hidden, and system files in the root directory of a system with DOS, Windows 3.1, and Windows 95 installed. Quite a few files are hiding in there!

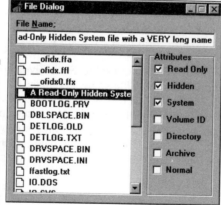

Figure 10-1: The file list box displays files whose attributes match the FileType property.

The file attribute group box was a flight of fancy; it isn't meant to be part of the final FILEDLG project. Delete it now, and the check boxes disappear as well. Flip to the Code Editor and delete the lines you entered in the OnClick event handler for the check boxes and the OnCreate handler for the form. Just delete what you typed; leave the begin..end pair alone. Now save the cleaned-up FILEDLG project.

File list boxes are good at undercover work, too. Whether they're visible or not, every time you change the Mask, Directory, or FileType properties, they immediately rebuild the list of names, and you can use that list in your programs.

Place a file list box on a new form, double-click its FileType property, and set all the types to False except ftDirectory. Place a panel on the form with the following properties:

Property	*Value*
Align	alTop
Alignment	taLeftJustify
Caption	One moment, please…
BevelInner	bvLowered

Size it so it's about the height of the form's title bar.

Now place an outline on the form and set its Align property to alClient. (It will hide the file list box.) Open the outline's Lines property and enter a single line containing c: (just *c* and a colon). Switch to the Events page and double-click the OnExpand event. Delete the begin..end pair supplied by Delphi, and substitute this code:

```
VAR
  S : String;
  N : Word;
begin
  IF Tag > 0 THEN Exit;
  WITH Sender AS TOutline, Items[Index] DO
    BEGIN
      S := FullPath;
      IF length(S) = 2 THEN S := S + '\';
      FileListBox1.Directory := S;
      FOR N := 0 TO FileListBox1.Items.Count-1 DO
        BEGIN(
```

(continued)

```
            S := FileListBox1.Items[N];
            S := Copy(S, 2, length(S)-2);
            IF S = '.' THEN Continue;
            IF S = '..' THEN Continue;
            Outline1.AddChild(Index, S);
         END;
     END;
end;
```

In the outline's OnClick method, put these lines:

```
WITH Sender AS TOutline DO
   Panel1.Caption := Items[SelectedItem].FullPath;
```

And replace the begin..end pair for the form's OnActivate event handler with these lines:

```
VAR N : Word;
begin
  Panel1.Refresh;
  WITH Outline1 DO
    BEGIN
      N := 0;
      REPEAT
        N := N + 1;
        Items[N].Expanded := True;
        Application.ProcessMessages;
      UNTIL N = ItemCount;
    END;
  Tag := 1;
  Panel1.Caption := '';
end;
```

When you run the program, it spends a few seconds building the directory outline. The OnActivate event handler steps through the outline's list of items, which initially contains just c:, and sets Expanded to True for each. This in turn causes an OnExpand event for the outline. The OnExpand event handler sets the directory for the hidden file list box to the current item in the outline. If it finds any subdirectories, it adds them as outline items under that current item. As the code steps through the outline's item list, the goal keeps receding because the list gets longer and longer. The end isn't reached until all directories have been expanded. At this point, the event handler sets the form's Tag property to 1, which is a signal to the OnExpand handler that its work is finished. Whew!

As Figure 10-2 shows, this directory outline has all the features of the outline component. Double-click the root to close the entire directory outline. Now press the asterisk key (*) to fully expand the outline, or press the plus key (+) to expand it by one level. Directories that contain subdirectories are represented as open or closed folders; directories without subdirectories show up as pieces of paper. When you click any item in the outline, its full path is displayed in the panel above. And all of this happens because of a file list box that you can't even see!

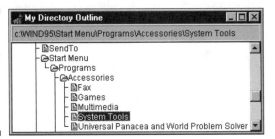

Figure 10-2:
This directory outline gets its data from a hidden file list box.

Directory Assistance

The directory list box lists the directories of the selected drive in an expandable tree form, just like the directory portion of a file common dialog. You could say it shows the current branch of the directory tree, along with a few twigs. Specifically, it shows the current directory, its parent, its parent's parent, and so on back to the root. And it shows any subdirectories of the current directory. Suppose the current directory is c:\foo\bar — the directory list box shows c:\ at the top, foo below it, and bar below foo. Any subdirectories of bar are also displayed. You can't ever see the whole tree, but you can navigate anywhere on the disk by backing up toward the root and following a different branch outward.

The DirLabel and FileList properties help integrate other components with a directory list box. The label specified in the DirLabel property displays the currently selected directory, and the file list box specified in the FileList property displays the list of files in the selected directory.

The run-time-only properties Drive and Directory are what rouse a directory list box to action. Change the Drive property and the list displays the current directory on the selected drive. And when you click a line in the list, the Directory property gets the full path for the selection. Like the file list box, the directory list box's main event is OnChange, which is called whenever the selected directory changes.

Load the FILEDLG project that you created earlier in this chapter. It has a column of components along the left: a label, an edit box, and a file list box. Make a second column to the right of the first column; the second column should contain two labels and a directory list box. Set the first label's caption to

&Directories: and set its FocusControl property to point to the directory list box. Set the directory list box's DirLabel property to Label3 (the name of the other label), and set its FileList property to FileListBox1 (the name of the file list box). If this is at all unclear, you can peek ahead at Figure 10-4, which shows the completed project.

When you run the updated FILEDLG project, you find that you can view the files in any directory that's on the current drive. The full path name of the selected directory appears in the label above the directory list box, and the file list box holds the contents of that directory. Save this enhanced file dialog project.

A Combo Box with Real Drive

You've probably guessed that the drive combo box is a drop-down combo box that's suspiciously similar to the drive list in the file common dialogs. It displays all drives available on your system with a cute little glyph signifying a floppy drive, a hard disk, a RAM drive, a CD-ROM, or a network connection.

A drive combo box already does the hard work of figuring out what drives are available on your system, as well as the drive type for each. If you need that information in a program, just use a hidden drive combo box. You can even "steal" the glyphs, as you can see later in this chapter.

The one significant property of a drive combo box is. . . you guessed it. . . Drive! At run time, this property returns the currently selected drive letter. And, of course, when the user chooses a new drive letter, the OnChange method is called. The DirList property holds the name of a directory list component. When the drive combo box's Drive property changes, the associated directory list box changes to display the directory structure of the new drive.

Load the good old FILEDLG project again. Add another label directly below the directory list box, and place a drive combo box below the label. All the components in this column should be the same width, aligned at their left edge. Set the caption of the label to Dri&ve:, and set its FocusControl to point to the drive combo box. Set the drive combo box's DirList property to the name of the directory list.

That's one more step toward a complete homemade file dialog. Run the program, pull down the drive list, and note the different icons next to the drive letters. When you choose a new drive, it starts a Rube Goldbergesque chain of events. The drive combo box sets the directory list box's drive property to the new drive letter. This causes the directory list box to update the directory label and the file list box's directory. The file list box in turn updates itself to show the files in the new directory. It all happens so fast you hardly notice. Once again, save the FILEDLG project.

About now, you might be asking why you're bothering to build a replica of the file common dialogs. Isn't it pointless? Well, the handmade version is more open to customization. For example, you can make a version that omits the file list box and its associated label and edit box, thus yielding a directory selection dialog.

Place a panel on a new fixed-size form and set its properties as follows:

Property	*Value*
Align	alTop
Alignment	taLeftJustify
BevelInner	bvLowered
Caption	(none)
Height	25

Drop a label on the panel, delete its caption, and set its Align property to alClient so that it fills the panel.

Below the panel, place two labels captioned &Directory: and Dri&ve:, and below them put a directory list box and a drive combo box, as shown in Figure 10-3. Set the FocusControl property of each label to the file component below it. Set the directory list box's DirLabel property to the name of the label on the panel, and set the drive combo box's DirList property to the name of the directory list. Place two bitmap buttons in the bottom right corner of the form with their Kind properties set to bkOK and bkCancel.

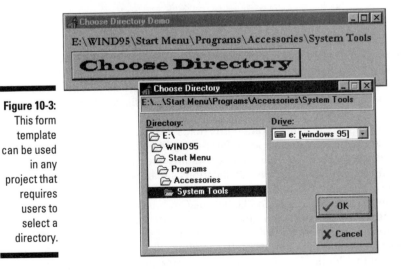

Figure 10-3:
This form template can be used in any project that requires users to select a directory.

Change the form's caption to Choose Directory and its Name property to ChooseDirForm. Right-click the form. If you're using Delphi 1.0, choose Save As Template... from the pop-up menu. Enter CHOOSDIR for the file name and Choose Directory Form for the title. Fill in any description you like and click OK. If you're using Delphi 2.0, choose Add To Repository... from the menu that pops up when you right-click the form. Enter Choose Directory Form for the title, fill in a description, and set the Page to Forms. Enter your own name as the Author and then click OK.

You've created a directory-selection dialog that you can use in any program. It should look something like Figure 10-3, although, of course, you can redecorate it to suit your own fashion sense.

Start a new project and choose New Form from the File menu in Delphi 1.0; under Delphi 2.0, choose New from the File menu and click the Forms tab. In either case, select the Choose Directory form template you just created. Place a label and a button on the main form. Delete the label's caption and then set the button's caption to Choose Directory. Put these lines in the button's OnClick event handler:

```
IF ChooseDirForm.ShowModal = mrOK THEN
   Label1.Caption :=
            ChooseDirForm.DirectoryListBox1.Directory;
```

Add Unit2 to the uses clause of the main form's unit.

Anytime you want to use a directory-selection dialog, all you have to do is add this template to your project and write a few lines of code.

Filter Your Files with a Combo Box

Your growing file dialog is coming along quite nicely, but it still lacks discrimination. You can choose any directory you want, but the file dialog insists on displaying all the files in that directory. By adding a filter combo box, you can give it the capability to choose files matching a set of file specifications.

The Filter property of a filter combo box holds a series of named file masks. Double-clicking it activates a special filter-entry dialog, with one column for the name and one for the mask. Each mask contains one or more wildcard file specifications, with multiple file specifications separated by semicolons. At run time, the Mask property holds the mask portion of the selected filter. I can hear you saying to yourself "Yeah, and I'll bet the OnChange event occurs when the user chooses a different filter, right?" It does get kind of predictable. . . . And of course the FileList property holds the name of a file list box whose Mask property is updated to match the selected filter. Oh, and one more thing. Delphi 1.0 omitted the PopupMenu property; Delphi 2.0 remedies this oversight.

Place a label directly below the file list box in the FILEDLG project and a filter combo box below the label. Set the label's caption to List files of &Type: and its FocusControl to the filter combo box. Double-click the filter combo box's Filter property — it already contains a filter for All files. Add a filter named Text files with the mask *.TXT. Set the filter combo box's FileList property to the name of the file list.

Add three bitmap buttons in a column along the right edge of the form with their Kind properties set to bkOK, bkCancel, and bkHelp. Enter these lines as the OK button's OnClick event handler:

```
IF ((Pos('*', Edit1.Text) > 0) OR
    (Pos('?', Edit1.Text) > 0)) THEN
  BEGIN
    FileListBox1.Mask := Edit1.Text;
    ModalResult := mrNone;
  END
ELSE
  BEGIN
    Filename := DirectoryListBox1.Directory;
    IF Length(FileName) > 3 THEN
      Filename := Filename + '\';
    Filename := Filename + Edit1.Text;
    ModalResult := mrOk;
  END;
```

Whoops! This code seems to be assigning a value to the Filename property, but your file dialog form doesn't *have* a Filename property. You can correct that. Page up through the unit in the editor until you see the comment { Public declarations }. Just below that line, insert:

```
Filename : String;
```

Click the file list box, flip to the Events page, and pull down the event list next to OnDblClick. Select the event handler you just wrote for the OK button. Change the form's Name property to MyFilDlg, and then right-click the form and save it as a template in Delphi 2.0 or add it to the repository in Delphi 2.0.

When you save a form in this way, it's automatically available anytime you choose New Form from the File menu in Delphi 1.0, or choose New from the File menu and click the Forms tab in Delphi 2.0.

When you select a filter, its mask becomes the mask for the file list box, and the mask gets copied into the file name edit box. Just what happens when you click OK depends on whether the file name edit box contains any wildcards. If the file edit box does contain wildcards, its contents become the new mask for the file edit box. If the file edit box doesn't contain wildcards, the dialog closes and returns mrOK for its modal result. When you double-click a file name, the first click selects the file name and copies it into the edit box, and the second click has the same effect as clicking the OK button.

Congratulations! You've successfully knocked off the look and feel of the Windows 3.1 file common dialogs! Figure 10-4 shows the resplendent result.

Figure 10-4:
This homemade equivalent to the file common dialogs is 100% customizable.

So how do you use this dialog in a program? I thought you'd never ask!

Place a label and a button on a new form. Delete the label's caption and set the button's caption to Choose File. Choose New Form from the File menu in Delphi 1.0, or choose New from the File menu and click the Forms tab in Delphi 2.0. Select the file dialog template you just created. Now back in the main form, add these lines to the button's OnClick event handler:

```
IF MyFilDlg.ShowModal = mrOK THEN
  Label1.Caption := MyFilDlg.Filename;
```

Press Ctrl+Home to go to the top of the unit and add Unit2 to the uses clause.

Incorporating the handmade file dialog into a program is as easy as that. And because you built the file dialog yourself, you can modify or enhance it in any way that suits you.

More Directory Assistance

The directory outline program you built at the beginning of this chapter was kind of fun, and it demonstrated the power of a hidden file list box. However, I have a confession to make — it wasn't entirely necessary. If you want a directory outline in your program, simply flip to the Samples page and use a directory outline component! Like the file list box, this component is a live wire. The minute you drop one on your form, you're viewing a directory outline for the current drive.

There are a few differences between the handmade outline and the directory outline component. The handmade one uses different glyphs to distinguish directories that can be expanded, can be collapsed, or can't be expanded. The handmade one also shows directories in sorted order, whereas the directory outline component doesn't. And the handmade outline correctly handles full expansion when you highlight the root and press asterisk. However, the handmade outline takes substantially longer than the directory outline component to initialize itself.

Properties and events

For the most part, the Delphi 1.0 directory outline's properties are a subset of the properties of its ancestor, the plain old outline. A directory outline always displays tree lines and glyphs, and you can't change the glyphs. There's just one added property, TextCase, which controls whether the directory names are displayed as-is or forced into upper- or lowercase. (If you think as-is and uppercase are the same, you're living in the past! In Windows NT and Windows 95, file names can include lowercase letters, so as-is doesn't necessarily mean uppercase!)

The directory outline in Delphi 2.0 still has a subset of the outline component's properties, but following Murphy's Law #42, it's a *different* subset. The Lines, OutlineStyle, PicturePlus, and PictureMinus properties disappear, and over a dozen other properties are present that weren't in the Delphi 1.0 directory outline. The new directory outline is a cleaner, spiffier component, but the changes could break code that relies on the old set of properties. The following examples stick to properties present in both versions.

The run-time-only Drive property tells the component which drive to display in outline form, and the Directory property holds the currently selected directory.

A directory outline's most important event is OnChange. This event occurs when the user changes directories; your programs normally use it to update a file list box. Yes, you have to write code to perform that update; there's no equivalent to the directory list box's FileList property.

At the end of the "Filter Your Files with a Combo Box" section, you created a simple project to demonstrate the use of the file selection dialog. If it's not still loaded in Delphi, take a minute to reconstruct it. In the file dialog, *delete* the directory list box and add a directory outline in its place. Select Replace from the editor's Search menu and replace all occurrences of DirectoryListBox1 with DirectoryOutline1. Create an OnChange event handler for the drive combo box; it should contain this line:

```
DirectoryOutline1.Drive := DriveComboBox1.Drive;
```

Put these lines in an OnChange event handler for the directory outline:

```
FileListBox1.Directory := DirectoryOutline1.Directory;
Label3.Caption := DirectoryOutline1.Directory;
```

The change you made to the file dialog in this program affects *only* this program. It doesn't change the template.

Didn't I say this handmade file dialog was customizable? With one stroke, you replaced its standard directory list with a fully expandable directory outline. Figure 10-5 shows how it looks now (compare it with the file dialog in Figure 10-4). The directory list box shows a single branch of the directory tree (the current directory, all of its ancestors, and one level of its subdirectories). The directory outline has the potential to show every little twig of the entire directory tree.

Figure 10-5:
This customized file dialog uses a directory outline instead of a directory list box.

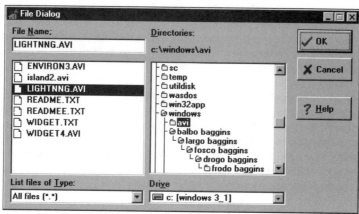

Steal This Bitmap!

The file common dialogs provide one way of looking at files on disk. They're oriented toward choosing one file or a few files in a directory. The same components can be assembled differently to yield a form that's more like a File Manager directory window.

Place a drive combo box on a new form and tuck it into the top left corner. Add a draw grid with properties set like this:

Property	*Value*
Align	alTop
ColCount	1
Color	clBtnFace
FixedRows	0
FixedCols	0
GridLineWidth	0
Height	26
Options.goHorzLine	False
Options.goVertLine	False
Options.goRangeSelect	False
RowCount	1

The draw grid hides the drive combo box; that's intentional. In the form's OnCreate event handler, insert these three lines:

```
DrawGrid1.ColCount :=
  DriveComboBox1.Items.Count;
DrawGrid1.Col := DriveComboBox1.ItemIndex;
```

Now create an OnDrawCell event handler for the draw grid, replacing the begin..end pair supplied by Delphi with these lines:

```
VAR Temp: TBitmap;
begin
  WITH DriveComboBox1, DrawGrid1.Canvas DO
    BEGIN
      IF (gdSelected IN State) THEN
        BEGIN
          Brush.Color := clWhite;
          FillRect(Rect);
        END
      ELSE Brush.Color := DrawGrid1.Color;
      InflateRect(Rect,-8,-3);
      OffsetRect(Rect,-6,0);
      Temp := TBitmap(Items.Objects[Col]);
      BrushCopy(Rect, Temp,
             Bounds(0,0,Temp.Width,Temp.Height),
         Temp.TransparentColor);
      Font := Self.Font;
      TextOut(Rect.Right+1, Rect.Top, Items[Col][1]);
    END;
end;
```

Add an OnResize event handler for the form:

```
WITH DrawGrid1 DO
  IF ClientWidth < ColCount * DefaultColWidth THEN
    Height := 47
  ELSE Height := 26;
```

Give the program a whirl, to make sure it works so far. You should see a row of icons across the top of the form representing the disk drives on your system. The images are hot property, stolen from the hidden drive combo box! When you make the form too narrow to hold all the drives, a scroll bar automatically appears across the bottom of the row of drive icons.

Now place a header component on the form, align it to alTop, and give it two sections called Directories and Files. Use the right mouse button to drag the header's dividing line so the sections are equal in width.

Drop a panel on the form with its properties set like this:

Property	Value
Align	alBottom
Alignment	taLeftJustify
BevelInner	bvLowered
Caption	(none)
Height	26

Place a directory outline on the form, align it on the left, and size it so its right edge is just under the dividing line in the header. Place a file list box and set its Align property to alClient. All the gears and gadgets are in place; you just need to connect them by attaching the pulleys and levers.

Put these lines in an OnSized event handler for the header:

```
DirectoryOutline1.Width :=
   Header1.SectionWidth[0];
```

Create an OnClick event handler for the draw grid using these lines:

```
WITH DrawGrid1 DO
   DirectoryOutline1.Drive :=
     DriveComboBox1.Items[Col][1];
```

In an OnChange event handler for the directory outline, enter these lines:

```
Caption := DirectoryOutline1.Directory;
FileListBox1.Directory :=
   DirectoryOutline1.Directory;
```

And finally, create an OnChange event handler for the file list box using this line:

```
Panel1.Caption := FileListBox1.Filename;
```

Figure 10-6 shows the completely different file-selection form displayed by this project. It's similar to one of File Manager's directory windows; in fact, it could serve as the jumping-off point to _build_ a directory window in a File Manager look-alike.

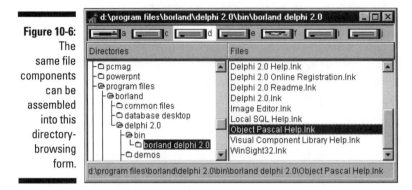

Figure 10-6:
The
same file
components
can be
assembled
into this
directory-
browsing
form.

Program files, text files, spreadsheet files . . . all kinds of files are on your system. These file components help you perform high-level, generalized actions such as locating and displaying files. When Delphi gets down to business, though, it deals with one very special variety of files — *database* files. That's what the next chapter is all about.

Chapter 11

Database Components

● ●

In This Chapter

▶ Learning the jargon behind database programming

▶ Building data-entry forms with help from Delphi

▶ Defining calculated fields whose values are supplied by your program at run time

▶ Building a universal database program

▶ Connecting data-aware components for instant access to database tables

▶ Experimenting with SQL (Structured Query Language)

▶ Using Delphi 2.0's new database features

▶ Creating a form template for selecting database tables

● ●

*W*hat's a computer for? What's its excuse for existence? You can make a pretty good argument that *computer* is the wrong name for these gadgets. Sure, they can compute, but the main thing they do is store and retrieve data. Aunt Tillie's phone number, Arnold Schwarzenegger's shoe size, or every parking ticket that's ever blessed your windshield — just about any piece of information you can think of is stored in a database somewhere. Modern databases can even include images, sounds, and video!

Because data management is so important, Delphi devotes two whole pages in the Component palette to it. The Data Access page holds components for connecting to databases and peeking at their innards. The Data Controls page is loaded with data-aware components that have been carefully trained to display and edit database data. The Delphi 2.0 Database Explorer makes finding and understanding your available databases easier than ever. And the new data module, a kind of nonvisual form for storing nonvisual database components, raises data worship to new heights.

Delphi relies on the near-omnipotent Borland Database Engine (BDE) to implement its database support. With the BDE (which comes with Delphi) you can just as easily connect to a remote Oracle database on a network server as to a local Paradox table on your hard disk. For simplicity, we use local databases in the examples in this chapter. Delphi insulates you from the painful details of database access so thoroughly that you can upsize a local database project to client/server with little effort beyond changing a few properties.

Walk the Walk, Talk the Talk

Quite a few ordinary English words take on special meanings in the techno-speak dialect used by database programmers. It's hopeless to try to avoid these words; all you can do is try to learn the language. Here's a basic dictionary:

- *Field* — The smallest element of data in a database. A field has a name and a type; for example, the type for a field named Company Name will probably be text. Some data types are text, numeric, currency, date, and time.

- *Record* — A collection of fields that contain related information. For example, a customer record might contain name and address information along with a unique customer ID number.

- *Table* — A collection of records that all have the same field structure. When a table is displayed in grid form, each row is one record and each column is one field.

- *Database* — A collection of related tables, usually identified by the directory that contains the tables or by an *alias* that names the database.

- *Index* — Just as the index to this book helps you find the topic you want, an index to a database helps locate records that have a particular field value.

- *Primary Index* — Required by many database functions, the primary index controls the order in which the records of the database are displayed. A primary index field must be unique; that is, no two records can have the same value in this field.

- *Secondary Index* — A more relaxed type of index that can be based on a combination of fields and need not be unique. Secondary indexes are used in linking tables, a topic I cover in this chapter.

- *Query* — A statement in SQL (Structured Query Language) that selects records and fields from one or more tables. You use a query to get information *from* the database, for example, a list of all customers with unpaid bills.

Different database programs store database tables and fields in different ways, but when you access the data with Delphi, you don't have to worry about that.

The concept of alias deserves special mention. Desperadoes in the old West used aliases to hide from the law. The BDE's aliases have a more benign purpose: After you use the Database Engine Configuration program (found in the Delphi group in the Windows 3.x Program Manager or in the Delphi menu under the Windows 95 Start menu) to establish an alias for a particular directory on disk, you can refer to tables in that directory through the alias. If you move the files, or install them on a different machine, or move them to a shared directory on a network server, you don't have to make any changes in your program. Just whip out the configuration program and change the directory for that alias!

In the Delphi group in Program Manager or the Delphi menu under the Start menu, find the Database Engine Configuration item and launch it. Select the Aliases page of the resulting dialog, and press the New Alias button. Fill in the name Demos, and leave the type set to Standard. In the Parameters panel, set the PATH for this alias to the directory that contains the Delphi database example files (C:\DELPHI\DEMOS\DATABASE, by default). If you have any other dBASE or Paradox databases on your system, give them aliases as well. Select Save from the File menu and then close the configuration editor. I'll use this Demos alias in examples throughout this chapter.

Nurture Your Relationships

We've defined a database as consisting of one or more tables. The simplest kind of database is just a single table filled with any number of identically laid-out records. This humdrum table is called a flat-file database. Let's look at how this kind of database evolves into something more complicated.

Suppose you want to devise a database to track your Christmas card list. You want to store the name and address of everyone you send cards to, and you also want to keep track of the cards you receive, noting when each arrived (before the Big Day or after), whether it included a handwritten note, and whether it included an Awful Xeroxed Christmas Letter. To start, you simply dump all of these data elements into one big table, adding a new record for each correspondent each year.

However, there's trouble right here in Delphi City, with a capital R — and that stands for Redundancy. If you've been exchanging Christmas cards with Bill Gates for ten years, he'll appear in ten different records in your database. At best, you're storing his name and address nine times more than you need to. At worst, you may have an inconsistent variety of addresses and names. Bill or William? WA or Wash.? Old address or new?

Here is the official motto of database designers everywhere:

Never Store Anything Twice

So the Christmas card database *should* store each name and address just once. In the simple-minded, one-table database, the name and address information is repeated with the specific data about each year's card exchange. A better solution is to store the name and address information in one table and the yearly card data in another. The two tables will be linked in such a way that *one* entry in the names table can be connected to *many* entries in the card data table. When a friend moves, you have to update the address only once. And if you get the urge to send a special Christmas message to anyone who blessed you with a Xeroxed Christmas Letter last year, you can easily find out who's naughty and who's nice.

This kind of *one-to-many relationship* is extremely important in database design. Delphi's database components devote special properties and methods to handling these relationships. Also, as you'll soon see, Delphi automates the process of creating database programs that link tables in this way.

Get Help from the Expert

Before going any further, let's consult the world's expert on Delphi database programming — Delphi itself!

Start with an empty project. On the Delplhi 1.0 Help menu or the Delphi 2.0 Database menu, select the Database Form Expert... item. Check the option to create a simple form and go on to the next page. Pull down the combo box labeled Drive or Alias name: and select the Demos alias. Or if you prefer, select another alias or navigate to a directory on your disk that contains database files. Highlight any table in the selected database and click Next.

The next page lets you choose and order fields from the database. Select them one at a time by double-clicking in the order you want or by highlighting them and pressing the arrow button. Or if you prefer, move them all to the right-hand list box and order them using the up and down arrows. In the next page, choose the Horizontal form type and press Next. When you press Create on the final page, Delphi creates a form for viewing or editing the selected database.

Run this program and you see a form similar to Figure 11-1, which shows an instant database form for the BIOLIFE database example that comes with Delphi. The database navigator component, the one that looks like a cassette player's buttons, lets you step through the records forward or backward or flip to the first or last record in the database. You can even edit the database fields (but don't make any drastic changes, please). Yes, Delphi did all that for you.

Figure 11-1:
This database editing form was created by Delphi's Database Form Expert.

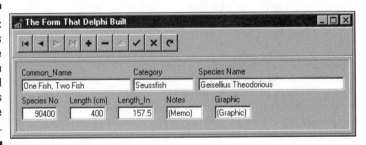

Start a new project, discarding the database application you just created. (Hey, you can build it again any time!) Again open the Database Form Expert; but this time, choose Create a master/detail form. On the next page, choose the Demos alias and select CUSTOMER.DB for the master table. Select any or all of the fields and, on the next page, choose Horizontal placement. For your detail table, choose ORDERS.DB, and again select any or all of the fields. Be very sure to choose grid-style placement for the detail data.

Now choose the field that will link the two tables. Pull down the combo box labeled Available Indexes and select ByCustNo or CustNo (this is a secondary index on the customer number in the ORDERS table). Select CustNo in each column, press the Add button, go on to the next page, and generate the form. If you're running Delphi 2.0, check the Form and Data Module radio button before pressing OK.

Because the orders table may well have many orders for a single customer number, it can't have a *primary* index on CustNo. A primary index must be unique; you can't have two records with the same primary index.

As Figure 11-2 shows, this is a much fancier data entry form than the one in Figure 11-1. As you navigate through the customer records, the grid at the bottom changes to list all orders for that customer. And you still haven't written a single line of code!

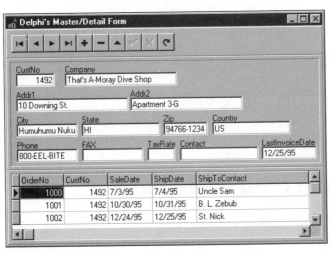

Figure 11-2:
You can create a master/ detail form like this one just by answering questions posed by Delphi's Database Form Expert.

If you're using Delphi 2.0, the Database Form Expert also creates a data module for your project. The first thing you notice is that all the nonvisual database components reside in the data module (see Figure 11-3) rather than in the main form in the Form Designer. Although tidiness may be next to godliness, the data module's *real* purpose is to add flexibility to database programming.

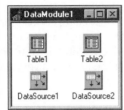

If multiple forms in the program must access the same tables, they can all refer to the table and data source components stored in the data module. To give a new form access to an existing data module's database components, you just choose Use Unit… from the File menu and select the unit containing the data module. If two forms access the same data with two different table components, unpleasant wrangling over who owns the data can result. The data module sidesteps these synchronization problems.

Just about any time you're developing a database project, it makes sense to use the Database Form Expert. You get a head start by using the form it generates as the starting point for your own efforts, and in Delphi 2.0, the Database Form Expert automatically creates a handy data module. The rest of this chapter delves deeper into Delphi's built-in database components.

DataBasics

Don't try to swallow everything about Delphi's database support at once. Just take a nibble, to start. Meet a few carefully selected components: table, data source, data-aware grid, and data navigator. You can build fully functional database applications using just these four components.

Lay your cards on the table

Different database programs store their information differently, but it all boils down to rows and columns in the end. Each column represents a field — information such as name, birth date, salary, or hat size. Each row represents one record of data. A set of columns and rows is called a table, and Delphi's table component is your program's link to a particular table of data.

In a table component, the DatabaseName property specifies the database that holds this table; it's either an alias or the name of a directory containing table files. TableName is the holographically derivative cornfluster . . . naw, just kidding, it's what you thought — the name of the table. Setting the Active property to True opens the table, even at design time. You won't believe how convenient it is to have live data available when you're designing a form or writing code! If your table has a primary key, the records show up in order sorted by that key. To use a secondary key instead, you specify it in the IndexName property. Delphi 2.0 enhances the table component with new features, the most significant of which are cached updates and filters.

Cached updates keep your program from constantly niggling the network for a little data here, a little update there. By storing changes locally and then blasting them back through the network all at once, the cached update feature can help your program be a good network citizen. There *is* a price — your program has to deal with the possibility that some other program may fiddle with the same records. If "transaction control" doesn't mean anything to you, leave CachedUpdates set to False. *Filters* let you temporarily put blinders on a table or query so that it sees only a subset of its data. When you take the blinders off, the whole data set is still available. If the Filtered property is True, the OnFilterRecord event handler that you supply is called for every record to determine whether or not that record will be accepted. This can be quicker than constructing a new query.

Place a table component on a new form and set its DatabaseName property to Demos or to any database on your system. (When you click the down arrow next to DatabaseName in the Object Inspector, you get a list of aliases.) Now click the TableName property, press the down arrow next to it, and make a choice from the list of tables in the selected database.

Set the Active property to True and try to change the DatabaseName or TableName; Delphi informs you in no uncertain terms that you can't change these properties when the table is open. Set Active to False and change either DatabaseName or TableName so that it's no longer valid. When you try to set Active to True again, Delphi won't let you; you can activate the table only when it has a valid DatabaseName and TableName.

Several of the table component's properties exist solely to set up two tables in a master/detail relationship. As you've seen, the Database Form Expert plugs values into these fields and voilà! A master/detail form! In the detail table, MasterSource is the name of the data source for the master table (hold on; I talk about data sources in just a minute), and MasterFields contains the name of the field or fields on which the two tables are linked. The linking field need not be the primary sorting key for the table, so the IndexName field holds the name of the index to be used.

If your table is hanging around a dark corner of some network server, someone else may want to access it at the same time you do. That's no problem; Delphi can share politely. If you set the Exclusive property to True, however, your program will hog the table for itself. Nobody else will be able to access the data while you're using it, and your program will run much faster. If you've chosen exclusive access and someone else is already using the data, you won't be able to open the table at all. If all you want to do is look at the data without making any changes, you can set ReadOnly to True.

Flip to the Events page in the Object Inspector, and you see a dizzying array of database events. The good news is, you can write complete and functional data-management programs that don't use these events at all! For now, forget 'em.

Get your data from the source

A table is a genteel component, much too sophisticated to hobnob with the riff-raff components that edit and display data. The data source component acts as a go-between in the exchange of data between a table and a data-aware component. Its DataSet property points to the table from which the fount of data flows. If AutoEdit is True, the data flows both ways. That is, changing data in a component connected to this data source automatically changes the data in the table. A data source receives notification events when data in a table or component changes and when its own state changes. For now, your programs can rely on the built-in handling for these events.

Instant view with a data grid

Displaying table data in a grid-style view is dead simple. Drop a data-aware grid on the form, set its DataSource property to a data source connected to the table, and you're ready to go. If you made the table active at design time, you see live data in the grid immediately. The data grid shares many properties with its cousins string grid and draw grid, so I just talk about properties special to a data grid.

The Options property explodes into a mass of True and False subproperties. dgTitles controls whether the field names appear as column titles, and dgIndicator controls whether the wedge-shaped current-row indicator appears at the left of the grid. You can press Ctrl+Del to delete the current row; if dgConfirmDelete is True, the grid asks for confirmation first. The remaining options should be familiar from your experience with the string grid in Chapter 9.

You can set the font for the titles separately using the TitleFont property. If the grid contains live data, you can drag column headings to reorder the columns or drag the lines between column headings to resize columns.

By default, a data-aware grid displays fields in the order they appear in the table, with the field names as column titles. However, you don't have to settle for the default. Double-click the table and the Dataset Designer dialog appears; it's shown in Figure 11-4. Using this dialog, you can control which fields are displayed and how.

Keep a live data grid hooked up to the table while you're using the Dataset Designer so that you can see the result of changes as you make them.

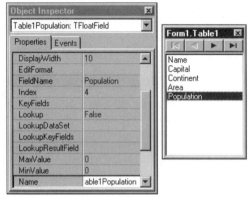

Figure 11-4:
The Dataset
Designer
lets you
individually
set
properties
for the fields
of a table.

Place a table, a data source, and a data grid component on a new form, and hook them up in series: grid to data source, data source to table. Set the table's database name to the Demos alias and choose the COUNTRY.DB table. Set the table's Active property to True. Set the grid's Align property to alClient. Now double-click the table to enter the Dataset Designer.

In Delphi 1.0, click the Add button; in Delphi 2.0, right-click the Dataset Designer and select Add fields from the pop-up menu. Highlight a few fields, and then click OK. Only the fields you added appear in the grid. You can drag fields up and down the list to change their order. Now add all the remaining fields.

Note that as you click fields in the list, the Object Inspector displays properties specific to each field. You can set the column heading for a field by filling in the DisplayLabel property, or you can set it to left, right, or center Alignment. Each field can be independently set to ReadOnly, or you can set Visible to False to hide the field (that is, to prevent it from showing in a grid). The exact set of properties present depends on the field type. For example, floating-point number fields have a True and False property to say whether they represent Currency. String fields have an EditMask property identical to that of a masked edit box.

Using the same form, return to the Dataset Designer, select the Population field, and set the Visible property to False. If you're using Delphi 1.0, click the Define... button; in Delphi 2.0, right-click the Dataset Designer and select New field from the menu. Under either version, enter a field named ShortPop. Select FloatField from the Field type list and check the Calculated check box. Click OK. Back in the Dataset Designer, arrange the fields so that the first three are Name, Capital, and ShortPop. Select ShortPop and set its DisplayLabel property to `Pop. (millions)` and its DisplayFormat to 0.0. Select the Area field and set its DisplayFormat property to

```
###,###,### "sq.mi."
```

Close the Dataset Designer. Create an OnCalcFields event handler for the table itself containing these lines:

```
Table1ShortPop.AsFloat :=
  Table1Population.AsFloat / 1000000;
```

Run the program and you see the names and capitals of various nations in the Americas, along with their populations in millions, as shown in Figure 11-5. Because of the special display format, the Area column shows, for example, 1,967,180 sq. mi. rather than the hard-to-read 1967180. You can change the capital of the U.S. from Washington to Washingtoon (Truth in Advertising requires this change!). Because the rounded-off population figure is a calculated field, it's not subject to change.

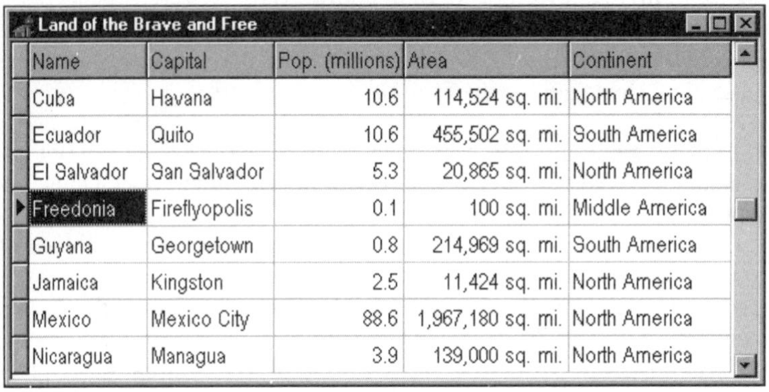

Figure 11-5:
This data grid's population column is a calculated field, and the area column was enhanced with a special display format.

Name	Capital	Pop. (millions)	Area	Continent
Cuba	Havana	10.6	114,524 sq. mi.	North America
Ecuador	Quito	10.6	455,502 sq. mi.	South America
El Salvador	San Salvador	5.3	20,865 sq. mi.	North America
Freedonia	Fireflyopolis	0.1	100 sq. mi.	Middle America
Guyana	Georgetown	0.8	214,969 sq. mi.	South America
Jamaica	Kingston	2.5	11,424 sq. mi.	North America
Mexico	Mexico City	88.6	1,967,180 sq. mi.	North America
Nicaragua	Managua	3.9	139,000 sq. mi.	North America

Land of the Brave and Free

Control columns for gorgeous grids

The data-aware grid in Delphi 2.0 has a nifty new property called Columns that gives you a huge amount of control over the display, along with some powerful aids to data entry. Columns is a megaproperty that has its own personal Columns Editor, as shown in Figure 11-6. Some of its capabilities overlap those of the Dataset Designer, but the Dataset Designer affects *all* components connected to the table.

The best way to get a handle on the Columns Editor is to use it. Limber up your fingers, because you're going to set a *lot* of properties!

Figure 11-6:
The
Columns
Editor sets
the font and
color of
each
column and
title
individually,
as well as
allowing
specialized
data entry
modes.

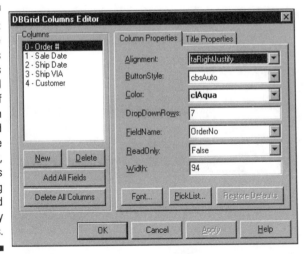

Figure 11-6: The Columns Editor sets the font and color of each column and title individually, as well as allowing specialized data entry modes.

Start a new application, and then choose New Data Module from the File menu. Place two tables in the data module, connecting Table1 to the ORDERS example table and Table2 to the CUSTOMER example table. Set Active to True for both, and connect a data source to each. Double-click Table1 to open the Dataset Designer, right-click, and choose Add fields from the menu. Add OrderNo, CustNo, SaleDate, ShipDate, and ShipVia. Now choose New field from the pop-up menu. Enter Customer for the field name and String for the type, and then click the Lookup radio button. Choose Table2 in the Dataset combo box and CustNo in the Key Fields and Lookup Keys combo boxes. Now choose Company in the Result Field combo box and press OK.

Just what did you *do* in the New Field dialog? You told Delphi to create a field called Customer, associated with Table1. The value of this field is obtained by a lookup into Table2. Delphi finds a record in Table2 whose CustNo matches the CustNo field in Table1. Then it returns the Company field from Table2. Why did you do that? Patience, patience — all shall be revealed!

Switch to the main form and choose Use unit... from the File menu to make the main form use the data module. Drop a data-aware grid on the form, set its Align property to alClient, and connect it to DataModule1.DataSource1. Take a moment to stop and marvel at the fact that the data source in a different unit appears in the pull-down list for the DataSource property.

Double-click the grid's Columns property to open the Columns Editor. Press the Add All Fields button, select CustNo, and then press the Delete button. Select SaleDate and set the ButtonStyle to cbsEllipsis; do the same for ShipDate. Select ShipVia, press the Pick List buttton, and enter the names of as many shipping companies as you can think of. Now go wild setting the color and font of each column and its title. The result should look vaguely similar to Figure 11-7.

Figure 11-7:
Four of the
five fields in
this grid
have special
powers
granted to
them by the
Columns
Editor.

Order #	Sale Date	Ship Date	Ship VIA	Customer
1003	4/12/88	2/6/96	PonyEx	Rölf Rülf Rålf
1004	4/17/88	4/18/88	PonyEx	Unisco
1005	4/20/88	2/6/96	UPS	Sight Diver
1006	11/6/94	2/6/96	Emery	Cayman Divers World Un
1007	5/1/88	5/2/88	US Mail	Rölf Rülf Rålf
1008	5/3/88	5/4/88	US Mail	Tom Sawyer Diving Cent
1009	5/11/88	5/12/88	US Mail	Blue Jack Aqua Center
				VIP Divers Club

Columns Demo

Just one more thing, and then you can play with the program! Create an
OnEditButtonClick event handler for the grid containing these lines:

```
DBGrid1.DataSource.DataSet.Edit;
DBGrid1.SelectedField.AsDateTime := Date;
```

Setting the ButtonStyle to bsEllipsis for the two date columns causes an ellipsis
button to appear in the cell during editing — pressing the button invokes this
event handler.

Because the Customer field is defined as a lookup field, it sports a pull-down list
displaying all the companies in the CUSTOMER table. Make a choice from the
list and the nonvisible CustNo field is updated automatically. The ShipVia field
has a more mundane pull-down list that simply displays the list of shipping
companies you entered in the Columns Editor. And when you press the ellipsis
button in either of the date columns, today's date is inserted automatically.
That's a lot of program for two lines of code!

If this section makes *no* sense to you, if you can't find the Columns Editor, if
Delphi won't create a data module on demand, there's probably a simple
explanation. You're using Delphi 1.0! The Columns editor and data module are
found only in Delphi 2.0.

The great navigator

You've already seen a database navigator component in the forms produced by
the Database Form Expert. This component is a collection of buttons that
resembles the Media Player (introduced in Chapter 9), but its buttons are
shortcuts for navigating through the database.

The database navigator's VisibleButtons property explodes into ten subproperties that determine which of ten buttons will appear. The most important buttons are those controlled by the properties nbFirst, nbLast, nbPrior, and nbNext. As you've surely discovered by fooling with them, these properties allow you to move to the beginning or end of the database and to the previous or next record.

If nbInsert and nbDelete are True, the navigator includes Insert and Delete buttons, symbolized by plus and minus signs. Clicking Insert adds a new blank row at the cursor; clicking Delete deletes the current row. If the ConfirmDelete property is True, the program asks for confirmation before deleting a row. The Edit button, the one with an up-pointing triangle, flips the associated table into edit mode. It's only needed when the data source's AutoEdit property is False.

Any changes you make to the data in a row are copied to the table as soon as you leave the row. The Post and Cancel buttons (checkmark and X, respectively) give finer control over this process. Clicking Post accepts changes immediately, without leaving the row, and clicking Cancel discards changes. Finally, the Refresh button, with a curved arrow on it, refreshes the table's data from disk. This is only necessary when the data may have been changed by another user (or another program on the same machine).

Closing the table does *not* automatically post a modified record. To be safe, post your programs before closing.

The skinny indicator column at the left edge of the grid does more than just point an arrow at the current row. If the row is new and hasn't been posted yet, the arrow changes to an asterisk. If the row has been changed and the changes haven't been posted, the arrow changes to an I-beam shape.

The average user can't decipher the hieroglyphics on the navigator's buttons. Set the ShowHint property to True to enable flyover help for them. If you don't like Delphi's default hint strings, you can fill in ten hints of your own in the Hints property. These hints correspond to the ten buttons, in order, even if not all of the buttons are visible in your particular program.

The most important navigator property is DataSource. Click the down arrow next to DataSource and you get a list of available data source components in the form. A navigator that isn't connected to a data source is utterly useless.

Build a Database Editor

Place a table and data source component and an Open File dialog on a new form, with the table as the data source's DataSet property. Set the table's ReadOnly property to True and the data source's AutoEdit property to False. Place a bevel component on the form, set its type to bsFrame, and set its Align property to alTop. Set the Open File dialog's properties like so:

Property	Value
DefaultExt	DB
Options.ofHideReadOnly	True
Options.ofFileMustExist	True
Title	Open Database File

Double-click the Filter property and create two filters named Database files and All files, with matching file specifications *.DB;*.DBF (for Database files) and *.* (for All files).

Put a single speed button at the left of the bevel component, with its Caption set to the digit 1 and its Font set to Wingdings. (Surprise! This produces a button with an open folder on it.) Place a database navigator to the right of it. Connect the navigator's DataSource property to the data source and set all but the first four VisibleButtons subproperties to False. Set the navigator's ShowHint property to True. Now place a data grid component on the form, set its Align property to alClient, and connect it to the data source as well. Change the form's caption to Universal Database Viewer. Double-click the speed button and put this code in its OnClick event handler:

```
WITH OpenDialog1 DO
  IF Execute THEN
    WITH Table1 DO
      BEGIN
        Close;
        DatabaseName := ExtractFilePath(Filename);
        TableName := ExtractFileName(Filename);
        Open;
      END;
```

That's it! You've built a viewer for all your database tables, simply by hooking up components and writing a few lines of code. As the following simple exercise shows, if you want to do more than look, all you have to do is change a few properties and your table viewer becomes a table editor.

In the database viewer project, set the table's ReadOnly property to False and the data source's AutoEdit property to True. Double-click the VisibleButtons property of the navigator and set the subproperties nbInsert, nbDelete, nbPost, and nbCancel to True.

With those simple changes, the database viewer becomes an editor. Figure 11-8 shows the finished product. The navigator lets you step through the records forward or backward, or jump to the start or end of the data. You can also navigate by scrolling around the grid. Save this project as DBVIEWER.

Figure 11-8:
Delphi's
database
components
do most of
the work in
this
database
viewer and
editor.

NAME	SIZE	WEIGHT	AREA	BMP
Angel Fish	2	2	Computer Aquariums	(Blob)
Boa	10	8	South America	(Blob)
Critters	30	20	Screen Savers	(Blob)
House Cat	10	5	New Orleans	(Blob)
Ocelot	40	35	Africa and Asia	(Blob)
Parrot	5	5	South America	(Blob)
Tetras	2	2	Fish Bowls	(Blob)

Universal Database Viewer — Next record

Run the program and try making *minor* changes to the sample databases that come with Delphi. The changes take effect as soon as you leave the current row. You can also click the Post button (checkmark) to post changes immediately, or click the Cancel button (X) to cancel changes before leaving a row.

Scroll to the bottom of the grid and press the down arrow to insert a new row, or click the Insert button (plus sign) to insert a new row anywhere in the table. If you leave the new row without entering anything, it disappears. In a table with a primary key, when you post the new record or leave the row, the row takes its place in order sorted on the primary key.

Remember that the changes you make in a Delphi database program get written to the file as soon as you leave the current row or click the Post button. There's no need to specifically save the file, though you should be sure to post before closing the table.

There's a Blob in Your Data

At first glance, the data grid seems to be a panacea for general database manipulation. A closer look, however, reveals some warts, most notably its failure to display BLOBs (Binary Large OBjects). Scan the BIOLIFE.DB sample table with the database viewer and look at the Notes and Graphic fields. These actually contain a variable-length memo and an image, but the general-purpose data grid can't display them.

For programs that work with one specific database, where the structure of the tables is known in advance, Delphi supplies a large group of data-aware components. (Visual Basic programmers like to call these *bound* components.) There are data-aware versions of the label, edit box, memo box, image, list box, combo box, check box, and radio group. Like the data grid, these all have a DataSource property that points to a data source within the project. They also have a

DataField property to identify which field they display. In addition to these simple bound components, Delphi offers super-smart data-aware list box and combo box components that can reach out and grab data from another table. Delphi 2.0 adds even smarter versions of the lookup list box and combo box but retains the original pair for backward compatibility.

The data-aware components are not actually restricted to one-database, predetermined structures. You *can* create and connect these components at run time using code. However, that's not what most database programs need to do.

Awakening components to data

The best way to understand data-aware components is to start working with them. For safety's sake, I'll work with a *copy* of one of the sample tables, not the original!

In the Delphi group in Program Manager, find and launch the Database Desktop application. Select Open Table from the File menu and open the BIOLIFE.DB sample database. Select Restructure Table... from the Table menu and immediately save the table as BIOLIFEX.DB. Now there's no chance that our experimenting will screw up the original table.

Bring up the Restructure Table dialog again and use the down arrow to go one row past the bottom of the list of fields. Enter **Large** for the name of the new field, set its data type to A for Alphabetic, and set its length to 3. Add another field called **Dominant Color,** set its data type to A, and set its length to 8. Save the table, and then close the Database Desktop.

Start a new project and choose Database Form Expert from the Help menu in Delphi 1.0 or from the Database menu in Delphi 2.0. Follow the prompts to create a simple form for BIOLIFEX.DB containing all fields in a horizontal layout. Click the table component in the resulting form and set its Active property to True.

Delphi's components are incredibly useful for viewing and modifying database table information. When you want to *create* a table or change a table's structure, however, it's easier to use the Database Desktop.

When you choose either of the nongrid layouts, the Database Form Expert generates a simple bound edit box for every field. Like the grid, the edit box can't display variable-length memos or images, so the Notes and Graphic fields still don't display properly. We'll deal with them shortly.

Run the program and enter values for the Large field in a few records. If the fish is 100 centimeters or more, enter Yes; otherwise, enter No. Now go to the first record and enter DUH. Lightning does not strike you. Although you may intend for this field to contain just Yes or No, the program accepts UGH, GUK, YAP, XX, or any string of up to three characters.

Below the edit box on the form, place a data-aware check box that represents the Large field. Set its properties like this:

Property	Value
Caption	Large
DataSource	DataSource1
DataField	Large
ValueChecked	Yes
ValueUnchecked	No

Delete the edit box and associated label, and then resize and move the data-aware check box into its place. Run the program again and flip through the records. The check box will be checked if the Large field contains Yes, or unchecked if the Large field contains No. If the field is empty or contains something other than Yes or No, the check box will be grayed. You can use the data-aware check box to force a field to have one of two specific values. It's a lot easier to search for large fish when you know the field contains either Yes or No, not Yea, Nay, or Duh.

Select the edit box and label for the Notes field and drag them to the start of a new row of components. Now select just the edit box and cut it to the Clipboard by pressing Ctrl+X. Switch to the Code Editor, go to the very end of the program, and press Ctrl+V to paste the component as text. Change TDBEdit to TDBMemo in the first line. Cut the text description of the component to the Clipboard, flip to the Form Designer, click edit box's previous location, and paste it back into the form. Enlarge the newly transformed field — you see the text of a note right away. Set its ScrollBars property to ssVertical.

Select the edit box and label for the Graphic field and move them down into the new row that holds the Notes field. As discussed in the preceding paragraph, cut the edit box to the Clipboard, paste it into the Code Editor, and replace TDBEdit with TDBImage. Delete the line containing MaxLength, cut the modified description to the Clipboard, click the form where the field used to be, and paste it back in. Resize the image so that you can see the picture.

You can always cut and paste between a component on the form and a text description of the component in the Code Editor. When two component types are similar enough, you can transform one into the other by editing the text description.

Wow! The program isn't even running, yet it displays useful information in the Notes field and a picture in the Graphic field. It's a big improvement over the simple form originally created by the Database Form Expert.

Delete the label that says Dominant Color, and then cut the Dominant Color edit box and paste it into the editor. Change the object type from TDBEdit to TDBRadioGroup. Delete the line that defines MaxLength — that's a TDBEdit property that does not exist in TDBRadioGroup. Now cut the modified description and paste it back into the form. Enlarge the data-aware radio button group and set its caption to Dominant Color. Double-click on its Items property and enter the four strings Red, Yellow, Green, and Black. Rearrange the components on the form so they look like Figure 11-9.

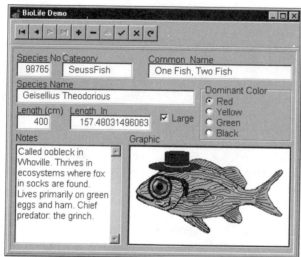

Figure 11-9:
Data-aware
components
tailored to
the table's
fields
enhance
this form.

Run the program and step through a few records. If the fish has a dominant color, choose the appropriate radio button in the Dominant Color group. If it's large (over 100 cm), check the Large check box; otherwise clear it. End the program and load the BIOLIFEX database into the Database Desktop. Wherever you checked a dominant color, the corresponding string has been inserted in the database! When only a few possible values exist for a field, the data-aware radio button group makes entering a wrong value impossible.

Before bidding this fishy form a fond farewell, we'll perform one more amazing feat of transmogrification. Select the radio button group, cut it to the Clipboard, and paste it into the very end of the Code Editor. Change the object type from TDBRadioGroup to TDBListBox, and delete the line that defines the Caption property. Now cut the description to the Clipboard and paste it back into the form.

When you run the program now, the dominant color for each fish is highlighted in the data-aware list box. If no dominant color has been entered, none of the items are highlighted. This component (and the very similar data-aware combo box) is useful when the number of possible values for a field is fairly small but too large for a data-aware radio button group.

You could look it up!

Don't confuse the data-aware list box (DBListBox) with the *lookup* list box (DBLookupList). In both, the user chooses the value of a field from a list, true. But in the data-aware list box, the programmer defines the list of values in advance, whereas the lookup list box rips its list of possible values from another table. This is extremely handy when, for example, two tables are linked on a common field. You don't want to let the user accidentally enter a value in the detail table that's not even present in the master; a lookup list makes that error impossible by forcing the user to choose from a list of existing values.

Place a table component and a data source on a new form. Connect the table to the example ORDERS.DB table and hook up the data source to the table. Set the table's Active property to True. Now place a second table and a second data source in the same way, connecting them to CUSTOMER.DB. Delphi 2.0 users may want to put both tables and both data sources in a data module. Put a data grid and a navigator on the form, connecting both to the first data source.

Double-click the first table to open the Dataset Designer. Add all the fields in the table, select CustNo, and set its Visible property to False. Close the Dataset Designer. Place a DBLookupCombo component on the form (in Delphi 2.0, this component lives on the Win 3.1 page of the Component palette) and set its properties like this:

Property	*Value*
DataSource	DataSource1
DataField	CustNo
LookupDisplay	Company;CustNo
LookupField	CustNo
LookupSource	DataSource2

Now run the program. As you scroll through the orders in the grid, the lookup combo box displays the name of the corresponding customer. When you enter a new order, you never type the customer number and thus never risk typing it *incorrectly*. Instead, you simply choose the customer name from the lookup combo box. Figure 11-10 shows a slightly fancier version of this same program that uses a lookup list box instead.

Delphi 2.0 users can try the new DBLookupListBox and DBLookupComboBox components, too. These two don't have the capability to display multiple fields, but they can be hooked directly to a lookup field that already exists in a table.

Try this: Take the preceding example program, delete the DBLookupCombo, and replace it with a DBLookupComboBox. Double-click Table1, right-click the

Figure 11-10:
This form
uses a
lookup list
box to
protect the
user from
mistyping
the all-
important
customer
number.

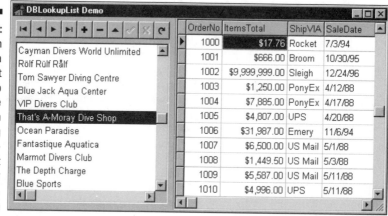

Dataset Designer that appears, and select New field from the menu. Enter CompanyLook for the field name, select String for the field type, and click the Lookup radio button. Select Table2 from the Dataset pull-down list, and select CustNo for both Key Fields and Lookup Keys. Now choose Company from the Result Field pull-down list. Click OK to create the lookup field. Back in the main form, set the DBLookupComboBox's DataSource to Table1 and its DataField to CompanyLook. Bingo! The component immediately fills with data.

This grid is in control

Sometimes you feel like a grid; sometimes you don't. That's why Delphi's Database Form Expert creates either a grid or a form full of separate data-aware components. If you wanted something pretty much like a grid, but with a few fields for each record, you used to be out of luck. With the Delphi 2.0 DBCtrlGrid, it's simple — that is, as long as you have the Developer or Client/ Server Suite version. The low-end Desktop version of Delphi 2.0 omits this super component.

Start a new project in Delphi 2.0, and right away select New Data Module from the File menu. Click the main form, select Use unit... from the File menu, and choose the unit containing the data module. Now select Explore from the Database menu to fire up the Database Explorer, shown in Figure 11-11.

Navigate into the Demos database and locate the EMPLOYEE table. Now drag the table from the Database Explorer into your data module. Amazing! Add a DataSource component to the data module, connect the data source to the table, and set the table's Active property to True.

Drop a DBCtrlGrid component on the main form and size it so that it nearly fills the form. Set its DataSource property to the data source in the data module, and set its RowCount to 4. Add a navigator component connected to the same

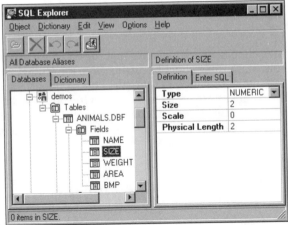

Figure 11-11:
The Delphi
2.0
Database
Explorer
makes
developing
database
applications
with Delphi
even easier.

data source. Flip back to the Database Explorer and fully expand the EMPLOYEE table so that you can see the list of fields. Now drag the fields one-by-one from the Explorer into the top section of the DBCtrlGrid. As you drop each one, it explodes into a data-aware edit box and a corresponding label. Rearrange these components so that they occupy two separate lines in the top section of the DBCtrlGrid. Now run the program. As Figure 11-12 shows, each record occupies one band of the component, and four records are visible at once.

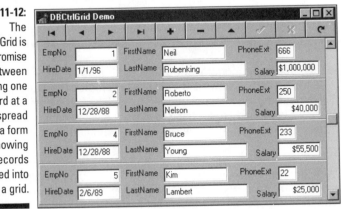

Figure 11-12:
The
DBCtrlGrid is
a compromise
between
showing one
record at a
time spread
out on a form
and showing
records
jammed into
a grid.

If you've ever programmed using Borland's Paradox for Windows, the DBCtrlGrid may look familiar. It's similar to Paradox's MRO (Multi-Record Object).

Getting Results

If you're a data entry clerk, you naturally feel that the database exists so that you can put data into it. Nothing could be further from the truth! Databases exist so that you can get information *out* of them. Putting the data in is just a necessary evil. The database proves its mettle when the boss comes and asks for a list of everyone who has placed an order over $500, but not ordered anything in the last two years, and lives anywhere in California except the San Francisco and Los Angeles areas.

Information please — the query

A query component is another way of hooking your Delphi program to a database. Like a table component, it has DatabaseName and Active properties, and it needs a data source as a go-between for connecting with data-aware components. When your program opens a query component, it grabs the information specified by the SQL (Structured Query Language) command in its SQL property. If you've set RequestLive to True, the query attempts to access the database so that edits made using the query will feed back into the database. This isn't always possible; the run-time property ResultSetLive indicates whether it worked or not. If ResultSetLive is False, the query gives you a copy of the *original data,* also known as canned, dead, or off-line data.

Delphi 2.0 enhances the query component with most of the same goodies it heaped on the table component. Most importantly, queries in Delphi 2.0 support cached updates and filters. A query involving multiple databases on a busy network can take hours to complete. If you need to view a subset of the query's result, filtering can be *much* faster than sending off a new query.

The good news is that a query component brings the full power of SQL into your Delphi programs. The bad news is that SQL is a complex language. (And even worse, SQL comes in many flavors, unique to each SQL server vendor.) The really good news is that you don't have to learn the whole language. All you really need to know is a few variations on the select command.

Place a push button on a new form and set its caption to &Go. Drop a memo box and set its Align property to alTop — don't worry if it covers the push button. Set its ScrollBars property to ssVertical. Now place a query component on the form with its DatabaseName property set to the Demos alias.

Put a data source on the form and set its DataSet property to the query. Add a data-aware grid with Align set to alClient, and connect it to the data source. Create an OnClick event handler for the hidden button containing these lines:

```
WITH Query1 DO
  BEGIN
    Close;
    SQL := Memo1.Lines;
    Open;
  END;
```

Save the project as SQLPAD. You've built a SQL scratch pad, a program you can use to fool around with SQL statements. Type a SQL statement in the memo box and press Alt+G; the results of the query show up in the data grid. Let's try a few statements that pull data from the Delphi demo databases. Run the SQLPAD program and enter this statement:

```
select * from biolife
```

Press Alt+G and the grid should fill with all the data from the biolife table. Now enter this:

```
select category, common_name from biolife
```

This time only the two specified fields show up. Try this:

```
select species name from biolife
```

Whoops! The query gags on that statement. The problem is that the field name consists of two separate words. To make such a name palatable to the query, you must surround it with quotation marks *and* prefix it with the table name followed by a period, like this:

```
select biolife."species name" from biolife
```

The query component may also gag on field names that are the same as SQL command words. Any time a SQL command is unexpectedly rejected, try this: Find each field name in the command, surround it with quotation marks, and prefix it with the table name and a period. The table name itself may require quotation marks, too, if it must include a file extension or special characters. For example, queries on dBASE files must include the .DBF extension in the file name.

So the select command selects fields from a specified table. Use an asterisk to represent all fields. If you want to see only certain fields, you simply list their names separated by commas. Let's fool with the SQLPAD some more. Take the preceding query and enter it with each word on its own line (but don't break up the quoted field name). Note that it works just jim-dandy. Now run this query:

```
select * from customer where state="HI"
```

As you'd expect, the grid now contains data only for customers in Hawaii. Now try this:

```
select * from customer where country<>"America" and
Company like "%SCUBA%"
```

You've selected all foreign customers with SCUBA in the company name.

The where clause is what makes the select command truly useful. With this clause, you can locate all records that match a simple or complex set of conditions. You can combine conditions logically using AND or OR. Let's try a few more where clauses. Here's a two-table query:

```
select orders.orderno, orders.itemstotal,
customer.company from orders,customer
where orders.custno=customer.custno and
customer.company like "%Dive%"
order by customer.company
```

This query pulls data from two different tables to display each order number, its total cost, and the company name, but only for customers whose name contains Dive. The last line contains a new SQL keyword, order by. As you might guess, this controls the sort order of the output. This particular command's output is sorted by company. If these SQL commands are making you dizzy, you may skip the next exercise. Still here? Good! Okay, for the grand finale, carefully enter this SQL statement:

```
select customer.company, items.orderno,
parts.description, vendors.vendorname
from parts, vendors, items, orders, customer
where parts.vendorno = vendors.vendorno and
items.partno = parts.partno and
items.orderno = orders.orderno and
orders.custno = customer.custno and
customer.company like "%SCUBA%"
order by customer.company, parts.description
```

That last massive query displays data drawn from four different tables based on conditions defining relationships between data elements drawn from *five* different tables. For each customer whose company name contains SCUBA, this query displays the name of each item ordered, the vendor who supplies that item, and the number of the order. Figure 11-13 shows the result, with rows sorted first by company and then by description.

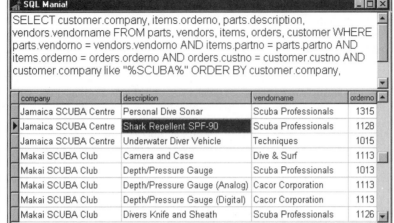

SQL Mania!

```
SELECT customer.company, items.orderno, parts.description,
vendors.vendorname FROM parts, vendors, items, orders, customer WHERE
parts.vendorno = vendors.vendorno AND items.partno = parts.partno AND
items.orderno = orders.orderno AND orders.custno = customer.custno AND
customer.company like "%SCUBA%" ORDER BY customer.company,
```

company	description	vendorname	orderno
Jamaica SCUBA Centre	Personal Dive Sonar	Scuba Professionals	1315
Jamaica SCUBA Centre	Shark Repellent SPF-90	Scuba Professionals	1128
Jamaica SCUBA Centre	Underwater Diver Vehicle	Techniques	1015
Makai SCUBA Club	Camera and Case	Dive & Surf	1113
Makai SCUBA Club	Depth/Pressure Gauge	Scuba Professionals	1013
Makai SCUBA Club	Depth/Pressure Gauge (Analog)	Cacor Corporation	1113
Makai SCUBA Club	Depth/Pressure Gauge (Digital)	Cacor Corporation	1113
Makai SCUBA Club	Divers Knife and Sheath	Scuba Professionals	1126

Figure 11-13: This alarming SQL statement pulls together data from five different tables.

Most of the time, your SQL statements won't come anywhere remotely near this level of complexity. The usual query is more like "Find me all the blacksmiths named Jones." But if you *need* to do something complicated, you can! Actually, a bona fide SQL-meister can use SQL statements to create new tables, delete rows, update fields based on a formula, and probably pay off the National Debt.

Get me that report!

Delphi's report component is an odd bird. It looks like almost any other component, and it has properties and methods like a component. But effectively it's just a door. Knock on the door by double-clicking and you find that you've activated ReportSmith, the reporting product that comes with Delphi. Call the Run method of a report component and you're really running ReportSmith Runtime. This is all a subtle way of leading up to the fact that we're not going to talk about the report component. ReportSmith is complex and powerful enough to merit a book all its own!

Database Guts

As you work with database components, you're constantly confronted with the seamy side of database society. You see lists of databases on the system, lists of tables in a database, lists of fields in a table, and so on. Because Delphi itself is written in Delphi, these lists must be available to your programs as well.

The list of databases and list of tables in a database emanate from the session component. The invisible and singular session component is present in any program that uses database components. It has methods that return a list of all database aliases on the system, or a list of all tables in a database. Add DB to your form's uses clause and you can call on the session component for help. The table and query components include a similar method that returns a list of field names. You can also request a list of indexes from a table.

A single-minded program that's obsessed with one particular database won't have any use for these methods. They only come into play in programs for generalized database access, like the database viewer you built earlier. Now you use them to create a table-selection form that lets the user make an informed choice.

Start a new project based on the fixed-size form template. Place an ordinary combo box near the top left corner, with a label captioned &Databases: above it. Set the combo box's Style property to csDropDownList. Below the combo box, place a label captioned &Tables: and below that, a list box with Sorted set to True. Connect the FocusControl property of the two labels to the corresponding component.

Place another sorted list box next to the first so that the tops of the two list boxes line up. Above the new list box, place a label captioned &Fields:. Below the new list box, place another label and a short list box, giving the label the caption &Indexes:. Again connect the FocusControl property of the two labels to the corresponding list box. Check your layout against Figure 11-14.

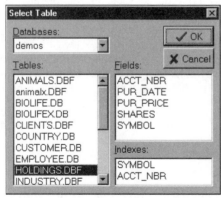

Figure 11-14: This database selection form relies on the session component.

Put two bitmap buttons at the top right of the form, setting their Kind properties to bkOK and bkCancel. Finally, drop a table component on the form and set its Name property to WorkTable. Create an OnActivate event handler for the form with these lines:

The database component

Did you notice we've gone through about 90% of this chapter without talking about the database component? Because we're covering local database access here, the database component is simply not necessary. It becomes truly useful only when you start upsizing your projects to work with remote databases. At that time, you'll have to be concerned with passwords and user log-in procedures, which are handled by the database component. It also has the capability to maintain a connection with the remote database even when none of the tables are open.

When you move up to client/server, you also get to worry about how your program interacts with other completely separate programs — usually on completely separate machines — accessing the same data. Delphi's tables already supply transaction processing for remote tables. Basically, that means that, even if your program dies a horrible death, it can't corrupt the database. It will never give up the ghost halfway through updating a record because it doesn't commit the update permanently until all the data has been transferred. The database component's TransIsolation property controls precisely when other programs accessing the same data can see your program's changes. Aren't you glad you don't have to understand this . . . yet?

```
Session.GetDatabaseNames(ComboBox1.Items);
ComboBox1.ItemIndex := 0;
ComboBox1Change(ComboBox1);
```

Put these two lines in an OnChange event handler for the combo box:

```
Session.GetTableNames(ComboBox1.Text,
  '', True, True, ListBox1.Items);
```

Now write an OnDeactivate event handler for the form using these two lines:

```
ListBox2.Clear;
ListBox3.Clear;
```

Double-click the first list box and enter these lines for its OnClick event handler:

```
WITH WorkTable, ListBox1 DO
  BEGIN
    DatabaseName := ComboBox1.Text;
    TableName := Items[ItemIndex];
    TheDatabase := DatabaseName;
    TheTable := TableName;
    GetFieldNames(ListBox2.Items);
```

(continued)

```
    ListBox3.Clear;
    GetIndexNames(ListBox3.Items);
  END;
```

Find the comment { Public declarations } near the top of the file. Just after the comment, insert this line:

```
TheDatabase, TheTable : String;
```

Set the form's Name to PickTable and its Caption to Select Table. Then right-click the form and save it as a template or, if you're using Delphi 2.0, add it to the repository.

Load the DBVIEWER project from earlier in this chapter. Choose New Form from the File menu or, in Delphi 2.0, choose New… from the File menu and flip to the Forms page. Choose the newly created table-selection template. Delete the Open File common dialog component. Replace the code in the speed button's OnClick event handler with these lines:

```
WITH PickTable DO
  IF ShowModal = mrOK THEN
    WITH Table1 DO
      BEGIN
        Close;
        DatabaseName := TheDatabase;
        TableName := TheTable;
        Open;
      END;
```

Note the name of the unit associated with the table-selection form and add that name to the main form's uses clause. With the addition of this table-selection form, your simple database editor program can browse and edit tables on a wide variety of remote databases as easily as files on the local disk drive.

You can use this table-selection form, shown in Figure 11-14, in any general database access program you write. It's a lot easier to choose between ZPHDBBRX.DB and SLRTBFST.DB when you can see a list of the fields in each.

Database programming is a huge subject. I could go on and on with more and more examples, but you know enough now to go ahead on your own. As for what's next, I have good news and bad news. The next chapter covers some truly phenomenal user interface components that encapsulate the Windows 95 look. What's the bad news? These components are present only in Delphi 2.0. Go ahead and read Chapter 12 even if you haven't started using version 2.0; maybe it will inspire you to make the leap!

Part IV
Real Programming

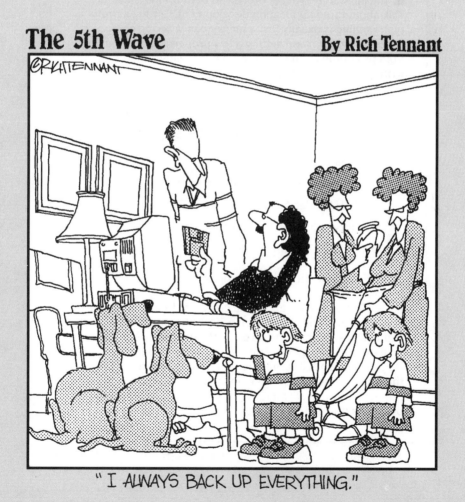

"I ALWAYS BACK UP EVERYTHING."

In this part . . .

In the previous parts, you had a field day tinkering with
the incredibly rich set of tools in Delphi's parts cabinet.
Talk about rapid application development! Getting a prototype running is usually just a matter of scattering components on the form and setting a few properties. And moving
from prototype to finished program is mostly a matter of
writing some event handlers.

So far, you've simply copied event handler code from this
book. You've gained a clear enough impression of Delphi's
language to pick it out in a police lineup:

- += ListPtr->ToppingPrice;
- Sumimasen ga, ima wa nanji desu ka?
- WITH Sender AS TListBox DO Clear;
- Budtye idyotom, a nye parasitom.
- LINE INPUT "Enter your name: ", Name$.

(You *did* choose the third item, right?)

In Part IV, you'll learn about the code that Delphi writes for
you, and study the elements. No, not antimony, arsenic,
aluminum, selenium, and so on — the elements that make
up a program! Sooner or later you *will* need to look at
Delphi's manuals, but these chapters will prepare you so
that the experience isn't too much of a shock. To round out
the section, we'll talk about what you can do when good
programs do bad things.

Chapter 12

Windows 95 Components

● ●

In This Chapter

▶ Giving your programs the true Windows 95 look and feel

▶ Tweaking numbers with track bar and UpDown components

▶ Displaying and editing a form's menu using a tree view

▶ Drawing bitmap images with transparent parts

▶ Using a list view to display and arrange a list of names

▶ Turning the simple text editor into a font-smart simple word processor

● ●

*E*very Windows program running under Windows 95 gets an instant makeover. The squared-off buttons, left-aligned caption, and tiny icon in the title bar combine to shout "This is *not* your father's Windows!" But that's what any old program looks like in Windows 95. If you want your programs to truly use the look and feel of this new Windows version, make use of the new and special user interface elements that Windows 95 brings to the game. As long as you're using Delphi 2.0, those components can be used in your programs. As an added bonus, the components work fine under Windows NT 3.51, too.

Choosing Windows 95 Components

Flip to the Win95 page in the Component palette and check out the new components. If you don't know quite what to *do* with them, look at Table 12-1.

Delphi Has Its Ups and Downs

Windows 3.*x* didn't include a spin button control in its repertoire of built-ins, but passionate programmers yearned to use this nifty interface gadget. Always obliging, Delphi 1.0 provided the spin button and spin edit components discussed back in Chapter 8. Windows 95 blows away these custom components with a built-in equivalent, which Delphi 2.0 presents as the UpDown component.

Table 12-1   Problems Solved by Windows 95 Components

Task	Component
Let the user tweak a numeric value up or down	UpDown. See "Delphi Has Its Ups and Downs."
Display status information at the bottom of the form	Status bar. See "Bar Hopping."
Display and adjust the value of a continuous numeric quantity	Track bar. See "Bar Hopping."
Display the progress of an ongoing process	Progress bar. See "Bar Hopping."
Allow direct entry of shortcut keys like those used in menus	Hotkey. See "Hot! Hot! Hotkey!"
Display bitmap images with "transparent" areas	Image list. See "The Strong, Silent Image List."
Store images for use with tree view and list view components	Image list. See "The Strong, Silent Image List."
Display and optionally edit hierarchical data outline form	Tree view. See "View from a Tree."
Create a form with multiple tabbed pages	PageControl. See "Keeping Tabs on Your Pages."
Display a set of selection tabs without associated pages	TabControl. See "Keeping Tabs on Your Pages."
Display a multisection header with resizable and clickable columns	HeaderControl. See "Two Headers Are Better Than One."
Display, organize, and edit a list of items, with icons representing each item	List view. See "The Amazing List View."
Edit unlimited-size documents using multiple font and paragraph styles	Rich text component. See "Get Rich (Text) Quick!"

Properties

Like a spin button, the UpDown component consists of two joined buttons with cuneiform wedges pointing up and down. Unlike the spin button, you can't change the triangular glyphs, but at least they resize along with the component. And by setting the Orientation property to udHorizontal, you can effectively transform it into a RightLeft component. (No, its name doesn't change!)

As the user clicks or holds one of the buttons, the Position property spins through the range of values defined by the Min and Max properties. If the Wrap property is True, trying to raise the Position property past Max will make it wrap back to Min (shades of Sisyphus).

UpDown components are gregarious; they like to hang out with their component buddies. Setting the UpDown component's Associate property to an edit box on your form produces the equivalent of a spin edit. The UpDown component leaps to a new position at the left or right of the edit box, depending on the value of the AlignButton property, and the "buddy" edit box displays the UpDown's Position property. If the Thousands property is True, the value shown in the edit box will include thousands separators. These are the essential properties for an UpDown component.

Events

The ever-popular OnClick event happens when the user clicks one of the UpDown component's buttons. The OnClick event is also triggered repeatedly if the user holds down one of the buttons to spin through possible values. The OnClick event carries a parameter that tells which of the buttons was clicked.

You'll occasionally write an event handler for the OnChanging event, perhaps to require the user's confirmation before raising the Position property past a certain danger level. An OnChanging event handler can prevent the UpDown component's Position property from changing, if necessary.

Let's take this component out for a spin. Drop two edit boxes and two UpDown components on a new form. Set the AlignButton property of the first UpDown component to udRight and set its Max property to 9999. Set the other's Min property to 50 and its Wrap property to True. Now associate one UpDown component with each of the edit boxes.

Add two list boxes to the form and fill their Items properties with names of friends, enemies, tutelary deities, or whatever strikes your fancy. Place two more UpDown components on the form and associate one with each list box — they stretch to fit. Set the Max property for each UpDown component to one less than the number of items in its "buddy" list box. Now select the two new UpDown components and write an OnClick event handler for them containing these two lines:

```
WITH Sender AS TUpDown DO
  (Associate AS TListBox).ItemIndex := Max - Position;
```

The result should look something like Figure 12-1.

Figure 12-1:
The
UpDown
component
combined
with an
edit box
replaces the
SpinEdit.

Run this program and try clicking the various UpDown components. The first UpDown paired with an edit box spins the value in its edit box from 0 to 9,999, adding thousands separators for numbers that need them. The other stays in the range from 50 to 100, wrapping back to 50 when it goes past 100 and vice versa. Clicking the UpDown that's associated with a list box selects the list box item corresponding to the UpDown component's position.

Actually, the connection between the UpDown component and the list box is reversed. If you literally set the list box item to the UpDown component's Position property, the up arrow would move the selection down and the down arrow would move it up. Confusing! To avoid this topsy-turvy situation, the OnClick handler subtracts the current position from the maximum value.

Bar Hopping

Like Las Vegas, Windows 95 has a lot of bars: status bars, progress bars, and track bars. All three of these components are similar to other components that you've already met. The progress bar works like a gauge, the track bar is a smarter and prettier scroll bar, and the status bar has a lot in common with a bottom-aligned panel. However, a program that uses these new-fangled components just *screams* Windows 95. Get used to grabbing one of these rather than an old-fashioned component in your Delphi 2.0 programs.

Progress bar properties and events

A progress bar's essential properties are Min, Max, and Position, corresponding to the gauge's MinValue, MaxValue, and Progress properties. A program can set the bar's Position, or it can call the StepIt method to advance the Position by the value of the Step property. If that seems too restrictive, free-spirited programmers can call the StepBy method to advance the position by any arbitrary amount. Events? Well, a progress bar does respond to the usual mouse and dragging events, but you'll rarely write event handlers for one.

Where, you may ask, is the Color property? As it turns out, you can't control the color of a progress bar. The colored rectangles that show progress always use the system highlight color (clHighlight in Delphi parlance).

Track bar properties and events

The Windows 95 track bar component looks like it belongs on the front of a fancy stereo. Like a scroll bar, the track bar lets the user slide a gadget back and forth or up and down. The Min and Max properties set the trackbar's range, and the Position property tells just where it's pointing. The Orientation property controls whether the trackball is horizontal or vertical.

That's where the similarity to a scroll bar ends, though. A number of other properties control the appearance and behavior of the track bar. The TickMarks property determines where the tick mark lines appear (one side, the other, or both), and the TickStyle property controls the spacing. If TickStyle is tsNone, no tick marks will appear. If it's tsManual, a tick mark will show up at each end and the program can set others with the SetTick method. And if it's tsAuto, tick mark spacing will be controlled by the Frequency property. If Frequency is 5, for example, a tick will appear at positions corresponding to 5, 10, 15, 20, and so on.

Sometimes highlighting part of a track bar's range is handy. For example, if the track bar controls a steam boiler's temperature, the low end will be too cold to function, the high end will be dangerously hot, and the highlighted middle will be *just* right. The SelStart and SelEnd properties define this highlight. A triangular tick mark appears at the position defined by each, and the bar itself is highlighted in between. Like a scroll bar, the track bar is controlled using the keyboard. The LineSize property defines how many ticks the arrow keys move the slider, and the PageSize property controls how far the PgUp and PgDn keys move it. The big event for a track bar is OnChange. This event is triggered when the slider gets moved using the mouse or the keyboard.

Status bar properties and methods

By default, the status bar is aligned at the bottom of the form that you drop it on, and it rarely makes sense to put it anywhere else. The status bar looks like a panel, but it has a kind of triangular tread in the bottom right corner that serves as an oversized resizing handle for the form. Setting the SizeGrip property to False hides the tread.

If all you want to do is display a simple line of text in the status bar, you can set the SimplePanel property to True and the SimpleText property to the text that you want. Simple! However, most of the time you want to create two or more subpanels within the status bar. For example, the first subpanel in Delphi 2.0's own Code Editor window displays the current cursor position.

To set up subpanels, you double-click the status bar's Panels property and use the Panels Editor dialog box (Figure 12-2) that appears. For each panel you create, you can set the text, width, and justification, as well as whether the panel's bevel edge is raised, lowered, or unchanged from the status bar itself. If you set the Style for a panel to Owner Draw, your program will draw just about anything on the panel in response to the OnDrawPanel event.

Figure 12-2:
You create the subpanels of a status bar component using the Panels Editor.

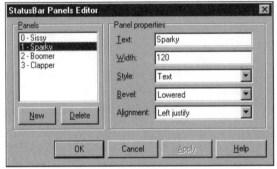

The user can click or double-click on a status bar, but your program has to do a bit of head-scratching to determine which subpanel was clicked.

Visiting a few bars

Place a status bar on a new form, and then add a scroll box with its Align property set to alClient. Drop a progress bar and a track bar on the scroll box, both with the same width. Set the Max property for both to 50, and set the track bar's Frequency to 5. Create an OnChange event handler for the track bar using this line:

```
ProgressBar1.Position := TrackBar1.Position;
```

Whenever you use a status bar, fill the rest of the form with a client-aligned scroll box, as in this program. Otherwise, if the user shrinks the form small enough so that scroll bars appear, the scroll bars will interfere with the status bar.

Double-click the status bar's Panels property. In the Panels Editor, create four subpanels and leave the Text property blank for all of them. Set the Width of the second subpanel to 120, and set the Style of the third to Owner Draw. Place a second track bar on the scroll box, again stretching it to the width of the form. Set its properties as follows:

Property	Value
Frequency	4
Max	212
Min	32
SelEnd	120
SelStart	80

Create an OnChange event handler for the track bar containing these lines:

```
WITH Sender AS TTrackBar DO
  BEGIN
    StatusBar1.Panels[0].Text :=
      Format('%d°', [Position]);
    IF Position < SelStart THEN
      StatusBar1.Panels[1].Text := 'Too cold'
    ELSE IF Position > SelEnd THEN
      StatusBar1.Panels[1].Text := 'Too hot'
    ELSE StatusBar1.Panels[1].Text := 'Juuust right!';
    StatusBar1.Panels[2].Text := StatusBar1.Panels[1].Text;
END;
```

Now put these lines in an OnDrawPanel event handler for the status bar:

```
WITH TrackBar2 DO
  IF Position < SelStart THEN
    StatusBar.Canvas.Brush.Color := clAqua
  ELSE IF Position > SelEnd THEN
    StatusBar.Canvas.Brush.Color := clRed
  ELSE StatusBar.Canvas.Brush.Color := clLime;
StatusBar.Canvas.FillRect(Rect);
```

Figure 12-3 shows the resulting program. When you slide the upper track bar's slider, the progress bar follows. Sliding the lower track bar reports the temperature of a theoretical bowl of porridge. The first panel shows the temperature, the second displays a message based on the temperature, and the third panel is icy blue for too cold, blazing red for too hot, or calm green for just right.

Figure 12-3:
The status
bar, track
bar, and
progress bar
add a
Windows 95
look to your
programs.

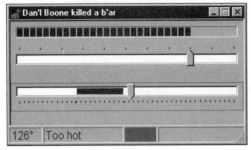

Are you still worrying about why the OnChange handler for the second track bar sets the Text property of the third subpanel, the one that's owner draw? Good! That shows you're thinking! As it happens, a *change* to the subpanel's Text property triggers the OnDrawPanel event. That's perfect, because there's no need to redraw the colored panel except when the track bar's position moves into or out of the selected area.

Hot! Hot! Hotkey!

Remember Windows 3.1? Remember Program Manager? The Program Item Properties dialog in Program Manager had a clever feature. To set the hotkey for a program item, you simply press the key combination. You use the Delphi 2.0 hotkey component to jam this functionality into any program.

Properties and events

In a fit of self-reference, the most important property of a hotkey component is Hotkey. The Hotkey property represents a specific key with a specific combination of Ctrl, Shift, and Alt modifiers, and it's encoded in the same way as the Shortcut property of a menu item (a fact you use later). The other two killer properties are InvalidKeys and Modifiers. By setting subproperties of InvalidKeys to True, you can prevent the user from entering hotkeys that use particular key combinations. By default, the hkNone and hkShift subproperties are True — meaning that a hotkey with no modifiers isn't valid, nor is a hotkey with only the Shift modifier.

The Modifiers property sits on the sidelines unless at least one of the InvalidKeys subproperties is true. If the user selects an invalid key combination, the set of keys specified in Modifiers is used instead. By default, only the hkAlt subproperty is True. Using the default values for both InvalidKeys and Modifiers, if the user pressed just *a* or *A*, the resulting hotkey would be Alt+A.

Be sure that you don't set the Modifiers property to the same key combination represented by the InvalidKeys property. For example, if hcAlt is the only True subproperty under InvalidKeys, don't make hkAlt the only True subproperty under Modifiers. Mismatching these properties won't do any harm, but it won't do any good, either!

The hotkey component doesn't have an OnChange event. Its event list is meager, consisting of just OnExit, OnEnter, and the three standard mouse events.

Drop a hotkey component on a new form and double-click its InvalidKeys property. Set the hcShift subproperty to False. Now double-click the Modifiers property and set all four subproperties to True. Run the program, click on the hotkey component, and try pressing various key combinations. Press the letter *X* alone and the hotkey changes to Ctrl+Shift+Alt+X. That's because InvalidKeys.hcNone is True, meaning an unmodified key isn't valid. Run the program again after tweaking the InvalidKeys and Modifiers properties, to get a feel for the possibilities.

The Modifiers property expands into hkShift, hkCtrl, hkAlt, and hkExt. The first three are clear, but what's hkExt? Delphi's help says it means the Extra key is used as a modifier, but you won't find the Extra key on your keyboard. In fact, hkExt distinguishes the extended Alt and Ctrl keys at the right of many keyboards from the original left-side Alt and Ctrl, and also distinguishes the extended navigation keys to the left of the numeric keypad from their numeric keypad equivalents.

The Strong, Silent Image List

Delphi's image list component stores a set of bitmap images and displays them on demand, optionally simulating a transparent background. The image list component is incredibly useful, but it does almost all its work at the bidding of other components. The various images that appear in list view and tree view components reside in image lists, for example. Its Width and Height properties control the size of the stored bitmaps. Most of the other important properties for an image list are set not through the Object Inspector but by using the ImageList Editor (Figure 12-4), invoked by double-clicking the image list component.

The only event an image list generates is OnChange, triggered by a change to the component. Most programs simply use the image list without attaching any event handlers.

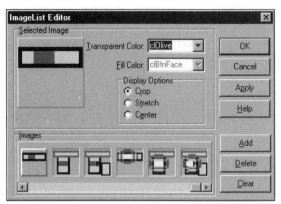

Figure 12-4:
The
ImageList
Editor is
used to
store one
or more
images in
an image list
component.

One image list feature is useful independent of any other component. Bitmaps are always rectangular, even when the images they contain are free-form. Displaying the bitmap draws the whole rectangle, including the useless background. An image list has the built-in capability to treat the background color as if it were transparent. All you do is call the image list's Draw method.

If you set an image list's BkColor property to a specific color, you'll disable the transparent-drawing feature. Leave BkColor set to clNone! Note too that, if you use 256-color bitmaps in an image list, they all have to have exactly the same palette. Sticking with 16-color bitmaps and avoiding the palette problem is best.

Start a new project and place an image list component on it, setting the Width and Height properties to 32. Double-click the image list to open the ImageList Editor, press the Add button, and select an icon whose image isn't rectangular. Pull down the Transparent color combo box and select the color that represents the icon's background. Now set the form's Color property to $B3B3B3. (This shows up as a grainy dithered pattern in 256-color mode.) Double-click the form and put this line in the resulting OnCreate event handler:

```
PtList := TList.Create;
```

Now page up until you see the comment { Private Declarations }, and add the line PtList : TList; immediately after.

Start an OnMouseUp event handler for the form, and replace the begin..end pair supplied by Delphi with this code:

```
VAR R : TRect;
begin
  PtList.Add(Pointer(SmallPoint(X, Y)));
  R := Bounds(X, Y, 32, 32);
  InvalidateRect(Handle, @R, True);
end;
```

Finally, create an OnPaint event handler for the form, delete the begin..end pair supplied by Delphi, and add these lines:

```
VAR N : Integer;
begin
  FOR N := 0 TO PtList.Count-1 DO
    WITH TSmallPoint(PtList[N]) DO
      ImageList1.Draw(Canvas, X, Y, 0);
end;
```

Figure 12-5 shows the resulting program.

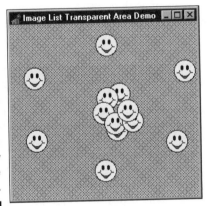

Figure 12-5:
The image list correctly draws these happy circular icons while letting the background show outside the circles.

Each click on the example form adds a point to the list stored in PtList. It also calls the Windows API function InvalidateRect, which triggers an OnPaint event. In response to this event, the form flips through the PtList list and draws the image list component's image at each point in the list. The background portions of the image don't cover the form's background or other images; they are effectively transparent. Many of the examples that follow use image list components.

View from a Tree

If you use the Windows 95 Explorer to poke around the files on your disks, you're already familiar with the tree view component. Explorer's left panel is a tree view representing all the drives and directories on your system. Explorer shows the hierarchical directory structure and uses a little icon at the left of the items to distinguish hard disks from directories, from CD-ROM drives, and so on.

The tree view component can represent any kind of data that has a hierarchical arrangement. You could define your company's organizational chart in a tree view — put yourself at the top! It's a lot more powerful than the Delphi 1.0 outline component, which it totally replaces.

Properties

The Images and StateImages properties of a tree view are both image lists. Images holds the bitmaps that represent the items themselves, like the disk drive images in Explorer. StateImages holds special images that indicate an item is in a particular state. What's a *state?* It's whatever you, the programmer, say it is!

The tree view's Items property is a collection of objects called TTreeNodes. The Items property has a whole set of methods named Add, AddChild, AddFirst, and so on for adding new nodes, each of which creates a node with the text you specify and returns the node in case you want to set some other properties. The most important properties of tree nodes are ImageIndex, SelectedIndex, and StateIndex. ImageIndex tells which image from the Images list represents the item, and SelectedIndex says which of those images gets used when the item is selected. Similarly, StateIndex is an index into the StateImages list. If StateIndex is something other than –1, the state image appears to the left of the regular image.

Other properties control the tree view's appearance. If HideSelection is True (as it is by default) the tree view's selection is hidden when it loses the focus. ShowButtons controls whether plus/minus buttons for expanding or collapsing parts of the tree appear. ShowLines determines whether or not the tree view displays lines connecting the nodes. If ShowRoot is True, the tree's root node is visible. There are loads of other properties, but trying to absorb them all at once could be dangerous to your health.

Events

Unless you set the ReadOnly property to True, the user can edit the item captions. Two separate clicks (not a double-click) on the same node opens an edit window and triggers an OnEditing event. When the user finishes editing, the OnEdited event occurs.

An attempt to select a different node sets off the OnChanging event; your program can imperiously forbid the change by responding to that event and setting AllowChange to False. When the selection *does* change, an OnChange event bursts forth. The tree view component also spews events when the user expands or collapses a branch of the tree.

Tree views can sort themselves, and there's built-in support for user-defined sorting through the OnCompare event. An OnCompare event handler receives two tree nodes as parameters and responds by indicating whether the first is less than, equal to, or greater than the second. If you want to rig the sorting mechanism so that your friends always come to the top of the list, OnCompare is the place to do it!

Growing a menu tree

The properties and methods of the tree view component can be overwhelming. Let's get down to some practical uses. First, start a new project and drop a main menu component on the form. Use the Menu Designer to add several templates. Let yourself go wild! Don't worry about creating event handlers for the menu items; all you're trying to do is make a complicated menu structure.

Create a new form, and then switch back to the main form and select Use Unit... from the File menu. Select the secondary form's unit and press OK. Drop a button on the main form and put the Form2.ShowModal; line in its OnClick event handler. The main form is now complete, so it's time to work on the secondary form.

First, use the Image Editor to create seven 16-x-16 bitmaps. The first should suggest the root of a menu tree, and the next three should represent a top-level menu item, a submenu item, and a cascading menu item, respectively. The last three represent the top-level menu item, submenu item, and cascading menu item when they're selected. You can look back at Figure 12-4 to see some ideas for the last six bitmaps. Choose a little-used color such as clOlive for the parts of the image you want to be transparent.

If you get the order wrong in an image list's bitmaps, you can just drag and drop them into the correct order in the ImageList Editor.

Place an image list on the secondary form and load the seven bitmaps into it, setting the transparent color for each to clOlive. Put a tree view on the form and set its Images property to the image list you just created. Now double-click the form itself to start an OnCreate event handler, and replace the begin..end pair supplied by Delphi with this code:

```
VAR
  Root : TTreeNode;
  N    : Integer;
  procedure StoreIt(TN : TTreeNode; TM: TMenuItem);
  VAR
    NewN : TTreeNode;
```

```
(continued)
  N    : Integer;
begin
  NewN := TreeView1.Items.AddChildObject(TN,
    TM.Caption, TM);
  IF TN = Root THEN NewN.ImageIndex := 1
  ELSE IF TM.Count = 0 THEN NewN.ImageIndex := 2
  ELSE NewN.ImageIndex := 3;
  IF NewN.ImageIndex > 0 THEN
    NewN.SelectedIndex := NewN.ImageIndex + 3;
  FOR N := 0 TO TM.Count-1 DO
    StoreIt(NewN, TM.Items[N]);
  end;
begin
  Root := TreeView1.Items.Add(NIL, 'Menu');
  WITH Application.MainForm.Menu DO
    FOR N := 0 TO Items.Count-1 DO
      StoreIt(Root, Items[N]);
  TreeView1.FullExpand;
end;
```

This event handler adds a root node to the tree view. Then it steps through the main menu of the main form and adds each menu item to the tree. For each node, the ImageIndex and SelectedIndex properties are set to the bitmaps that represent the corresponding menu item type, whether it's a top-level menu, a lone submenu item, or a cascading submenu. Next, you must perform a seemingly pointless ritual. Drop a main menu onto the secondary form, save the project, and then delete that main menu.

When you add a component to a form and save it, Delphi puts any necessary units in the uses clause automatically. Deleting the component doesn't change the uses clause. By adding and deleting a main menu, you gain access to the Menus unit, which is needed by the event handler you just wrote.

Place a bitmapped button component on the form and set its Kind property to bkClose. Then run the program. You find that, when you press the button on the main form, the secondary form appears with the main form's menu structure displayed in a tree view. Each item has an image representing its type, and the selected item gets a special image. Wow!

But wait! There's more! Exit the program and choose the secondary form again. Add a hotkey component and set its Hotkey property to None. Place an ordinary button captioned Assign Hotkey on the form. Create three more 16-x-16 bitmaps, one representing changed text, one representing a changed hotkey, and one representing both. I used simple circles containing *T* (for Text), *K* (for

Key), and *TK*. Place a second image list on the form and double-click it to open the ImageList Editor. Add the first image twice, and then add the other two; set the Transparent color for each to whatever color you used for the background. Set the tree view's StateImages property to this second image list.

Create an OnChange event handler for the tree view component and insert these lines:

```
IF Node.Data <> NIL THEN
  HotKey1.HotKey := TMenuItem(Node.Data).Shortcut;
```

This sets up the hotkey component to display the hotkey of the selected menu item. Now use these lines to replace the begin..end pair of an OnClick handler for the Assign Hotkey button:

```
VAR P : Pointer;
begin
  P := TreeView1.Selected.Data;
  IF P <> NIL THEN
    BEGIN
      TMenuItem(P).Shortcut := HotKey1.HotKey;
      WITH TreeView1.Selected DO
        IF (StateIndex = 1) OR (StateIndex = 3) THEN
          StateIndex := 3
        ELSE StateIndex := 2;
    END;
end;
```

When you press the Assign Hotkey button, the menu item on the main form that matches the selected item in the tree has its Shortcut property changed to match the hotkey. Also, the tree node has its StateIndex set to 2 or 3, meaning the hotkey changed or the hotkey and the text changed.

Start an OnEdited event handler for the tree view, and insert these lines:

```
IF Node.Data <> NIL THEN
  BEGIN
    TMenuItem(Node.Data).Caption := S;
    WITH Node DO
      IF StateIndex >= 2 THEN StateIndex := 3
      ELSE StateIndex := 1;
  END;
```

When the user edits an item in the tree view, the matching item in the main form's menu changes, and the tree node has its state set to 1 or 3, meaning the text changed or the text and hotkey changed.

Whee! You're finished! Figure 12-6 shows the resulting program. The secondary form displays the main form's menu as a tree. Selecting an item in the tree pours the shortcut key for that item into the hotkey component. Pressing the Assign Hotkey button dumps the hotkey component's hotkey back into the selected menu item. And editing an item's text in the tree view changes the caption of the corresponding menu item. A state icon appears to show that an item has had its hotkey, text, or both changed. And when you close the secondary form, you find the changes have indeed taken place in the main menu.

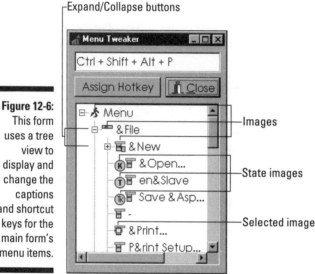

Figure 12-6: This form uses a tree view to display and change the captions and shortcut keys for the main form's menu items.

To sum up, each item in the tree has an image that's drawn from the tree view's Images property; the selected item has a special image. If an item's StateIndex property is greater than zero, an extra image drawn from the tree view's StateImages property will appear to the left of the main image. The expand/collapse buttons appear when the ShowButtons property is True, and the connecting lines appear when the ShowLines property is True.

Keeping Tabs on Your Pages

The TabControl and PageControl components resemble the familiar TabSet and TabbedNotebook, but they're built into Windows 95. You want to use these for the Windows 95 look. The PageControl actually has some advantages over TabbedNotebook. As for TabControl, well, it's just another pretty face.

Properties

The TabControl's most important property is Tabs, a list of strings that become the tab captions. TabIndex is the index of the selected tab, and MultiLine controls how the TabControl reacts when it's too narrow to show all the tabs. If MultiLine is True, the tabs reorganize into multiple lines. If not, the control sprouts a pair of tiny arrow buttons pointing left and right. These buttons enable you to scroll all the tabs into view. Unlike the Delphi 1.0 TabSet, there's no provision for owner-draw tabs.

The PageControl has a MultiLine property that works in the same way, and its ActivePage property holds the name of the selected page. Surprisingly, it doesn't have a Pages property, at least not in the way the TabbedNotebook does. To add a new page, you right-click the control itself and choose New Page from the pop-up menu. Each new page is itself a component — a TabSheet. The essential properties for a TabSheet are Caption, TabVisible, and Enabled. Yes, you can easily hide or disable individual pages. By contrast, the TabControl's tabs are inseparable; you can't hide or disable one without the others.

Events

Like the TabSet component, a TabControl generates an OnChanging event when the user clicks a new tab and generates an OnChange event when the change takes place. The OnChanging event handler can refuse to permit the user to switch tabs, perhaps because data entry is incomplete in the current tab.

The PageControl has the same set of events as the TabControl. The TabSheet's event collection is limited to the simplest mouse and dragging events.

Drop a TabControl on a new form and set its Align property to alTop, and then double-click its Tabs property and add six or eight items. Give it enough tabs so that they won't all fit on the form. Set its MultiLine property to True, and adjust its height to just barely show all the tabs. Now place a PageControl on the form, aligned to fill the rest of the client area. Repeatedly right-click it and choose New Page, until again you have too many tabs to fit in the form's width. Leave MultiLine set to False. On the first page, place two check boxes captioned *Sheet 2 visible* and *Sheet 3 enabled*. Set the Checked property to True for both. Put this line in the OnClick event handler for the first check box:

```
TabSheet2.TabVisible := (Sender AS TCheckBox).Checked;
```

Use this line as the OnClick event handler for the second check box:

```
TabSheet3.Enabled := (Sender AS TCheckBox).Checked;
```

Place one or two components on TabSheet3, and then run the program. The result should look something like Figure 12-7.

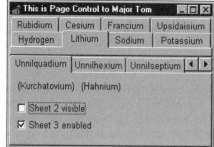

Run the program and experiment. When you choose a tab in the back row of the MultiLine TabControl, that row moves to the front. Pressing the left and right buttons near the top right corner of the PageControl scrolls through the available tab sheets. If you remove the check from the first check box, the second tab sheet disappears. And if you remove the check from the second check box, the components on the third tab sheet are disabled, though the sheet itself can be selected.

No, the names on the tab sheets in Figure 12-7 don't represent a new line of microchips. They're the current names for the unstable elements with atomic numbers 104, 106, and 107. Unnilpentium (the hidden number 105) is also called neilsbohrium and rutherfordium. Whatever happened to short names such as lead, tin, or zinc?

Two Headers Are Better Than One

The Delphi Header component works, but it doesn't quite match the Windows 95 style — hence the new HeaderControl component. Like the Header component, HeaderControl holds column headings in its multiple sections and permits resizing of the sections. As an added bonus, the HeaderControl's sections can function as push buttons.

Properties

Sections is the only significant property of a HeaderControl. Double-click it to open the special Sections Editor. Each section has its own set of properties, including Text, Width, Alignment, and Min and Max (which constrain the resizing of the section). The Style property can be Text or Owner Draw, and if the Allow Click box is checked, the section will function as a button.

Events

If a particular section is marked as Owner Draw, you put code in the OnDrawSection event handler to draw it. OnSectionClick is triggered when the user presses a section that allows clicks, and OnSectionResize occurs after a section has been resized by the user. The OnSectionTrack event is more complex. It occurs once when section resizing begins, repeatedly during the resizing process, and once when section resizing ends.

What's the difference? Well, if you resize other components on your form in response to the OnSectionTrack event handler and the components are graphically complicated, your redrawing may be jerky. On the other hand, if you wait to resize other components until the OnSectionResize event occurs, your program may seem less responsive. It's a trade-off.

Time to get a feel for what's happening here. Drop a HeaderControl on a new form and double-click its Sections property. Add four sections named One, Two, Three, and Four. Set the Min and Max properties for One to 50 and 100. Remove the check next to Allow Click for section Two. Set section Three's Alignment to Right justify. Finally, set Section Four's Style to Owner Draw.

Create an OnDrawSection event handler for the header using these lines:

```
HeaderControl.Canvas.Brush.Color := clRed;
HeaderControl.Canvas.Ellipse(Rect.Left+2, Rect.Top+2,
   Rect.Right-2, Rect.Bottom-2);
```

Run the program and give it a whirl. You can resize all the sections, but the range of the first one is limited. All but the second can be pressed like push buttons. And the fourth section has a red ellipse instead of a caption.

Drop an image component on the form, load a bitmap into it, and set its Stretch property to True. Move it to just below the header, and match its left edge and width to section Two. Now put this code in an OnSectionResize handler for the HeaderControl:

```
IF Section.Text = 'One' THEN
  Image1.Left := Section.Left + Section.Width
ELSE IF Section.Text = 'Two' THEN
  Image1.Width := Section.Width;
```

In an OnSectionClick handler for the HeaderControl, use this single line:

```
Image1.Visible := NOT Image1.Visible;
```

Run the program again. Each time you resize the sections, the image moves to directly below section Two. Pressing any of the clickable sections toggles the image from visible to invisible and back.

Let's try one more trick. Create an OnSectionTrack handler for the HeaderControl, and put these lines into it. Be careful — they're not quite the same as the lines in the OnSectionResize handler:

```
IF Section.Text = 'One' THEN
  Image1.Left := Section.Left + Width
ELSE IF Section.Text = 'Two' THEN
  Image1.Width := Width;
```

Delete the lines you previously put into the OnSectionResize handler.

Don't delete the header portion of an event handler that you want to get rid of. Delete only the lines of code *you* added. Next time you save or run the program, Delphi will neatly dispose of the empty event handler.

Now when you run the program, the image moves or resizes while you're resizing section headers, instead of snapping into place when the resizing operation finishes. However, unless the image is very small or simple, it probably displays a pronounced flicker as it moves.

The Amazing List View

You've met the tree view, which forms the left panel of the Windows 95 Explorer. What's in the right panel? A list view, of course. It's something like a list box, in the same way a jumbo jet is something like an oxcart. A list view can display a columnar list of items, but that's just one of its four display modes. In the large icons mode, it looks like an old Program Manager group window showing icons with titles beneath. In small icons mode, the titles appear to the right of the icons, which are arranged left-to-right in rows. You can move the icons around in either large or small icons mode (as long as the program includes code to move 'em). List mode is like small icons mode, but the items appear in columns and can't be moved around. Finally, details mode provides a multicolumn listing of any subitems associated with the items.

If these display modes aren't clear to you, just fire up Explorer and try them out. In Explorer, the details mode lists file date, time, size, and such trivia.

Properties

The Items property is the heart of a list view. It contains the list of items displayed by the component and their subitems as well. Double-clicking this property displays a specialized Items Editor. However, you're much more likely to create the item list under program control; you'll see how to do that in a moment.

The Columns property, which controls the columns displayed in details mode, also has its own special editor. For each column, you can set the Caption and Alignment. You can also specify whether the column width should initially match the widest item, the width of the header, or a fixed value.

As for those various display modes, they're controlled by the ViewStyle property. The icons and other images are stored in three image list properties named LargeImages, SmallImages, and StateImages. The first two clearly hold the images for the large icons and small icons display modes. StateImages is used to provide an extra icon indicating an item's state, like the same-named property in a tree view.

Events

The list view generates tons of events. Naturally, when the user selects an item, the OnChange event occurs. OnChanging is triggered first and allows a program to prevent the new selection. Item editing is built in, just as in the tree view, and the OnEditing and OnEdited events occur at the start and end of the editing process. The OnColumnClick event indicates that the user has clicked on a column header. (You can set the ColumnClick property to False if you don't want to permit this scandalous behavior.) In Explorer, you click on a column's header to sort by that column. Handily, the OnCompare event allows your program to define how sorting will take place. Many more properties and events are associated with a list view, but we have enough of them now to give the list view a test drive.

A Liszt of composers

Place a list view on a new form and set its ViewStyle property to vsReport, set ReadOnly to True, and set DragMode to dmAutomatic. Double-click its Columns property to fire up the Columns Editor. Enter the column names Composer, First Name, and Birth Year. Choose the Item Width radio button for the first two and the Header Width radio button for the third. The columns look all squished together after you're finished, but don't worry. They'll straighten out as soon as the list view has some data to display. Double-click the form to start an OnCreate event handler, and replace the begin..end pair supplied by Delphi with this impressive block of code:

```
CONST
  Composers : ARRAY[0..9] OF String = ('Albinoni',
    'Buxtehude', 'Corelli', 'Dowland', 'Elgar',
          'Frescobaldi',
    'Grainger', 'Handel', 'Ives', 'Joplin');
  FirstNames : ARRAY[0..9] OF String = ('Tomaso', 'Dietrich',
    'Arcangelo', 'John', 'Sir Edward', 'Girolamo', 'Percy',
    'George', 'Charles', 'Scott');
  BirthYears : ARRAY[0..9] OF Word = (1671, 1637, 1653, 1562,
    1857, 1583, 1882, 1685, 1874, 1868);
  Countries : ARRAY[0..9] OF Integer = (2,3,2,1,1,2,0,4,0,0);
VAR N : Integer;
begin
  WITH ListView1.Items DO
    FOR N := 0 TO 9 DO
      WITH Add DO
        BEGIN
          Caption :=  Composers[N];
          ImageIndex := Countries[N];
          StateIndex := 0;
          SubItems.Add(FirstNames[N]);
          SubItems.Add(IntToStr(BirthYears[N]));
        END;
end;
```

Whoops! I lied. There's actually very little code here. Most of what you typed is data. If you like, you can substitute your own favorite composers, but be sure to keep all four arrays in synch. Each number in the Countries array represents the composer's country of origin; in order from 0 to 4, the countries are U.S., U.K., Italy, Denmark, and Germany.

Now we need some images to display next to these names. Place an image list component on the form and set its Width and Height properties both to 32. Set the list view's LargeImages property to this image list. Now find or draw 32-x-32 icons or bitmaps representing the flags of the United States, England, Italy, Denmark, and Germany, and add them to the image list in that order.

Place a second image list on the form and set the list view's SmallImages property to point to it. Find or draw 16-x-16 bitmaps representing the same five countries and add them to this second image list. You can add yet another image list. This one should contain a 16-x-16 blank image, followed by a 16-x-16 image of musical notes. Set the list view's StateImages property to this third image list.

Place a radio group on the form, set its caption to View, set its Align property to alTop, and double-click its Items property. Add four lines to the Items property: Large, Small, List, and Details. Set its Columns property to 4 and its ItemIndex to 3. Use these lines as an OnClick event handler for the radio group:

```
WITH Sender AS TRadioGroup DO
  ListView1.ViewStyle := TViewStyle(ItemIndex);
```

Set the list view's Align property to alClient. Start an OnMouseDown event handler for it, and replace the Delphi-supplied begin..end pair with this code:

```
VAR TheItem : TListItem;
begin
  IF Shift = [ssShift, ssLeft]THEN
    BEGIN
      TheItem := (Sender AS TListView).GetItemAt(X,Y);
      IF TheItem <> NIL THEN
        TheItem.StateIndex := TheItem.StateIndex XOR 1;
    END;
end;
```

Put these two lines in an OnColumnClick event handler for the list view:

```
SortCol := Column.Index;
ListView1.AlphaSort;
```

Now page up until you find the comment { private declarations }, and insert this line immediately after it:

```
SortCol : Integer;
```

Back at the list view, create an OnCompare event handler and fill it with these lines:

```
CASE SortCol OF
   0 : Compare := AnsiCompareStr(Item1.Caption,
      Item2.Caption);
   1 : Compare := AnsiCompareStr(Item1.SubItems[0],
         Item2.SubItems[0]);
   2 : Compare := AnsiCompareStr(Item1.SubItems[1],
         Item2.SubItems[1]);
END;
```

You're almost ready to roll; you have just a few more details to take care of. Put this line in an OnDragOver event handler for the list view:

```
Accept := (Source = Sender);
```

Now create an OnDragDrop event handler containing these two lines:

```
(Sender AS TListView).Selected.SetPosition(Point(X,Y));
(Sender AS TListView).Arrange(arDefault);
```

All right, all right, I know you're champing at the bit. Go ahead and run the program. Figure 12-8 shows two possible views of this program.

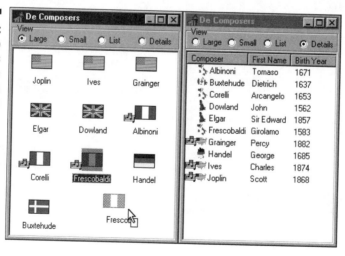

Figure 12-8:
Two instances of the composers program show the large icons view and the details view; note the large icon being dragged.

Experiment with all four views. Notice that you can reorder the icons only by dragging in the large and small icons views. Switch to the Details view and click on each of the column heads. As you do so, the list is sorted by the column you chose. Shift-click on an item in any view to toggle the state marker on and off. You can't edit the text, though, because the ReadOnly property is True. Hey, these guys are famous; they're not going to change their names just because you say so.

Get Rich (Text) Quick!

In this modern world, the editing capabilities of the memo box component are just too-too old hat. If you can't use four fonts in every sentence, why write at all? And if you're going to hit the wall with a mere 32,768 bytes of text, why bother? The Delphi 2.0 rich text component zooms to the rescue. The good news is, a rich text component handles every task a memo box can. The other good news (hah! got you!) is that it does a lot more. Its capacity is virtually unlimited, it lets the user apply different font styles throughout the text, it includes paragraph formatting, and it even takes care of searching and printing its text for you.

Properties

As far as properties listed in the Object Inspector, the rich text component is a little different from a memo box. The PlainText property is new; set it to True and you eliminate the capability to use multiple fonts and styles (and speed up the component's performance). That's about it for interesting new properties. Or is it?

The spiffiest new properties show up only at run time. The SelAttributes property holds the font attributes of the currently selected text. It has all the same properties as a TFont object, along with a new one called ConsistentAttributes. This property indicates which font attributes are consistent throughout the selection. What's that mean? If half the selection is 12-point Arial and half is 14-point Arial, the font name is consistent but the font size isn't. If you change the properties of the rich text component's SelAttributes property, the change affects the entire selection.

Properties can themselves be objects, so it's not crazy or redundant to talk about the properties of the SelAttributes property.

A similar property named DefAttributes defines the attributes for newly inserted text. And the Paragraph property contains formatting information for the selected paragraph or paragraphs. Paragraph formatting includes bullets, tabs, alignment, and indentation.

Events

The rich text component generates all the events a memo box does, plus a number of new ones. The simplest and most easily used is OnSelectionChange. This event is triggered any time the selection or cursor position changes. It's handy for reflecting the selection's formatting in a status bar.

Enriching the simple editor

Remember the simple editor project, last seen in Chapter 8? It's not so simple any more, and it's about to make another Great Leap Forward. Load that project now, delete the memo box that fills its main form, and replace it with a rich text component. In the Code Editor, press Ctrl+R and replace all occurrences of Memo1 with RichEdit1. Now set the rich text component's Align property to alClient, its ScrollBars property to ssBoth, and its HideSelection property to False.

Pull down the File menu and click the Font item. You are tossed into the Code Editor right at that item's OnClick event handler. Delete the event handler's code and replace it with these lines:

```
WITH RichEdit1.SelAttributes DO
  BEGIN
    FontDialog1.Font.Name := Name;
    FontDialog1.Font.Size := Size;
    FontDialog1.Options := FontDialog1.Options +
      [fdNoFaceSel, fdNoSizeSel];
    IF caFace IN ConsistentAttributes THEN
      FontDialog1.Options := FontDialog1.Options -
        [fdNoFaceSel];
    IF caSize IN ConsistentAttributes THEN
      FontDialog1.Options := FontDialog1.Options -
        [fdNoSizeSel];
  END;
WITH FontDialog1 DO
  IF Execute THEN
    BEGIN
      RichEdit1.SelAttributes.Name := Font.Name;
      RichEdit1.SelAttributes.Size := Font.Size;
```

```
      RichEdit1.SelAttributes.Style := Font.Style;
      RichEdit1.SelAttributes.Color := Font.Color;
      SpeedButton3.Down := fsBold IN Font.Style;
      SpeedButton4.Down := fsItalic IN Font.Style;
      SpeedButton5.Down := fsUnderline IN Font.Style;
   END;
```

Delete the single line of code in the font dialog's OnApply method. Now double-click one of the font style speed buttons to reach the event handler they share. In the first line of code within that event handler, change RichEdit1.Font to RichEdit1.SelAttributes. Double-click one of the text alignment speed buttons, and in their shared event handler, replace RichEdit1.Alignment with RichEdit1.Paragraph.Alignment. Now click the Print item under the File menu to go to its OnClick event handler. Delete the code in this event handler and replace it with these two lines:

```
IF PrintDialog1.Execute THEN
   RichEdit1.Print('My Document');
```

Click the find dialog, flip to the events page of the Object Inspector, and double-click the OnFind event. Delete all the code from the existing event handler, including the begin..end pair and the variables preceding the begin line. Then insert this code:

```
VAR
   ST   : TSearchTypes;
   Rslt : Integer;
begin
   ST := [];
   WITH Sender AS TFindDialog DO
     BEGIN
       IF frWholeWord IN Options THEN ST := [stWholeWord];
       IF frMatchCase IN Options THEN ST := ST +
            [stMatchCase];
       Rslt := RichEdit1.FindText(FindText, RichEdit1.SelStart
            +
         RichEdit1.SelLength, RichEdit1.GetTextLen, ST);
       IF Rslt > -1 THEN
         BEGIN
           RichEdit1.SelStart := Rslt;
           RichEdit1.SelLength := Length(FindText);
         END;
     END;
end;
```

Place a status bar on the form and double-click its Panels property. Add two panels with the text Row and Col, and add a third panel with no text. Start an OnSelectionChange event handler for the rich text component. Delete the begin..end pair that Delphi created and add this code:

```
VAR ro, co : Integer;
begin
  WITH RichEdit1.SelAttributes DO
    BEGIN
      SpeedButton3.Down := (fsBold IN Style) AND
        (caBold IN ConsistentAttributes);
      SpeedButton4.Down := (fsItalic IN Style) AND
        (caItalic IN ConsistentAttributes);
      SpeedButton5.Down := (fsUnderline IN Style) AND
        (caUnderline IN ConsistentAttributes);
  END;
  CASE RichEdit1.Paragraph.Alignment OF
    taLeftJustify  : SpeedButton6.Down := True;
    taCenter       : SpeedButton7.Down := True;
    taRightJustify : SpeedButton8.Down := True;
  END;
  ro := RichEdit1.Perform(EM_LINEFROMCHAR,
          RichEdit1.SelStart,
    0);
  co := RichEdit1.SelStart - RichEdit1.Perform(EM_LINEINDEX,
    ro, 0);
  StatusBar1.Panels[0].Text := Format('Row: %d', [ro+1]);
  StatusBar1.Panels[1].Text := Format('Col: %d', [co+1]);
end;
```

Now when the cursor moves, the status bar displays the current row and column, the font style speed buttons reflect the selection's style, and the alignment speed buttons change to match the current paragraph alignment.

You're almost finished! Click the file open dialog, double-click the Filter property, and add a new filter called Rich Text Files, with the mask *.RTF. For the save dialog, double-click the Filter property, and change the Text Files filter to Rich Text Files and change its mask to *.RTF. Select both and change the DefaultExt property to RTF. You've given the simple editor the capability to read either text files or rich text files and to save rich text files. You can change the font style for portions of the text, and control the alignment of paragraphs. With this, your introduction to Delphi 2.0's Windows 95 components is complete.

Chapter 13

Learn Programming from the Master

• •

In This Chapter

▶ Code Delphi writes for you

▶ Basic structure of programs and units

▶ Code you can edit and code you should leave alone

▶ Changes Delphi handles for you and changes you have to take care of yourself

• •

*B*y now, you've built dozens of programs while becoming intimate with Delphi's components. Each time you start a new project, Delphi generates a project file for you, and each time you add a form to the project, Delphi whips up a unit file for it. When you plop a component on the form, Delphi inserts code to integrate it into your program. And when you're ready to write an event handler, Delphi provides the infrastructure.

Sounds like Delphi's doing all the work, doesn't it? Well, there's plenty more for you to do; but by first scrutinizing the things Delphi does for you, you get a good head start in understanding how to write your own great programs.

Dissecting an Empty Program

The moment a new, blank project appears on your screen, busy beaver Delphi has already written two pages of program code. The first page, initially named Unit1, is the code that handles the main form and all its components. The second, titled Project1 by default, isn't visible until and unless you select Project Source from the View menu. Project1 — the main project file — pulls together all the forms in your program.

So start a new project now, and hone your scalpel, because you're going to dissect the files that make up an empty program. It's a lot cleaner than dissecting frog or cow's eyes, and there's no lingering smell of formaldehyde.

What's inside an empty unit?

Click on the Unit1 tab in the Code Editor and expand the window until you can see all (or most) of the code. It should look roughly like Figure 13-1.

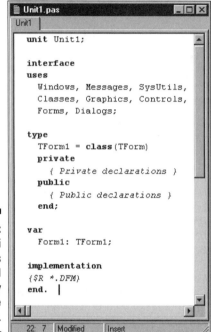

```
unit Unit1;

interface
uses
   Windows, Messages, SysUtils,
   Classes, Graphics, Controls,
   Forms, Dialogs;

type
   TForm1 = class(TForm)
   private
      { Private declarations }
   public
      { Public declarations }
   end;

var
   Form1: TForm1;

implementation
{$R *.DFM}
end. |
```

Figure 13-1: Every Delphi form starts its life linked to an empty unit like this one.

The first line in a Delphi file generally tells you what kind of file you're dealing with. This one is a *unit,* a code module that always depends on the kindness of strangers: It exists only to be used by a main program or by another unit, and can never stand alone. The unit name (in this case, Unit1) immediately follows the *unit* keyword. When Delphi creates a unit to go with a new form, Delphi always tries to call it Unit1. If that name is taken, it tries Unit2, Unit3, and so on.

Julius Caesar said that all Gaul is divided into three parts; the same is true of every unit (and it takes a lot of Gaul to make that comparison). The three parts are the *interface section,* the *implementation section,* and the *initialization section.* The interface section is the smiling face the unit shows to the world; whatever is in this section can be seen and accessed by any program or unit that uses this unit. (So don't put anything incriminating in the interface section!) Anything that appears solely in the implementation section, on the other hand, is private, accessible only within the unit itself. Finally, any commands that you put in the initialization section are executed automatically at the start of any program that uses the unit.

The interface section starts with the lone word *interface*. It continues until the start of the implementation section, which is a line that contains only the word *implementation*. Every unit must include these two sections, even if they're empty. It's not just a good idea; it's the law!

The initialization section is optional, and Delphi doesn't build it into the form-based units it creates. If present, it starts with *initialization* and ends with *end.,* including the period. A unit that doesn't have an initialization section still ends with *end.,* but there's no matching *initialization* preceding it.

The interface section: the inside story

The first line in the interface section is the *uses clause* — a list of the other units this unit relies on. The units Delphi builds for you are not rugged individualists; they're quite content to get along with a little help from their friends.

The units in the initial uses clause are standard ones that come with Delphi, and each has its own special gift:

- ✔ *SysUtils* — a variety of system utilities such as string handling routines, date/time conversions, and file management functions

- ✔ *WinProcs* — in Delphi 1.0, provides access to functions in the Windows libraries GDI, USER, and KERNEL (the ruling triumvirate of Windows)

- ✔ *WinTypes* — in Delphi 1.0, holds data types and constant values used by the Windows functions defined in WinProcs

- ✔ *Windows* — in Delphi 2.0, replaces both WinProcs and WinTypes

- ✔ *Messages* — Windows message number constants and data types associated with particular messages

- ✔ *Classes* — low-level nuts-and-bolts elements of Delphi's component system

- ✔ *Graphics* — graphical elements such as fonts, pens, brushes, and bitmaps

- ✔ *Controls* — mid-level elements of Delphi's component system

- ✔ *Forms* — the form component and the invisible application and screen components

- ✔ *Dialogs* — the common dialog components

Delphi 2.0 replaces the WinTypes and WinProcs units with a single unit called Windows. Rather than force you to make that substitution in every single existing Delphi 1.0 unit, though, the designers kindly defined WinTypes and WinProcs as aliases for the Windows unit. When you're writing code that needs to compile under either version of Delphi, be sure that the uses clause contains WinTypes and WinProcs, not Windows.

After the uses clause is a *type declaration block,* introduced by the word *type*. A type declaration block contains one or more definitions for *data types*. What are those? Well, deep down inside, all the data in your computer is stored as bits and bytes. You use data types to tell your program how to interpret those bytes. For example, the same four bytes could represent

- ✔ 78, 101, 105, and 108
- ✔ 25,934 and 27,753
- ✔ 1,818,846,542
- ✔ 1.128632 E+27
- ✔ 'Neil'

You find out everything you need to know about data types in the next chapter.

The particular unit that we're dissecting defines just one data type, an *object class* named TForm1. The two-bit definition of an object is a collection of data elements combined with functions that act on the data. Sound familiar? Yes, forms and components are examples of objects. The process of wrapping up data in a nice package — an object — with the functions that act on that data is called *encapsulation* by object mavens.

The first line of the type definition:

```
TForm1 = Class(TForm);
```

says that the TForm1 object *inherits* all the features and capabilities of the generic TForm object. Anything TForm can do, TForm1 can do, too. For example, TForm has Caption and Color properties, so TForm1 has them, too. And because TForm has a Close method, TForm1 has a Close method, too.

This particular object class definition is effectively empty. It has a *private* section and a *public* section, but each just contains a comment. (We talk about comments shortly.) If there were any lines of code here, they would define the ways in which TForm1 is different from TForm. TForm1 extends TForm by adding new data fields, defining new methods, or overriding existing methods. Fields and methods in the private section are accessible only to the object itself; those in the public section are visible to any program or unit that uses this unit.

Programmers like to say that TForm1 is a *descendant* of TForm and that TForm is an *ancestor* of TForm1. If TForm1 had its own descendants, they would also be descendants of TForm, and TForm would be their ancestor. After hearing these warm fuzzy terms, you won't be surprised to learn that programmers say objects have a family tree (technically, an object hierarchy).

Next comes a *variable declaration block*, signaled by the word *var*. A variable is a chunk of memory that your program reserves to store data. Every variable has a name so it doesn't get lost in the crowd and a data type, to let Delphi know what kind of stuff this variable stores. The next chapter has a lot to say about variables.

In the unit in Figure 13-1, Delphi declares a single variable whose name is Form1 and whose data type is TForm1. In object-speak, Form1 is an *instance* of the object class TForm1. Notice that this variable declaration comes after the definition of the data type TForm1. That's the rule in Delphi: You can't use anything until after you've defined it!

The type definition and variable declaration I just reviewed come after the interface line and before the implementation line, so they're within the interface section of the unit. That means they are accessible to any program or unit that uses this unit.

The implementation section: deep, dark secrets

A unit's implementation section is the back room where the real work happens; there's no distraction coming from outside influences. All contact with other code modules is funneled through the interface section. A variable declared in the implementation section cannot be examined or changed by code outside the unit; a function declared only in the implementation section cannot be called by any code outside the unit.

The empty unit in Figure 13-1 contains only one line in its implementation section, the *compiler directive* {$R *.DFM}. This line tells Delphi to include all the hard work you put into designing the form; property information for the form and every component on it resides in the .DFM file. Delphi replaces the asterisk with the name of the unit, so this particular line includes UNIT1.DFM in the program. Never delete or change the {$R *.DFM} line! Never!

Compiler directives are orders that go directly to Delphi, as opposed to commands that get translated into machine code for the final program. Remember the compiler options you set way back in Chapter 1? Each of those options has a corresponding compiler directive. For example, {$S+} in a Delphi source file turns stack checking on, regardless of how you've set the compiler options.

You can also add a second uses clause at the start of the implementation section, for units that are required only by code in the implementation section. The only time you have to do this is when two units depend on each other. If unit Alfonse uses unit Gaston and unit Gaston uses unit Alfonse, it can make Delphi go around in circles. The solution is to add an implementation uses clause to one of the units.

The initialization section: last-minute preparations

Some units need to warm up their engines or do last-minute touch-up work at the start of a program. Program statements in the initialization section are executed at the beginning of any program that uses the unit, or uses a unit that uses the unit, or uses a unit that uses a unit that uses the unit. . . . If there's anything in the unit that must be initialized in some way before it can be used, you do it in the initialization section. There's no example for this section because Delphi doesn't need to create one. In fact, not a single example program in this book uses the initialization section. In general, if there is an initialization section it will be just a few lines.

The innards of an empty program

Now click the Project1 tab in the Code Editor to review the ridiculously tiny main program generated by Delphi. It should look like Figure 13-2.

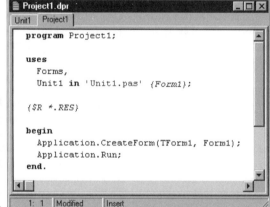

Figure 13-2:
Delphi's standard main program is a mighty mite.

```
Project1.dpr
  Unit1   Project1

  program Project1;

  uses
    Forms,
    Unit1 in 'Unit1.pas' {Form1};

  {$R *.RES}

  begin
    Application.CreateForm(TForm1, Form1);
    Application.Run;
  end.

  1: 1    Modified    Insert
```

The first line tells us this file defines a program whose name is Project1. Unlike a unit, a program can and does stand alone. Immediately after the program line comes a uses clause, just like in the unit. This program uses two units, Forms and Unit1. Forms is the built-in Delphi unit that defines the form and application components. Unit1 is, of course, the unit you just looked at in the other page of the Code Editor.

Note that Delphi has graciously placed the name of the form corresponding to Unit1 in a comment after the unit name. This comment has no effect on the program code, but Delphi *does* use it to help associate the unit with its form. Never modify the comments Delphi inserts in the main program's uses clause.

Any text surrounded by braces {like this} or by parenthesis-asterisk pairs (*like this*) will be ignored by Delphi when it compiles the program. With the exception just noted, comments exist for you! You can and should add comments to the programs you write. Otherwise, when you go to modify the code six months later, you may have no idea what it's supposed to do. Delphi's editor displays comments in a special color and font so that they stand out.

You can also use comment characters to comment out portions of your code. For example, if a certain part of your program is causing problems and you don't know why, you can try commenting out different parts to see what makes the problem disappear. For consistency, I suggest you stick to braces {like this} for regular comments, and use parenthesis-asterisk pairs (*like this*) for commenting out code.

Comment delimiters surrounding a text string almost always mean a comment. The one exception is when the very first character of the string is a dollar sign. In that case, you have a compiler directive, not a comment.

After the uses clause is a compiler directive that loads the resource file for the program. A resource file contains data that's compiled into the final executable program file; the .DFM file included in a Delphi-built unit is a kind of resource file. In a new empty program, the resource file contains nothing but the default icon.

Next comes the *main body* of the program, starting with *begin* and ending with *end.* (The period after *end* must be included.) It looks a lot like the initialization section of a unit, but in this case, it's not optional. In a typical Delphi program, the main body is really puny because all the activity takes place in the units. This program has just two lines, one to initialize Form1 and associate it with the application, and one to run the application.

One way Delphi uses data types is to keep you from passing the wrong kind of variable to a method. If a certain method works on numbers, Delphi won't let you pass it a string of characters. If it works only on whole numbers, Delphi won't permit a number with a fractional part. But when it comes to objects, things get a little weird. Delphi methods that expect a TForm don't raise a fuss when they receive a TForm1 instead. Why not?

The answer lies in *polymorphism,* a ten-dollar word that means "many shapes." If a method expects to receive a certain kind of object, you're allowed to pass it any descendant of that object instead. It's not obvious at first, but this is one of the most powerful features of object-oriented programming.

A program by any other name . . .

As discussed earlier, Unit1 is a default name Delphi gives to a unit. You can easily change it to something more interesting (and mnemonic). Choose Save Project from the File menu, enter Barney for the unit name, and type Fred for the project name. Look at the Code window and you see that Delphi has updated the tabs — they now read Barney and Fred. The first line of the unit is now `unit Barney;` and `program Fred;` is the first line of the project file. Also, the project's uses clause now has Barney and BARNEY.PAS where it used to have Unit1 and UNIT1.PAS. Delphi has updated the source code files to reflect their new names.

Now switch to the Object Inspector window and change the form's Name property from Form1 to Rubble. Again Delphi changes the source code to match. The object type for the form changes to TRubble, and in the main project, even the comment has been updated. Because the form's caption was *exactly* the same as its name, Delphi changed the caption, too. Figure 13-3 shows the main program as updated by Delphi.

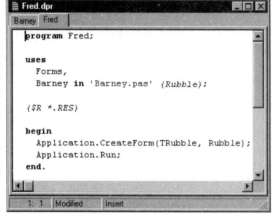

Figure 13-3:
When you rename the form or save files under new names, Delphi handles all the internal changes.

Anything Delphi does for you is something you shouldn't do for yourself in the code. For instance, if you want to give a unit or program a new name, don't edit the name by hand. Instead, use Save As. . . or Save Project As. . . to save it under the new name. And don't change the form object's name in the unit code — do it in the Object Inspector window. If you make these changes yourself, Delphi won't compile your program!

What a Difference a Component Makes

Building a framework for the main program and unit is just the beginning of Delphi's programming work. Every time you add or rename a component, Delphi is there, integrating that component into your program.

Arrange the Form and Code Editor windows on the screen so that you can see both of them at once. Cover up the Object Inspector window if you have to. In the Code Editor, flip to the Barney page and make sure that the type declaration section for TRubble is visible. Click the button icon in the Standard page of the Component palette and move the mouse over the form, but don't place the button yet. Focus your gaze on the TRubble definition, and click the mouse.

Did you see what happened? The definition of TRubble expanded to include the `Button1: TButton;` line. This line is a declaration of independence for the TRubble object type; it now marches to a different drummer. It is different from a plain blank TForm because it has a data field named Button1 whose data type is TButton.

Delphi deals with dependencies

When you add a component, Delphi sticks a line into the form object's definition. That gives your program a name to holler when it wants to call on the component. There's a tad more preparation required, but Delphi doesn't do it until you save the program.

Scroll the Code Editor so that the uses clause is visible. Fix your eyes on the uses clause as you press Ctrl+S to save the file. Now delete the button from the form.

When you saved the file, the unit name StdCtrls popped into the uses clause. This is the name of the unit that supports standard controls such as buttons, edit boxes, and list boxes. When you deleted the button from the form, the Button1 line in the TRubble object type declaration disappeared. StdCtrls, however, is still present in the uses clause.

Why doesn't Delphi remove the unit name, too? First, the StdCtrls unit supports many Delphi components — not just TButton and not just the one specific TButton named Button1. To decide whether it's safe to remove the unit from the uses clause, Delphi would have to review every other component in the form. Second, and more importantly, *you* may have written code that requires that unit. Delphi knows all about its own code, but it doesn't psychoanalyze your code. Thus, it's just not safe for Delphi to delete the unit from the uses clause.

Just about any component you place on a form expands the uses clause, unless the support unit for that component is already present. When you're starting out with a new program, you may be in a creative frenzy, adding and removing components from the form with wild abandon. Chances are good that your final version includes units you don't need, and some of the code and data for those units can wind up in your compiled program. To avoid program-bloat, delete all units from the uses clause that Delphi added to support particular components. Leave all the units that are present in a brand new form's uses clause (you can see them in Figure 13-1), and don't delete any unit names that you typed in yourself. Next time you save the file, the ones that are still necessary magically reappear.

There's a slight possibility that following this advice could give Delphi indigestion, as in Figure 13-4. If Delphi suddenly starts complaining that your code contains an unknown identifier, it means you've deleted one unit too many. Don't panic! Simply consult the help system about the offending identifier to see which unit supports it, and then add that name back to the uses clause.

Figure 13-4:
Here
TButton is
an unknown
identifier to
Delphi
because you
deleted
StdCtrls
from the
uses clause.

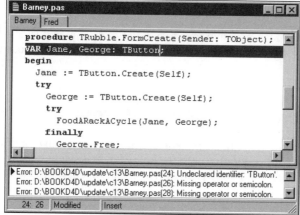

If you use Delphi 1.0, you'll notice that you don't get a list of error messages as shown at the bottom of Figure 13-4. The Delphi 1.0 compiler screeches to a halt when it hits a syntax error, dropping you into the editor at the error location. Because of the compiler's incredible speed, detecting and correcting errors one at a time was never a serious problem. Delphi 2.0, however, detects as many errors as it can before stopping, and lists them all. Clicking an item in the error list displays the line of code that caused the problem. Not only that, it warns you about code that has fine syntax but whose logic is suspect, and it even gives you hints for better programming. What won't they think of next!

What's in a name?

If you change the Name property of a component using the Object Inspector window, you'll see it change in the Code Editor. Delphi even renames any event handlers whose default names were based on this component. If you change Button1 to TikTok, Button1Click will change to TikTokClick. However, Delphi won't meddle with the code you wrote. If your code calls a component by its name, it will stop working when you change the name.

The easiest way around this problem is to accept the default names supplied by Delphi. On the other hand, giving components names that relate to their function helps you keep track of what's going on in your program. The intended purpose of FormatHardDiskButton is obvious; Button42 is not. If you decide to use descriptive names, one simple rule saves you aggravation: Always name a component at the time you create it, before writing any code that refers to the component. If you do change your mind about the name later on, be sure to change it in any code you've written yourself!

There's another way around the name problem, one that we've already used quite a bit in example programs. Every event handler has a parameter called Sender that identifies the component that caused the event. Instead of referring to, say, Edit1, your code can use: `(Sender AS TEdit)`

You get a double benefit this way. First, there's no dependence on the name of the component button. Second, the same event handler can now easily service multiple components of the same type (in this case, TEdit). Like the song says, "Avoid any possible embarrassment or blame. Don't ever call your component by his name!"

Handling Event Handlers

You've written dozens of event handlers by now, and you surely take it for granted that Delphi generates the proper skeleton for each type of event. Let's take a closer look at some of those skeletons and see what we can scare up.

Easy come, easy go . . .

Delphi creates empty event handlers at the drop of a hat, or at least at the click of a button. But if you don't use 'em, you lose 'em! Starting with a new project, select the Events page of the Object Inspector window and double-click the OnClick event for the main form. In the Code Editor, scroll up until you can see the object class definition. Besides supplying you with the framework for an OnClick event handler, Delphi adds that event handler to the definition of the main TForm1 object. With an eagle eye on the Code Editor, press Ctrl+F9 or select Compile from the Compile menu.

The event handler skeleton and its line in the object type definition appeared like magic, and they vanished just as quickly when you compiled the program. When an event handler contains no code, not even a comment, Delphi deletes it before compiling the program.

Add a button to the form, double-click it, and put an empty comment {} in the OnClick event handler. Now delete the button and compile the program.

Notice several things here. For one thing, the event handler is part of the form object's definition; it actually belongs to the form, not to the button. When you delete the button, the event handler remains behind — another sign that it doesn't belong to the button. And because the handler wasn't 100% empty, Delphi doesn't wipe it out at compile time.

If you want to delete an event handler, delete all the code except the skeleton Delphi originally provided. Delphi takes care of removing the skeleton and the declaration line the next time you compile.

But are we compatible?

In several of the sample programs you worked with earlier, you've connected more than one component to the same event handler. For example, the interface for the simple editor project you built in Chapter 5 was initially based on push buttons. You transferred the OnClick handlers for those buttons to menu items in Chapter 6, and then connected speed buttons to some of them in Chapter 8, all without any change to the event handlers. You can connect an event handler to events from multiple components, or multiple events from the same component, as long as the events are compatible. What are compatible events? You'll see.

Starting again with a new form, create an OnClick event handler. Now select OnDblClick in the Events page and press the down-arrow button next to this event's value. A list appears, containing the single item FormClick. Do the same for OnClose, though, and the list is empty. What's happening?

Go down the list of events and create an event handler for every single one of them. Don't bother putting any code in the handlers; we're just interested in the skeletons Delphi builds. Maximize the Code Editor so that you can see as much code as possible.

Figure 13-5 shows part of the TForm1 object's declaration after performing this exercise. Note that several groups of handlers have the same parameter list (the stuff in parentheses after the procedure name). The most popular parameter list is `(Sender : TObject);`

FormDragDrop and FormDragOver have the same set of parameters, as do FormKeyDown and FormKeyUp.

Now if you click the down arrow next to the OnClick method in the Object Inspector, you get quite a list of choices (Figure 13-6). Look back at the Code Editor and you see that all the handlers in the list have the same set of parameters. That's all Delphi requires. If the parameter list matches, the event handler

```
Unit1.pas                                                    _ □ ×
Unit1
    procedure FormActivate(Sender: TObject);
    procedure FormClick(Sender: TObject);
    procedure FormClose(Sender: TObject; var Action: TCloseAction);
    procedure FormCloseQuery(Sender: TObject; var CanClose: Boolean);
    procedure FormCreate(Sender: TObject);
    procedure FormDblClick(Sender: TObject);
    procedure FormDeactivate(Sender: TObject);
    procedure FormDestroy(Sender: TObject);
    procedure FormDragDrop(Sender, Source: TObject; X, Y: Integer);
    procedure FormDragOver(Sender, Source: TObject; X, Y: Integer;
      State: TDragState; var Accept: Boolean);
    procedure FormHide(Sender: TObject);
    procedure FormKeyDown(Sender: TObject; var Key: Word;
      Shift: TShiftState);
    procedure FormKeyPress(Sender: TObject; var Key: Char);
    procedure FormKeyUp(Sender: TObject; var Key: Word;
      Shift: TShiftState);
11: 1              Insert
```

Figure 13-5: If you create event handlers for every event, you'll notice a pattern emerging.

is compatible, even if you went behind Delphi's back and built it by hand. Remember: Delphi creates the event handlers' parameter lists, so you must never change them.

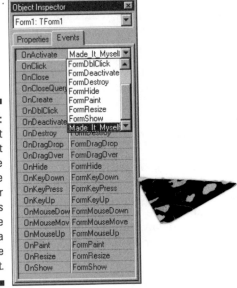

Figure 13-6: Any event handler that has the same parameter list as OnActivate is a compatible replacement.

The fact that Delphi lists a particular event handler as compatible is no guarantee that you can use it successfully. That depends entirely on the code in the event handler. The code might assume that the handler is being called by a particular component or a particular type of component.

What Can You Edit in the Code?

To redundantly reiterate once more: Leave Delphi's work to Delphi. With some specific exceptions, if Delphi wrote a line of code, let Delphi handle it. If you wrote the code, it's your responsibility. Now just what is under your control?

Event handler innards

Obviously you can create event handlers — you've been doing that for ages. Delphi builds a skeleton for you and adds the declaration line to the form object definition, and you fill in the rest. But never change the method header (the first line of the framework containing the method name and parameter list), and never change the declaration line in the form object definition. Within the event handler, you can do anything that's legal in Delphi's programming language.

All right, all right, if you're just desperate to rename an event handler, here's how you do it. Suppose you want to rename Button1Click to GoSpeedRacerGo. Click on Button1, and then flip to the Events page in the Object Inspector. Highlight the event handler name Button1Click and change it to GoSpeedRacerGo. That's all you have to do. Delphi will take care of changing the code, and it will even make the change for any other components that share this same event handler. The only time you'd need to edit the code yourself is if it includes a direct call to Button1Click from another event handler.

Adding units to the uses clause

Several of the sample programs have required you to add something to your program's uses clause. Delphi starts you off with units that most programs need, and automatically adds units to support the components you place on the form. However, if you start poking around in the Delphi manual and using the functions you find there, Delphi may hit you with an Unknown identifier error message. Just look up the offending identifier in the help system to get the name of the unit it's in. Insert the name into the uses clause and you're ready to roll.

You also need to add units to the uses clause when you start using Windows functions that don't live in the three core Windows DLLs — GDI, USER, and KERNEL. Delphi has an import unit for just about every Windows library, including COMMDLG, DDEML, LZEXPAND, MMSYSTEM, OLE, PENWIN, SHELLAPI, STRESS, TOOLHELP, VER, and WINMEM32. Again, look up the function in Delphi's help system to find the unit name.

If your main form needs to call on a secondary form, you'll also have to add that secondary form's unit to the main unit's uses clause. The main form doesn't know anything about a secondary form unless you give it access to the secondary form's unit.

Touch not the body!

By default, the main body of the project file contains only commands to create one or more forms and run the application. You hardly ever need to change this code, and if you do, Delphi may lose the capability to automatically maintain it.

When you become expert enough at programming that you need to make changes to the main program's body, be circumspect. Wait until the program is stable enough that you're sure you won't need to add or rename any forms.

My object all sublime

A few of the sample programs have required you to add a data field or two to the object definition. Nobody told you that's what was happening; you were just instructed to find the public or private declarations section near the top of the file and insert a specific line or two. You were busily extending an object definition without even realizing it!

You can add your own data fields to the object definition, define your own methods, or override existing methods. A method here, a method there . . . and pretty soon you're talking about real programming! That's the next chapter.

Always add fields or methods in the public or private declarations section, never to the top part of the form class declaration. That's where Delphi generates its own declarations. If you put your declarations in the middle of Delphi's, Delphi will complain about the infiltrators and ask whether it's okay to delete them.

Quick Review: Your Personal Crib Sheet

There won't be a pop quiz on what you've learned in this chapter — we haven't managed to make the print medium interactive yet! But the chapters that follow assume you absorbed at least most of the material. If you're unsure, here's a quick review.

For each project you start, Delphi writes a *program* file that gets turned into a self-contained EXE and one or more *unit* files that must be used by a program or another unit. Delphi program files tend to be small, with all the real action taking place in units.

A unit has three parts. The *interface section* holds variables, functions, and type definitions that are available for all the world to see. Stuff in the *implementation section* is private to the unit. And any lines of code in the optional *initialization section* are executed at the start of a program that uses the unit.

The *uses clause* at the beginning of a code module (program file or unit file) identifies other units this file depends on. A code module may have one or more *type definition blocks,* which define data types. It may also include one or more *variable declaration blocks*. Among the possible data types is the *object class*. An object is a collection of data fields *encapsulated* with functions that act on the data.

An *object class* (or just *object*) is almost always defined in terms of an existing object. It *inherits* the features and capabilities of the existing object, and *extends* the object by adding new data fields, adding new methods, or overriding existing methods. The new object is called a *descendant* of the object it inherits from (its *ancestor*).

Normally, Delphi functions insist that the data passed to them match the data type of their parameters. If the type in question is an object type, however, any descendant is also acceptable. That's called *polymorphism*.

Next time the topic of object-oriented programming comes up at a cocktail party, remember the big three words: inheritance, encapsulation, and polymorphism. Just say them a lot, in various combinations, and people will think you're a genius.

Well, you made it! The lightning round is over, and you've all won. You've wrung dry the code that Delphi writes for you, and perhaps have a greater appreciation for the work it does. The next chapter is a primer on programming principles. Ready? Let's go!

Chapter 14

Elements of Programming

· ·

In This Chapter

▶ Naming variables

▶ Choosing data types for maximum flexibility

▶ Making decisions in code

▶ Creating statements that repeat over and over and over . . .

▶ Keeping your programming skills growing

· ·

Did you ever take a radio apart when you were a kid? It sure was a lot easier than putting it back together! We've picked apart the program code that Delphi writes, but putting a program together is going to require knowledge of all the nasty little pieces.

On the other hand, you received quite a stack of manuals with Delphi, and the help system will tell you about any particular aspect of Delphi's programming language. So maybe I don't have to write this chapter?

Well, before you can get answers from a manual or a help system, you have to know the right questions to ask. That's where this chapter comes in. I won't waste your time regurgitating factoids from the manuals; rather, I'll help you reach the point where manuals become useful.

The techno-geek quotient of this chapter is above average, and the concepts you need to learn are all wound up with each other, so it's hard to lay them out in any kind of order. If you find it tough sledding, try to plow through to the end regardless, to pick up the general ideas. Take a break, walk the guinea pig, practice your figure skating, and then try reading through it again. It *will* be easier the second time, I promise!

Data's De Way It Goes

You say DAY-ta, I say DAT-ta, let's call the whole thing off . . . but we can't! Computers were invented to process data, and a big part of programming is finding the right way to represent the data.

Delphi's data storage lockers are called *variables,* and each variable represents a specific *type* of data. In addition, Delphi programs use immutable data elements called *constants,* also with a particular data type.

It depends on several variables . . .

What do Delphi variables have to do with the price of gum in Singapore? Well, the price of gum in Singapore *is* a variable. Today it may be 50¢ and a week in jail; tomorrow it may be 75¢ and a public caning. We can say that chewing tobacco costs twice as much as gum without specifying today's price. It's the same in Delphi. When you want to refer to a particular piece of information without concern for its current value, you use a variable.

If time is nature's way of keeping everything from happening at once, variables are Delphi's way of keeping everything from happening in the same place. When you declare a variable in your program, Delphi reserves space in memory for that variable and makes sure that no other variable occupies the same space.

The word *var* begins a block of one or more variable declarations. Each declaration associates a variable name with a particular data type. (I'll discuss data types shortly.)

Scoping out variables

The dictionary says *scope* means "breadth or opportunity to function," and Delphi variables have the opportunity to function only within their scope. A variable declared outside any function has *global* scope; it can be used anywhere in the program. The main form variable in a Delphi unit is an example of a global variable. A variable declared inside a function, on the other hand, is *local* in scope. It's inaccessible outside the function that defines it. Global variables grab space in memory and hog it the whole time your program is running. Local variables exist only while the function that contains them is active.

Figure 14-1 shows an event handler from Chapter 9's CD player project. In this event handler and many others, you were instructed to *replace* the begin..end pair supplied by Delphi rather than just typing lines between begin and end. Surprise! When you typed these event handlers, you were defining local variables!

Figure 14-1:
This event
handler
uses three
local
variables
named Trk,
Min, and
Sec (for
Tracks,
Minutes,
and
Seconds).

```
CDPlayru.pas                                            _□✕
CDPlayru
  procedure TForm1.Timer1Timer(Sender: TObject);
  VAR Trk, Min, Sec : Word;
  begin
    WITH MediaPlayer1 DO
      BEGIN
        Trk := MCI_TMSF_TRACK(Position);
        Min := MCI_TMSF_MINUTE(Position);
        Sec := MCI_TMSF_SECOND(Position);
        Label1.Caption := Format('%.2d', [Trk]);
        Label2.Caption := Format('%.2d:%.2d', [Min, Sec]);
      END;
  end;

  1: 1            Insert
```

Use local variables whenever you can. Doing so conserves memory and makes it easier to keep track of what your program is doing. And, of course, always assign a value to a variable before you try to refer to its value!

What to name the new variable

Any combination of letters, digits, and the underscore character is a valid Delphi variable name, as long as the first character isn't a digit. You could name your variables _1, _2, _3, or VariableA, VariableB, VariableC, or Shadrach, Meshach, Abednego. Delphi won't mind!

However, you should give some thought to a variable's name and choose one that helps you remember the purpose of the variable. An expression such as IF X > Y doesn't have nearly as much punch as

```
IF ReactorCoreTemp > MeltdownDisasterLevel
```

The only time a nondescript name such as *N* really makes sense is when the variable *does* something nondescript, such as counting repetitions in a loop:

```
FOR N := 1 TO 12 DO Omelette.Add(Egg[N]);
```

Delphi won't let you use the same variable name twice in the same scope. You can't declare two global variables named SewageFlow, or one named STENCH and one named stench. (Delphi ignores the distinction between uppercase and lowercase.) If there's a conflict between global and local variables with the same name, the home team wins. For example, say you have a global variable called UnmatchedSocks and the current function declares a variable with the same name. When the function refers to UnmatchedSocks, it means the local one.

She's not my (data) type

Here's a quick quiz for you:

- ✔ What's "Cake" plus pi?
- ✔ How much is True times seven?
- ✔ What's the square root of "DUTT"?

Did you come up with any answers? Then you're thinking like a computer. If you answered 6.947, 7, and 37614, you're *really* thinking like a computer! Computers are famous for wasting time trying to answer the wrong questions. Delphi's data types help keep you out of this trap by squawking when, say, you try to take the natural logarithm of Tuesday. Every data type also has a particular size, so the data type tells Delphi how much memory to reserve.

A type declaration block in a Delphi program begins with the word *type*.

Choosing data types

Like the famous donkey sitting equidistant between two bales of hay, you could starve to death trying to decide which of Delphi's myriad data types to use. To cut through this muddle, memorize the half-dozen most important types:

Type	Data
LongInt	A whole number (no fractional part)
Extended	A number that may have a fractional part
Boolean	A True or False value
Char	One character, such as 'A'
String	A string of characters, such as 'Delphi'
PChar	A character string for use with a Windows API function

Whole numbers count

Computers, like people, do math fastest when they don't have to worry about fractions. Delphi has many whole number data types, but LongInt is the biggest and most flexible. It can represent any number from –2,147,483,648 to 2,147,483,647. That's over 4 billion values!

A LongInt takes 4 bytes of memory. The other whole number data types (Word, SmallInt, Byte, and ShortInt) use 2 bytes or 1, but their ranges are much smaller. 386 and better CPU chips talk to themselves internally in 4-byte numbers. Windows NT and Windows 95 are called 32-bit operating systems because they use 32-bit (4-byte) numbers internally. The Integer data type is adaptable — it uses 2 bytes (16 bits) in a 16-bit environment and 4 bytes (32 bits) in a 32-bit environment. The Cardinal type adapts in the same way, but it's an unsigned quantity. A Delphi 1.0 Cardinal is equivalent to a word; a Delphi 2.0 Cardinal can range from 0 to 2,147,483,647. However, LongInts are dependable 4-byte integers in either environment. LongInts rule!

I'll have just a fraction more

Whole numbers are nice, but a huge amount of scientific and business data can't be expressed in nice, whole numbers. To represent interest rates, pork-belly prices, or the weight of an electron, you need numbers with a fractional part. Delphi represents these as floating-point numbers. That means that the decimal point isn't fixed in one place, so it's just as easy to represent 1 trillion or 1 trillionth.

Here's the catch. Think back to grade school, when you learned about decimals. To convert a nice, clean fraction such as $1/3$ into decimal, you wrote 0.3 and then kept adding 3s until your pencil wore out. A decimal expression for $1/3$ will never be perfectly accurate. Other numbers, such as pi or the square root of 42, don't even have a repeating pattern.

The computer's floating-point numbers have the same problem, and they wear out their pencils after a fixed number of significant digits. To minimize the fuzziness of floating-point data, you want as many significant digits as possible. The 10-byte Extended data type has more significant digits and a larger range than Delphi's other floating-point types (Single, Real, Double, and Comp). Its maximum possible value is roughly 10^{4932}. How much is that? Well, one estimate puts the number of subatomic particles in the measurable universe at a mere 10^{74}!

An Extended type variable is accurate to 19 significant digits. To get an idea of how accurate that is, consider the distance of the Earth from the Sun, which is roughly 93 million miles, or 5,892,480,000,000 inches. An Extended type variable could represent the number of inches with six significant digits to spare. Therefore, you could store the distance from the Earth to the Sun accurate to around a millionth of an inch — that is, if the Earth and the Sun would hold still for the measurement. . . .

Most modern computers have an $80x87$ math coprocessor. If the main processor is an 80487 DX or Pentium, the coprocessor is built into the main processor. Internally, the math coprocessor does its calculations using data in the same format as Delphi's Extended type.

That sounds logical!

Delphi's components are busting with properties that have just two possible values, True and False. The data type for these properties is called Boolean, after George Boole, who was such a nut for logic puzzles that he invented symbolic logic to solve them. Delphi uses 1 byte to store a Boolean variable; a byte with the value 1 stands for True, and a byte with the value 0 represents False.

A real character

Computers also have to store text — gobs and gobs of text! Text is made of characters, and the Char type stores a single character. A Char occupies 1 byte, and it can have 256 different values. The values from 0 to 31 are control characters, such as Tab and carriage return. In most fonts, characters 32 to 127 are letters, numbers, and punctuation, and those from 128 to 255 are foreign and other special characters. Try the following exercise to see a list of all characters from 32 to 255.

Place a draw grid component on a new form and set its FixedRows and FixedCols properties to 0. Set ColCount to 2 and RowCount to 224. Insert these lines in the OnDrawCell event handler:

```
WITH DrawGrid1.Canvas DO
  IF Col = 0 THEN
    TextOut(Rect.Left, Rect.Top,
      IntToStr(Row+32))
  ELSE
    TextOut(Rect.Left, Rect.Top,
      Char(Row+32));
```

Run the program and you'll get a list like the one in Figure 14-2, showing each character and its corresponding numeric value. Note that in the last line of the event handler, we use Char as if it were a function, to convert the number that represents the current row into a character. That street runs both ways — Byte('A') is 65, for example.

The character sets represented by the Char data type were obviously invented by English-speaking people, with a few crumbs tossed to the European languages. Displaying Sanskrit or Cyrillic characters has always been difficult, if not impossible. The Unicode standard, used internally by Windows NT, allots 2 bytes to every character, allowing 65,536 different characters — enough for every known alphabet and then some. Delphi's WideChar data type represents a Unicode character. However, neither Delphi nor Windows 95 uses Unicode internally. For now, writing a Delphi application that uses Unicode falls into the realm of "Delphi Programming for Rocket Scientists."

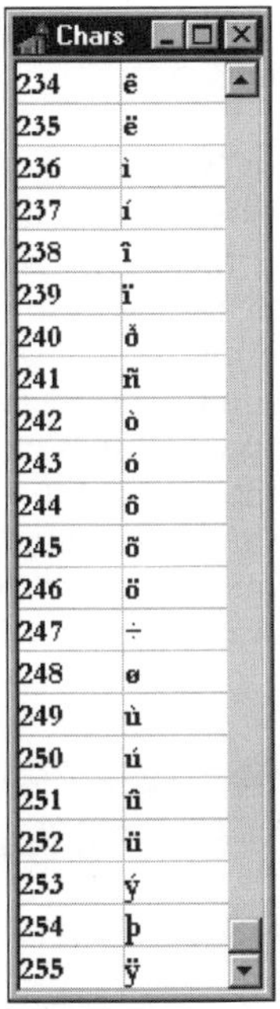

Chars		
234	ê	
235	ë	
236	ì	
237	í	
238	î	
239	ï	
240	ð	
241	ñ	
242	ò	
243	ó	
244	ô	
245	õ	
246	ö	
247	÷	
248	ø	
249	ù	
250	ú	
251	û	
252	ü	
253	ý	
254	þ	
255	ÿ	

Figure 14-2:
Each value for a Char type variable corresponds to a numeric value from 0 to 255.

There are some strings on me

If you're representing the Sex field in a personal data record, a single character may be enough, so you'd use the Char type. (That's M or F, not Y or N!) For text-based data in general, though, you use a whole string of characters at once. The Delphi 1.0 String data type can hold up to 255 characters, which is enough for most purposes.

A Delphi 1.0 string is an array of characters that takes up 256 bytes of memory, but most of the strings your program uses won't be 256 characters long. So Delphi 1.0 reserves the first byte of a string variable to hold a value representing the length of the text string it contains. (Delphi 2.0 strings are different; we'll look at them in a minute.) If the value of the string is 'Stromboli', the length byte will hold character number 9.

Old-time Turbo Pascal users know that you can fiddle with the length byte by referencing the 0th element of the array. For example, this line shortens a string variable by one character:

```
Dec(MarieAntoinette[0]);
```

However, Borland recommends against this practice because code written using this technique will *not* work with Delphi 2.0 strings.

Delphi also supports another type of string called a *PChar* (pronounced "pee char"). A PChar is an array of characters, like a String, but it doesn't have a length byte at the start. Instead, it has a null (zero) character after the last in-use character, from which it gets the alternate name ASCIIZ ("askee zee") string. Just to confuse you further, the terms *zero-delimited string* and *null-terminated string* are also used. Figure 14-3 shows how the same text string would be stored as a String and as a PChar. The dash at the beginning of the String variable is character #45 because the string is 45 characters long. The PChar data ends at the #0 character. The AnsiString has both a preceding length value and a terminating #0. The only reason to use a PChar rather than a string is if you need more than 255 characters or you're passing text to a Windows function.

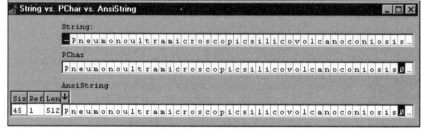

Figure 14-3:
Storing a string as String and as PChar.

You can declare a PChar in one of two ways:

```
VAR
  MyNonPointerPChar : ARRAY[0..300] OF Char;
  MyPointerPChar : PChar;
```

The first variable can be used immediately by your program. The second is a pointer (more about those shortly) and can't be used until you set aside some memory for it to point at.

A PChar can hold lots more text than a string, up to 65,535 characters! On the other hand, PChars are more awkward to use. A simple task such as assigning one PChar's value to another requires a call to StrCopy, one of the many PChar-specific functions Delphi offers. (They all begin with *Str.*) Delphi uses strings rather than PChars wherever possible; you should do the same. See Chapter 16 for some gory stories about the consequences of misusing PChars.

Honey, I blew up the string

People have problems with PChars, period. Yet Windows wants to wallow in them. Delphi 2.0 defangs this dilemma by defining AnsiString, a new type of string with the best characteristics of both. Like a PChar, the AnsiString ends in an ASCII zero character. Like a Delphi 1.0 string (now called a ShortString), it has its length stored at the beginning. However, the stored length is a 32-bit quantity, and the length of a AnsiString is limited only by available memory.

Figure 14-3 shows the layout of an AnsiString. Three numbers are before the actual string. The size allotted to the string is first, and the amount of that allotted size that's in use is third. In between is a reference count — when you set one AnsiString equal to another, Delphi raises the reference count rather than making another copy of the whole string. That means working with AnsiStrings can be quite a bit faster than working with the older length-byte strings.

Almost all standard string manipulation routines work with AnsiStrings. The only significant thing you can't do is tweak their length by fiddling with the length byte. Delphi 2.0 provides the SetLength procedure to handle cases when you want to set an AnsiString's length to a specific value. When you need to convert an AnsiString to a PChar, you just typecast it. (We'll talk about typecasting later in this chapter.)

By default, "String" in Delphi 2.0 means AnsiString — old-fashioned length-byte strings are called ShortString. You can set a compiler option to bring back the good old days, so that String has the old-fashioned meaning. But why would you want to?

As if that weren't enough, Delphi 2.0 has another jumbo-size string type, PWideChar. PWideChar is a zero-delimited character string, like a PChar, but it's composed of 2-byte Unicode characters. As noted previously, neither Windows 95 nor Delphi uses Unicode internally, so programming with PWideChars is for experts only.

Roll your own types

The data types for many properties of Delphi components are complete fabrications. Really! They're made up. In Delphi code, you can define new types based on the ones that are built into the compiler, or create new data types out of thin air. The simplest fictitious data type is the subrange. The NumGlyphs property for a bitmap button is an example. It's defined like this:

```
type TNumGlyphs = 1..4;
```

Delphi's range-checking code will reject any attempt to assign a value outside the range from 1 to 4.

In a similar vein, you can define string data types that occupy fewer than 255 bytes of memory. Simply follow the word String in the declaration with the maximum number of characters enclosed in brackets. For example, the code for the common dialog components defines the file extension as a 3-character string:

```
type TFileExt = String[3];
```

Use a smaller string type to save memory only if you know that a particular string variable will *never* use more than that number of characters. What, never? No, never! If your *never* turns into *hardly ever,* you'll have big trouble.

Delphi 2.0 users don't have to worry about the difference between ShortString and AnsiString. When you follow the word String with a length limit as shown here, Delphi 2.0 knows that you're asking for a ShortString. Ain't it smart?

Finally, there are data types defined simply by listing (or enumerating) the possible values. You'll find a lot of these enumerated types in Delphi's components. For example, the form styles are defined internally as

```
TYPE TFormStyle = (fsNormal, fsMDIChild,
   fsMDIFOrm, fsStayOnTop);
```

Generally, properties that show up in the Object Inspector as drop-down lists of values are enumerated types.

Any simple type that can be matched one-for-one to a whole number data type is called an ordinal type. This includes all the whole number types and the Char, Boolean, subrange, and enumerated types. Remember the name "ordinal type" because we'll use it in describing other aspects of Delphi programming.

The typecasting couch

Delphi uses data types to keep you from making mistakes. If you assign a value of one type to a variable of an incompatible type, Delphi will gripe. Sometimes, though, you really want to do that. All you have to do is tell Delphi you know what you're doing by using the name of the desired type as if it were a function. This is called a *typecast,* and as long as it's possible, Delphi will permit it. TFormStyle(0) equals fsNormal, and Word(fsMDIChild) is one, for example.

A typecast is always possible when the variable's actual type and the desired type are the same size. You can typecast a LongInt to a Single (a 4-byte floating point type) or to an array of four Chars, because they're all 4 bytes in size. That doesn't guarantee such a typecast makes sense, of course!

You've used typecasting extensively in the sample programs, but in a slightly different way. The AS keyword tells Delphi to treat an object AS if it were a particular type. The Sender parameter for event handlers is defined as a simple TObject, but if you know that every component using this handler is really a TButton, you can typecast it with an expression like this:

```
WITH Sender AS TButton DO
```

Constant as the northern star

The rule is simple: Use variables to hold values that may change during the running of your program, and use constants for values that won't change. When Delphi compiles the program, constants are hard-coded directly in the machine code. Numbers such as 42 and $C0FFEE are constants, as are literal strings such as 'Beware the Ides of March'.

You can also declare named constants, to make your code easier to understand. Defining WM_ENTERMENULOOP equal to the number 529 doesn't make your final program any bigger, and it's a lot clearer. Named constants are defined in a constant block beginning with the word *CONST*.

```
CONST AnswerToUltimateQuestion = 42;
```

Check the WinTypes unit (or the Windows unit in Delphi 2.0) for a zillion named constants used in calling Windows functions!

Scientific breeding of variables and constants has produced a hybrid of the two: the typed constant. A typed constant starts life with an initial value, like a regular constant. But that value can be changed in the program, just as a variable can. And a typed constant defined inside a function does not disappear when the function isn't active.

We used a typed constant in Chapter 9's Icon Viewer program to hold the number of the next icon. Its declaration looks like this:

```
CONST CurItem : LongInt = 0;
```

When the program starts, CurItem's value is 0. When the event handler containing this declaration is called, one or more icons are added to the collection, and CurItem's value is changed to match. Next time the event handler is called, CurItem retains the changed value.

Just to add to the confusion, in Delphi 2.0, typed constants can be changed only if you've checked the compiler option called Assignable typed constants. If you turn off this option, typed constants can't be changed, but VAR declarations containing a single global variable can include a value, like so:

```
VAR CurItem : LongInt = 0;
```

To preserve compatibility (and sanity), the programs in this book assume the Assignable typed constants option is ON.

Arrays, records, and sets: Building structured data types

A structured data type is one that's cobbled together from a bunch of simple data types (or other structured types), and there are three main cobbling styles. An *array* is made up of identical elements, whereas a *record* is a crazy quilt of different types. Delphi's *set* type is like the mathematical sets you may remember from New Math homework. You won't have to tinker up your own structured data types right away, but you'll find plenty of them in Delphi's own code.

Array of hope

Delphi's SYSUTILS unit defines a general-purpose array of bytes like this:

```
TYPE TByteArray = ARRAY[0..32767] OF Byte;
```

Here 0 and 32767 are the lower and upper bounds of the array. (They must be constants, not variables.) In Delphi 1.0, the total size of the array (the element size times the number of elements) must be less than 65,536 bytes. In Delphi 2.0, array size is limited only by available memory, but you still shouldn't use more than you need. Like the mess hall cook says, "Take all you need, but use all you take!" The elements of an array can be any type, even another array type. To refer to the *N*th element of the array named Foo, you'd use the expression

```
Foo[N]
```

Here *N* is an *index* into the array Foo.

When it comes to passing arrays as parameters to functions, Delphi cuts you some slack. You don't have to say exactly what the lower and upper bounds are, as long as the element type of the array matches. The built-in functions Low and High return the lower and upper bounds. That means you can define functions like this:

```
FUNCTION Min(TheArray : ARRAY OF LongInt) : LongInt;
VAR N : LongInt;
BEGIN
  Result := MaxLongInt;
  FOR N := Low(TheArray) TO High(TheArray) DO
    IF TheArray[N] < Result THEN
      Result := TheArray[N];
END;
```

You can pass any array of LongInts into this function, and it will return the smallest one. An array parameter like this, where the bounds aren't specified, is called an *open array parameter*. Open arrays can appear only in parameter declarations, not in type or variable declarations.

A new world record

Visualize a database record in a file — it might store name, age, and salary using a string, a whole number, and a floating-point number, respectively. This Record type declaration defines a single data type holding those three disparate elements:

```
TYPE
  DataRecord = RECORD
    Name : String[20];
    Age : Byte;
    Salary : Single;
  END;
```

To access an individual field of a variable that's a record type, you simply add a period and the field name to the variable name. For example, if ActionRec is a variable of the type shown here, ActionRec.Salary refers to the salary field. (Yes, this is identical to the way you reference a property of a component.)

You may have noticed that this record doesn't follow the rules for choosing data types. It has String[20], Byte, and Single instead of String, LongInt, and Extended. Why? Using the default data types, the record's size would be 270 bytes. With the selected smaller types, it's 26 bytes — less than a tenth as big. Multiply that difference by, say, 1,000 records and you've got a *substantial* difference in file size.

The Delphi 2.0 AnsiString type doesn't even have a fixed size, so the compiler steps in to keep you out of trouble. If you attempt to define a file of a certain record type and the record type contains one or more fields that are AnsiStrings, the compiler will gag and refuse to process your code. The error message confusingly says the record type needs "finalization." Don't worry about that — just redefine the string field as a ShortString or an ARRAY OF Char.

When just a single variable is involved, use the default choices, which are large and flexible. But when you'll have lots of variables in a file or array, use the smallest type that will hold the needed data.

Set 'em up

Star Wars, The Empire Strikes Back, and *Revenge of the Jedi* (whoops! I meant *Return of the Jedi*) make a set. Your video collection may include all of them, none of them, or any one or two. You may have multiple copies of one or all, but that's not important in determining whether you have a complete set. For each possible element in the set, either you own it or you don't. Delphi's sets are just like this!

Consider the BorderIcons property for a form. It explodes into four True or False subproperties: biSystemMenu, biMinimize, biMaximize, and biHelp. (Delphi 1.0 has only the first three.) The value of BorderIcons is displayed as a pair of square brackets [] enclosing the names of the subproperties that are True. BorderIcons is a set. Specifically, its type is defined like this:

```
TYPE
    TBorderIcon = (biSystemMenu, biMinimize, biMaximize,
            biHelp);
    TBorderIcons = Set OF TBorderIcon;
```

In this case, the possible elements of the set are all values in the enumerated type TBorderIcon. A set can also be defined using a subrange. For example, in the DB unit we find

```
TYPE TDBFlags = Set OF 0..15;
```

The TDBFlags type is defined with 16 possible members. A set can be defined to have up to 256 possible members of any ordinal type. It'll be a *long* time before your *Star Wars* video collection overruns the capacity of a Delphi set!

An ordinal type is one that can be matched one-for-one with a whole number data type. All whole number, Char, Boolean, and enumerated types are ordinal. Strings, floating-point numbers, and structured types are not.

Delphi generates especially fast and efficient code for set types defined with a limited number of possible elements. Remember, each possible element of a set takes 1 bit in memory. In 16-bit Delphi 1.0, the most elements a set type can include and still get super-speedy service is 16; in 32-bit Delphi 2.0, the limit is (as you've already guessed) 32.

Figure 14-4 is the event handler for the font speed buttons that you added to the simple editor project in Chapter 8. (A blast from the past!) Each button's Tag property contains the numeric equivalent of one of the font styles. If the button is down, the code adds that style to the font's Style set; otherwise, it removes it.

You can observe two different kinds of typecasting in Figure 14-4. The first line after begin uses AS to typecast the Sender parameter to TSpeedButton. The two lines that change the font style typecast the Tag property (a LongInt) to the enumerated type TFontStyle. That's necessary because Style is defined as a Set of TFontStyle.

```
MyEditor.pas                                          _ □ ×

MyEditor

  procedure TForm2.SpeedButton5Click(Sender: TObject);
  begin
    WITH Sender AS TSpeedButton, Memo1.Font DO
      IF Down THEN
         Style := Style + [TFontStyle(Tag)]
      ELSE
         Style := Style - [TFontStyle(Tag)];
  end;

  242: 1                    Insert
```

Nailing your files

You've written code by using Delphi components that load and save their own data to files on disk, and you've worked with database files, again using components. You'll probably find that it's easiest to use components for file access whenever you can. For example, read small to medium text files by loading them into a memo box and flipping through the lines.

On the other hand, when you do come to a file problem that can't be solved with a component, Delphi offers three types of file variables: TextFile, typed, and untyped. They're defined like this:

```
VAR
  MyTextFile    : TextFile;
  MyTypedFile   : File OF MyType;
  MyUntypedFile : File;
```

If the file you want to read is human-readable text, use a TextFile file type. If it consists of many identical chunks of data, use a typed file of a record type that matches the layout of the data chunks. And if it has a complex structure or no structure, use an untyped file. You'll find example code for reading and writing all three types in Delphi's own manual and help system.

Let me give you a pointer

Pointers are the bane of budding programmers. They're single-handedly responsible for the majority of hard-to-find bugs, and some programmers never master them. That's the bad news. The good news is, Delphi frees you from most of the aggravation surrounding pointers. (Technically, Delphi components are pointers, but you never have to think about that fact.)

So, what is a pointer? It's an address of a location in memory. A pointer variable points to another variable. You define a pointer type by putting a caret (^) in front of an existing type name. To refer to the variable pointed to by the pointer, put a caret after the variable name, like so:

```
VAR MyPointer : ^LongInt;
...
MyPointer^ := -1161889074;
```

But there's a catch: The variable the pointer points to doesn't exist; there's no memory allocated to it. (When a programming concept spawns convoluted phrases such as "the variable the pointer points to," you just *know* it must be trouble!) Global variables occupy memory throughout the run of your program, and local variables are automatically created when the function that contains them executes. But the variable a pointer points to is created only when you, the programmer, write code to allocate memory for it. Once you do, it's like feeding a stray dog: *You* are also responsible for cleaning up the mess. You have to write code that frees up the memory the pointer was using and returns it to the general pool, like this:

```
VAR MyPointer : ^LongInt;
...
GetMem(MyPointer, 4);
MyPointer^ := -1161889074;
DoSomethingWith(MyPointer);
FreeMem(MyPointer, 4);
```

You've already met the PChar data type, which is a pointer to a zero-delimited array of characters. The AnsiString data type is actually a pointer, too, but it's a really weird one. A normal pointer points to the beginning of a chunk of memory; an AnsiString points to a location in the chunk. Specifically, an AnsiString's data consists of a header made of three 4-byte Integers representing the allocated length, the reference count, and the in-use length of the string, followed by the characters of the string itself. The pointer points to the beginning of the character data, *not* to the header. (Look back at Figure 14-3 if this is confusing.) That's why you can get away with simply typecasting an AnsiString to a PChar when you need to pass a PChar to a Windows function. Never meddle with AnsiString innards; the compiler handles it all behind the scenes.

Putting It All Together

By now you should have a pretty good handle on the kinds of data Delphi programs can store. So now we have data — but no data processing. To do anything with the stored data, you have to write code (no shock!). You've experienced writing Delphi code throughout the first part of this book; now we'll talk about why the code you wrote works.

Idiomatic expressions and hot operators

Operators operate on operands. More specifically, they modify or combine variables or constants in a way that's dependent on the data type. The + operator between two numbers returns their sum, for example. But if you put it between two strings, whether they're old-fashioned length-byte strings or modern Delphi 2.0 strings, it glues them together. 'Two' + 'Two' equals 'TwoTwo'.

An *expression* is an operator with its operands. Here are some expressions:

```
X * Y
'Happy' + ' Birthday'
Bob = Leland
```

You can use an expression in place of a variable just about anywhere you're not trying to *change* that variable.

The four math operators (+, -, /, and *) work on any numeric type, as do the comparison operators (=, >, >=, and so on). If either operand in a math operation is a floating-point number, the result is a floating-point number. For whole numbers only, the DIV operator returns the whole number quotient of a division, and MOD returns the remainder.

Boolean operators combine logical expressions — the operators are AND, OR, XOR, and NOT. Suppose the Boolean variables A and B represent "Ivan is tall" and "Ivan is fat," respectively. A AND B is True only if Ivan is both tall and fat. A OR B is True if he's either tall or fat or both. A XOR B is True only if he is tall and thin, or short and fat — tall or fat, but not both. Finally, NOT A is True only if Ivan is not tall.

Figure 14-5 is a Delphi form that displays a truth table for AND, OR, and XOR. The cells in each table contain the result of combining the logical values in the row and column headers using the specified logical operator.

The logical operators can be applied also to whole numbers. In that case, they operate on each corresponding pair of bits in the two numbers. The most common use for this technique is to see whether a particular bit is set to 1, like this:

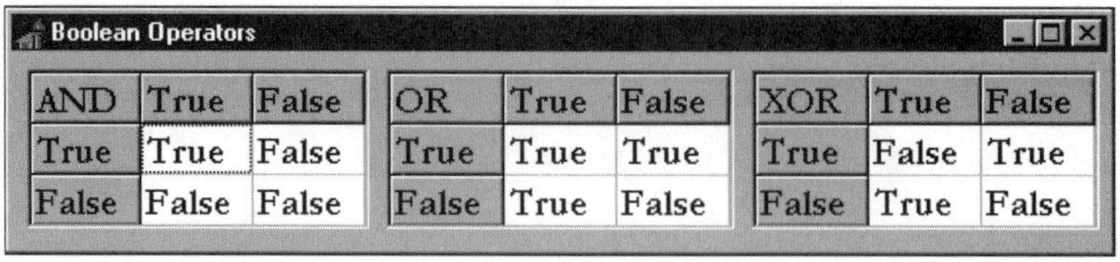

Figure 14-5:
This form displays the result of combining True and False using each of three Boolean operators.

Boolean Operators

AND	True	False
True	True	False
False	False	False

OR	True	False
True	True	True
False	True	False

XOR	True	False
True	False	True
False	True	False

```
IF Flags AND WF_ENHANCED > 0 THEN
```

You almost never need to know that NOT $COFFEE equals $FF3F0011, or that $BEEF XOR $FACE is $4421.

99.44 percent of set operations use the *in* operator to determine whether a particular member is present in a set. For example:

```
IF fsBold IN Font.Style
```

For those rare occasions when you have to perform gory mathematical operations on sets, the +, –, and * operators mean union, intersection, and difference, respectively. Thinking again of sets as video collections, the union of your set and mine includes all the videos that either of us own. The intersection is the ones we both have. The difference is the set of videos that you have but I don't — those are the ones I want to borrow!

The + and – operators have yet another set of meanings when used with PChars. Add 1 to a PChar and you get a pointer into the same text string, but one character further along. For example, if the PChar variable Yahoo contains 'Neil', then Yahoo+1 is 'eil'. If I now change 'Neil' to 'Nell', Yahoo+1 is 'ell'. Crazy? You bet! And misusing PChar math can make your program spew General Protection Faults. The more you learn about PChars, the better plain Delphi 1.0 strings look. And of course Delphi 2.0 AnsiStrings are the best of both worlds.

Making a statement

An old-fashioned DOS-based program is like a simple list of instructions for the computer to follow, one after another, whereas a Windows program is a set of contingency plans that are activated in response to events. When you start to pick apart those contingency plans, however, you find that deep down inside, each one is . . . a list of instructions for the computer to follow, one after another. In either case, the instructions on the list are called *statements*. Just as you end an English sentence with a period, you end a Delphi statement with a semicolon. Statements come in two flavors, simple and compound.

Just a simple statement

There are two kinds of simple statements: assignments and calls. An *assignment* gives a value to a variable. A *call* executes a procedure, function, or method elsewhere in the program, and then returns to the line that called it.

You've used quite a few assignments in the sample programs you built earlier in this book. For example:

```
Button1.Enabled := False;
```

The := symbol is the assignment operator. It takes the variable that's to its left and gives it the value that's to its right. The value on the right can be any expression that's compatible with the data type of the variable.

A procedure call is an instruction to go execute a bundle of statements elsewhere in the program and then return. For example, when you defined a button's OnClick method with the single statement

```
Close;
```

you were telling the computer to go execute the method called Close. A function call is the same as a procedure call, except a function brings back a result value when it returns to the caller.

There is actually a third kind of simple statement. It's similar to a line that's common in opinion polls — "If your answer is no, skip to question 42." The *Goto* statement jumps to another statement in the program, such as a procedure call. However, it never returns. Gotos are considered gauche and ill-mannered, and you're better off pretending that they don't exist.

Compounding statements

Suppose that you want to tell your Delphi program to wash and wax the floor if it's dirty. You might write code like this:

```
IF IsDirty(Floor) THEN Wash(Floor);
Wax(Floor);
```

However, this doesn't do what you wanted. The floor gets washed if it's dirty, but it gets waxed whether it's dirty or not. A compound statement will solve the problem:

```
IF IsDirty(Floor) THEN
  BEGIN
    Wash(Floor);
    Wax(Floor);
  END;
```

To turn a series of statements into one big compound statement, you put *begin* before the first statement and *end;* after the last statement. You can use a compound statement anywhere that a simple statement is permitted. For example, this is a valid (if pointless) Delphi statement:

```
BEGIN
  BEGIN
    BEGIN
      BEGIN
        BEGIN
        END;
      END;
    END;
  END;
END;
```

You'll use compound statements most often with the IF and WHILE statements (they're coming right up) and with the familiar WITH statement.

Conditional statements: Decisions, decisions

The IF statement has made frequent appearances in our sample programs:

```
IF Odd(Index) THEN Height := 2*Height;

IF odFocused IN State THEN Brush.Color := 0;

IF Bevel1.Height = 8 THEN
  Self.ClientHeight := Bevel1.Top
ELSE
  Self.ClientHeight := Bevel1.Height +
    Bevel1.Top + 8;

IF OpenDialog1.Execute THEN
  BEGIN
    ...
  END;
```

The basic framework is always the same:

```
IF <Boolean expression> THEN
  statement
ELSE
  statement;
```

The ELSE portion is optional, and either or both of the statement parts can be a compound statement. If the Boolean expression (called the *condition*) is True, the first statement gets executed; otherwise, the optional ELSE statement gets executed.

When you start to type an IF statement, first type the framework:

```
IF THEN
  BEGIN
  END
ELSE
  BEGIN
  END;
```

Now go back and fill in the condition between IF and THEN, and type the appropriate statements between the two BEGIN..END pairs. By doing this, you ensure that your BEGIN..END pairs will be matched up correctly and that they'll be aligned in the text, so you can easily see what matches what.

You can nest IF statements by using another IF statement as the statement part of the first IF. However, it's easy to mix up which ELSE goes with which IF. To avoid confusion, always use a BEGIN..END pair around nested IF statements.

Sometimes you need to test a particular variable against a bunch of different values. If the variable is an ordinal type, the CASE statement is more effective than stacking up dozens of IF statements.

A CASE statement looks like this:

```
CASE <variable> OF
  <Label1> : statement;
  <Label2> : statement;
  <Label3> : statement;
  ...
  ELSE statement;
END;
```

The variable part can be any variable, expression, or function result that's ordinal. The labels must be one or more constants or ranges of constant values separated by commas. For example, these are all valid:

```
'A' :
False, True:
fsBold..fsStrikeOut:
1..4, 6..10 :
```

The CASE statement is more efficient than multiple IF statements, and also easier to read.

Loops: Going around in circles

Computers are good at doing stuff over and over again, performing repetitious tasks that would bore a human to death. Delphi provides three kinds of looping statements:

Purpose	Loop type
Repeat a statement a specified number of times	FOR..DO loop
Execute a statement once and keep doing it until a condition becomes True	REPEAT..UNTIL loop
Execute a statement only while a condition remains True	WHILE..DO loop

A FOR loop requires a local control variable of some ordinal type. It looks like this:

```
FOR N := lower TO upper DO
   statement;
```

You can look, but don't touch. That is, your program must not try to change the value of the control variable. After the FOR loop is over, Delphi makes no promises about the value of the control variable, so don't make any assumptions. Delphi 2.0 adds the additional restriction that the control variable must *not* be a field of a record type — it has to stand alone.

The statement (simple or compound) will be executed once for each number, starting with lower and going all the way to upper. You can also reverse it by putting the upper limit first and replacing TO with DOWNTO. The control variable *N* is available within the statement:

```
FOR N := 0 TO Memo1.Lines.Count-1 DO
   WriteLn(POutput, Memo1.Lines[N]);
```

A REPEAT..UNTIL loop always executes its statement part once. After executing the statement, it checks to see whether the UNTIL condition is True yet. If not, it does it all over again:

```
REPEAT
  statement;
UNTIL condition;
```

A WHILE..DO loop checks its condition first and repeatedly executes the statement part while the condition is True. If the condition is False to begin with, the statement is never executed.

```
WHILE condition DO
  statement;
```

What if you've just told the computer to do something a million times, and a problem occurs the third time through? The Break statement helps here — it breaks out of any of the three types of loop. A related statement, Continue, jumps to the next repetition without finishing the loop. Figure 14-6 shows the OnReplace event handler from Chapter 5's simple editor project. It uses a WHILE True DO loop, with Break statements to break out of the loop when the search text isn't found or when one replacement has been made and the Replace All option wasn't chosen.

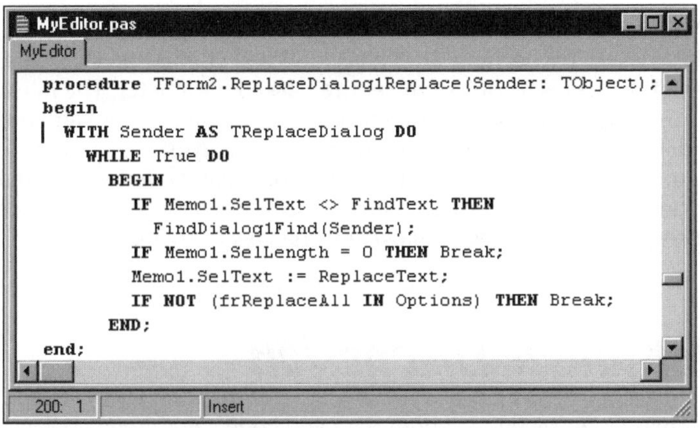

Figure 14-6:
The WHILE
True DO
loop would
execute
forever, but
the Break
procedure
breaks out
of the loop.

```
MyEditor.pas
MyEditor

procedure TForm2.ReplaceDialog1Replace(Sender: TObject);
begin
  WITH Sender AS TReplaceDialog DO
    WHILE True DO
      BEGIN
        IF Memo1.SelText <> FindText THEN
          FindDialog1Find(Sender);
        IF Memo1.SelLength = 0 THEN Break;
        Memo1.SelText := ReplaceText;
        IF NOT (frReplaceAll IN Options) THEN Break;
      END;
end;

200: 1          Insert
```

What's my function?

You've called many different functions that are built into Delphi, and a few built-in Windows functions. Delphi's help system lists and explains all the built-in Delphi and Windows functions. If you don't find a ready-made function to suit your purpose, you can write your own.

For example, if you find that several different event handlers in your program repeat the same chunk of code, you can move that code into a function and call the function from those several event handlers. Your program's size is reduced, and replacing straight code with a function call will have no noticeable effect on your program's performance. Also, if you need to change the code later, you can do it in just one place.

A function header starts with the word FUNCTION followed by the function name, parameter list, and returned data type. A procedure header starts with the word PROCEDURE followed by the name and parameter list only. The main body of the function consists of a begin..end pair surrounding one or more statements. Optional TYPE, VAR, and CONST blocks may precede the begin statement.

The purpose of a function is to return a value, so *somewhere* in the function's code you *must* assign a value to the function or to the implicit variable Result. If you forget this step, your function will return garbage!

Parameters are values passed by the code that's calling your function. Each parameter has a name and data type, like a variable. If the name is preceded by the word VAR, the calling code must pass a variable, not a constant, and the function can *change* the actual passed variable by changing the parameter. If the name doesn't have VAR before it, the calling code can pass a variable, a constant, or a function result, and any changes the function makes to the value won't affect the calling code.

When you're passing big variables, VAR parameters are more efficient because only the address of the variable is passed. When you use a value parameter, your function makes a copy of the entire passed parameter. The function can modify this copy, but not the original. Copying a number here and there isn't a big deal, but copying a 1,000-element array certainly is! If you want the efficiency of a VAR parameter without the risk of making unintended changes, put CONST in front of the parameter name. CONST parameters are passed as addresses, but Delphi doesn't allow any changes to them.

The Object under Discussion

In this chapter, we've talked about data and code separately; now we're back to objects, which meld the two. Delphi's forms and components are objects, and programming in Delphi is mainly a matter of combining and extending those objects. Now that you know more about the data and code that go into those objects, you have more freedom to extend them.

Strawberry data fields forever

When Delphi creates a form-type object, it automatically fills in the data fields that define the components on the form and the methods that implement their event handlers. Just before the end of the object type declaration, it inserts the keywords private and public. When you add data fields (and methods), this is where you put 'em. If a field is meant for communication with the outside world, put it in the public section. Any fields that are just for your form's internal consumption go in the private section.

Data field declarations are just like variable declarations. You start with the variable name, add the data type after a colon, and finish with a semicolon.

Data fields in the main form object are like global variables, but better. You can keep them private to your form yet have them freely accessible in the form. And if the program has multiple instances of the form (for example, child windows), each gets its own copy of the data fields. Anytime you're tempted to use a global variable, see if you can simply create a new data field instead.

A method to your madness

You've created a zillion methods with Delphi's help, but you can also build methods from scratch. Methods have the same advantage over functions that data fields have over global variables: You can make methods private or public, and the methods you write are accessible in any other method of your object. No matter how many instances of an object your program uses, there's only one copy of the code for its methods.

To declare a new method, first enter a normal procedure or function header right *in* the object declaration, in the public or private section. Copy it to the Clipboard, move down into the implementation section, and paste the copy. (Don't stick it inside another method!) Now insert the object's name and a period just before the function name, so Delphi knows who this method belongs to. Add a begin..end pair, enter your code between, and go-go-go!

Let's lock in a few of these concepts with a concrete example. We'll rewrite a simple program from Chapter 9, the one that teases group window names out of Program Manager.

Place a list box on a new form and set Align to alTop and Sorted to True. Place another sorted list box, this one with Align set to alClient. Drop a DdeClientConv on the form and set its DdeService and DdeTopic both to ProgMan. (So far, this is déjà vu all over again, but that will change soon.)

Put the following line in an OnCreate method for the form:

```
GetTheData('Groups', ListBox1);
```

Insert the following line in an OnClick event handler for the first list box:

```
WITH ListBox1 DO
  GetTheData(Items[ItemIndex], ListBox2);
```

Page up to the private declarations section of the form object and add the following line:

```
PROCEDURE GetTheData(Item : String; ListB : TListBox);
```

Copy this line to the Clipboard, page down to the start of the implementation section, and paste in a copy. Insert TForm1 and a period just before the procedure name in the copy and add code so that the final method looks like this:

```
PROCEDURE TForm1.GetTheData(Item : String; ListB : TListBox);
VAR P : PChar;
begin
  P := DdeClientConv1.RequestData(Item);
  ListB.Items.SetText(P);
  StrDispose(P);
end;
```

This program does the same thing as the original example, but the duplicated code is now efficiently combined into the single method GetTheData.

Learning to Learn

If you just sit back and gawk at the sheer volume of stuff there is to learn about programming, you'll probably freeze up in horror. So, don't look: Do! Seriously, if you want to learn programming, the important thing is to *do* programming. When your ability is small, do something simple. When you get that working, build on it.

Think up something you'd like your computer to do, and just start working on it in Delphi. It doesn't have to be a simple project, as long as you have patience. Start adding components and building event handlers, within the realm of your ability. Most important, always leave yourself with a program that compiles and runs.

When you get stuck, go snooping. Peek into the source code for Delphi's components. Study the code for the sample projects in this book. Download code from your favorite on-line service. And of course, ask for help in the on-line forums. Borland has a considerable presence on CompuServe, but you'll find you can exchange tips with fellow Delphi users just about anywhere in cyberspace.

As for the manuals, there's no way you can memorize them, but try to at least page through them all. Keep one by your hammock, your bathtub, your favorite chair, or wherever you like to read. You don't have to understand the whole thing; just pass the contents in front of your eyes. Later, when you're trying to puzzle out some programming problem, a key word or phrase you've seen may pop into your memory. Look it up!

Many distinguished authors of prose and poetry set themselves a goal of writing something every day. Should an author of Delphi programs do any less? Keep programming, snoop through any code you can find, get at least moderately friendly with the manuals, and find a forum to ask for help. You'll learn!

Of course, one of the most famous learning methods is trial and error. You'll find out about some errors right away because Delphi will stop compiling your program and berate you. The tough mistakes are the ones that result in a program that runs but doesn't do what you meant it to. In other words, the program has a bug. In the next chapter, we'll work with Delphi's built-in debugging resources.

Chapter 15

Debugging

• •

In This Chapter

▶ Why compiler error messages deserve hearty applause

▶ Why the hints and warnings in Delphi 2.0 merit a standing ovation

▶ How Delphi programs keep from crashing when errors happen at run time

▶ How to peek at your data while the program is running

▶ How to step through your code line by line

▶ Techniques for applying bug-repellent to your code

• •

*A*ccording to modern legend, the original computer bug was a real, live (well, dead) insect found fried in a relay by the late Admiral Grace Hopper. Modern computers don't have any such gross physical components, but when they do what we *tell* them to do instead of what we *mean* for them to do, we still blame the problem on "bugs." *Debugging* a program means correcting it so that it does exactly what you intended it to do.

Some errors are so glaringly obvious that Delphi can catch them when it tries to compile the program. If you make a language mistake, Delphi never says "Aw, shucks, I know what you mean." It digs in its heels and refuses to continue until you correct the error. Other errors come up at run time when your program does something you didn't plan for, like dividing by zero or switching to a nonexistent directory. Delphi comes to the rescue again by posting a run-time error box (but still attempts to continue with the program).

Logic bugs are the worst — silent, but deadly. The program compiles and runs just fine, but the results are plain wrong. When you run into a logic bug, you'll be very thankful for Delphi's substantial built-in debugging features.

Grammar Lessons

About the twentieth time Delphi interrupts the compile process to grumble about an unknown identifier or something it "expected," you may be tempted to rub your magic lamp and wish all error messages to oblivion. Don't! Every message is helpful; every one is great! If a message is ignored, the compiler gets quite irate. Delphi speaks a very particular language, and if you make a grammatical mistake, you do not want Delphi guessing what to do. If you tell the program "Throw the baby down the stairs a cookie," it darn well better ask precisely what you meant by that!

When Delphi hits a snag during the compile process, it puts the cursor on the error and displays an error message on the status line. By pressing F1, you get detailed help information about the error (though the information may or may not be useful).

Unfortunately, Delphi can't truly tell you the error location. All it can do is show you where it noticed the error. It's like making a mistake in a long math problem. You may notice that the answer's wrong, but that doesn't tell you which calculation contains the error. In Figure 15-1, Delphi reports that it expects to see a semicolon instead of a period in the program's final line. But the real culprit is the extraneous BEGIN line above, marked with {<===}.

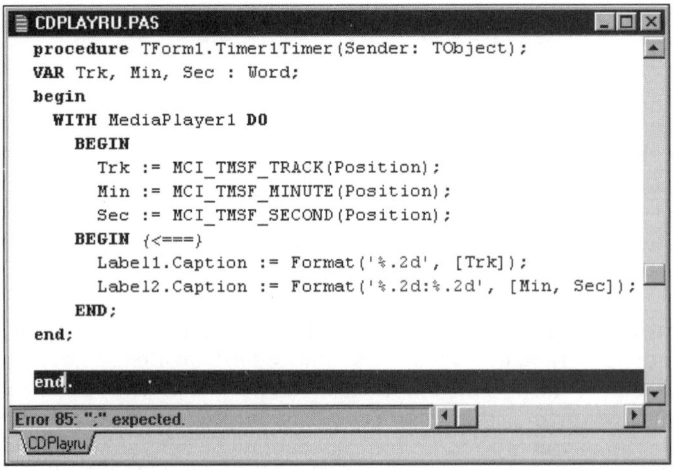

Figure 15-1:
Delphi tries
to point out
the location
of errors,
but it
doesn't
always hit
the target.

```
CDPLAYRU.PAS
procedure TForm1.Timer1Timer(Sender: TObject);
VAR Trk, Min, Sec : Word;
begin
  WITH MediaPlayer1 DO
    BEGIN
      Trk := MCI_TMSF_TRACK(Position);
      Min := MCI_TMSF_MINUTE(Position);
      Sec := MCI_TMSF_SECOND(Position);
    BEGIN  {<===}
      Label1.Caption := Format('%.2d', [Trk]);
      Label2.Caption := Format('%.2d:%.2d', [Min, Sec]);
    END;
  end;

end.
Error 85: ";" expected.
CDPlayru
```

If Delphi claims that a perfectly valid built-in function, variable, type, or constant is an Unknown identifier, it usually means you forgot to add a unit name to the uses clause. Click on the identifier in question to clear the error message, and press F1. The help system should tell you which unit contains the identifier.

The Delphi 2.0 compiler is smarter than its predecessor. When it hits a syntax error in the code, the compiler continues checking for errors until it just *has* to stop. Instead of a single error message, you may get several, as Figure 15-2 shows. Each error message includes the file name and line number where the error was detected; if you double-click a message, the program jumps to the corresponding source line.

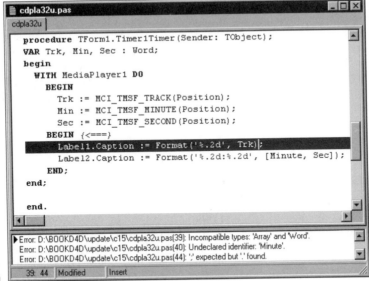

Figure 15-2:
Delphi 2.0
catches
multiple
errors at
once, so you
can correct
them all
before
trying to
compile
again.

The code in Figure 15-2 has the same erroneous BEGIN line as the example in Figure 15-1, but that's not all. The sloppy programmer has omitted the brackets around the variable Trk in line 44 and accidentally typed Minute instead of Min in the next line. The compiler not only catches all three errors, but also gives a clearer explanation. Whereas Delphi 1.0 merely said it expected a semicolon, Delphi 2.0 points out that a period was found in the spot where a semicolon should have been.

Many of Delphi's compiler error messages are self-explanatory. WHILE and DO go together like a horse and carriage, so Delphi won't let you forget the DO. If you use a variable where Delphi expects a type or vice versa, Delphi points out your error. Put a colon instead of an equal sign in a type declaration, omit the final bracket in an array, write an IF statement with no THEN . . . in every case, Delphi halts and complains that you haven't met its expectations.

If the error message doesn't make sense to you and the F1-invoked help isn't any better, look for something wacky in your code. The most common source of confusion is mismatched BEGIN..END pairs. This kind of error can be confusing because the point of discovery is often many statements past the actual cause. Perhaps you commented out some code and removed an END without its BEGIN. If eyeballing the code doesn't turn up the problem, try this solution. Print the offending function, circle all the BEGINs and ENDs, and draw lines connecting the matching pairs, starting at the outside and working inward. Then post the resulting abstract artwork on your refrigerator.

Anytime you write code that includes a BEGIN..END pair, type the BEGIN and END first, and then go back and insert lines of code between them.

When you're new to programming, you're bound to suffer through a lot of compiler error messages. They're annoying, but they both force you and help you to learn Delphi's rules of grammar. You *will* spend time poring over code, bitterly convinced that Delphi is lying about the error, right up to the moment when you discover the problem. Trust me — using code gets easier. Before long, you'll routinely dash off code that compiles on the first try!

Can You Take a Hint?

If your program has multiple syntax errors (and many programs do!), Delphi 2.0 can catch several at a time. But the 32-bit compiler's skill at analyzing programs doesn't stop there. Given the chance, Delphi 2.0 warns you about elements of your code that are syntactically correct but may not be complete or may not do what you expect. And it will give you hints about improving your code. All you have to do is check the Show Hints and Show Warnings boxes on the Compiler page of the Project Options dialog. Figure 15-3 illustrates the difference between hints and warnings.

Figure 15-3:
The Delphi 2.0 compiler warns about possible problems and offers hints for better programming.

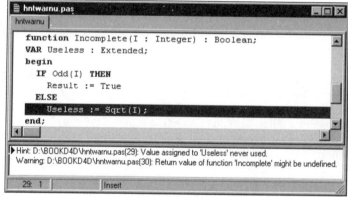

The aptly named Incomplete function returns True if its *I* parameter is odd. If not, it sets the local variable Useless to the square root of *I.* The Delphi 2.0 compiler notes a problem here — if *I* is not odd, the function's result is not defined. A problem exists, though the function doesn't generate any syntax errors as such. Delphi 2.0 gives you a warning that the function's return value may be undefined.

Because the program doesn't *do* anything with the variable named Useless, in expending computing power to set Useless to the square root of *I* is silly. That power could be better used for some other task, such as calculating winning lottery numbers in the background. Delphi 2.0 hints that your program is more efficient if you avoid wasting effort on the Useless variable.

Pay attention to Delphi's warnings — they help you improve your programming. Whereas compiler error messages catch flagrant syntax errors, warnings alert you to potential logic errors. Strive to write your programs so that Delphi doesn't need to give you any hints, and you end up writing better programs.

I Take Exception to That!

After your code passes Delphi's nit-picking grammatical scrutiny, it compiles and runs. That's when run-time error messages kick in. In Turbo Pascal, Delphi's ancestor, a run-time error usually brought the whole program to a screeching halt. Delphi programs are much more robust. They can survive most run-time errors, because of an ultra-modern feature called *exception handling*. I'll show you how to put this feature through its paces.

In a new project, start an OnCreate method for the form. Then replace the begin..end pair with the following local variable declarations and lines of code:

```
VAR
  X, Y : Extended;
  Z : 1..4;
  F : File OF Byte;
begin
  {$S+}
  X := 1/0;
  Z := 5;
  Y := 0;
  X := 1/Y;
  Caption := FloatToStr(X);
  Z := 4;
  Z := Z + 1;
  Caption := IntToStr(Z);
  AssignFile(F, 'NOGOOD.BUM');
  Reset(F);
  FormCreate(Sender);
end;
```

When you try to run this program, the Delphi 1.0 compiler detects and rejects the division by zero in the first line. (Delphi 2.0 allows the division, assigning X a value that represents an infinite number — but as soon as you try to use the number, you have problems.) So, delete the line containing division by zero and try again. This time, the compiler flags the line that assigns variable Z a value that doesn't fit in its range. Delete that line too. Note that Delphi caught this error at compile time — Delphi reserves run-time error checking for problems that it can't detect at compile time!

Try once more to run the program, and you find the compiler accepts it with no error messages. However, problems crop up at run time. Nothing is grammatically wrong with assigning variable X the value of $1/Y$, but when Y is 0, no finite number can represent the answer. Computers hate division by zero, so this line triggers the error box shown in Figure 15-4. The rest of the code in the event handler gets skipped, but the program does keep running.

Figure 15-4:
For most
run-time
errors,
Delphi posts
a warning
message
and
continues.

You'll notice that the program uses the value of X as the program's caption immediately after assigning the illegal value $1/Y$ to it. Method does exist in this madness! The Delphi 2.0 compiler can optimize your programs by eliminating useless code and never-used variables. If the value of X weren't *used* in the program, no exception would need to be demonstrated, because the Delphi 2.0 compiler would effectively throw away the offending calculation!

Choose Environment from the Options menu, click the Preferences tab, and put a check next to the Break on exception option in the Debugging panel. Run the program again and you get the message box shown in Figure 15-5. This message comes straight from Delphi, not from your program. It's a bit more detailed, because it's aimed at the programmer rather than the user. To correct this error, you can use the exception name EZeroDivide in your code.

When you close this message box, your program goes into suspended animation. You can use the techniques described later in this chapter to poke and pry at the variables involved and find out what caused the error. When you revive the suspended program, the user-style error box appears.

Figure 15-5:
The
message
Delphi
displays
when you
check the
Break on
exception
option box.

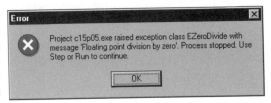

Comment out the $X := 1/Y$ line and run the program again. This time, you get a range-check exception on the line that attempts to give variable Z a value outside its range. Comment out *that* line and try once more. Now, unless you happen to have a file named NOGOOD.BUM (perhaps data on an ex-spouse?) you'll see a File not found error box. In each case, your program reports the error, skips the remainder of the method, and keeps on ticking.

To comment out one or more lines of code, surround them with braces {like these} or with parenthesis-asterisk pairs (*like these*).

Delphi 1.0 programs just can't handle some errors through exceptions. To see one, comment out the Reset(F) line and run the program one more time. This time, you get the stark and unfriendly error box shown in Figure 15-6. If you're running Delphi 1.0 under Windows 95, you may see something even weirder — the same error message box, but without the box. That's right; you may see the text from the two labels and the button shown in Figure 15-6 superimposed on your screen, without a message box to hold them! If that happens, you can click on the invisible button to put away the invisible box (shades of street mime artistry).

Figure 15-6:
Delphi 1.0
programs
can't
recover
from **every**
run-time
error.

A peek into Delphi's help system reveals that run-time error 202 is a "stack overflow error." That means your program started chasing its own tail and couldn't stop. The last line of the FormCreate method makes another call to FormCreate, which makes another call to FormCreate, and so on. As you'll remember from Chapter 1, each call uses up a little bit of stack space for local variables, and eventually no stack space is left. Still, almost all run-time errors get trapped and tamed by Delphi 1.0's default exception handling. And Delphi 2.0 tames the runaway stack overflow error as well.

If you're running Delphi 2.0, try this experiment. Drop a label on a new form, start an OnCreate event handler for the form, and replace the begin..end pair supplied by Delphi with this code:

```
procedure Overflow(I : Integer);
  begin
    try
      Overflow(I+1);
    except
      On EStackOverflow DO
        Label1.Caption := 'Repetitions before overflow: ' +
          IntToStr(I);
    end;
  end;
begin
  OverFlow(1);
end;
```

The Overflow procedure is a victim of runaway tail-chasing (called *recursion* at computer nerd cocktail parties). It calls itself over and over, upping the ante each time by adding one to the parameter it received. When the stack overflows, though, the exception handler catches it and reports just how many repetitions *were* possible. Don't try to run this program under Delphi 1.0, because the compiler won't even recognize EStackOverflow. And if you're running Delphi 2.0, be aware that although Windows NT is rock-solid, Windows 95 can be shaky when challenged by stack overflows.

By default, when your program traps an exception, it reports it and skips the rest of the active function, but you don't have to settle for that behavior. If you prefer, you can tell the program precisely how to respond to each exception.

Back in the OnCreate event handler you were working on, delete the tail-chasing last line and rewrite the rest of the code so it looks like the following:

```
Y := 0;
Try
  X := 1/Y
```

```
Except
  ON EZeroDivide DO X := 1.1E+4932;
End;
Caption := FloatToStr(X);
Z := 4;
Try
  Z := Z + 1;
Except
  ON ERangeError DO Z := 1;
End;
Caption := IntToStr(Z);
AssignFile(F, 'NOGOOD.BUM');
Try
  Reset(F);
Except
  ON EInOutError DO Rewrite(F);
End;
Caption := 'Success!';
```

For each potentially risky statement, you've given Delphi contingency instructions for exceptions. It will try to set X equal to 1 divided by Y, except if division by zero occurs, in which case X is just set to a Very Large Number. It will try to add 1 to Z, except if the result is out of range, in which case it will "wrap" back to 1. And it will *try* to open the file NOGOOD.BUM, unless the file doesn't exist, in which case it will create a new file with that name.

Now turn off the Break on exception option on the Preferences page of the Environment Options dialog and run the program. You'll see that the three lines that previously caused problems have been neutralized by your exception-handling code! The event handler runs all the way to its final statement, which sets the form's caption to "Success!"

A try..except exception handler reacts when an exception occurs. Another type of exception handler exists, however, that's proactive rather than reactive. This handler ensures that a particular block of code is executed whether or not an exception occurs. This type uses the keyword *finally* rather than *except*. Here's an example:

```
VAR TempStr : TStringList;
begin
  TempStr := TStringList.Create;
  try
    TempStr.LoadFromFile(InputFilename);
    DoSomethingWith(TempStr);
```

(continued)

```
    TempStr.SaveToFile(OutputFilename);
  finally
    TempStr.Free;
  end;
end;
```

The code that creates the TempStr variable is responsible for freeing up the memory it occupies when it's no longer needed. Because the line that frees memory is in the protected block that follows the keyword *finally*, it will be executed regardless of whether an exception occurs in the try block.

Try..finally blocks are useful any time your program takes some action that requires a follow-up. Allocating and deallocating memory, opening and closing files, creating and destroying temporary objects — these are all candidates for try..finally exception handling.

Alas, no help is available for the stack overflow problem in Delphi 1.0, because the exception-handling mechanism needs some stack space itself! But in most cases, Delphi's default exception handling prevents a run-time error from causing an ugly program crash. And by writing simple exception handlers for risky code sections, you can make your code nearly bulletproof.

Tiptoe through the Code Lines

Really blatant problems in your programs cause exceptions or run-time errors. Those are the easy ones to find and correct. But what if the program compiles without error, runs smoothly . . . and produces the wrong result? The problem is with your logic, and only *you* can solve it. You need one of those miniature submarines that can cruise your program's bloodstream and spot clots in the code. Of course, Delphi provides you with all the equipment you'll need for that little expedition.

Gimme a breakpoint

If your mouse gestures tend to be on the wild side, you may have already discovered breakpoints by accident. Click in the very leftmost column of the Code Editor to set or clear a breakpoint on that line. The line turns red (unless you've changed the default colors) and a stop sign appears in the left column. Press the F5 key to set or clear a breakpoint on the current line.

When you run the program, it halts just before it executes the breakpoint line. This action gives you an opportunity to examine your variables or to step through the code a statement at a time and watch for trouble. Figure 15-7 shows a breakpoint in a procedure that mysteriously locks up the system.

Figure 15-7:
Just before
the
highlighted
breakpoint
line is
executed,
Delphi stops
the program
so you can
have a look
around.

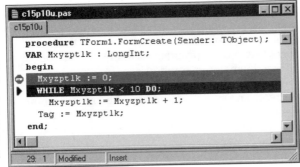

For a one-shot instant breakpoint, press F4. Delphi runs until it reaches the current line in the editor, and then halts. You can also select Program Pause from the Run menu (or press the Pause speed button) to suspend the program at whatever line it's currently executing.

Hot on the trace

Okay, your miniature submarine has surfaced at a breakpoint. What now? You could just choose Run again to put the program back in gear and wait for the next breakpoint. Most likely you want to cruise along slowly, one statement at a time.

When you press F7, choose Trace Into from the Run menu, or press the Trace speed button, Delphi executes just the current line of code and then halts again. If the current line is a function call and the source code for that function is accessible, Delphi dives right into it. You can trace through the lines of the function, and of any functions it calls, and so on. The current line is always highlighted and marked by a triangle in the left margin. (You can see it just below the breakpoint line back in Figure 15-7.)

Step on it

Sometimes Delphi's capability to trace into functions is a bane, not a boon. To avoid taking a pointless detour into a bug-free function, Step, don't Trace. Press F8 or choose Step Over from the Run menu. The whole function executes at full speed, and the program halts at the line after the function call.

The Trace Into speed button looks like a flea jumping into a box. The Step Over speed button looks like a flea jumping over a box.

Advanced breakpoints

What if you suspect trouble on the thousandth time through a particular code loop? You *could* put a breakpoint in the loop and run to that spot a thousand times. (Hey, you *could* carve the program on stone tablets, too!) But a pass-count breakpoint is a much better solution.

In a new project, create an OnClick method for the form with nothing in it but an empty comment, {}. Click in the far left column of the method's end line, or move the cursor to the line and press F5. Run the program and click the form; this should trigger the breakpoint.

Now choose Breakpoints from Delphi's View menu. You should see one breakpoint in the Breakpoint list window. Highlight it, and then right-click and select Edit Breakpoint… from the pop-up menu. If you're running Delphi 2.0, choose Properties from the pop-up menu. In the Pass count line of the resulting dialog, enter 10 and press the Modify button.

Run this program and click the form repeatedly. The breakpoint is triggered every tenth time it's reached. When you reach the breakpoint, press F9 to get the program rolling again, and keep clicking.

What if you suspect there's a problem when variable BabyBop is larger than variable Barney? You can use the same Edit breakpoint dialog to set a *condition* for the breakpoint. In this case, you'd simply enter BabyBop > Barney on the Condition line. Now each time this line is reached, Delphi checks the condition and breaks only if it's True. Figure 15-8 shows a sample program, its breakpoint list, and the Edit breakpoint dialog.

After you set up a fancy pass-count or conditional breakpoint, you may want to keep it even when you're not debugging. Instead of deleting the breakpoint at the end of a debugging session, highlight it in the Breakpoint list window, right-click, and choose Disable Breakpoint. In the Code Editor, the stop sign and the line's highlight will turn gray.

If you close the Edit breakpoint box by pressing the New button rather than Modify, you're creating a brand new breakpoint on the same line. Doing so lets you set a conditional breakpoint and a pass-count breakpoint on the same line. If you put both in the same breakpoint, the pass count advances only when the breakpoint is reached and the condition is true.

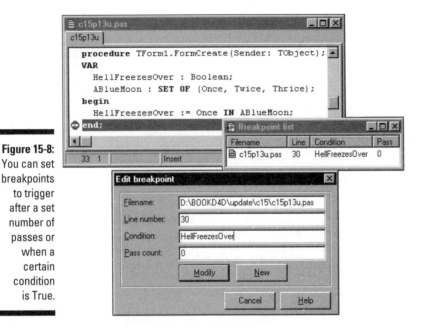

Figure 15-8:
You can set
breakpoints
to trigger
after a set
number of
passes or
when a
certain
condition
is True.

Demystifying Data

Now you know how to navigate through your program's code, how to stop at a particular line of code, and how to run your program one line at a time. But *why* would you want to do so? The main reason is to check on the values of variables. Delphi can squawk when a variable's value goes completely out of range, but it takes a human operator to spot more subtle problems. You've learned how to navigate through your code and follow the sequence of execution; now it's time to raise the periscope and have a look around.

Don't hesitate — evaluate

Way, way back many chapters ago, not long after this book began, I discussed the Evaluate/Modify dialog box. Ctrl+F7 displays this dialog any time (or choose it from the Run menu); you can use it to perform simple calculations or to convert numbers from hexadecimal to decimal. But its real purpose is revealed in a hot and heavy debugging session — it lets you peek at (and even modify!) variables.

When the program is stopped, you can get the value of any global variable or any local variable accessible to the current line. Not only that, if you suddenly realize the value is wrong, you can patch it up and continue debugging the program. Of course, you have to remember to go back and correct the *code* so that the variable doesn't get the wrong value the next time around.

You can also evaluate expressions combining multiple variables and constants. Of course, you can't change this result. If you want to change the sum of Foo and Bar, you'll have to change Foo, or Bar, or both!

Watch it!

Suppose you can see that a variable has the wrong value but can't figure out how it got that value. You could try various breakpoints until you find a spot where the variable looks right, and then step, step, step through the lines of code, evaluating the variable after each step. (Some people actually enjoy this process!) But if you'd rather just solve the problem as fast as possible, open the Watch list window instead.

When you press Ctrl+F5 or choose Add Watch from the Run menu, Delphi asks for a variable name. Once you add a watch variable, the Watch list window appears. (You can also choose Watches from the View menu.)

A variable in the Watch window has no more privacy than a goldfish. Every time the program stops at a breakpoint, every time you step into or over a line of code, Delphi updates the variable's value in the Watch window. *Now* it's practical to step through the program watching for suspicious changes! Just tap, tap, tap on the F7 key and keep your eye on the Watch window.

How'd I Get Here?

Delphi programs are surprisingly straightforward. Almost all the code *you* write is in the form of event handlers, and the event handler gets called when an event occurs. Rarely does any doubt exist about the sequence of function calls that led to a particular line of code being executed.

If you ever *do* wonder about the path your program took to reach the current line, choose Call Stack from the View menu. The list in the Call Stack window, shown in Figure 15-9, starts with the currently active function. Next comes the function that called the active function, then the function that called it, all the way back to the granddaddy function that represents the main program. If you find anything unlikely in the call stack, you can select a line and right-click to view or edit the corresponding source code.

Figure 15-9:
This is the
series of
function
calls that
lead to a
simple
OnClick
event.

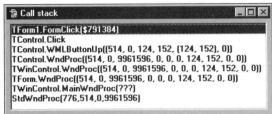

What about Turbo Debugger?

Borland sells a separate high-powered debugging product called Turbo Debugger for Windows — there's a 32-bit version as well, to go with Delphi 2.0. Go ahead and try it, if you like. But you'll probably find that any additional features it offers are beyond the ken of mortal man. For programming wizards, Turbo Debugger is fantastic! It's just overkill for the average person.

Delphi's integrated debugger should handle almost all of your debugging needs. It's a polite debugger that peacefully coexists with Windows and with the program that's being debugged. Turbo Debugger operates at a lower level; you can't even switch to another window when Turbo Debugger is active. It runs in character mode because it can't rely on Windows for its display. It's a brute!

If you decide to try it despite these dire warnings, you need to prepare your program. Choose Project from the Options menu, flip to the Linker page, and check the box that says Include TDW debug info. If you skip this step, Turbo Debugger still runs, but it displays assembly language gibberish and gripes that your program has no symbol table.

Almost all the features Turbo Debugger shares with the integrated debugger have the same menu names and shortcut keys. You still press F9 to run, F8 to step, and F7 to trace, for example. If you poke around the menu, though, you'll find it

has a lot of unfamiliar features, such as data dumps in hexadecimal, CPU register views, and a window that shows your program in assembly language.

The two features in Turbo Debugger that are most useful and least incomprehensible are global breakpoints and data debugging. Sometimes you'll find that a variable's value is changing and you absolutely can't figure out how. A "global changed memory breakpoint" (what a name!) solves that problem by breaking on any line that changes the specified variable. You can also set a global breakpoint that will kick in anywhere in the program when a specified condition is True.

Data debugging is to the Evaluate/Modify dialog as MIT is to the little red schoolhouse. Try the following. Choose Inspect from Turbo Debugger's Data menu and enter the main form variable's name (Form1 by default). Maximize the resulting window and every aspect of the variable is laid out in front of you. You see all the data fields with their values, and all the methods. And you can highlight a data field and inspect it, drilling down as far as you care to, or farther.

Despite these benefits, your time is probably more productively spent becoming proficient with the integrated debugger. When you've earned your wizard's hat, that's the time to buy a copy of Turbo Debugger.

Bug-Repellent Programs

Nobody writes buggy programs on purpose. Bugs creep in because people are careless or don't understand exactly what they're doing. Spending a little extra time *thinking* about the code you're writing is far better than to wasting days tracking down problems later on.

You can do some things to armor your programs against bugs. For example, whenever you can, turn logic errors into run-time errors. Really! If the variable Smee should always be in the range –12 to 12, define it to have that range. Now if an error in the program sets Smee to 42, you'll be alerted by a range-check error. This method sounds a little like testing for land mines by clomping around in heavy boots, but an exploding run-time error truly is better than a lurking logic error.

Many program statements aren't fully under your control because they process the user's data. When possible, don't give the user the chance to enter invalid data. And use try..except blocks to protect any risky statements. What's risky? You'll learn as you go along, but for starters always protect statements involving division by a variable and input/output statements.

Delphi attempts to protect you from pointers, the world's biggest supplier of bugs. Mistakes with pointers can trash completely unrelated data in your program, and they're hard to track down because the tiniest change to your code may change their behavior. If you have a choice, don't use pointers; but if you must use them, *triple*-check your code. Make sure that you always allocate the necessary amount of memory, and always deallocate precisely the same amount when you're through. Never access the variable before you've allocated its memory or after you've freed its memory. Do all this and you still may have some pointer-related bugs, but they'll be fewer.

You learn programming by programming, and you learn debugging by debugging. Believe me, you'll have plenty of opportunities to learn debugging. Keep writing code and debugging any errors you make. The remainder of this book is devoted to pointing out interesting facts and functions that you may want to try, and warning you about common errors. You should find lots of ideas for your own programs in the following chapters.

Part V

The Part of Tens

The 5th Wave

"THE PRINTER AND DISK DRIVE ARE CONTAINED IN THE HAT. IT'S GREAT FOR KEEPING AN UNCLUTTERED DESK, BUT IT'S HARD GETTING MORE THAN THREE OF US ON AN ELEVATOR AT THE SAME TIME."

In this part . . .

There's so much to say about Delphi, this book could go on forever. But then you'd keep reading forever, and you'd never get around to programming. That's no fun! So Part V simply hits some of the high and low points you'll encounter along your path, and then lets you get on with your life. For example, by now you know how to debug Delphi programs — perhaps you'd like to *avoid* the most common bugs? Well, you'll get the low-down on their modus operandi in Chapter 16!

Windows is euphemistically called a "rich" programming environment. That means it contains more function calls than any sane person could possibly remember, with names that nobody can spell. And of course 32-bit Windows ups the ante with more functions and still longer names. Delphi's components and built-in functions handle almost all the programming tasks you'll run into, but occasionally you do need to dive down to the Windows API (Application Program Interface) level. When you do, start by checking out the ten fascinating functions you'll meet in Chapter 17.

The secret of Delphi programming in three words is: components, components, components! But the code that defines those components and the code you write yourself to enhance them — well, that code uses a bunch of functions that are built into Delphi. And after you get past the brouhaha of components demanding your attention, you'll find some demure objects lurking in the background, objects that can do quite a lot for you. You'll get an introduction to these fabulous functions and obscure objects in Chapters 18 and 19.

So when you feel the urge to expand your horizons, flip to this section and take off!

Chapter 16
Ten Common Mistakes

In This Chapter

▶ Recognizing and avoiding common programming errors

▶ Comparing floating-point numbers without being thrown for a loop by tiny errors

▶ Understanding range, stack, and integer overflow errors

▶ Observing the destruction that misused PChars can cause

▶ Preventing input/output errors from turning into time bombs

*W*hen you start debugging your programs, you're bound to find some real bloopers. Here's a preview of ten mistakes that every programmer invariably makes at one time or another. When you pull one of these yourself, think of it as a rite of passage!

Fencepost Errors

Suppose you need to put up a 100-foot free-standing fence between your swimming pool and the freeway, so passing motorists don't lose control while checking out your tan. The elegant Art Deco fencing you've chosen needs a post every 10 feet. How many posts do you buy? If you said 10, you just committed a *fencepost error,* more mundanely called an *off-by-one* error. You need a post at one end and then another post every 10 feet, for a total of 11 posts, not 10.

The equivalent question in Delphi might be: How many buttons are in an ARRAY[0..10] of TButton? Again, the answer is 11, not 10. If you want an array with 10 buttons, you need to set the array bounds to [0..9] or [1..10].

Another off-by-one problem surfaces in REPEAT..UNTIL loops:

```
Commandment := 1;
REPEAT
  Commandment := Commandment + 1;
  EngraveOnTablet(Commandment);
UNTIL Commandment = 10;
```

This loop looks like one that will handle engraving each commandment from 1 to 10, but it's not! In fact, it acts on *nine* commandments, from 2 to 10. The correction in this case is to set Commandment equal to 0 initially.

Most of the time, you can ferret out fencepost errors by "shrinking" the problem. For instance, to put up a 20-foot free-standing fence with posts every 10 feet, you need three posts, one at each end and one in the middle. Every additional 10-foot section requires one more post, so the 100-foot fence will need 11 posts. In the REPEAT..UNTIL example, suppose the condition were UNTIL Commandment = 2. The condition will be True the very first time through the loop, so the loop executes once, not twice. Whenever you suspect a fencepost error, try shrinking the problem down to something more manageable.

Empty Statements and Spurious Semicolons

As discussed in Chapter 14, every statement in Delphi's language must end with a semicolon. Delphi also permits completely empty statements, so lines like these are valid:

```
;;;;;;;;;;;

(* World.Problems.Solve(Now) *);

begin end;
```

Empty statements are harmless, because the compiler doesn't generate any code for them. They can even be helpful! An empty statement for a particular value in a CASE statement makes it clear that you didn't *forget* that value — you really, truly meant for the CASE statement to do *nothing*.

However, adding a semicolon where it doesn't belong can replace an important statement with an empty statement, and the consequences can be lethal. To show you what I mean, place a spin edit box, a push button, and a list box on a new form, one below the other, all with the same width, as in Figure 16-1. Set the push button's caption to &Hail and its Default property to True. Insert this line in its OnClick event handler:

```
Hailstone(SpinEdit1.Value);
```

Because the SpinEdit component is a second-class citizen from the Samples side of the tracks, Delphi 2.0 users may want to build this program a bit differently. Delete the SpinEdit and put a plain edit box in its place. Add a modern Windows 95 UpDown component and set its Associate property to the edit box. In the button's OnClick event handler, use this single line of code:

```
HailStone(StrToIntDef(Edit1.Text, 0));
```

The result looks almost the same as a SpinEdit — in fact, Figure 16-1 shows a program built using an edit box and UpDown component.

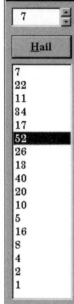

Figure 16-1: With the extra semicolon removed, this program demonstrates the peculiar Hailstone function.

Insert this line in the private section of the main form's object definition:

```
PROCEDURE Hailstone(N : LongInt);
```

Now page down to just after the implementation line and enter this code:

```
PROCEDURE TForm1.Hailstone(N : LongInt);
BEGIN
  ListBox1.Clear;
  ListBox1.Items.Add(IntToStr(N));
  WHILE N > 1 DO;
    BEGIN
      IF Odd(N) THEN N := 3*N + 1
      ELSE N := N DIV 2;
      ListBox1.Items.Add(IntToStr(N));
    END;
END;
```

As written, this program can completely lock up Windows 3.1. Do you see why?

The WHILE loop in this function is supposed to repeat the three lines of code between the BEGIN and END that follow for as long as *N* is greater than 1. However, the semicolon following DO turns the WHILE loop into a no-exit existentialist nightmare. The WHILE loop now executes the empty statement repeatedly as long as *N* is greater than 1. Because the empty statement doesn't change *N*, this loop runs forever (or until you press Ctrl+Alt+Del). The defective Hailstone procedure compiles just fine, but as soon as it's called with *N* greater than 1, it goes into a tailspin. Because multitasking in Windows 3.1 depends on the cooperation of every program, one program stuck in a loop can bring down the whole system. A Delphi 2.0 program that's locked in a loop won't do you much good, but at least it won't take Windows 95 or Windows NT down with it!

You can use a compound statement anywhere a simple statement is valid, so the "orphan" BEGIN..END block after the short-circuited WHILE loop is not a problem.

By the way, the Hailstone function is way cool. The rule is simple: If your number is odd, triple it and add 1. If it's even, divide it by 2. Repeat until the number reduces to 1. Graph the result and you'll see that it goes up and down wildly before converging on 1, like a hailstone bouncing up and down in storm winds. No way exists to predict how long a particular number will take to reach 1, or even to prove that every possible number *will* reach 1.

Put a semicolon at the end of every statement, but never insert a semicolon where it isn't needed. In the words of a famous patron of the arts, "Should these commands be ignored, a disaster beyond your imagination will occur!"

The Myth of Floating-Point Equality

Floating-point variables are fuzzy. No way exists to represent the vast majority of numbers with absolute precision, so we settle for as many significant digits as possible. Delphi's Extended data type offers 19 significant digits — enough to measure the distance from here to Alpha Centauri with just a few millimeters of error. Still, two numbers that differ by only that tiny margin are *not* equal.

Don't believe it? Try this! Place four labels on a new form, one below the other, and set the Alignment property for all four to taRightJustify. Set their captions to *X:*, *Y:*, *Y=X?*, and *Y-X:*. Add four more labels in a parallel second column. Replace the begin..end pair for the form's OnCreate event handler with these lines:

```
VAR X, Y : Extended;
begin
  X := 1995;
```

```
   Y := Sqr(Sqrt(X));
   Label5.Caption := FloatToStr(X);
   Label6.Caption := FloatToStr(Y);
   IF Y=X THEN Label7.Caption := 'YES'
   ELSE Label7.Caption := 'NO!';
   Label8.Caption := FloatToStr(Y-X);
 end;
```

Figure 16-2 shows the result. Squaring the square root of a number *should* give you back the same number, and it *seems* as if it does. But the expression $Y=X$ isn't True, and in fact, a teeny tiny difference exists between X and Y. The difference, about 0.0000000000000001, isn't *important,* but it *is* a difference. This problem can be hard to catch, because it depends on the exact numbers used. For example, change 1995 to 1996 in the example and the diminutive discrepancy disappears.

Figure 16-2:
You don't
need a
faulty
Pentium to
gather tiny
errors in
floating-
point
calculations.

```
The Quite Fatal Monty Python Fig Oil      _ □ X

  X : 1995

  Y : 1995

X=Y ? NO!

  Y-X : 1.11022302462516E-16
```

Once you're over the shock of realizing that 1995 isn't always equal to 1995, you'll be wondering what to do. Simply decide how close is close enough. Then instead of testing whether two numbers are equal, test whether they're close enough.

Returning to the previous example, insert this line right after the line that declares variables X and Y:

```
CONST epsilon = 0.000000001;
```

Now replace *IF Y=X* with the following:

```
IF Abs(X-Y) < epsilon
```

The absolute value of the difference between X and Y is much less than one billionth, so the program now reports that X does indeed equal Y.

Don't Forget the Function Result

Picture this: You've worked all night to finish your tax return before the April 15th deadline. As the sun rises, you rub your eyes and carefully seal the envelope — without enclosing the tax forms! Doing the same thing is easy when you're writing a function, especially if you stay up all night programming. Your code may carefully calculate a dozen intermediate values, meticulously combine them into one temporary variable, and then neglect to assign that variable to the function's return value. Such a function returns pure unadulterated garbage, nothing but random bytes skimmed from your system's memory.

The best cure is to *avoid* that temporary variable entirely. Every Delphi function has an implicit local variable named *Result,* and you can and should use Result instead of a temporary variable. Here's a simple example:

```
FUNCTION DefaultExt(const FileName, Extension :
   String) : String;
BEGIN
   Result := UpperCase(FileName);
   IF Pos('.', Result) = 0 THEN
      Result := Result + '.' + Extension;
END;
```

This function converts the file name to uppercase and assigns it to Result. Then, if the Result variable does *not* contain a period, it appends a period and the passed extension to the Result. No temporary variable needed here!

Ever vigilant, Delphi 2.0 catches this mistake. When you compile the program, a warning politely appears suggesting that the function result *may* be undefined. Don't mistake politeness for uncertainty! If the compiler says your function result may be undefined, you had better look long and hard at the function to see what's wrong.

Home In on the Range Errors

You should always do your development with the Range checking compiler option turned on. This built-in safety net catches an amazing number of errors ! Yes, you're allowed to turn it off when you compile the final production version of your program; turning off the various run-time error-checking options shrinks the final EXE file substantially. But when your users report bugs and you have to dive back into the code, grit your teeth and turn those options back on.

You learned back in Chapter 1 that the Range checking check box on the Compiler page of the Project Options dialog controls range checking. Well, you can also turn range checking on or off with a compiler switch in your code.

{$R+} turns it on for subsequent lines of code, and {$R-} turns it off. These switches supersede the state set by the Range checking check box.

The simplest range errors occur when your program tries to set a variable to a value that's just not in its range. With range checking on, a run-time error occurs. With checking off, the results can be surprising. If you try to pour the four bytes of a LongInt into a two-byte container, the extra two bytes are simply lost. For example, dump the number 987654321 into a Word variable and what's stored is 26,801. Who'd have thunk it? But wait, there's more! If you have range checking turned off and you try to access elements outside the bounds of an array, you can destroy the lives of innocent variables!

In a new project, build an OnCreate event handler for the form, replacing Delphi's begin..end pair with this code:

```
VAR
  Lawyer        : LongInt;
  Perpetrator   : ARRAY[1..2] OF LongInt;
  Bystander     : LongInt;
  Addr1, Addr2  : Pointer;
begin
  {$R-}
  Lawyer    := 0;
  Bystander := 0;
  Addr1     := @Bystander;
  Addr2     := @Perpetrator[Lawyer];

  Perpetrator[Lawyer] := $DADABABA;
  Caption   := Format('%p =?= %p', [Addr1, Addr2]);
end;
```

Set a breakpoint on the line of code that begins with the word Perpetrator. Press Ctrl+F5 and add Addr1, Addr2, and Bystander,x to the Watch window. Run the program to the breakpoint. Now press F7 to execute that one line of code.

Figure 16-3 shows the dirty deed — the innocent Bystander variable's pristine zero value was stomped into the dust by a range error. The variables Addr1 and Addr2 have the same value, indicating that the nonexistent 0th element of the Perpetrator array occupies the same location as the Bystander variable. This kind of thing happens all the time when you forego the protection of range checking. You Have Been Warned!

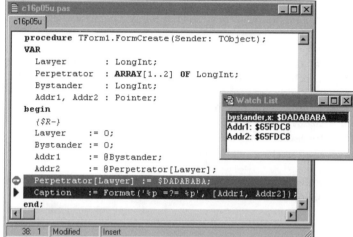

Figure 16-3:
Range
errors can
wreak
havoc on
nearby
variables.

Stacking Up Errors

Every program running on your system has a memory hunk reserved to hold its code, another hunk for global data, and a third hunk called the stack. This third hunk gets its name from the spring-loaded dish stacks in old-fashioned cafeterias. Take a dish off and the spring pushes the stack up so the next dish is at the top. Add some clean dishes and they sink down again so the top dish is at the same height.

Delphi programs don't wash dishes (too bad!), but they do stack *function calls.* When a function gets called, its local variables are pushed onto the stack. If it calls another function, the variables remain on the stack — they just get pushed down further to make room for the second function's variables. And when each function ends, its variables pop off the stack.

The Stack checking check box on the Compiler page of the Project Options dialog controls stack checking for your program. The compiler switch {$S+} forces stack checking on for lines of code that follow; {$S-} turns it off. These switches override the compiler options setting.

The only time you have to think about this stack thingie is when a stack error happens. If your program seizes up with a stack error, it might actually need more stack space. You can adjust your functions to use fewer or smaller local variables, or you can tweak the Stack size setting on the Linker page of the Project Options dialog. Thirty-Two-bit programs compiled under Delphi 2.0 have loads more stack space available, which is a good thing, because stack checking can't necessarily protect a 32-bit whose stack runneth over.

Most of the time, though, a stack error means your program is stuck chasing its tail in a recursive loop. The dictionary entry for *recursion* says "See recursion."

When a function calls itself, or calls another function that calls it back, that's recursion. When you forget to include a way for the function to break *out* of recursion, that's a stack error. Each time the function calls itself, it uses a little bit of stack space, and eventually the stack is just used up. You'll usually remember to provide a way out in a function that's supposed to be recursive. You run into trouble when the recursive call is accidental.

Make sure that you've checked the Stack checking check box on the Compiler page of the Project Options dialog. Then start an OnResize event handler for a new form, replacing the begin..end pair supplied by Delphi with these lines:

```
VAR BigWaste : ARRAY[0..1023] OF Integer;
begin
  BigWaste[1023] := Width;
  IF Odd(Width) THEN Width := Width + 9
  ELSE Width := Width - 9;
end;
```

Run the program, and it crashes with a stack overflow. The BigWaste variable ensures that even the expanded stack of a Delphi 2.0 program overflows. What happened? Well, any change to the dimensions of a form, whether it's from mouse action by the user or code in the program, causes an OnResize event. This OnResize event handler changes the Width value, which generates another OnResize event, which changes the width, *et cetera ad nauseam*.

Windows 3.1 and Windows 95 don't react *at all* well to stack overflows. If your program has stack checking turned off, a stack overflow could occur *inside* a Windows function. In that situation, Windows itself can crash. Leave stack checking turned on during development, and consider leaving it on in your production code as well. Windows NT is invulnerable to application stack overflows because NT system functions run on a system stack, not the application's stack.

Overflowing Integers

An integer overflow is like a range error, but sneakier. If you run your program with integer overflow checking off, you can suffer mysterious errors in calculations involving whole number variables. Cheer up! If you follow the recommendation in Chapter 14 and use LongInts for all your whole numbers, you'll almost never experience this one! The compiler switch to turn overflow checking on is {$Q+}; turn it off with {$Q-}.

Here's the deal. When you add, subtract, or multiply two whole numbers, they first get "promoted" to the smallest whole number data type that fits them both. If the result of the calculation doesn't fit in that data type, the extra bits are simply tossed out. I'll show you this problem in action.

Put six labels on a new form and then replace the begin..end pair of an OnCreate method for the form with this code:

```
VAR
  B, B1, B2 : Byte;
  I, I1, I2 :SmallInt;
  W, W1, W2 : Word;
begin
{$Q-,R-}
  B := 255;
  I := 32767;
  W := 65535;
  B1 := B*B; B2 := B+B;
  I1 := I*I; I2 := I+I;
  W1 := W*W; W2 := W+W;
  Label1.Caption := Format('%u*%u=%u',[B,B,B1]);
  Label2.Caption := Format('%u+%u=%u',[B,B,B2]);
  Label3.Caption := Format('%d*%d=%d',[I,I,I1]);
  Label4.Caption := Format('%d+%d=%d',[I,I,I2]);
  Label5.Caption := Format('%u*%u=%u',[W,W,W1]);
  Label6.Caption := Format('%u+%u=%u',[W,W,W2]);
end;
```

Figure 16-4 shows just what can happen when you turn off overflow checking. Weird, huh? You're better off leaving overflow checking on and using LongInt variables wherever possible.

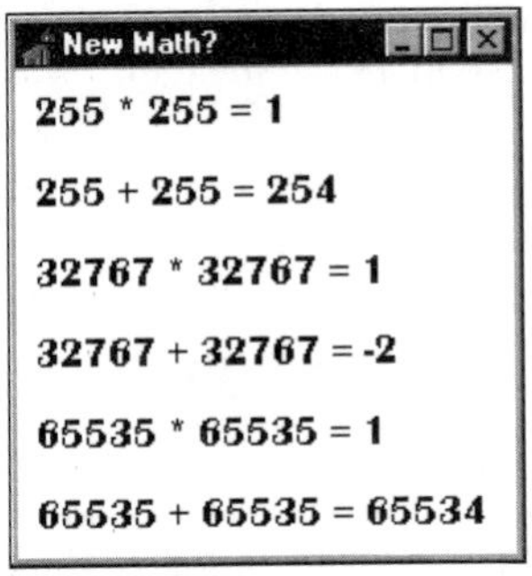

Figure 16-4:
Delphi's
overflow
checking
protects you
from bizarre
results like
this.

```
New Math?                    _ □ X
255 * 255 = 1

255 + 255 = 254

32767 * 32767 = 1

32767 + 32767 = -2

65535 * 65535 = 1

65535 + 65535 = 65534
```

PChar Panic — GPFs Galore

Delphi 1.0 String variables and Delphi 2.0 AnsiString variables are easy as pie to use because they're no different from other types of variables. The moment you declare one, it's available for use. You can assign the value of one String or AnsiString variable to another, or glue several together with the + operator.

```
ZooString := 'orang' + 'utan';
```

Once you're familiar with Strings and AnsiStrings, you're likely to try using PChar variables in the same way. DON'T! That's about the most dangerous thing you can do in Delphi!

Start an OnCreate event handler for the main form of a new project and replace the begin..end pair supplied by Delphi with these lines:

```
VAR Curly, Larry, Moe, Shemp : PChar;
begin
  Shemp := 'Nyuk nyuk nyuk!';
  Curly := 'Ow!';
  StrCopy(Curly, Shemp);
  Larry := StrNew('Woo-woo woo-woo!');
  Moe := Larry;
  StrCopy(Moe, 'Oh, a wise guy, eh?');
  IF (Moe=Curly) OR (Larry=Curly) THEN;
end;
```

Set a breakpoint on the first line of code, and add Curly, Larry, and Moe to the Watch window. Run the program and step through the event handler, keeping an eye on the Watch window. See Figure 16-5.

Figure 16-5:
Treating
PChars as if
they were
Strings
makes this
function
extremely
dangerous.

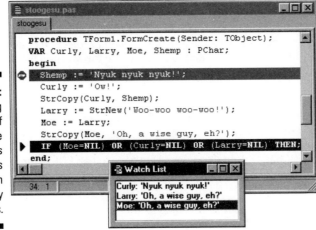

This event handler is a real comedy of errors. The code says to set Larry to the string 'Woo-woo woo-woo!', but as you step through it, you'll see it actually gets set to a portion of 'Nyuk nyuk nyuk!' And when the last line of code assigns a value to Moe, Larry gets the same value. Poor Larry!

The first two lines of code contain the same big mistake. They each set a PChar variable equal to a literal string constant. Remember, PChars are pointers, so the pointers now point to those literal strings *in the program's data segment.* The third line is a legitimate function that copies one PChar's value to another. Unfortunately, Curly's string has room for only the three characters 'Ow!' The rest of the copied string spills over into the next part of your program's data segment in memory. Specifically, it trashes the string 'Woo-woo woo-woo!' The line that sets Larry's value is a legitimate way to give a value to a PChar. The StrNew function allocates enough memory to hold the literal string and copies the string into that memory, and Larry points to that copy in memory. Unfortunately, the literal string that gets copied is the one that was trashed by the previous command.

For your next really big mistake, set Moe equal to Larry. When you set one String variable equal to another, the characters in the string get copied over. But PChars are pointers, so setting one PChar equal to another just gets them both pointing at the same *place* in memory. When the last line legally copies a value into Moe, it changes Larry, too.

What's the point of the last line, the one that checks whether any of the three PChars are NIL? Without that line, the Delphi 2.0 optimizing compiler wouldn't keep all three variables visible for us in the Watch window! One or more would be inaccessible at any given moment.

Under Delphi 1.0, this program compiles and runs without a noticeable problem. If you use the more exacting Delphi 2.0, the program probably crunches to a halt with an Access Violation after the OnCreate method finishes. Choose Program Reset from the Run menu to clear up the mess. Actually, these problems are pretty mild. Pointer errors can just as easily overwrite more significant parts of your program, causing inexplicable *General Protection Faults* (GPFs) or Access Violations in seemingly unrelated areas. Be forewarned: If you treat PChars like Strings, you turn your program into an accident waiting to happen.

In Delphi 2.0, String by default means AnsiString, the new PChar/String hybrid. You can use an AnsiString in place of a PChar when you need to pass a string of characters to a Windows API function. All you have to do is typecast the AnsiString to a PChar. But don't go wild! Don't try to use PChar functions to *change* the value of an AnsiString! Treating an AnsiString as a PChar can be just as big a problem.

Let Sleeping I/O Errors Lie

When your program performs any kind of input/output task, such as reading a file or creating a directory, you risk having it interrupted by an I/O exception.

That can be a shock to the user! To keep things running smoothly, your program can take over the handling of I/O errors. The {$I-} compiler directive turns off I/O error checking; {$I+} turns it back on.

If you do turn off I/O checking, your code must check the built-in IOResult variable after each I/O operation and deal with any errors. If you forget this step, an I/O error can get stuck in Delphi's gears and go dormant, only to come flying out at the next I/O operation anywhere in your program.

Start a new project and put these lines in the form's OnCreate event handler:

```
{$I-}
ChDir('C:\I\LOVE\YOU\YOU\LOVE\ME');
{$I+}
```

Put this single line in an OnClick event handler for the form:

```
ChDir('C:\');
```

When you run the program, nothing happens. The invalid directory name in the OnCreate method doesn't cause any trouble, because you turned off I/O checking. But because you didn't check the IOResult variable, the I/O error is still lurking. Click the form and an Invalid file name exception box pops up, even though nothing is wrong with the directory in *this* ChDir statement.

See the problem in this simple program is easy, but what if you had a big project with dozens of forms? If you must turn off I/O checking, your code needs to check IOResult after every I/O operation!

Chapter 17

Ten Windows API Functions

In This Chapter

▶ Why you don't have to memorize hundreds of Windows functions

▶ Launching other Windows programs from your programs

▶ Building a utility to exit or restart Windows quickly

▶ Locating important Windows files

▶ Quizzing Windows about important system information

▶ Building fancy 16-bit and 32-bit About boxes that display useful system information

---

*W*indows makes hundreds and hundreds of API (Application Program Interface) functions available to the programmer. This seeming largesse is actually a mind-numbing disaster. You can spend hours, even days, paging through reference books looking for just the right function. The names get unwieldy, too, with tongue-twisters such as GetMenuCheckMarkDimensions, IsClipboardFormatAvailable, and DlgDirSelectComboBoxEx.

Delphi 2.0 opens up the world of 32-bit Windows programming for Windows 95 and Windows NT. Scads of additional functions are available, with even longer names such as MultinetGetConnectionPerformance, DestroyPrivateObjectSecurity, and SystemTimeToTzSpecificLocalTime. Almost all Windows 3.1 functions are still present for backward compatibility, and many have new "extended" versions named by adding the suffix *Ex*. GetVersion becomes GetVersionEx, ExitWindows becomes ExitWindowsEx, and so on.

Delphi's components mostly insulate you from contact with this prickly style of programming. When you call on a component to load itself from a file or display itself on the screen, it may call dozens of Windows functions, but it politely keeps them out of sight. On the other hand, all the Windows functions are still completely available for your programs if you need them, and some are still useful even with Delphi, as you'll see in this chapter.

The WinProcs unit that appears in the uses clause of every unit Delphi 1.0 builds gives direct access to the majority of the Windows API functions. The Delphi 2.0 Windows unit serves the same purpose. Others are contained in special units such as MMsystem (for Multimedia functions) and OLE (for Object Linking and Embedding functions).

Where's the BEEP?

If you've enabled the Windows system sounds, each Windows session can start with the sound of a brass band and end with a lullaby. How about a bomb sound or a breaking window to go with critical errors? Four system sounds are tied to the four standard icons for a message dialog box. So how come you never hear them unless you're running Windows 95? Windows 3.1 doesn't automatically add sound to its message boxes, and neither Delphi 1.0 nor Delphi 2.0 gives voice to its message dialogs. The programmer has to call the API function MessageBeep before displaying the message box.

If you're unsure whether a particular event handler is getting called, insert a call to MessageBeep. If it squawks, clanks, or neighs, the handler was called!

Start a new project with a fixed-size form captioned Beep Test. Place four bitmap buttons and two regular buttons in a vertical column. Assign these captions to the buttons, from top to bottom: MB_ICONINFORMATION, MB_ICONEXCLAMATION, MB_ICONQUESTION, MB_ICONSTOP, Default Beep (0), and Speaker Beep (65535). Assign these six values to the Tag property of the buttons, from top to bottom: 64, 48, 32, 16, 0, 65535. Select all four bitmap buttons and set their Height to 49, their Width to 257, and their Margin to 4. Now select all six buttons and create an OnClick event handler for them containing just these two lines of code:

```
WITH Sender AS TButtonControl DO
  MessageBeep(Tag);
```

Write an OnCreate event handler for the form and replace the begin..end pair supplied by Delphi with these lines:

```
VAR
  Ico : TIcon;
  N   : LongInt;
BEGIN
  FOR N := 1 TO 4 DO
    WITH FindComponent('BitBtn' + IntToStr(N)) AS TBitBtn DO
      BEGIN
        Glyph := TBitmap.Create;
        Ico := TIcon.Create;
        try
          CASE Tag OF
            64 : Ico.Handle := LoadIcon(0, IDI_ASTERISK);
            48 : Ico.Handle := LoadIcon(0, IDI_EXCLAMATION);
            32 : Ico.Handle := LoadIcon(0, IDI_QUESTION);
            16 : Ico.Handle := LoadIcon(0, IDI_HAND);
          END;
```

```
            WITH Glyph DO
              BEGIN
                Height := Ico.Height;
                Width := Ico.Width;
                Canvas.Draw(0,0,Ico);
              END;
          finally
            Ico.Free;
          end;
        END;
  END;
```

Whew! That OnCreate handler was complicated, but worthwhile. It sets the glyph for each of the first four buttons to the corresponding icon, as Figure 17-1 shows. Run the program and press each button to hear the corresponding system sound. To use one of the sounds in a program, just call MessageBeep and pass the constant indicated on the button.

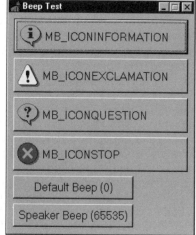

Figure 17-1: This program lets you audibly review the four dialog box system sounds.

Bossing Other Programs Around

If you're a take-charge kind of programmer, why not have your application take charge of launching other applications? Who knows — if Godfather Program Manager loses his edge and the Windows 95 Explorer gets lost in the jungle, *your* program may be able to take over! Even if your ambitions aren't quite so grandiose, knowing how to fire up other programs is useful, and you can do so in three ways.

A quick launch with WinExec

The WinExec function is a bit creaky; it's been around since Windows 3.0. Still, it's adequate for launching programs.

Start a fixed-size form project with the caption Launcher. Place an edit box on the form, delete its text, and stretch it the entire width of the form. Below the edit box, put a push button with the caption Launch, and set its Default property to True. Use these lines for the button's OnClick event handler:

```
VAR Command : String;
begin
  Command := Edit1.Text + #0;
  IF WinExec(@Command[1], SW_SHOWNORMAL) < 32 THEN
    MessageDlg('Failed to execute ' + Edit1.Text,
      mtError, [mbOK], 0);
end;
```

That's it! Run the program and type a command such as NOTEPAD.EXE WIN.INI, and then press Enter or click the Launch button. Poof! Notepad appears, with WIN.INI loaded. You can run DOS-based programs as well. WinExec searches the current directory, the Windows directory, the Windows system directory, the directory containing the Launcher program, local directories in the PATH, and any mapped network directories in the PATH, in that order.

Here's a technical note you *can't* skip. Sorry! You learned in Chapter 14 that when you pass string data to Windows API functions, it has to be a PChar. A PChar is a pointer to an array of characters, with an ASCII zero to signal the end. The code in the Launcher project creates a PChar *in* the String variable named Command. First it copies the edit box's text to Command and appends an ASCII zero, and then it passes the expression @Command[1] to WinExec. @Command[1] refers to the first character in the string Command, and the @ operator returns the *address* of the variable that follows it. This expression is a pointer to a zero-terminated array of characters: a PChar! As long as you have room to tack the #0 character on at the end, and the function you're calling won't modify the PChar data you send it, this command is a dandy way to convert Strings to PChars that works in both Delphi 1.0 and Delphi 2.0. If this program didn't need to be compatible with Delphi 1.0, we could eliminate the Command variable and the line that sets its value. Instead of @Command[1] in the WinExec function call, we'd use PChar(Edit1.Text).

ShellExecute eats WinExec's launch

The ShellExecute function, new in Windows 3.1, is WinExec with all the bells and whistles needed to emulate Program Manager. You can specify a working directory, automatically load the program associated with data files, even auto-print data files. Now *that* is a launcher!

Start a new fixed-size form project and again set its caption to Launcher. Add a column of three labels captioned Command:, Parameters:, and Working Dir:. Now place a parallel column of three edit boxes, all with blank Text properties. Dump a push button on the form and set its caption to Launch and its Default property to True. Use these lines for the button's OnClick event handler:

```
VAR Command, Params, WorkDir : String;
begin
  Command := Edit1.Text + #0;
  Params := Edit2.Text + #0;
  WorkDir := Edit3.Text + #0;
  IF ShellExecute(Handle, 'open', @Command[1],
    @Params[1], @WorkDir[1], SW_SHOWNORMAL) < 32 THEN
    MessageDlg('Failed to execute ' + Edit1.Text,
      mtError, [mbOK], 0);
end;
```

Find the uses clause near the top of the program file and add ShellApi to it.

Fool with this program to get a feel for ShellExecute. Enter NOTEPAD.EXE for the command and C:\DOS for the directory, for example, and Notepad comes up with C:\DOS for its current directory. Enter a bitmap's file name as the command and launch; it automatically comes up in Paintbrush. If you change `open` to `print` in the event handler, the program prints any data file that has a program associated with it!

CreateProcess for control freaks

You've seen that ShellExecute is decidedly more sophisticated than WinExec, yet it remains fairly understandable. The next step up to the 32-bit CreateProcess function is a quantum leap in complexity. WinExec takes two parameters, ShellExecute takes six, and CreateProcess takes ten, one of which is a record with 18 fields to control the initial appearance of the program! Fortunately for the sanity of programmers everywhere, ignoring many of CreateProcess's parameters is possible by passing NIL as their value.

CreateProcess is a 32-bit function, and as such it's available only to Delphi 2.0 programs.

Start a new fixed-size form project just like the one you used to demonstrate ShellExecute, with three labels captioned Command:, Parameters:, and Working Dir:, three edit boxes in another column, and a button labeled Launch. Add a radio group component to the right of the edit boxes. Set its caption to Mode and add the three strings Normal, Minimized, and Maximized to its Items list property. Now set its ItemIndex to 0, so Normal is checked.

Place a label on the form and set its Alignment property to taRightJustify. Add a skinny edit box next to the label; it has to hold only four characters. Place a Windows 95 UpDown component just to the right of the edit box. Select the label, edit box, and UpDown component, press Ctrl+C to copy them to the Clipboard, and then paste them back three times. Set the captions of the four labels to Left:, Top:, Width:, and Height:, and set each UpDown component's Associate property to the adjacent edit box. (Look ahead at Figure 17-2 to see how the form should appear.)

Set the form's caption to Launcher32 and give it an OnCreate event handler containing these lines:

```
UpDown1.Max := Screen.Width;
UpDown2.Max := Screen.Height;
UpDown3.Max := Screen.Width;
UpDown4.Max := Screen.Height;
```

Start an OnClick handler for the button, and replace the begin..end pair supplied by Delphi with this imposing chunk of code:

```
CONST Modes : ARRAY[0..2] OF Integer = (SW_SHOWNORMAL,
   SW_SHOWMINIMIZED, SW_SHOWMAXIMIZED);
VAR
   TSI     : TStartupInfo;
   TPI     : TProcessInformation;
   WorkDir : PChar;
   Success : Boolean;
   Mssage  : String;
begin
   IF Edit3.Text = '' THEN WorkDir := NIL
   ELSE WorkDir := StrNew(PChar(Edit3.Text));
   FillChar(TSI, SizeOf(TSI), 0);
   TSI.wShowWindow := Modes[RadioGroup1.ItemIndex];
   TSI.dwFlags := STARTF_USESHOWWINDOW;
   TSI.dwX := StrToIntDef(Edit4.Text, -1);
   TSI.dwY := StrToIntDef(Edit5.Text, -1);
   IF (TSI.dwX > -1) AND (TSI.dwY > -1) THEN
      TSI.dwFlags := TSI.dwFlags OR STARTF_USEPOSITION;
   TSI.dwXSize := StrToIntDef(Edit6.Text, -1);
   TSI.dwYSize := StrToIntDef(Edit7.Text, -1);
```

```
  IF (TSI.dwXSize > -1) AND (TSI.dwYSize > -1) THEN
    TSI.dwFlags := TSI.dwFlags OR STARTF_USESIZE;

  Success := CreateProcess(NIL, PChar(Edit1.Text + ' ' +
    Edit2.Text), NIL, NIL, FALSE, NORMAL_PRIORITY_CLASS,
    NIL, WorkDir, TSI, TPI);
  IF WorkDir <> NIL THEN StrDispose(WorkDir);
  IF Success THEN
    Mssage := Format('"%s"'#13'Process Handle: %.4x'+
      #13'Thread Handle: %.4x'#13'Process ID: %.8x'#13+
      'Thread ID: %.8x', [Edit1.Text, TPI.hProcess,
      TPI.hThread, TPI.dwProcessID, TPI.dwThreadID])
  ELSE
    Mssage := Format('Failed to execute %s. Error %d',
      [Edit1.Text, GetLastError]);
  MessageDlg(Mssage, mtInformation, [mbOK], 0);
end;
```

Whew! To set up for the big call to CreateProcess, this event handler sets a PChar variable either to a copy of the working directory string or to NIL if no working directory was specified. It initializes a TStartupInfo structure and fills its data fields to select the initial size, state, and position of the program being launched. Then it calls CreateProcess, passing NIL for as many parameters as possible and simple default values for the rest.

If all went well, the event handler displays arcane information about the program that was just launched, as Figure 17-2 shows. Wizards are reputedly able to control you if they know your true name; wizard-level programmers can take control of a program using this process information. However, in the Launcher32 program it serves simply as decoration. If CreateProcess failed, the program reports that fact, along with an error code.

Should you use CreateProcess or ShellExecute in your Delphi 2.0 programs? In one sense, you don't have a choice, because the 32-bit version of ShellExecute itself calls CreateProcess deep down inside. But unless you need some of the power granted by CreateProcess, sticking to ShellExecute is probably easier for now. You get a bonus if you do — your programs remain compatible with Delphi 1.0.

Lemme Outta Here!

You've seen t-shirts with the motto "$#!+ Happens." Well, the programmer's version says "Programs Crash." When you're developing programs, they *are* going to crash, and they may take a portion of your Windows memory or other

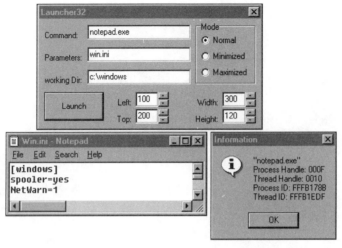

Figure 17-2:
This
program has
precisely
controlled
the size and
location of
the Notepad
it launched.

resources with them. The only cure is to restart Windows. You also find the occasional DOS game, um, I mean, essential business application that won't run under Windows. The ExitWindows function shows you a way out, along with its 16-bit cousin ExitWindowsExec and its 32-bit replacement ExitWindowsEx.

Exit, stage left

You *can* exit Windows 3.1 by bringing up Program Manager and engaging in its tiresome confirmation dialog, but why wait? Here's a little program that will not only exit, but also restart or reboot the system at the touch of a button.

Place four buttons across the top of a new form with the captions X, E&xit, &Restart, and Re&boot. Reduce their height to the minimum that looks good, and set the first button to have the same width as its height. Set the remaining three buttons to the same width, just wide enough to show all the captions. Set the Tag property of the Exit, Restart, and Reboot buttons to 0, 66, and 67, respectively. Pack the buttons so they touch, and shrink the form so it precisely encloses them. Now set the form's BorderStyle property to bsNone. Put the single command Close; in the OnClick event handler for the X button. Select the other three buttons and enter these two lines in an OnClick event handler for all three:

```
WITH Sender AS TButton DO
  ExitWindows(Tag, 0);
```

Put these two lines in the OnCreate event handler for the form:

```
Left := Screen.Width - Width;
Top := Screen.Height - Height;
```

Save the project as SKIDOO.PAS.

The Skidoo program takes almost no space on-screen, as Figure 17-3 shows, and it stays out of the way in the bottom right corner of the screen. Click one of the three larger buttons to exit Windows, restart Windows, or reboot the whole system. Press the small X button to terminate Skidoo itself. Chances are good you'll want to put SKIDOO.EXE in Program Manager's Startup group or the Startup submenu of the Windows 95 Start Menu!

Figure 17-3:
The Skidoo
program
gives you
three fast
ways out of
Windows.

Windows 95 users may find that the default position for the Skidoo program's window overlaps the taskbar. No problem — just change the second line of the OnCreate event handler to `Top := 0;`. If you compile this program with Delphi 2.0, though, you run into a different problem. No matter what button you press, the system simply offers to log you on as a different user. When you use the 32-bit compiler, you need a 32-bit solution!

Fifty ways to leave your windows

Changing the Skidoo program to work under Delphi 2.0 is relatively simple. Start by changing ExitWindows to ExitWindowsEx in the OnClick handler for the buttons. Rename the three buttons to &LogOff, &ShutDown, and &Reboot and set their Tag properties to 0, 1, and 2, respectively. That would make for a minimal 32-bit transformation. To really take advantage of the ExitWindowsEx function, however, you need a brand-new program. And because it's strictly for Delphi 2.0, we can take advantage of some features not found in Delphi 1.0.

Set a new form's BorderStyle property to bsToolWindow, and set its caption to a single space. Place a speed button in the top left corner of the form. Set the speed button's caption to N, and change its font to 16-point Wingdings (yielding a skull and crossbones!). Set the form's ClientHeight property to the speed button's height. In the form's OnCreate event handler, insert these lines:

```
ClientWidth := SpeedButton1.Width;
ShowWindow(Application.Handle, SW_HIDE);
```

The first line shrinks the form's width to fit the speed button, and the second hides the button that would normally appear on the taskbar.

Select New Form from the File menu, and set this form's BorderStyle to bsToolWindow as well. Give it the caption Properties. Back in the first form, select Use Unit... from the File menu and choose the newly-created form. Double-click the speed button to start an OnClick event handler, and enter this line:

```
ExitWindowsEx(Form2.goFlags, 0);
```

You also need an OnMouseUp event handler for the speed button containing this line:

```
IF Button = mbRight THEN Form2.ShowModal;
```

Can you guess what it does? If you right-click the skull-button, the second form is displayed. I'll show you how to design that form now.

Place four radio buttons down the left side of the form, with captions &Shut down, &Power down, &Reboot, and &Log off. Set their Tag properties to 1, 8, 2, and 0, respectively. Add a check box captioned Force and a bitmap button with Kind set to bkOk. Page up into the form definition and find the comment { Public declarations }. Right after it, insert this line:

```
GoFlags : Integer;
```

In an OnClick event handler shared by all four radio buttons, use this line:

```
goFlags := CheckBox1.Tag OR (Sender AS TRadioButton).Tag;
```

The OnClick handler for the check box needs a few more lines:

```
IF CheckBox1.Checked THEN CheckBox1.Tag := EWX_FORCE
ELSE CheckBox1.Tag := 0;
GoFlags := GoFlags AND (NOT EWX_FORCE);
GoFlags := GoFlags OR CheckBox1.Tag;
```

That does it! Figure 17-4 shows the result. The tiny skull-button window can be placed anywhere on the desktop, and right-clicking the button lets you control what happens when the button is pressed. The Force checkbox tells the program to shut down even if one or more programs refuse. (Normally one refusenik can prevent a shutdown.) And the new Power down option shuts down the system and then turns off its power, but only if the computer supports automated power shut-off.

Figure 17-4:
The tiny window on the right is the only part that normally shows; pressing the skull-button ends your Windows 95 session.

When good programs go bad

Some DOS-based programs (especially games) just plain refuse to run under Windows 3.1. In Windows 95, you can simply set the properties for the program's icon to make it run in MS-DOS mode, but Windows 3.1 never learned how to do that. If everything *else* runs under Windows 3.1, exiting for the one bad boy of the bunch is a pain. Here's a program you can use to execute those bad programs from an icon, just like the *nice* programs.

Start a new project, open the Project Manager view, and remove the main form. Select Project Source from the View menu, and replace Forms with WinProcs in the uses clause of the project source module. Insert this variable declaration block before the main `begin` line:

```
VAR
   Command, Params : String;
   N               : LongInt;
```

Now replace the main `Application.Run` line with these lines of code:

```
IF ParamCount < 1 THEN Exit;
Command := ParamStr(1) + #0;
Params := '';
FOR N := 2 TO ParamCount DO
   Params := Params + ' ' + ParamStr(N);
Params := Params + #0;
ExitWindowsExec(@Command[1], @Params[1]);
```

Save the program as BADBOY.PAS and then compile it. *Do not* run the program from within Delphi. And don't try to compile it under Delphi 2.0. Microsoft is so sure that they've solved the problem of boorish programs that they eliminated the ExitWindowsExec function from 32-bit Windows!

Here's an oddity — a Delphi program with no main form. To run an ill-behaved program using BADBOY.EXE, select a group in Program Manager and then choose New from the File menu. Fill in a description, and for the command line use BADBOY.EXE followed by the name of the program and any command line parameters. For example:

```
BADBOY.EXE C:\BLASTEM\BLASTEM.EXE -MEGABLAST
```

Include the full path name for both BADBOY.EXE and the program. Note that if the program you want to run is a batch file, you must insert the following between BADBOY.EXE and the batch file name:

```
C:\DOS\COMMAND.COM /C
```

Now you can click an icon to automatically shut down Windows, run the program, and restart Windows.

Where's Windo (ws)?

Most of the time, the Windows directory is C:\WINDOWS, but your programs don't dare assume that's always right. If you need to locate INI files, for example, the GetWindowsDirectory function always returns the correct Windows directory, be it C:\WINDOWS or D:\FENESTRA. For locating DLLs and other system files, a GetSystemDirectory call is better than hard-coding C:\WINDOWS\SYSTEM.

Place two labels on a new form, one below the other, captioned Windows Directory and System Directory. Place two more labels in a second column. Use these lines for the form's OnCreate event handler:

```
VAR Buffer : ARRAY[0..255] OF Char;
begin
  GetWindowsDirectory(Buffer, 255);
  Label3.Caption := StrPas(Buffer);
  GetSystemDirectory(Buffer, 255);
  Label4.Caption := StrPas(Buffer);
end;
```

Here we're not passing text *into* the Windows function; rather, we're supplying it with a buffer into which it can dump text. The buffer is a zero-based array of characters, which Delphi happily treats as a PChar. The built-in StrPas function converts the filled buffer's contents into a string. Presto change-o, we have the Windows and system directories!

Take Your System's Measurements

You can get the screen's width and height in pixels using Delphi's Screen object, but Windows is dying to reveal more through the GetSystemMetrics function. This function reports on the dimensions of 33 on-screen elements, and on whether or not 6 Windows features are enabled. Looking up the dozens of constants used by GetSystemMetrics can be a pain, so I use a little program instead.

Place a list box on a new fixed-size form and set the form's caption to System Metrics. Double-click the list box's Items property to open the string list editor. Enter the following 43 strings, 1 per line. (Yes, 43! A tedious process, but you have to do it only once.) Here are the system metrics constant names, in order:

```
SM_CXScreen, SM_CYScreen, SM_CXVScroll, SM_CYHScroll,
       SM_CYCaption, SM_CXBorder, SM_CYBorder,
       SM_CXDlgFrame, SM_CYDlgFrame, SM_CYVThumb,
       SM_CXHThumb, SM_CXIcon, SM_CYIcon, SM_CXCursor,
       SM_CYCursor, SM_CYMenu, SM_CXFullScreen,
       SM_CYFullScreen, SM_CYKanjiWindow,
       SM_MousePresent, SM_CYVScroll, SM_CXHScroll,
       SM_Debug, SM_SwapButton, SM_Reserved1,
       SM_Reserved2, SM_Reserved3, SM_Reserved4,
       SM_CXMin, SM_CYMin, SM_CXSize, SM_CYSize,
       SM_CXFrame, SM_CYFrame, SM_CXMinTrack,
       SM_CYMinTrack, SM_CXDoubleClk, SM_CYDoubleClk,
       SM_CXIconSpacing, SM_CYIconSpacing,
       SM_MenuDropAlignment, SM_PenWindows,
       SM_DBCSEnabled
```

Whew! Those were the system metrics constants for Windows 3.1. If you're running under Windows 95 or Windows NT, take a deep breath, wave your fingers vigorously in the air, and then enter 33 more constant names:

```
SM_CXScreen, SM_CMouseButtons, SM_Secure, SM_CXEdge,
       SM_CYEdge, SM_CXMinSpacing, SM_CYMinSpacing,
       SM_CXSmIcon, SM_CYSmIcon, SM_CYSmCaption,
       SM_CXSmSize, SM_CYSmSize, SM_CXMenuSize,
       SM_CYMenuSize, SM_Arrange, SM_CXMinimized,
       SM_CYMinimized, SM_CXMaxTrack, SM_CYMaxTrack,
       SM_CXMaximized, SM_CYMaximized, SM_Network,
       SM_Reserved5, SM_Reserved6, SM_Reserved7,
       SM_CleanBoot, SM_CXDrag, SM_CYDrag,
       SM_ShowSounds, SM_CXMenuCheck, SM_CYMenuCheck,
       SM_SlowMachine, SM_MidEastEnabled, SM_CMetrics
```

Make the list box wide enough to hold the longest constant name, which is SM_MenuDropAlignment. Place a bitmap button below the list box, aligned at the left. Set its Kind property to bkHelp and set Enabled to False. Put a label below the list box aligned at the right, set its Alignment property to taRightJustify, and delete its caption.

Double-click on the list box and put these lines in the resulting OnClick event handler:

```
BitBtn1.Enabled := True;
Label1.Caption := IntToStr(
  GetSystemMetrics(ListBox1.ItemIndex));
```

Choose Options from the Project menu in Delphi 2.0 (or Project from the Options menu in Delphi 1.0), and flip to the Application page. Press the Browse button next to the Help file line, choose Delphi's own WINAPI.HLP file, and then click OK. Even if you're using Delphi 2.0, use the WINAPI.HLP file from the Delphi 1.0 directory. Alas, the Delphi 2.0 help file doesn't devote a separate help page to each system metrics constant.

Now create an OnClick event handler for the Help button, replacing the begin..end pair supplied by Delphi with these lines:

```
VAR Buffer : ARRAY [0..255] OF Char;
begin
  WITH ListBox1 DO
    StrPCopy(Buffer, Items[ItemIndex]);
  Application.HelpCommand(HELP_KEY,
    LongInt(@Buffer));
end;
```

Run the program and click various items in the list. The label below the list box displays the current value of the selected item. Better yet, pressing the Help button brings up a description of the particular constant, as Figure 17-5 shows.

Some Windows functions promiscuously accept either a LongInt (a four-byte number) or a PChar (a four-byte pointer). The function called by Delphi's Application.HelpCommand is one such, so you can convert the String to a PChar using StrPCopy and then typecast the PChar to a LongInt.

Figure 17-5:
The System Metrics program shows that the vertical spacing for icons on this system is 75 pixels. Note that items starting with SM_CMouse Buttons aren't present in Windows 3.1.

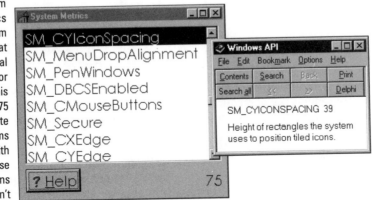

Free the System Resources!

You can have multimegabytes of RAM free yet still get Out of Memory errors if you're short on system resources. What are those? Well, suffice it to say that they belong to Windows itself, they're drawn from fixed-size memory blocks totaling just a few hundred kilobytes, and every program needs them. Windows 95 manages system resources much better; you'll rarely run low. And Windows NT, with its pure 32-bit architecture, *never* runs out. But in Windows 3.1 running out of system resources long before you run out of memory is quite common. Running programs when system resources are very low, say, under 10 percent, can yield bizarre results. To check the current percentages, you pass one of three values to the GetFreeSystemResources function:

- GFSR_GDIRESOURCES — returns the percentage of free GDI resources
- GFSR_USERRESOURCES — returns the percentage of free USER resources
- GFSR_SYSTEMRESOURCES — returns the smaller of the other two

The GetFreeSystemResources function doesn't exist in 32-bit Windows, so this example program is strictly for Delphi 1.0. Place three labels in a column at the left edge of a new fixed-size form and set their captions to G, U, and S. Set the form's FormStyle property to fsStayOnTop. Place three gauge components to the right of the three labels, making them quite small from top to bottom, as shown in Figure 17-6. Drop a Timer component on the form and put these lines in its OnTimer event handler:

```
Gauge1.Progress := GetFreeSystemResources(
  GFSR_GDIRESOURCES);
Gauge2.Progress := GetFreeSystemResources(
  GFSR_USERRESOURCES);
Gauge3.Progress := GetFreeSystemResources(
  GFSR_SYSTEMRESOURCES);
```

If you keep this tiny program running, you'll always know how close you're getting to running out of resources. Because you gave it the fsStayOnTop style, it has to be very small so as not to obscure other programs (as Figure 17-6 shows).

Earlier, I mentioned that the GetFreeSystemResources function doesn't exist in 32-bit Windows. That's no problem for Delphi 2.0 users because the Delphi 2.0 package includes the Delphi 1.0 compiler. But if you want, you can morph the FSR program into a roughly equivalent 32-bit program.

Figure 17-6:
The FSR program floating over Delphi's Code Editor shows plenty of free system resources.

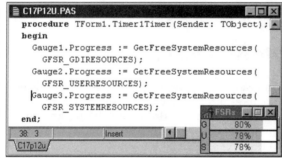

Starting with the previous project, change the form's caption to Memory and set its BorderStyle to bsToolWindow. Change the three label captions to L, R, and S. Delete the code you entered for the timer's OnTimer event handler and replace it with these lines:

```
VAR TMS : TMemoryStatus;
begin
  TMS.dwLength := SizeOf(TMS);
  GlobalMemoryStatus(TMS);
  Gauge1.Progress := TMS.dwMemoryLoad;
  Gauge2.Progress := (100*TMS.dwAvailPhys)
    DIV TMS.dwTotalPhys;
  Gauge3.Progress := (100*TMS.dwAvailPageFile)
    DIV TMS.dwTotalPageFile;
end;
```

That's it! The gauge labeled L shows "memory load" from 0 (meaning the Memory Manager is laying around in its boxer shorts doing nothing) to 100 (meaning the Memory Manager is busier than a past-deadline programmer). The R and S gauges show the percentage of free RAM (actual physical memory) and swap-file memory. You can expect your system's performance to degrade when the percentage of free RAM goes to 0 because swapping data to and from the disk is a lot slower than reading bits from chips.

A-Version Therapy

Some programs need to know the Windows or DOS version you're running to avoid calling on a feature that's not *in* that version. Others just want to show off by displaying the version numbers. The Windows 3.1 API function GetVersion gives you both the Windows and DOS version numbers packed into a single LongInt. Each of the LongInt's four bytes represents a major or minor version number, in a peculiar order: Windows major version, Windows minor version, DOS minor version, and DOS major version. Windows 95 reports its version as 3.95, to avoid bothering 16-bit programs that refuse to run unless the major version number is 3. I'll use this in a sample program in just a minute.

The 32-bit GetVersionEx function returns slightly different information than its 16-bit predecessor. The DOS version isn't present because DOS itself may not be present. Besides providing the major and minor Windows version numbers, it specifies precisely which 32-bit platform is active (Windows 95, Windows NT, or Win32s under Windows 3.1).

Flag Waving

A program that whips out calculations in seconds on a machine with an 80x87 coprocessor may take minutes on a machine without an 80x87 coprocessor. And other Windows features are unavailable unless you're running in 386 Enhanced mode. It'd be nice to know ahead of time about situations like this. The GetWinFlags function in 16-bit Windows returns a LongInt that's packed with this kind of information — literally! Every bit has its own meaning, and every bit has a named constant assigned to it in the WinTypes unit. Using this function and a few of the previous ones, you can build a nifty custom About box.

Start a new project with a fixed-size main form and set the form's caption to About [*program name*]. Place an image component near the top, left corner of the form with Width and Height set to 32, and place a bevel component so it makes a border around the image. Put a label component next to the icon with the caption [*program name*], Version x.xx. Add another label below it with the caption Copyright © 1996 by [*author*].

TIP

To enter the copyright symbol in the second label, hold down the Alt key, tap 0 1 6 9 on the numeric keypad, and release Alt. No kidding!

Put six more labels on the form in a column, giving them captions to match Figure 17-7. Place three labels in a second column, as shown in the figure, and set the first one's caption to Present. In the top right corner of the form, put a small push button with the caption OK, the Default property set to True, and the ModalResult property set to mrOK.

Start an OnCreate event handler for the form and replace Delphi's begin..end pair with these lines:

```
VAR L : LongInt;
begin
  Image1.Picture.Graphic := Application.Icon;
  L := GetVersion;
  Label3.Caption := Format('Windows %u.%.2u',
    [LoByte(LoWord(L)), HiByte(LoWord(L))]);
  Label4.Caption := Format('DOS %u.%.2u',
    [HiByte(HiWord(L)), LoByte(HiWord(L))]);
  L := GetWinFlags;
  IF L AND WF_ENHANCED = 0 THEN
    Label5.Caption := 'Standard Mode';
  IF L AND WF_80x87 = 0 THEN
    Label9.Caption := 'Absent';
end;
```

Create an OnActivate event handler for the form containing these few lines:

```
Label10.Caption := FormatFloat('#,',
  MemAvail DIV 1024) + 'KB Free';
Label11.Caption := IntToStr(
  GetFreeSystemResources(GFSR_SYSTEMRESOURCES)) +
  '% Free';
```

Finally, change the main form's name to MyAbout.

Run the program to make sure that it's working right. The result should resemble Figure 17-7. Now save it as a template for use in any project that needs an About box. All you have to do is adjust the form's caption and the first two labels to reflect the program's name and copyright information. The About box even grabs the application's icon automatically!

About 32 bits...

When you dive into 32-bit programming with Delphi 2.0, you'll occasionally hit a submerged rock. The About box form contains a few of these hidden snags. First, the program needs to use the GetVersionEx function rather than GetVersion. And the GetWinFlags function is gone. It's more or less replaced by a new function, GetSystemInfo. An About box form for Delphi 2.0 will have to be rebuilt from the ground up.

Figure 17-7:
This is the custom About box, adapted for use with an imaginary program that answers all questions.

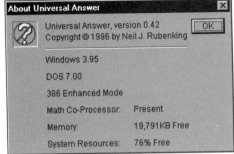

Follow the instructions for the 16-bit About box form up to and including placing the label that holds the copyright notice. Now place four more labels in a column below the copyright label, setting the captions of the last two to Memory: and Memory Load:. Place two more labels in a second column, as shown in Figure 17-8. Start an OnCreate event handler for the form and replace the begin..end pair supplied by Delphi with this code:

```
CONST PlatNames : ARRAY[0..2] OF String =
  ('Win32s', 'Windows 95', 'Windows NT');
VAR
  OVI : TOsVersionInfo;
  SI  : TSystemInfo;
begin
  Image1.Picture.Graphic := Application.Icon;
  OVI.dwOSVersionInfoSize := SizeOf(OVI);
  GetVersionEx(OVI);
  Label3.Caption := Format('%s, version %u.%.2u',
    [PlatNames[OVI.dwPlatformID], OVI.dwMajorVersion,
     OVI.dwMinorVersion]);
  GetSystemInfo(SI);
```

```
(continued)
  CASE SI.dwProcessorType OF
    386 : Label4.Caption := '80386';
    486 : Label4.Caption := '80486';
    586 : Label4.Caption := 'Pentium';
    ELSE Label4.Caption := 'Unknown processor ' +
      IntToStr(SI.dwProcessorType);
  END;
end;
```

Also create an OnActivate event handler for the form, and enter the following code in place of the Delphi-supplied begin..end pair:

```
VAR TMS : TMemoryStatus;
begin
  TMS.dwLength := SizeOf(TMS);
  GlobalMemoryStatus(TMS);
  Label7.Caption := FormatFloat('#,"KB Free"',
    (TMS.dwAvailPhys + TMS.dwAvailPageFile) DIV 1024);
  Label8.Caption := Format('%d%% Load', [TMS.dwMemoryLoad]);
end;
```

As you can see in Figure 17-8, this About box form is better suited to the 32-bit Windows environment. It reports which Windows platform it's running on, and the correct version number. And it reports the processor type and the amount of free memory.

More useful Windows API functions exist, and still more are available that aren't much use. On nights when you're having trouble sleeping, try flipping through the Windows Software Developers Kit manual, to get a feel for the vast and sometimes awkward set of choices. Now, though, you're ready to take a look at the consistently handy functions that Delphi offers!

Figure 17-8:
The 32-bit version of the About box form displays memory information, the active Windows platform, and CPU type.

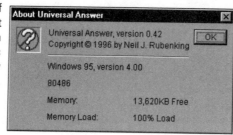

Chapter 18

Ten Fabulous Function Families

*W*indows has hundreds of functions, it's true, but Delphi is no slouch when it comes to built-in functions. I've used quite a few of them in the sample programs already. These built-in Delphi functions can convert variables from one type to another, deal with files and disks, manipulate strings, and even generate random numbers. You don't need to know all of them at once — start with the groups discussed in this chapter. To know them better, check their dossiers in the Help system.

A Conversion Experience

If you count each function call in our sample programs as a vote, the IntToStr function wins by a landslide. Delphi is touchy about data types; you can't pass a number if a string is expected or vice versa. So before you can display a number as a label's caption or add it to a list, you must process it through IntToStr. Want to impress (or at least confuse) your coworkers? Use the IntToHex function instead of IntToStr. IntToHex turns a number into a hexadecimal string using as many digits as you specify (usually 2, 4, or 8). For example, IntToHex(12648430, 8) yields the string 00C0FFEE. The "00" here is not an exclamation of glee; IntToHex jammed two zeros in at the front because you asked for 8 digits.

Occasionally we've used StrToInt to go from a string to an integer. That's a little tricky, because passing a string such as four or 3.14159 causes a run-time exception. To handle conversions cleanly, you may want to use StrToIntDef. Pass it a string and a default value; if the string isn't correctly numeric it returns the default.

```
L := StrToIntDef(Edit1.Text, -1);
```

L gets the numeric value of the edit box's text, or –1 if the text was no good as a number. Delphi has dozens of conversion routines for strings, numbers, and even the date and time. If you need to convert one type of data to another, check the Help system — Delphi probably has a function for it.

Big numbers look better with commas separating every three digits: 2,147,483,648 is easier to read than 2147483648. Surprisingly, Delphi's FormatFloat function inserts those commas for you. Its official purpose is to format floating-point numbers, but it comma-izes LongInts perfectly if you use the following format string:

```
',#'
```

Some Random Thoughts

Suppose you're writing a screen saver that bounces tennis balls around the screen. If the balls always bounce in the same pattern they'll bore you, so you want to vary their bouncing unpredictably. You need a function to generate random numbers, and the aptly-named Random function does the job. Random is two functions in one. Call it with no parameters and it returns a random nonnegative floating-point number less than 1. Pass a whole number from 2 to 65535, and it returns a random nonnegative whole number that's less than the number you passed. For example, Random(2) returns either 0 or 1.

Now for the exposé — Random, along with its equivalent in every other programming language, is a fraud! The numbers it returns aren't random at all. They're generated by a pseudorandom function inside Delphi. Each number is based on the number before, and the function goes through billions of repetitions before the same number repeats. At the start of any program that uses Random, make one call to the Randomize procedure. This "seeds" the random-number generator based on the exact current time. Start a new project and give the form the caption Random-Eyes. Set the form's Ctl3D property to False. Drop a timer component on the form and put these lines in its OnTimer event handler:

```
VAR X, Y, Delta : LongInt;
begin
  WITH Canvas DO
    BEGIN
      Delta := Random(8) + 3;
```

```
      X := Random(ClientWidth-16*Delta) + 4*Delta;
      Y := Random(ClientHeight-8*Delta) + 4*Delta;
      Brush.Color := RGB(Random(256), Random(256),
        Random(256));
      Pen.Width := 3;
      Ellipse(X-4*Delta, Y-4*Delta, X+4*Delta,  Y+4*Delta);
      Ellipse(X+4*Delta, Y-4*Delta, X+12*Delta, Y+4*Delta);
      Brush.Color := clBlack;
      Ellipse(X+2*Delta, Y-Delta, X+4*Delta-2, Y+Delta);
      Ellipse(X+4*Delta+2, Y-Delta, X+6*Delta, Y+Delta);
      MoveTo(X+2*Delta, Y-4*Delta);
      LineTo(X+4*Delta, Y-2*Delta);
      LineTo(X+6*Delta, Y-4*Delta);
    END;
end;
```

This program draws pairs of eyes whose size, position, and color are random. The variable Delta, which determines the size, can take any value from 3 to 10. In general, to get a random number from *A* to *B* inclusive, you use:

```
Random(B-A+1) + A;
```

Run the program several times and you may notice something odd; the "random" pattern of eyes is the same every time. Whoops! We forgot to Randomize. Put this single line `Randomize;` in an OnCreate event handler for the form:

That does the trick! Unless your system's clock is moribund, each run of the program displays a different pattern of eyes.

The Commando Line-o

Some DOS-based programs don't enable you play until you learn dozens of command-line switches. Windows programs don't hold with that kind of foolishness, but plucking a file name from the command line can be useful. Delphi's ParamCount function returns the number of parameters on the command line, and ParamStr(N) returns the *N*th parameter. I grab strings from the command line in the next section.

Here's a nice surprise — ParamStr(0) returns the full path name of the program that's running! If your program needs to locate helper files that reside in its own directory, this can be very handy.

The Secret Life of Files

If Delphi's components can handle the file tasks you're interested in, use them. If not, well, you have plenty of other choices. Before you tell a component to load data from a file, for example, check with FileExists to make sure the file exists. You've already seen several functions for slicing and dicing file names. ExtractFilename, ExtractFilepath, and ExtractFileExt take a file name as their one parameter and return just a portion of it. You can go the other way, too. ExpandFilename takes a file name with no path or a partial path and expands it to a full path name. We'll use some of these functions to update the simple editor project that you built in Chapter 5 (and added features to in Chapters 6, 8, and 12).

Load the simple editor project into Delphi and put these lines in an OnCreate event handler for the form:

```
VAR FileHandle : Integer;
begin
  IF ParamCount < 1 THEN Exit;
  IF NOT FileExists(ParamStr(1)) THEN
    BEGIN
      FileHandle := FileCreate(ParamStr(1));
      IF FileHandle >= 0 THEN
        FileClose(FileHandle)
      ELSE
        BEGIN
          MessageDlg(ParamStr(1) +
            ' is not a valid filename',
            mtError, [mbOK], 0);
          Exit;
        END;
    END;
  SaveDialog1.Filename := ParamStr(1);
  Memo1.Lines.LoadFromFile(ParamStr(1));
  Memo1.Modified := False;
  OpenDialog1.HistoryList.Add(ParamStr(1));
  Caption := 'My Editor - ' +
    ExtractFilename(ParamStr(1));
end;
```

If you're using Delphi 2.0, you convert the simple editor to a rich text editor in Chapter 12. If so, find the two occurrences of Memo1 in the OnCreate event handler you just wrote and change them to RichEdit1. If the command-line parameter isn't an existing file name, try to create it by using FileCreate. If you succeed, you close the new file; otherwise you report that the file name is bad and exit. Of course if this program is compiled under Delphi 2.0, long file name support means more difficulty in coming up with an invalid file name! If all is well, load the file into the editor just as if it had been chosen from the Open File dialog. Open File Manager or Explorer and locate the name of the simple editor's EXE file. Try dragging a data file onto the EXE file. It launches and loads the file!

Anytime you write a program that processes data files, give the program the capability to load whatever file is specified on the command line.

Old-timers may be wondering what's become of the FindFirst and FindNext functions. Ever since DOS was a pup, programmers have used these two functions to find files that match a particular specification. Well, they exist in Delphi, too, but it's just so much easier to use a file list box that these functions don't get much exercise! If you do use them in a 32-bit program, you must clean up afterward by calling FindClose.

Disk Must Be the Place

Before your program starts a lengthy task that needs acres of disk space, you better make sure enough space is available. If your program runs out of space after running for an hour, the user is not going to thank you. Delphi's DiskFree and DiskSize functions take a disk number and return the free space or total capacity in bytes. What's a disk number? Well, 1 means A, 2 means B, 3 means C, and so on. Pass a 0 and the function acts on the current drive. A return value of –1 means the disk number isn't valid. Drop a gauge component near the bottom of a new form with its BorderStyle set to bsDialog, and set its Kind property to gkPie. Set the gauge's ForeColor property to clFuchsia, BackColor to clBlue, and ShowText to False. Place three labels, one below the other, and set their captions to Used space:, Free space:, and Capacity:, respectively. Add two more columns of labels parallel to the first column, select them all, and set their Alignment property to taRightJustify. Place a paint box to the left of the first label, set its Color to clBlue, and set its width and height to 14. Use these lines as an OnPaint event handler for the paint box:

```
VAR R : TRect;
begin
  WITH Sender AS TPaintBox DO
    BEGIN
      R := ClientRect;
      Frame3D(Canvas, R, clDkGray, clWhite, 1);
      Canvas.FillRect(R);
    END;
end;
```

Click the paint box and then press Ctrl+C and Ctrl+V to make a duplicate of it. Put the duplicate to the left of the second label and change its Color property to clFuchsia. Start an OnCreate event handler for the form and replace Delphi's begin..end pair with these lines:

```
VAR Siz : LongInt;
begin
  Siz := DiskSize(3);
  Gauge1.MaxValue := Siz DIV 1024;
  Label6.Caption := FormatFloat(',# "bytes"', Siz);
  Label9.Caption := FormatFloat(',#.# "MB"',
    Siz / 1048576);
  Timer1Timer(Timer1);
end;
```

Drop a timer on the form and use these lines for its OnTimer event handler:

```
VAR Fre, Used : LongInt;
begin
  Fre := DiskFree(3);
  Used := DiskSize(3) - Fre;
  Gauge1.Progress := Fre DIV 1024;
  Label14.Caption := FormatFloat(',# "bytes"', Used);
  Label17.Caption := FormatFloat(',# "MB"',
    Used / 1048576);
  Label15.Caption := FormatFloat(',# "bytes"', Fre);
  Label18.Caption := FormatFloat(',# "MB"',
    Fre / 1048576);
end;
```

The resulting program displays the free space on drive C: both numerically and as a pie slice, with the data updated every second. The form's layout is modeled after the Windows 95 dialog that displays disk drive properties, but the Windows 95 dialog is static — no updates! Try making a copy of a very large file (perhaps DOOM.WAD) while this program is running and watch the display change!

Casing the Strings Joint

What's the absolute, number-one most popular activity with Strings? No, it's not *cat*'s cradle; it's con*cat*enation. That means gluing one string onto another, such as 'horse' + 'carriage.' The vast majority of sample programs in this book use concatenation in one spot or another. A few of the sample programs have used the substring functions Copy and Pos. Pos returns the position of one string within another, or 0 if it's not found. For example:

```
Pos('cat', 'communicate')
```

is 8. Copy takes the string you pass as its first parameter and returns a chunk of it. The second parameter says where the chunk starts, and the third says how long the chunk will be. For example:

```
Copy('pusillanimous', 6, 3)
```

is 'lan.' You may occasionally find a use for the related functions Insert and Delete. The former inserts one string into another; the latter deletes a chunk.

Several of the string functions have the same name as Delphi component methods. If Delphi objects to the way you're using these functions, stick System and a period in front, such as System.Delete.

Users often enter text higgledy-piggledy, without regard for uppercase or lowercase. You can clean up after them with UpperCase, LowerCase, AnsiUpperCase, and AnsiLowerCase. The latter two work on "foreign" characters; the former two don't. On the other hand, the latter two are much slower than the former two. Place five labels on a new form and set the caption of the first to DÉJA vù. To enter the É, hold Alt, press 0 2 0 1 on the numeric keypad, and release Alt. For the ù, do the same with the numbers 0 2 4 9. Now put these lines in an OnCreate event handler for the form:

```
Label2.Caption := UpperCase(Label1.Caption);
Label3.Caption := LowerCase(Label1.Caption);
Label4.Caption := AnsiUpperCase(Label1.Caption);
Label5.Caption := AnsiLowerCase(Label1.Caption);
```

In the resulting program, the plain UpperCase and LowerCase functions fail to change the É and ù, but they're handled correctly by the ANSI versions.

Delphi also gives you plenty of ways to *compare* strings. CompareStr compares two strings and returns 0 if they're precisely equal. A negative result means that the first string is less than the second; a positive result means the reverse. CompareText does the same, but it compares without regard to case. CompareText('NeUrOtIc','nEuRoTiC') returns 0. Again, for strings containing foreign characters, you use the ANSI versions, AnsiCompareStr and AnsiCompareText. AnsiCompareText('AÑO NUEVO', 'año nuevo') returns 0, where the non-ANSI version doesn't. The power of these comparison functions is enhanced if you're using Delphi 2.0. Remember, Delphi 2.0 AnsiString variables can hold immense amounts of text, vastly more than Delphi 1.0 String variables. These four comparison functions chug right along in Delphi 2.0, comparing strings as large as you care to throw at them. Delphi 2.0 also adds handy functions for trimming extraneous characters from strings. TrimRight trims trailing spaces from a string, along with any trailing control characters. TrimLeft does the same for leading spaces and control characters. Total cleanup is handled by Trim, which trims at both ends. Unwanted spaces can be messy if you're converting a user-entered string to a number or treating such a string as a file name. Trim eliminates errors caused by spaces hanging around the start or end of the string (though it can't do anything about unwanted characters in the middle). If you *want* a string with lots of spaces, try the new Delphi 2.0 StringOfChar function. Want a string containing 10,000 spaces? StringOfChar(' ', 10000) does the job.

PChar "Pculiarities"

PChars are poison, one hundred percent. Well, almost. You do need to use them when calling Windows functions in Delphi 1.0 programs, but you don't need to hassle with most of the PChar functions. A few do have some redeeming social value. Pass a literal string or another PChar to the StrNew function, and it returns a shiny new PChar containing a copy of the string. After you finish with the copy, hand it off to StrDispose for destruction.

Never, ever, copy a longer string into a string created by StrNew. StrNew allocates just enough memory to hold the string you passed. And never use StrDispose on a string that wasn't created with StrNew.

StrPas is a great function — it takes a PChar and returns a String! If you need to go the other way, StrPCopy does the job, but it's tricky. The function declaration for StrPCopy looks like this:

```
function StrPCopy(Dest: PChar; Source: String): PChar;
```

The Dest parameter is the destination for the copy, and *your* program must supply it. StrPCopy does not create a PChar the way StrPas creates a String. Almost all the PChar functions work this way — you must to provide any necessary buffers. The function's return value is the PChar you passed into it, which makes some really horrendous nested function calls possible. Even better than StrPCopy is StrPLCopy. StrPLCopy takes one more parameter that specifies the length of the destination PChar. This enables you to avoid the problems that arise if you copy a 256-character string into a 42-character buffer. You get only the first 42 characters of the string, but that's a lot better than having the rest of the characters overwrite unknown locations in memory!

Two other essential PChar functions are StrLCopy and StrLCat. StrLCopy copies one PChar to another, up to a specified maximum length. StrLCat appends one PChar to another, again up to a maximum length. Both functions come in nonlength-limited versions, which you should avoid like the plague. Copying more characters than a PChar can hold is a recipe for disaster!

Just to show PChars *can* be useful, here's a program that displays the DOS environment. Don't try to use this one in Delphi 2.0, though — the 32-bit Windows API doesn't support the GetDOSEnvironment function. Drop a list box on a new form and set its Align property to alClient. Replace the begin..end pair for the form's OnCreate event handler with these lines:

```
VAR P : PChar;
begin
  P := GetDOSEnvironment;
  WHILE P[0] <> #0 DO
    BEGIN
      ListBox1.Items.Add(StrPas(P));
      P := StrEnd(P) + 1;
    END;
end;
```

This program calls a Windows API function to get a pointer to the environment. As it turns out, the environment is like a bunch of PChars jammed together, with an empty PChar to end it. The WHILE loop in this program adds the current PChar to the list box and then sets it to point one character beyond its end.

New Math

Delphi comes with a whole wad of math functions for doing all the things you hated in high school. I've used Sqr and Sqrt already, to get the square and square root of a number. Ln returns the log of a number, and Exp(X) returns the exponential. That's e to the X power, where e is a weird special floating-point constant such as pi. Those awful trig functions are here, too, in the form of Sin, Cos, and ArcTan (sine, cosine, and inverse tangent).

The excitement comes when you try to use a function that isn't supplied: Delphi 1.0 supplies the minimum number of math functions necessary, and leaves you to derive the rest. Before you start banging your head against the wall, here are a few formulas that may help:

Math function	*Delphi expression*
tangent(*X*)	Sin(X)/Cos(X)
inverse sine(*X*)	ArcTan(X/Sqrt(1–Sqr(X)))
inverse cosine(*X*)	ArcTan(Sqrt(1–Sqr(X))/X)
X to the *Y* power	Exp(Y*Ln(X))

Just plug these expressions into your programs as needed, add a little protection against numeric naughtiness such as dividing by 0 or taking the square root of –1, and you're ready to calculate.

Newer Math

Add the Math unit to the uses clause of a Delphi 2.0 program and you've got so many functions at your fingertips you don't know what to do. That is, as long as you have the Developer or Client/Server version; Delphi Desktop doesn't include this marvelous unit. Trig functions, angle conversions, hyperbolic trig functions (hyper-WHAT?), logarithmic and exponential functions are just the beginning. Those who know that standard deviation has nothing to do with the level of weirdness out on the streets can find a whole slew of statistical functions. These functions are hand-crafted (by elves?) to take advantage of special features in the Pentium chip, so they're both speedy and small. And the financial functions enable you to calculate really important stuff, such as the payment on a million-dollar house.

To try that last one, place four edit boxes one below the other along the right side of a new form, and put a label below the last one. Delete the Text property of the edit boxes and the Caption property of the label. Now place a column of five labels to the left of the components you already placed, with their Alignment property set to taRightJustify and with the caption shown in Figure 18-1. Select the four edit boxes and connect them all to an OnChange event handler in which these lines replace the Delphi-supplied begin..end pair:

```
VAR
  PercentDown, PercentInterest,
  TotalCost, MonthlyPayment : Extended;
  MortgageLength            : Integer;
begin
  try
    TotalCost := StrToFloat(Edit1.Text);
```

```
   PercentDown := StrToFloat(Edit2.Text) / 100;
   MortgageLength := StrToInt(Edit3.Text) * 12;
   PercentInterest := StrToFloat(Edit4.Text) / 100;
 except
   Exit;
 end;
 MonthlyPayment := -Payment(PercentInterest / 12,
   MortgageLength, TotalCost*(1-PercentDown), 0,
    ptStartOfPeriod);
 Label1.Caption := FloatToStrF(MonthlyPayment,
   ffCurrency, 18, 2);
end;
```

Figure 18-1:
Got $9,000 a
month lying
around? Buy
a million-
dollar
house!

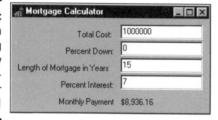

Before you sit down to code a complicated math routine, double-check the Math unit. You don't want to reinvent the wheel!

Dangerous Moves

Delphi has a few extremely powerful functions that are pure poison if you use them incorrectly. You should probably be forced to sign a waiver before you can use them because the destruction they can wreak if misused is almost beyond belief. On the other hand, they're fast and they're powerful, so what the heck!

The Move procedure is a bulldozer — it pushes a copy of a bunch of bytes from one location to another. You use Move to do things such as take up the slack in an array when you delete an element. But woe betide you if the destination variable isn't big enough. Move pushes the whole block of bytes regardless, and data after the destination is trashed. FillChar fills a variable with copies of a specified Byte or Char. A command such as

```
FillChar(MyString, SizeOf(MyString), 'A');
```

yields a string of 65 *A*'s, if MyString is a Delphi 1.0 string variable. Actually all 256 bytes of the string now contain that same character, but the very first byte is the length byte, and *A* corresponds to a 65-character string. FillChar fills as many bytes as you tell it to, blithely ignoring the size of the destination variable. If FillChar overflows, it spews into other data elements of your program.

Never use Move or FillChar on objects — never! You find situations for which these razor-edged power tools are essential or at least way cool. Whenever you use them, triple-check to make sure the number of bytes to move or fill fit in the destination variable. The SizeOf function returns the size of a variable in bytes — use it! And if something goes wretchedly wrong with your program, make these two functions your prime suspects.

Appendix
Delphi and VB Controls

Why switch from Visual Basic to Delphi? Well, just for starters, Delphi applications are fully compiled EXE programs, whereas VB, even VB 4.0, produces interpreted p-code. In English, that means Delphi programs run faster, by a long shot. Also, every VB programmer eventually runs into one of several frustrating limitations. For example, a VB program can respond to Windows messages only if a response is built into an existing control; Delphi programs can easily respond to any Windows message. VB programs can't use Windows functions that require a special kind of function known as a callback function; Delphi programs can. VB3 can use Dynamic Link Libraries (DLLs) but can't create them; Delphi can use *and* create them. VB4 can create DLLs, but programs in other languages can't use them in the usual way; they communicate only via OLE. And if you want to graduate from writing VB programs to writing VB controls, you must throw away all your knowledge of VB and start over with some other programming language such as Pascal or (ugh!) C++. Delphi components are written *in* Delphi, so the step from using components to writing components is an evolution, not a revolution.

Must be a catch, right? Well, if you've been doing any serious development in Visual Basic, you've surely shelled out good money for specialized third-party VBX or OCX controls. Hundreds of them are out there, for every purpose from speech recognition to video editing, from WinWord wannabes to telecommunicators. If you switch to Delphi, isn't your investment in VB-style controls wasted? Of course not!

What's the difference between a VBX control and an OCX control? The most significant difference for a Delphi programmer is that VBXs can be used in 16-bit programs but not in 32-bit programs and OCXs can be used in 32-bit programs but not in 16-bit programs. That means Delphi 1.0 programs can use VBXs and Delphi 2.0 programs can use OCXs but not the other way around. To avoid wearing out the forward slash key, I don't refer to the two kinds together as "VBX/OCX" — I'll just say "VB controls."

Adding a VBX control to the Delphi 1.0 Component palette is no more difficult than adding a new Delphi component! The same is true of adding an OCX control to the Delphi 2.0 Component palette. In fact, the Component palette already *has* a page for VB controls with a few example components on it. Step through the process of adding a VBX control to the palette in Delphi 1.0 so that you can see how easy it is.

If any of the programs installed on your system were written in Visual Basic 3.0, you have some VBX controls in your Windows system directory. These "visiting" controls are *not* automatically available for use in your own programs! If you try to install a VBX that floated in with one application or another, you get a message saying that you need a license. The license is a special file that's installed when you *buy* the component that gives you, well, the license to create and distribute applications that use that particular VBX. It has the extension LIC and usually the same name as the component. For example, if you want to use the VBX controls that come with Visual Basic itself, VB.LIC must be present.

Almost all the controls that come in VB 3.0 Professional are already duplicated by existing Delphi components, but a few have unique capabilities. The mhState control (contained in KEYSTAT.VBX) is one — it both reflects and controls one of four keyboard shift states. Assuming Visual Basic 3.0 is installed on your system, the following paragraphs tell you how to make the mhState control available to your Delphi 1.0 programs. (Don't worry; I tell you how to add the corresponding OCX to Delphi 2.0, too!)

Close the current project, if one is open, and choose Install Components from the Options menu. Click the VBX button and browse until you find the file KEYSTAT.VBX. Click OK. At this point, if you don't have a license for the control, you can't continue. If you have a license, the Install VBX dialog appears, as shown in Figure A-1.

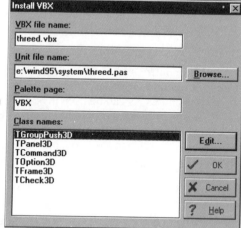

Figure A-1: This particular VBX file contains six different controls.

The file name in the Unit file name text box identifies the source file Delphi *creates* as a "wrapper" for the VBX. In effect, Delphi builds a component with properties and methods that precisely match those of the VBX. You can choose a different location for this file, but the default is the same directory as the VBX.

If you look at the wrapper Delphi builds for a VBX, you see almost no code — only enough to define a type that makes the "alien" VBX appear as a native Delphi component. Like the Borg of *Star Trek* fame, Delphi simply assimilates the VBX. VBX controls normally reside in the palette page named VBX. If this page is overflowing, or if you just prefer another name, type the name you prefer on the Palette page line. Finally, the Class names list box shows the Delphi class names for the controls found in the VBX. (Yes, one VBX can have multiple controls.) Leave these at their default values, which are the control's internal name prefixed with a *T*. Now click OK. Add more VBX controls, if you want. After you finish, click OK in the Install Components dialog. Delphi takes a few moments to recompile the component library; after it finishes, the VBX controls are available for use.

The process of adding an OCX control to Delphi 2.0 is even simpler, if that's possible. Choose Install from the Component menu and press the OCX button. You get a list of OCX controls that are registered on your system. Generally, the process of installing an OCX control also registers it. If you don't see the one you want, press the Register button and browse until you find it. Description lines for all the registered OCX controls are listed; choose one. From this point, the process is identical to installing a VBX in Delphi 1.0. Figure A-2 shows the Delphi 2.0 Import OLE Control dialog.

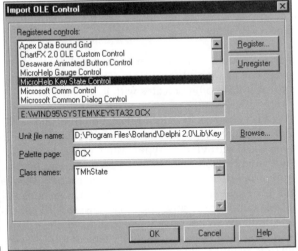

Figure A-2: "MicroHelp Key State Control" is a lot easier to interpret than "KEYSTAT.VBX"

You can add any or all of the VB controls that come with VB (except the components built into VBRUN300.DLL or VB40032.DLL) as well as any third-party VB control. As long as a VBX control remains compatible with the VBX 1.0 specification, Delphi 1.0 programs can use it. However, Delphi 1.0 can't use features specific to later versions of the VBX specification, most notably data-awareness. Because Delphi has its own style of database support and its own set of data-aware components, that's no big loss. And Delphi 2.0 gives full access to OCX controls. Try this after installing KEYSTAT.VBX in Delphi 1.0 or the MicroHelp Keyboard State Control in Delphi 2.0. Drop four mhState controls on a new fixed-size form, and set the form's caption to Toggles. Set the Style property of each of the four mhStates to a different number from 0 to 3. Select all four and set their TimerInterval property to 100. Figure A-3 shows the resulting program. Press the CapsLock, ScrollLock, NumLock, or Ins key on the keyboard and the corresponding button changes to match. Or press the mhState button to turn the shift state on or off.

Figure A-3:
Four
instances of
the mhState
VBX control.

Delphi gives the advanced programmer more power over VB controls than VB itself does! After Delphi creates a wrapper for the control, you can write a new component that *extends* the resulting Delphi object. Add new data fields, or new methods or change the way existing methods work. It's not simple, but in Delphi it's possible. In VB, no way!

If your Delphi programs use VB controls, you must distribute the VBX or OCX file with the program, just as with a VB program. The Delphi wrapper doesn't replace the VB control; it just communicates with it.

Unfortunately, using VBX controls in Delphi 1.0 isn't all beer and skittles. Scan the BIVBX and VbxCtrl units and you see dozens of data types and specialized conversion functions used with VB data types. Much of the conversion is handled for you, but you probably want to avoid certain areas, such as directly manipulating picture properties. That's a consequence of the VBX specification, not a fault in Delphi 1.0. Fortunately, the OCX specification enables Delphi 2.0 to integrate OLE controls quite thoroughly. The most powerful VB controls are like black boxes — self-contained wonder-machines that do whatever you order them to without exposing their inner workings. These components work jim-dandy with Delphi! Give Delphi a whirl; you will find it similar enough to VB that you know how to use it right away. You may stumble over the language differences but will marvel at the similarities. And you can still use your favorite VB controls.

Index

Title	Author	ISBN	Price
The Internet For Macs® For Dummies® 2nd Edition	by Charles Seiter	ISBN: 1-56884-371-2	$19.99 USA/$26.99 Canada
The Internet For Macs® For Dummies® Starter Kit	by Charles Seiter	ISBN: 1-56884-244-9	$29.99 USA/$39.99 Canada
The Internet For Macs® For Dummies® Starter Kit Bestseller Edition	by Charles Seiter	ISBN: 1-56884-245-7	$39.99 USA/$54.99 Canada
The Internet For Windows® For Dummies® Starter Kit	by John R. Levine & Margaret Levine Young	ISBN: 1-56884-237-6	$34.99 USA/$44.99 Canada
The Internet For Windows® For Dummies® Starter Kit, Bestseller Edition	by John R. Levine & Margaret Levine Young	ISBN: 1-56884-246-5	$39.99 USA/$54.99 Canada

MACINTOSH

Mac® Programming For Dummies®	by Dan Parks Sydow	ISBN: 1-56884-173-6	$19.95 USA/$26.95 Canada
Macintosh® System 7.5 For Dummies®	by Bob LeVitus	ISBN: 1-56884-197-3	$19.95 USA/$26.95 Canada
MORE Macs® For Dummies®	by David Pogue	ISBN: 1-56884-087-X	$19.95 USA/$26.95 Canada
PageMaker 5 For Macs® For Dummies®	by Galen Gruman & Deke McClelland	ISBN: 1-56884-178-7	$19.95 USA/$26.95 Canada
QuarkXPress 3.3 For Dummies®	by Galen Gruman & Barbara Assadi	ISBN: 1-56884-217-1	$19.99 USA/$26.99 Canada
Upgrading and Fixing Macs® For Dummies®	by Kearney Rietmann & Frank Higgins	ISBN: 1-56884-189-2	$19.95 USA/$26.95 Canada

MULTIMEDIA

Multimedia & CD-ROMs For Dummies® 2nd Edition	by Andy Rathbone	ISBN: 1-56884-907-9	$19.99 USA/$26.99 Canada
Multimedia & CD-ROMs For Dummies® Interactive Multimedia Value Pack, 2nd Edition	by Andy Rathbone	ISBN: 1-56884-909-5	$29.99 USA/$39.99 Canada

OPERATING SYSTEMS:

DOS

MORE DOS For Dummies®	by Dan Gookin	ISBN: 1-56884-046-2	$19.95 USA/$26.95 Canada
OS/2® Warp For Dummies® 2nd Edition	by Andy Rathbone	ISBN: 1-56884-205-8	$19.99 USA/$26.99 Canada

UNIX

MORE UNIX® For Dummies®	by John R. Levine & Margaret Levine Young	ISBN: 1-56884-361-5	$19.99 USA/$26.99 Canada
UNIX® For Dummies®	by John R. Levine & Margaret Levine Young	ISBN: 1-878058-58-4	$19.95 USA/$26.95 Canada

WINDOWS

MORE Windows® For Dummies® 2nd Edition	by Andy Rathbone	ISBN: 1-56884-048-9	$19.95 USA/$26.95 Canada
Windows® 95 For Dummies®	by Andy Rathbone	ISBN: 1-56884-240-6	$19.99 USA/$26.99 Canada

PCS/HARDWARE

Illustrated Computer Dictionary For Dummies® 2nd Edition	by Dan Gookin & Wallace Wang	ISBN: 1-56884-218-X	$12.95 USA/$16.95 Canada
Upgrading and Fixing PCs For Dummies® 2nd Edition	by Andy Rathbone	ISBN: 1-56884-903-6	$19.99 USA/$26.99 Canada

PRESENTATION/AUTOCAD

AutoCAD For Dummies®	by Bud Smith	ISBN: 1-56884-191-4	$19.95 USA/$26.95 Canada
PowerPoint 4 For Windows® For Dummies®	by Doug Lowe	ISBN: 1-56884-161-2	$16.99 USA/$22.99 Canada

PROGRAMMING

Borland C++ For Dummies®	by Michael Hyman	ISBN: 1-56884-162-0	$19.95 USA/$26.95 Canada
C For Dummies® Volume 1	by Dan Gookin	ISBN: 1-878058-78-9	$19.95 USA/$26.95 Canada
C++ For Dummies®	by Stephen R. Davis	ISBN: 1-56884-163-9	$19.95 USA/$26.95 Canada
Delphi Programming For Dummies®	by Neil Rubenking	ISBN: 1-56884-200-7	$19.99 USA/$26.99 Canada
Mac® Programming For Dummies®	by Dan Parks Sydow	ISBN: 1-56884-173-6	$19.95 USA/$26.95 Canada
PowerBuilder 4 Programming For Dummies®	by Ted Coombs & Jason Coombs	ISBN: 1-56884-325-9	$19.99 USA/$26.99 Canada
QBasic Programming For Dummies®	by Douglas Hergert	ISBN: 1-56884-093-4	$19.95 USA/$26.95 Canada
Visual Basic 3 For Dummies®	by Wallace Wang	ISBN: 1-56884-076-4	$19.95 USA/$26.95 Canada
Visual Basic "X" For Dummies®	by Wallace Wang	ISBN: 1-56884-230-9	$19.99 USA/$26.99 Canada
Visual C++ 2 For Dummies®	by Michael Hyman & Bob Arnson	ISBN: 1-56884-328-3	$19.99 USA/$26.99 Canada
Windows® 95 Programming For Dummies®	by S. Randy Davis	ISBN: 1-56884-327-5	$19.99 USA/$26.99 Canada

SPREADSHEET

1-2-3 For Dummies®	by Greg Harvey	ISBN: 1-878058-60-6	$16.95 USA/$22.95 Canada
1-2-3 For Windows® 5 For Dummies® 2nd Edition	by John Walkenbach	ISBN: 1-56884-216-3	$16.95 USA/$22.95 Canada
Excel 5 For Macs® For Dummies®	by Greg Harvey	ISBN: 1-56884-186-8	$19.95 USA/$26.95 Canada
Excel For Dummies® 2nd Edition	by Greg Harvey	ISBN: 1-56884-050-0	$16.95 USA/$22.95 Canada
MORE 1-2-3 For DOS For Dummies®	by John Weingarten	ISBN: 1-56884-224-4	$19.99 USA/$26.99 Canada
MORE Excel 5 For Windows® For Dummies®	by Greg Harvey	ISBN: 1-56884-207-4	$19.95 USA/$26.95 Canada
Quattro Pro 6 For Windows® For Dummies®	by John Walkenbach	ISBN: 1-56884-174-4	$19.95 USA/$26.95 Canada
Quattro Pro For DOS For Dummies®	by John Walkenbach	ISBN: 1-56884-023-3	$16.95 USA/$22.95 Canada

UTILITIES

Title	Author	ISBN	Price
Norton Utilities 8 For Dummies®	by Beth Slick	ISBN: 1-56884-166-3	$19.95 USA/$26.95 Canada

VCRS/CAMCORDERS

Title	Author	ISBN	Price
VCRs & Camcorders For Dummies™	by Gordon McComb & Andy Rathbone	ISBN: 1-56884-229-5	$14.99 USA/$20.99 Canada

WORD PROCESSING

Ami Pro For Dummies®	by Jim Meade	ISBN: 1-56884-049-7	$19.95 USA/$26.95 Canada
MORE Word For Windows® 6 For Dummies®	by Doug Lowe	ISBN: 1-56884-165-5	$19.95 USA/$26.95 Canada
MORE WordPerfect® 6 For Windows® For Dummies®	by Margaret Levine Young & David C. Kay	ISBN: 1-56884-206-6	$19.95 USA/$26.95 Canada
MORE WordPerfect® 6 For DOS For Dummies®	by Wallace Wang, edited by Dan Gookin	ISBN: 1-56884-047-0	$19.95 USA/$26.95 Canada
Word 6 For Macs® For Dummies®	by Dan Gookin	ISBN: 1-56884-190-6	$19.95 USA/$26.95 Canada
Word For Windows® 6 For Dummies®	by Dan Gookin	ISBN: 1-56884-075-6	$16.95 USA/$22.95 Canada
Word For Windows® For Dummies®	by Dan Gookin & Ray Werner	ISBN: 1-878058-86-X	$16.95 USA/$22.95 Canada
WordPerfect® 6 For DOS For Dummies®	by Dan Gookin	ISBN: 1-878058-77-0	$16.95 USA/$22.95 Canada
WordPerfect® 6.1 For Windows® For Dummies® 2nd Edition	by Margaret Levine Young & David Kay	ISBN: 1-56884-243-0	$16.95 USA/$22.95 Canada
WordPerfect® For Dummies®	by Dan Gookin	ISBN: 1-878058-52-5	$16.95 USA/$22.95 Canada

Fun, Fast, & Cheap!™

NEW!

NEW!

SUPER STAR

SUPER STAR

The Internet For Macs® For Dummies® Quick Reference
by Charles Seiter

ISBN:1-56884-967-2
$9.99 USA/$12.99 Canada

Windows® 95 For Dummies® Quick Reference
by Greg Harvey

ISBN: 1-56884-964-8
$9.99 USA/$12.99 Canada

Photoshop 3 For Macs® For Dummies® Quick Reference
by Deke McClelland

ISBN: 1-56884-968-0
$9.99 USA/$12.99 Canada

WordPerfect® For DOS For Dummies® Quick Reference
by Greg Harvey

ISBN: 1-56884-009-8
$8.95 USA/$12.95 Canada

Title	Author	ISBN	Price
DATABASE			
Access 2 For Dummies® Quick Reference	by Stuart J. Stuple	ISBN: 1-56884-167-1	$8.95 USA/$11.95 Canada
dBASE 5 For DOS For Dummies® Quick Reference	by Barrie Sosinsky	ISBN: 1-56884-954-0	$9.99 USA/$12.99 Canada
dBASE 5 For Windows® For Dummies® Quick Reference	by Stuart J. Stuple	ISBN: 1-56884-953-2	$9.99 USA/$12.99 Canada
Paradox 5 For Windows® For Dummies® Quick Reference	by Scott Palmer	ISBN: 1-56884-960-5	$9.99 USA/$12.99 Canada
DESKTOP PUBLISHING/ILLUSTRATION/GRAPHICS			
CorelDRAW! 5 For Dummies® Quick Reference	by Raymond E. Werner	ISBN: 1-56884-952-4	$9.99 USA/$12.99 Canada
Harvard Graphics For Windows® For Dummies® Quick Reference	by Raymond E. Werner	ISBN: 1-56884-962-1	$9.99 USA/$12.99 Canada
Photoshop 3 For Macs® For Dummies® Quick Reference	by Deke McClelland	ISBN: 1-56884-968-0	$9.99 USA/$12.99 Canada
FINANCE/PERSONAL FINANCE			
Quicken 4 For Windows® For Dummies® Quick Reference	by Stephen L. Nelson	ISBN: 1-56884-950-8	$9.99 USA/$12.99 Canada
GROUPWARE/INTEGRATED			
Microsoft® Office 4 For Windows® For Dummies® Quick Reference	by Doug Lowe	ISBN: 1-56884-958-3	$9.99 USA/$12.99 Canada
Microsoft® Works 3 For Windows® For Dummies® Quick Reference	by Michael Partington	ISBN: 1-56884-959-1	$9.99 USA/$12.99 Canada
INTERNET/COMMUNICATIONS/NETWORKING			
The Internet For Dummies® Quick Reference	by John R. Levine & Margaret Levine Young	ISBN: 1-56884-168-X	$8.95 USA/$11.95 Canada
MACINTOSH			
Macintosh® System 7.5 For Dummies® Quick Reference	by Stuart J. Stuple	ISBN: 1-56884-956-7	$9.99 USA/$12.99 Canada
OPERATING SYSTEMS:			
DOS			
DOS For Dummies® Quick Reference	by Greg Harvey	ISBN: 1-56884-007-1	$8.95 USA/$11.95 Canada
UNIX			
UNIX® For Dummies® Quick Reference	by John R. Levine & Margaret Levine Young	ISBN: 1-56884-094-2	$8.95 USA/$11.95 Canada
WINDOWS			
Windows® 3.1 For Dummies® Quick Reference, 2nd Edition	by Greg Harvey	ISBN: 1-56884-951-6	$8.95 USA/$11.95 Canada
PCs/HARDWARE			
Memory Management For Dummies® Quick Reference	by Doug Lowe	ISBN: 1-56884-362-3	$9.99 USA/$12.99 Canada
PRESENTATION/AUTOCAD			
AutoCAD For Dummies® Quick Reference	by Ellen Finkelstein	ISBN: 1-56884-198-1	$9.99 USA/$12.99 Canada
SPREADSHEET			
1-2-3 For Dummies® Quick Reference	by John Walkenbach	ISBN: 1-56884-027-6	$8.95 USA/$11.95 Canada
1-2-3 For Windows® 5 For Dummies® Quick Reference	by John Walkenbach	ISBN: 1-56884-957-5	$9.95 USA/$12.95 Canada
Excel For Windows® For Dummies® Quick Reference, 2nd Edition	by John Walkenbach	ISBN: 1-56884-096-9	$8.95 USA/$11.95 Canada
Quattro Pro 6 For Windows® For Dummies® Quick Reference	by Stuart J. Stuple	ISBN: 1-56884-172-8	$9.95 USA/$12.95 Canada
WORD PROCESSING			
Word For Windows® 6 For Dummies® Quick Reference	by George Lynch	ISBN: 1-56884-095-0	$8.95 USA/$11.95 Canada
Word For Windows® For Dummies® Quick Reference	by George Lynch	ISBN: 1-56884-029-2	$8.95 USA/$11.95 Canada
WordPerfect® 6.1 For Windows® For Dummies® Quick Reference, 2nd Edition	by Greg Harvey	ISBN: 1-56884-966-4	$9.99 USA/$12.99/Canada

scholastic requests & educational orders please Educational Sales at 1. 800. 434. 2086

FOR MORE INFO OR TO ORDER, PLEASE CALL ▶ 800. 762. 2974

For volume discounts & special orders please call Tony Real, Special Sales, at 415. 655. 3048

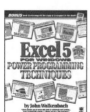

"A lot easier to use than the book Excel gives you!"

Lisa Schmeckpeper, New Berlin, WI, on PC World Excel 5 For Windows Handbook

Official Hayes Modem Communications Companion
by Caroline M. Halliday

ISBN: 1-56884-072-1
$29.95 USA/$39.95 Canada
Includes software.

1,001 Komputer Answers from Kim Komando
by Kim Komando

ISBN: 1-56884-460-3
$29.99 USA/$39.99 Canada
Includes software.

PC World DOS 6 Handbook, 2nd Edition
by John Socha, Clint Hicks, & Devra Hall

ISBN: 1-878058-79-7
$34.95 USA/$44.95 Canada
Includes software.

PC World Word For Windows® 6 Handbook
by Brent Heslop & David Angell

ISBN: 1-56884-054-3
$34.95 USA/$44.95 Canada
Includes software.

PC World Microsoft® Access 2 Bible, 2nd Edition
by Cary N. Prague & Michael R. Irwin

ISBN: 1-56884-086-1
$39.95 USA/$52.95 Canada
Includes software.

PC World Excel 5 For Windows® Handbook, 2nd Edition
by John Walkenbach & Dave Maguiness

ISBN: 1-56884-056-X
$34.95 USA/$44.95 Canada
Includes software.

PC World WordPerfect® 6 Handbook
by Greg Harvey

ISBN: 1-878058-80-0
$34.95 USA/$44.95 Canada
Includes software.

QuarkXPress For Windows® Designer Handbook
by Barbara Assadi & Galen Gruman

ISBN: 1-878058-45-2
$29.95 USA/$39.95 Canada

Official XTree Companion, 3rd Edition
by Beth Slick

ISBN: 1-878058-57-6
$19.95 USA/$26.95 Canada

PC World DOS 6 Command Reference and Problem Solver
by John Socha & Devra Hall

ISBN: 1-56884-055-1
$24.95 USA/$32.95 Canada

Client/Server Strategies™: A Survival Guide for Corporate Reengineers
by David Vaskevitch

ISBN: 1-56884-064-0
$29.95 USA/$39.95 Canada

"PC World Word For Windows 6 Handbook is very easy to follow with lots of 'hands on' examples. The 'Task at a Glance' is very helpful!"

Jacqueline Martens, Tacoma, WA

"Thanks for publishing this book! It's the best money I've spent this year!"

Robert D. Templeton, Ft. Worth, TX, on MORE Windows 3.1 SECRETS

For scholastic requests & educational orders please call Educational Sales, at 1. 800. 434. 2086

FOR MORE INFO OR TO ORDER, PLEASE CALL ▶ 800. 762. 2974

For volume discounts & special orders please call Tony Real, Special Sales, at 415. 655. 3048

ORDER FORM

IDG BOOKS WORLDWIDE™

Order Center: **(800) 762-2974** *(8 a.m.–6 p.m., EST, weekdays)*

3/26

Quantity	ISBN	Title	Price	Total

Shipping & Handling Charges

	Description	First book	Each additional book	Total
Domestic	Normal	$4.50	$1.50	$
	Two Day Air	$8.50	$2.50	$
	Overnight	$18.00	$3.00	$
International	Surface	$8.00	$8.00	$
	Airmail	$16.00	$16.00	$
	DHL Air	$17.00	$17.00	$

*For large quantities call for shipping & handling charges.
**Prices are subject to change without notice.

Ship to:

Name _____

Company _____

Address _____

City/State/Zip _____

Daytime Phone _____

Payment: ☐ Check to IDG Books Worldwide (US Funds Only)

☐ VISA ☐ MasterCard ☐ American Express

Card # _____ Expires _____

Signature _____

Subtotal _____

CA residents add
applicable sales tax _____

IN, MA, and MD
residents add
5% sales tax _____

IL residents add
6.25% sales tax _____

RI residents add
7% sales tax _____

TX residents add
8.25% sales tax _____

Shipping _____

Total _____

Please send this order form to:

IDG Books Worldwide, Inc.
Attn: Order Entry Dept.
7260 Shadeland Station, Suite 100
Indianapolis, IN 46256

Allow up to 3 weeks for delivery.
Thank you!